ecpr PRESS

Globalisation of Nationalism
The Motive-Force Behind Twenty-First Century Politics

Edited by Liah Greenfeld

ecprPRESS

The ECPR Press is the publishing imprint of the European Consortium for Political Research (ECPR), a scholarly association, which supports and encourages the training, research and cross-national co-operation of political scientists in institutions throughout Europe and beyond.

ECPR Press
Harbour House
Hythe Quay
Colchester
CO2 8JF
United Kingdom

Typeset by Lapiz Digital Services

Printed and bound by Lightning Source

British Library Cataloguing in Publication Data

A catalogue record for this book is available from the British Library

HARDBACK ISBN: 978-1-785-522-14-7
PAPERBACK ISBN: 978-1-785-522-64-2
PDF ISBN: 978-1-785-522-15-4
EPUB ISBN: 978-1-785-522-16-1
KINDLE ISBN: 978-1-785-522-17-8

www.ecpr.eu/ecprpress

ECPR Classics:

Beyond the Nation-State: Functionalism and International Organization
(ISBN: 9780955248870) Ernst Haas

Citizens, Elections, Parties: Approaches to the Comparative Study of the Processes of Development
(ISBN: 9780955248887) Stein Rokkan

Comparative Politics: The Problem of Equivalence
(ISBN: 9781907301414) Jan Van Deth

Democracy
(ISBN: 9780955248801) Jack Lively

Electoral Change: Responses to Evolving Social and Attitudinal Structures in Western Countries
(ISBN: 9780955820311) Mark Franklin, Thomas Mackie and Henry Valen

Elite and Specialized Interviewing
(ISBN: 9780954796679) Lewis Anthony Dexter

Identity, Competition and Electoral Availability: The Stabilisation of European Electorates 1885–1985
(ISBN: 9780955248832) Peter Mair and Stefano Bartolini

Individualism
(ISBN: 9780954796662) Steven Lukes

Modern Social Policies in Britain and Sweden: From Relief to Income Maintenance
(ISBN: 9781907301001) Hugh Heclo

Parties and Party Systems: A Framework for Analysis
(ISBN: 9780954796617) Giovanni Sartori

Party Identification and Beyond: Representations of Voting and Party Competition
(ISBN: 9780955820342) Ian Budge, Ivor Crewe and Dennis Farlie

People, States and Fear: An Agenda for International Security Studies in the Post-Cold War Era
(ISBN: 9780955248818) Barry Buzan

Please visit www.ecpr.eu/ecprpress for information about new publications.

Table of Contents

List of Figures and Tables

Figures

Tables

Contributors

DMITRI BYKOV is the preeminent dissident poet in Russia today, a biographer of Pasternak and Okudzhava, and author of several novels. He is a regular political commentator on "Ekho Moskvy."

LEONE CAMPOS DE SOUSA is an assistant professor of social science at the Federal University of the State of Rio de Janeiro (UNIRIO) in Rio de Janeiro, Brazil. She is the author of *The Myth of Raciual Democracy and National Identity in Brazil* (2009) and does research on the topics of nationalism and national identity, race and ethnicity, as well as on culture and politics in Brazil.

JOCELYNE CESARI is Professor of Religion and Politics at the University of Birmingham and Senior Research Felllow at the Berkley Center for Religion, Peace and World Affairs at Georgetown University. Her most recent book: The Awakening of Muslim Democracy: Religion, Modernity and the State, Cambridge University Press, 2014.

LEE COJOCARU holds a PhD in Political Science of the Boston University. He is currently a Researcher at Boston University and Oslo University as member of the Varieties Democracy Project. His studies focus on identities and economic development in Eastern Europe.

EMMANUEL DALLE MULLE is Swiss National Science Foundation post-doctoral fellow at the Centre for Sociological Research of the Catholic University of Leuven (Belgium). Emmanuel holds a PhD in International History and Politics from the Graduate Institute of International and Development Studies, Geneva, and he is currently working on a research project on the cultural premises of welfare producerism in Catalonia, Flanders and Northern Italy. His research interests include nationalism and ethnic politics, Western European minorities and welfare nationalism.

KATRINA DEMULLING is the US Operations Manager at Symphony Ventures and a member of the Institute for the Advancement of the Social Sciences. Her PhD from the University Professors Program at Boston University explored the emergence and development of nationalism in Tanzania.

JONATHAN EASTWOOD is the Laurent Boetsch Term Professor of Sociology at Washington and Lee University.

MARC-OLIVIER GAGNÉ, teacher of philosophy, Centre collégial de Mont-Tremblant, Cégep Saint-Jérôme, QC, Canada.

IRENEUSZ PAWEL KAROLEWSKI is professor of political science in the Willy Brandt Centre for German and European Studies at the University of Wroclaw (Poland). He holds a Ph.D. in political science from the University of Potsdam, his research interests include European identity and and nationalism in Europe; recent publications: *European Identity Revisited* (Routledge, 2016), *Citizenship and collective Identity in Europe* (London: Routledge, 2010)

NINA KHRUSHCHEVA is professor of international affairs at New School University in New York City. Her latest book is The Lost Khrushchev: A Journey into the Gulag of the Russian Mind.

AXEL MARION holds a PhD in International History of the Graduate Institute of International and Development Studies, Geneva. He is currently Associate Researcher at the Pierre du Bois Foundation for current history, and has been visiting scholar in Boston University and Université libre de Bruxelles. His study field focuses on the European borders, identity and citizenship.

AAYESHA NOOR MIAN holds a PhD in Economics from City University of Hong Kong. She is currently a fellow at the Institute for the Advancement of the Social Sciences Boston and has been visiting scholar in Boston University. Her study area focuses on the role of political Islam in the creation of Pakistani Identity and Citizenship.

CHANDLER ROSENBERGER is Assistant Professor of International and Global Studies and Sociology at Brandeis University and chair of Brandeis's International and Global Studies program. A historical sociologist specializing in the cultural foundations of politics, Mr. Rosenberger is especially interested in the intellectual roots of political revolutions, especially nationalist movements. From 1992 to 1994, he covered the collapse of Czechoslovakia and the war in Yugoslavia as a journalist and as a fellow of the Institute of Current World Affairs. Mr. Rosenberger has written about post-Communist Central Europe for scholarly journals and for such publications as *Critical Review, Human Rights Watch, World Policy Journal*, and *The Wall Street Journal*. He is now writing an intellectual biography of former Czech dissident and president, Václav Havel.

WEI WAN-LEI received his PhD in Intellectual history of China from Tsinghua University and is an associate professor at China Youth University of Political Studies.

YIU CHUNG WONG, currently a professor in the Department of Political Science, Lingnan University, Hong Kong. Research interests include: China's political reform, cross Strait relations, democratic transition in HK, and 'one country, two systems': concept and implementation.

YU PEIJI is the Juris Doctor candidate in Law School, Chinese University of Hong Kong. Peiji was born in Shanghai, educated in Mainland China and Hong Kong. He received his bachelor degree in International Studies and Mhpil degree in Political Science from Lingnan University, Hong Kong. His MPhil research is about the Chinese nationalism and cross Strait relations. His research interests include law, politics in the Greater China Area and China's modernization since 1840.

ZU GUO-XIA holds a PhD in world history from Beijing Normal University and is now an associate professor at Beijing Forestry University.

Introduction

Collected Volume as an Experiment

Liah Greenfeld

We live in a time of confusion. So many changes occurred in our political world that contradict the image we had created of it just a quarter of a century ago, that we, political scientists, the presumed possessors of objective knowledge of politics on which its practitioners and participants can confidently rely, are reduced to the position of bewildered observers, reporters – weathermen keeping the record of yesterday's snowfalls and trying to describe as best we can what we see from the window today.

What happened in this short quarter of a century? The Cold War that defined our understanding of politics – and much of political science – during the previous forty-five years was (ostensibly) won by the West, the Soviet Union collapsed, and the bipolar world disappeared. Politics writ large was no longer the ideological opposition between liberal democracy and communist totalitarianism, representing the social forces of good and evil. History itself, it was said, reached its end and what we had understood of its course until then became of no use to us. The focus of much of political science shifted onto the process of democratisation, primarily in Eastern Europe and the formerly Soviet areas, but elsewhere as well, because now it was expected everywhere. In the meantime, what was seen as the emergence of capitalism as the victorious economic system gave a major boost to the theory and studies of globalisation in political economy.

These flavours of the first post-Soviet months were from the start embittered, however, because both democratisation and globalisation lacked the douceur that the end of history led one to expect. While the end results of the two processes were assumed to be positive, the means chosen to achieve them in the overwhelming majority of cases were those of violent nationalist conflict. Indeed, the resurgence, following the collapse of communism, in Europe and Central Asia of virulent ethnic nationalism of the kind not seen since World War II was a major surprise for political observers, second only to that collapse itself. Nationalism, generally disregarded before in the social sciences as a subject of mainly historical interest, therefore, also emerged as a fashionable specialisation in both political science and political sociology.

In general, developments in Western Europe appeared to be more in line with the globalisation theory than the claim that nationalism – and national conflict – was returning as the major political force. The newly independent republics of the Soviet Union were rocked by nationalist passions, which seemed only to have waited for the lifting of imperial controls to erupt, and such long-existent transnational entities as Czechoslovakia and Yugoslavia (just years ago regarded by the neighbouring Italy as the model for transcending provincial rivalries) were disintegrating, whether peacefully or violently, into ethnic national units. Meanwhile, France, Germany, Italy, and the Benelux countries established the European Union, dedicated to the principles of liberal democracy, with its own transnational citizenship and, within a decade, common currency, and growing membership, eventually reaching a population of over half a billion. But, in Western Europe too, nationalist passions would run high in the Basque country and Catalonia in Spain, among the Flemish in Belgium, and in Scotland.

Before we could figure out the logic behind these contradictory trends, several other international developments contributed to our confusion. The spectacular terrorist attack on American soil on 11 September 2001, which was within hours interpreted as religiously motivated, virtually wiped out the Cold War and the Soviet Union from our collective memory, temporarily eclipsed the optimistic projections of democratisation and globalisation, born out of the latter's collapse, and diverted attention from the resurgent and ever-present nationalism which rendered them problematic. Suddenly, the world seemed to be structured along another historical divide and riven by another fundamental conflict: the divide and conflict between modernity and Islam, which was resistant to it. Since September 2001, international politics – and history – was, therefore, in addition to democratisation, globalisation, and nationalism, framed by the confrontation of modern, secular, and pre-modern, religious, identities and cultures. The very large numbers of immigrants from North African, Arab, and other Muslim societies in Western European and North American countries that were considered standard bearers of liberal democracy made this international conflict a central issue in domestic Western politics. Governments and publics would attempt to reconcile their humanitarian commitments with security considerations.

In the meantime, Russia has recovered from its recent embarrassment and reverted to the old authoritarian ways. Its infatuation with liberal democracy, if such it was, proved short lived, its nuclear arsenal indestructible, its natural resources inexhaustible. With the West otherwise engaged it has had the opportunity to flex its imperial muscles in Moldova, Georgia, and the Ukraine, among other things annexing the Crimea. On the other side, in the United States, the temporary demise of its Cold War antagonist paradoxically resulted in a loss of self-confidence and dilution of identity, as if, no longer seeing constantly what they were opposed to, Americans forgot what distinguishes them. American liberals, young and old, would have equality at the expense of liberty, and the democracy to which the great republic continues to profess allegiance is more and more often understood, if not named, as the Soviet-type, i.e., social (or socialist) democracy. Thus, after all, the West and the (European/post-Soviet) East do meet and, as political scientists predicted in the 1960s, converge, but with the East standing its ground and the West, befuddled, drawing closer to it. Our victory of a quarter of a century ago turns out to be Pyrrhic.

And if it is not Pyrrhic, it turns out to be irrelevant. For these twenty-five years had more in store for us, already numb from the quickly succeeding developments which contradicted all our political notions and each other, and unable to process (or even register) them. In this quarter of a century, we have been forced to discover China. Our notion of its existence before was purely theoretical. In the course of a few recent years, it has risen before our eyes, colossal, impassive, and enigmatic, like a giant mountain range suddenly erupting out of the earth in place of rolling plains. This tectonic change in our political geography demands the redrawing of every conceptual map by which we have ever been guided in our understanding. China's population is four times larger than that of the United States, which has lost its direction, almost three times larger than the half-a-billion strong but wobbling European Union, ten times the size of the dwindling population of Russia. It is a monolith determined to play a role commensurate with its powers on the world stage. It has entered our politics. This new presence presupposes the redefinition of both the West and the East.

Contrary to what we believed twenty-five years ago, is political reality a disordered coexistence of heterogeneous processes, each driven by its own logic or is there, after all, a method even behind the madness of this quarter of a century, packed with surprises? What, if anything, unites:

- the Cold War and the contradictory post-Cold War trends of regional disintegration and integration;
- the struggles for national sovereignty and the willing devolution of national sovereignties to transnational bodies;
- the Eastern European transitions from the social democracies in politics and socialism in the economy of the age of communism to the liberal democracies in politics and capitalism in the economy, and the simultaneous drift in the opposite direction in traditionally liberal democratic and capitalist societies;
- secession and unification;
- increasing stress on particularistic identities and globalisation;
- downplaying of religious affiliations in civic life and the emergence of militant religion as a major political force
- and the tremendous, reality-transforming expansion of our political world due to the ascendancy of South-East Asia, especially China?

The argument of this volume is that, behind all these seemingly heterogeneous developments, lies nationalism – that they all result, specifically, from the globalisation of national consciousness.

It is unusual for edited volumes such as this to have an argument. It is also unusual to present an argument as this volume does. Indeed, this volume breaks away from convention in several ways. Its contributors represent a truly global community, escaping '-centrisms' of any kind and bringing to bear on the overall discussion numerous rarely combined cultural perspectives. The plurality of the authors are Europeans, three Western Europeans – Jocelyne Cesari, Emmanuel Dalle Mulle, and Axel Marion, who come from France, Italy, and Switzerland, respectively; two Eastern Europeans – the Pole Pawel Karolewski and the Romanian Lee Cojocaru; and two Russians – Nina Khruscheva and Dmitri Bykov. Four chapters are written by South-East Asians: one, by the Pakistani Ayesha Noor Mian, representing the Indian sub-continent, and three, by Y. C. Wong, Zu Guo-xia and Wei Wan-lei, and Yu Peiji, China. The remaining five participants are American, three of them – Katrina Demulling, Jonathan Eastwood and Chandler Rosenberger – from the US, Leone Campos de Sousa from Brazil, and Marc-Olivier Gagné from Quebec, Canada. To limit the volume to one particular discipline, or even to social sciences in general, would reflect a totally unwarranted assumption that academic disciplines and intellectual discourse are defined and classified uniformly in different countries, not to speak of different civilisations. Thus, the group is as broadly transdisciplinary as it is international: there are obviously political scientists and sociologists, but also economists, historians, philosophers, activists, poets and writers; the goal of the collection is to contribute to the understanding of the perplexing political world, not to force all its authors to adopt the standards of the Euro-American academic discourse shared by some of them. Contributors also range considerably in age, some of them having reached the peaks of success in their pursuits in or outside academia and, as the reader in some cases would readily recognise, great fame, some, younger ones, only beginning their careers. Collectively, the volume covers most of the hot spots of post-Cold War politics around the globe. Its authors discuss transformations of identity in post-Soviet Eastern Europe and Africa (Cojocaru, Demulling), European transnationalism (Karolewski, Marion), independence movements in Catalonia, Scotland, and Quebec (Dalle Mulle, Gagné), Russian nationalism and imperialism (Bykov, Khruscheva), Chinese nationalism (Zu and Wei, Wong, and Yu), ideologies of Islamic states and movements (Cesari, Mian, Rosenberger), and state and anti-state ideologies in Latin America (Eastwood, de Sousa).

In addition to the intrinsic interest of the data and analysis of each individual contribution, they represent collectively a set of primary sources. The volume was conceived as an experiment. I wished to assemble – from among people in one way or another engaged with nationalism, and given the optimal length of analogous ECPR collections – as heterogeneous a team as possible. The structure of the experiment was to ensure the cohesion of the pieces, necessarily tying each chapter to the argument in this introduction, and unifying all the chapters as tests for the same hypothesis. When invited to take part in the project, the authors were asked to write about nationalism in the context of central political and identity-formation processes, either in the area of their academic expertise, reflecting their research, or based on their experience as participants in these processes. Their contributions were then used to test the 'globalisation of nationalism' argument and the underlying theory of nationalism. This underlying theory, based on over thirty years of comparative historical research in the field, has been summarised in numerous essays and the trilogy of books on nationalism and political, economic, and psychological implications of modern culture I have published since 1992.[1] As will be clear to the reader, not all of the authors in the present volume were familiar with my theory and, among those who were, not everyone shared it. None of the chapters in the book was written to prove the argument or to support the theory. They could as easily have refuted them. In the words of the great French historian Marc Bloch, they were all to represent that most valuable sort of evidence: testifying, for or against, these arguments and theory without intending to do so, or 'despite themselves'. There was an element of adventure in this. In the end, when all the contributions were written, I would have to take the consequences as they came: it was possible that my hypothesis that nationalism lies behind all the major political developments of the last quarter of a century, uniting the seemingly contradictory trends, would be proven wrong. As it happened, it has been unanimously – yet, still clearly unintentionally – supported. But the Chinese essays introduced an important corrective into my theory of nationalism. I shall address this later. Let me present the theory and the hypothesis of 'globalisation of nationalism', based on it, first.

What makes nationalism the major global political force that it is, the force behind seemingly unconnected developments in far-apart regions? Nationalism is, first and foremost, national consciousness, i.e. the way of thinking and feeling which reflects a very specific image of reality. This image is secular – in the sense that it is focused on this world of our living experience to almost complete exclusion of the transcendental spheres, and, in its social core, it presumes that this world is naturally divided into sovereign communities of fundamentally equal members. We refer to this image of reality by the term 'nationalism', because the English, who created it in the sixteenth century and first constructed a society based on it, named this society a nation.

Envisioning one's community as fundamentally egalitarian and sovereign means that it is imagined as a democracy. The world of nations, by definition, is a world of democracies, whether these nations are individualistic and civic, collectivistic and civic, or collectivistic and ethnic. These different types of nationalism, however, result in different kinds of democracy: individualistic nationalism, which is necessarily civic, and collectivistic and civic nationalism produce liberal democracies, while ethnic nationalism, which is necessarily collectivistic, produces authoritarian democracies (referred to as popular or socialist). Classical liberalism and socialism/communism are, therefore, products and self-representations of different kinds of nationalism, which means that the Cold War, no less than World War II, was a national conflict. Thus, the logic of (and driving forces behind) politics during and after the Cold War remain the same.

The main reason for national conflicts – and for conflicts within nations – is wounded pride or threat to dignity. National identity, which derives from membership in a sovereign community of equals, is a dignifying identity. This is what distinguishes it from most other identities – all other inclusive identities, cutting across status lines – what makes it so attractive (explaining the spread of nationalism over much of the Earth's surface) and makes national mentality so competitive. Nations are in constant pursuit of prestige, always on the look out for signs of superiority to others or at least equality to those whose superiority is recognised, whether in military or economic power, in intellectual and cultural achievement or in sports, in quality of its products or beauty of its women – but invariably in its moral standing. Members' personal identities necessarily reflect the prestige of the community from which their national identity, a central element in modern personal identities, derives. Thus, they are extremely protective of their nations' dignity, especially in ethnic collectivistic nations, in which the dignity of individual identity is a direct function, reflection, of the dignity of the nation. Ethnic nationalists experience the indignity of their nation (for instance, its defeat in war, its comparative underachievement in whatever competitive pursuit is of significance to their national consciousness, and its moral failings) as personal inferiority, with a profound effect on their mental comfort. They are wounded in their national pride by, and likely to perceive threats to national dignity from, the mere existence of nations they recognise as superior. What is primarily at stake in national conflicts between or involving ethnic nations is equality of respect due to one's nation, or unconditional national dignity.

In collectivistic and civic nations, where the ties between national prestige and personal dignity are more convoluted, and especially in individualistic nations, in which the dignity of the nation is believed also to reflect the achievements of the individuals who compose it, fluctuations in national prestige do not have such a direct effect on individual self-respect, but preoccupation with personal dignity is far more intense. This explains the brutally competitive nature of individualistic nations domestically as well as the character of their internal politics. While the institutions in liberal democracies safeguard individual liberties, which, among other things, make it possible for individuals to achieve distinction and contribute to the dignity of the nation, oppositional movements in them, as a rule, insist on ever greater group equality, superimposed on the equality of individuals before the law (equality of opportunity) and at the expense of individual rights. Dignity of personal identity in nations derives from membership in a sovereign (i.e., self-governing, free) community of equals – those who share in sovereignty or freedom, which in individualistic nations implies the right to distinguish oneself. The goal of oppositional movements in individualistic nations is to assure the dignity implicit in this equality without exercising this right, thus escaping competition and personal responsibility for one's possible failure in it.

Because nationalism implies dignity of both individual and collective identity, it is likely to replace other forms of consciousness precisely in the periods of humiliation and loss of dignity and to appeal in the first place to groups that experience such humiliation and loss and that, therefore, were in possession of dignity earlier. This explains why the architects of every new nationalism come from privileged groups whose status is in some way threatened. This also explains why, in cases of contested national identity, the one that offers more dignity to more people is likely to carry the day, and that the success of transnational initiatives to develop transnational identities and secure the allegiance of the constituent populations ultimately depends on the ability of the proposed transnational identities to secure more dignity than membership in the nations they propose to transcend would. Transnational identity, in other words, must be worth more than national identity in the coin of dignity; whatever other benefits it offers, it must have more "dignity capital," in the first place. It is, clearly, these calculations, however inexplicit and seemingly contradictory, that have been behind the splits, unifications, tensions, and conflicts that have characterised the European political scene in the past quarter of a century in Eastern as well as Western parts of the continent.

The very same – essentially secular – calculations lie behind the rise of militant and, more generally, political Islam. This too is an aspect of nationalism's globalisation: in this case, its expansion into the sphere of religion. The Cold War was perceived in terms of the natural opposition between the universal ideological alternatives of liberal democracy and socialism/communism, but was in actual fact a bloody competition for prestige between the nationalisms of two superpowers (one of which happened to be individualistic and civic and the other collectivistic and ethnic, thus indeed representing two fundamentally opposed worldviews). In a similar way, the unconventional but very real war between the indisputably modern (in the parlance of an earlier era, 'First World') – i.e., technologically developed, fully industrialised, and generally prosperous – societies and the terrorist organisations waving the flag of religion, such as ISIL, Al Qaeda, Hezbollah, Hamas, Boko Haram, etc., often, surreptitiously or not, supported by Islamic states, is a secular nationalist conflict. It is a conflict between developed and prosperous modern societies and those who see themselves as members of ethnic national communities that they themselves consider inferior (because technologically undeveloped and economically backward, because, in other words, they compare badly to those societies) and are therefore deeply humiliated by their very existence. At stake in this conflict, again, dignity, and its psychological underpinning, as the underpinning of ethnic nationalism as such is resentment or existential envy of those believed to have such dignity. The conflict is fundamentally secular: Islamic terrorist organisations are concerned exclusively with the mundane hierarchy of community status and relations between people. But religion – and, importantly, religious history – provides the basis for their demands for international, secular, respect. (Islam is a great religion, in the eyes of its believers: by definition morally superior to its alternatives. On its emergence at the time of the Christian Dark Ages, for several centuries it was not only a major political power in the monotheistic world, drawing into it through conquest, among others, significant chunks of India, but arguably the vanguard of the monotheistic – that is, Western – civilisation). The dignity capital, or dignity quotient, of Islam is very high. It is from their membership in its community, once powerful, respected, and, what is more, eminently respectable, that the great majority of the participants in the militant Islamic organisations derive their identity, not from the relationship between each one of them and God, and it is because this community has lost its former power and respect that they feel humiliated, assailed in their dignity. This identity, and their grievance, is secular, not religious. This does not mean that their religious proclamations are just rhetoric, that they are not sincere in declaring that they are doing God's work, or that they do not really believe that they are going to be rewarded for their deeds by eternal life. The majority, probably, truly believe all that (and the few who do not are either Machiavellian geniuses, willing to sacrifice everything for the glory of their nation, or sadists, using the beliefs of others to satisfy their desire to kill with impunity). But their religious faith is itself secularised; it is brought down to earth; it becomes a conduit for secular ideas and aspirations, rather than inspiring – and explaining – them. To understand militant Islam, in other words, we must address the national consciousness behind it.

The ethnic nations that these radical Islamic organisations represent are obviously not the makeshift political entities created by Western imperial powers in the course of pursuing their own rivalries and distributed among their client families of native aristocracy, which are today represented in the United Nations – Iraq, Jordan, Syria, etc. Instead, these are the imagined Arab (mostly) and Persian nations, seen through the lens of national consciousness as emerging in the distant past and from the beginning distinguished by certain exemplary characteristics and propensities (the expression of which may be under some circumstances compromised). As these characteristics and propensities are collective and ethnic – that is, as they are characteristics of the collective individual – insofar as individual members of the nation are concerned, they are natural, independent of individual volition, given, even in such evidently cultural cases as those of language and religion. Individual members can only compromise their expression, just as cancerous cells can compromise the expression of one's genetic code, and, when they do, must be excoriated from the collective organism.

Islam, which, with its glorious history, contributes most to the dignity of the Arab and Persian nations, is seen as their distinguishing ethnic characteristic. This explains the multi-front war of the dedicated Arab and Persian nationalists: they are engaged in a war with developed Western societies, such as the US, Britain, France, Israel, the very existence of which is intolerable and humiliating to them; with Christians and Jews more broadly; with the opposing interpretations of Islam; with governments of Muslim societies which do not share their agenda; and against all slacking Muslims, whom they consider traitors.

Religion has been utilised as an important tool for the promotion of the national and nationalist agenda by almost every ethnic nationalism, not only in the Islamic world. Suffice to recall 'Orthodoxy, Autocracy, Nationality', the motto of official nationalism in Tsarist Russia. The central cultural tradition uniting the populace with the ruling strata, it naturally recommends itself as an ethnic characteristic. Thus it has been very often politicised, commonly becoming the preferred instrument of ideological mobilisation in the hands of the state. In this sense, the Soviet Union offered ethnic nationalism a seventy-year-long parenthesis, in which this ideological role was performed by Marxism, while religion lay dormant, practised by the people where this was not explicitly discouraged, but generally unarticulated and largely irrelevant for political elites within the state as well as among anti-establishment activists. Only Catholicism remained a political, secular, force in nations such as Poland and Lithuania, resisting Russian domination, or Northern Ireland, whose conflict was defined in religious terms. National projects of both the states and opposition activists in countries of what was then called the 'Third World', whose dignity was offended by the existence of the 'First' one, were served perfectly well by the irreligious rhetoric of historical materialism. Indeed, not a few Jihadist leaders were schooled as the vanguard of the proletarian struggle first. The ill-advised Soviet invasion of Afghanistan threw a spanner into the works of the proletarian brotherhood, and the collapse of the Soviet Union undermined the appeal of Marxism among Muslims, though well into the new century there have remained some die-hard socialists among their heads of state. The Cold War thus quite naturally morphed into the current confrontation, with some reshuffling of allies and adversaries but very little change in fundamental motivations.

This continuity of international political processes discussed thus far, behind their seeming heterogeneity, has been due, among other factors, unquestionably to the little remarked upon fact that these processes have been contained within one, our, civilisation – the civilisation regularly misnamed Western and Judeo-Christian, but embedded within the monotheistic tradition and properly called monotheistic. In this sense, both the opposition between Western and Eastern blocks earlier, and the conflict of the last twenty-five years, which pits Judeo-Christian against Muslim societies, have been family feuds, quarrels between people (and peoples) whose separate cultures share the same first principles and who, therefore, fundamentally, think and feel alike.

The monotheistic civilisation, however, is only one among several, most likely three, currently existing civilisations, the other two being the Chinese and the Indian civilisations. Between them, they probably contain about half the world's population (with the countries of China and India alone containing 2.5 billion people), leaving the other half to us. This makes the monotheistic civilisation the most populous of the three. It is also the most widespread, with societies on all five continents, while the other two civilisations exist only in Asia. Peers in age – all three civilizations are between five and six thousand years old – they followed different historical trajectories, among which the monotheistic seems to be the most eventful. For at least the first three thousand years of its existence, it was so small that only the steady development through the millennia of its foundational traditions and the codification of their first principles justified calling it a civilisation. Its spread, which began only two thousand years ago – when both the Chinese and Indian civilisations had already reached their territorial limits – first, under the aegis of Christianity, then both Christianity and Islam, however, was extremely rapid. Yet, it was only during the last 500 years that the monotheistic civilisation expanded to the Western Hemisphere and most of Africa. It was the addition of South American and African populations that made that civilisation the most populous of the three.

The spread of the monotheistic civilisation in the last two thousand years of its existence has been aggressive: none of the cultures it came into contact with outside the other two civilisations (which during these two thousand years remained almost entirely self-contained) were able to resist its thrust. At the borders of the other civilisations, however, this thrust stopped. Existing side by side for two millennia, the Chinese and the monotheistic civilisations might be compared to similarly charged magnets that repel each other: they could as well be populating different planets. Until very recently we simply did not include China in our concept of 'the world'. The space of the Indian civilisation, by contrast, has been repeatedly invaded by Islam, and parts of it were for centuries under Muslim rule. In distinction to the Chinese civilisation, which, were it not in fact, would still seem to be walled off from Western influences, the Indian one was able to recede before them like oil before metal: it was pliable, but it remained immutable. (It is significant that, as a major factor in shaping individual and group identities in India, dividing Indians' political commitments, and pitting Muslim Indians against the huge majority of others, Islam emerged only when absorbed in the national consciousness.)

While the drive behind the monotheistic civilisation during the first millennium and a half of its aggressive spread was the spirit of religious proselytism, much of its expansion in the last 500 years was motivated by, and at the same time spread, national consciousness. Until the middle of the twentieth century, nationalism developed almost exclusively within the monotheistic civilisation: the only nation outside it was Japan. Humiliated by the forcible opening of their country, self-sufficient and completely uninterested in the rest of the world, Japan's unusually large upper class of the samurai, to reassert their dignity, decided to reconstruct their society on the national model of the invading Westerners. This reconstruction was astonishingly rapid and successful. By the beginning of the twentieth century, the little Asian country without natural resources, which less than half a century earlier did not know firearms[2] and was satisfied with a subsistence economy, entered both military and economic competition with the major Western powers. Propelled by nothing but its national motivation, committed to the dignity of the nation above all else, it has been counted among the major powers ever since.

Fully aware of Western military and economic superiority, architects of Japanese nationalism considered Western peoples barbarian and looked down on their religion and moral values. Their motto was 'Western knowledge, Eastern values'; they wished to learn Western methods of doing things, not to pursue the same goals. The Japanese never measured themselves by Western standards; in other words, they never wanted to be 'like' the West. And, conscious of being unlike, they did not envy us and did not develop ressentiment.

The distance Japan kept between itself and the world which would force itself on the country channelled its people's energies and they acquired Western knowledge very quickly. War, as they learned from the West among other things, was the surest way of making a nation respected. Thus, just forty years after American 'black ships' sailed into Uraga Harbour, Japan invaded and defeated China. China's defeat at the hands of its erstwhile 'dwarf' vassal, far more humiliating for the Middle Kingdom than the irritations caused by contemptible yongueidz – foreign devils – (the Japanese were devils too, but the Chinese did not consider them foreign), sowed the first seeds of Chinese nationalism. With the even more spectacular victory over Russia, 'the Great White Power', in 1905, hailed all over South-East Asia, Japan opened the way to the spread of national consciousness throughout the two Eastern civilisations – or its true globalisation.

It took about a century for these seeds to germinate and bear fruit. But in the last quarter of a century they did bear fruit. And this fruit – the spread of nationalism to China and India, which made these two colossal and near monolithic cultures enter into competition with the nations comprising our civilisation for dignity – is what the eventful and confusing post-Cold War period has offered us for dessert.

The volume is organised along two continua: the magnitude of political change due to developments of/in national consciousness and identity, and how unexpected this change has been among observers. Placed along them, the chapters are grouped by area and subject: Europe, Africa, the Americas, North and South, and Asia; and the stability/instability of national consciousness and identity, their development, and their spread behind an ostensibly unrelated political agenda, under (cover of) Islam, and, finally, into China. Thus it starts with a discussion of Russian national consciousness, the most unexpected aspect of which is the lack of change in it in over three centuries and, specifically, despite what appears from outside as a dramatic transformation, over the most recent twenty-five years. The authors of the two chapters in this section are likely to make the volume as a whole an important primary source for Russian specialists one day, because of their insider status in Russian culture. Nina Khruscheva, Professor of International Affairs at the New School for Social Research, is the great-granddaughter (brought up as a granddaughter) of the Soviet Leader Nikita Khruschev. Thanks to her family connections, she has been privy from a young age to discussions and ruminations within the most exclusive circle of the country's leadership on Russia's national aspirations and position in the world. Dmitri Bykov is perhaps the foremost oppositional literator – a prolific and famous poet, writer, and literary biographer – in Russia today, a frequent political commentator on the relatively free TV station Echo Moskvy viewed by millions of the educated Russian public. Both authors independently insist on the immutability of Russian national consciousness in the face of repeated revolutions. As if caught in a time warp, it remains morbidly defensive of its dignity, which it presumes is constantly under attack by Western democracies, and, as a result, is permanently resentful and aggressive. Perpetually trying to model itself on the West and failing, it turns against western values and those (in the first place, Jews) representing these values inside the country. Today's Russians still argue (or agree with) their nineteenth-century compatriots, who were the first to formulate their national agenda. These arguments are as passionate as before the revolution of 1917 a century ago, but, as in the state of mania, incessant agitation and a sense of urgency produce no movement forward, just the same, dangerous, milling about. It is impossible to understand Russia's political positions and actions without taking into consideration the nature of its nationalism and the psychological dynamics underlying it.

From Russia we move to the former Soviet Socialist Republic of Moldavia, today the independent country of Moldova, and its people's struggles to define their national identity, analysed by Lee Cojocaru. Is it to be Moldovan or Romanian? Moldovans are Romanians under Russian rule: same history, customs, and language (though using the Cyrillic, instead of the Latin, alphabet). Their consciousness is unmistakably national: essentially secular, it presupposes that the world is divided into sovereign communities of equal members – nations – and that theirs is one such community. What is in dispute is its name, and the upper classes, at least, the intelligentsia and the political elite, are split on this issue. To identify as Romanian is more dignified: this is the identity of an independent European country with its own (high) culture language, literature, political history – whereas Moldovan culture is artificially carved out of Romanian by Russian/Soviet rulers of the province, underdeveloped, and heavily Russified. Culturally active and proficient people consider themselves Romanian; those less proficient and/or with vested interests in Russian education prefer national identity to be termed Moldovan.

Which of the available identities has a higher dignity quotient is also a central issue in the chapters focusing on Western Europe and the European Union. This is clearly an extremely important consideration in the cases of Scottish and Catalan separatism, discussed by Emmanuel Dalle Mulle. Among activists, it is probably the most important consideration, although, when appealing to broader publics in Scotland and Catalonia, they stress the economic and political benefits of independence. These evidently arouse less passion, as attested by the undemonstrative behaviour of those unconvinced, who vote 'No' in successive referenda. In both Scotland and Catalonia, the question of dignity becomes enmeshed in the interpretations of equality, which, interestingly, attracts much more attention in independence-related discussions than liberty. Not being recognised within the United Kingdom as a fully equal partner to England is experienced as humiliating in Scotland, as is not being treated, commensurate with its contributions to Spain as a whole, as superior to other Spanish communities in Catalonia: thus the insistence on being regarded as fully fledged nations. This eclipses the importance of the equality of individuals across communities. As in the Moldovan–Romanian identity dispute, the consciousness of all involved, the 'Yes' and the 'No' voters alike, remains unmistakably national.

The chapters by Axel Marion and Pawel Karolewski address problems in constructing the transnational identity of the European Union. The process so far has been unsuccessful. Marion suggests that this is because Europe lacks an essential territorial dimension of nations, and, as a result, there is no tangible entity with which its citizens can identify. The transnational identity, it appears, is only possible, if it remains, in effect, national; the EU, in other words, attempts to double the national commitments of Europeans, arranging them in two concentric circles. Karolewski argues that this is done with explicit intention and with the help of 'identity technologies' borrowed from traditional nationalism and deployed through the cooperation of individual nations. What is thereby achieved is 'nationalism lite' – an imitation, surface nationalism without passion; a legal, purely rational affiliation which does not penetrate to the deep psychological layers of – and so does not affect – one's identity. And, indeed, why would it? The club in which half a billion Europeans are offered membership offers certain material benefits, but it is not exclusive. Its dignity quotient is low. Being formally recognised as European could boost the morale of the educated sectors in the Eastern bloc countries immediately following the collapse of communism (and the denial of such recognition can still be experienced as a gratuitous offence in Turkey), but what could European identity ever add to the national identities of the French or Italians? Who are Europeans, if not they? Who, if not they, makes European identity dignified, to begin with?

We follow nationalism from the continent of its birth to Africa. 'Dignity for All' is what Katrina Demulling calls her chapter on Tanzania. In this case, too, it is dignity that makes national identity attractive and allows national consciousness to spread. The first to be converted to it are members of local elites, exposed to Western values through their education. The anomic situation of status-inconsistency in which they are placed in the colonial environment and which offends the dignity they acquire with national consciousness inclines them to its collectivistic, socialist, variant. To start with, this new consciousness – reflected in national identity – is unattached: the sovereign community of equal members, as such deserving respect of other communities, is black Africa in its entirety. Historical contingencies eventually narrow it to particular territory and ethnic groups, making the nation of Tanzania.

Similar to Demulling, Marc-Olivier Gagné recognises the formative role of the original English nationalism in his discussion of nationalism in French Canada and Quebec. His contribution is an apology as much as an analysis, and his analysis reflects the influence of Quebec nationalist philosopher Michel Seymour. As is common to nationalist thinkers, Gagné equates national identity with a sense of community in general, but his chapter allows one to trace how, among French Canadians and, specifically, Quebeckers, this sense of community, in confrontation with the British, evolved into a national consciousness and identity, internalising the values of equality and popular sovereignty, as well as the fundamentally secular image of reality (despite the centrality of Catholicism in the original French Canadian sense of community), and was spurred on by the pursuit of dignity. As in so many other cases of collectivistic nationalism, the search for dignity involves problematising the understanding of equality. Pro-independence Quebeckers justify their agenda by arguing that an independent Quebec would be a more egalitarian, thus more democratic, thus morally superior society, by comparison to today's Canada. The demand for independence is at its root a demand for the recognition of the Quebec nation, equal as such to the Canadian nation, from which it differs in language. However, defining the nation essentially as a linguistic community raises for civic-minded Quebeckers the spectre of ethnic nationalism, discriminating against linguistic minorities in Quebec. Quebec remains conflicted.

None of the developments described in the chapters following the discussion of Russia, almost shocking in its lack of change, require a significant revision of our political understandings: changes are minor and not particularly surprising. The political identities on which they focus evolve in accordance with the nature of nationalism, moving between its traditional types, intensifying and waning. Both the magnitude of change and the element of surprise, however, grow in the chapters that follow. The two chapters on Latin America by Leone de Sousa and Jonathan Eastwood independently discover nationalism under movements and ideologies which would not be connected to it as a rule and, in the case of Bolivia, are even explicitly dissociated from it. The June Days spontaneous mass protests in Brazil in 2013, de Sousa argues, on the face of it identical in their concerns with public services to demonstrations organised by parties on the Left, in fact were motivated by disappointment with the nation's 'stray dog' status in the world, its lack of international prestige, for which the public blamed the government. Increases in transportation fares and poor public health provisions were just additional manifestations of this humiliating position, incommensurate with Brazil's size and potential. Similarly, Eastwood, analysing the rhetoric of Left-leaning political regimes in Venezuela and Bolivia, sees in it reformulations, in one case less, in the other more original) of the national consciousness, which leads him to consider the (unexpected among Latin Americanists) staying power of nationalism and attempt an original explanation.

Nationalism presenting as civic protest or Marxist (internationalist, transcending nationalism) ideology, however, is less surprising than nationalism under the guise of Islam, which is the subject and the conclusion of the next three chapters, by Jocelyne Cesari, Ayesha Noor Mian, and Chandler Rosenberger. Armed with her extensive research on several Arab societies and Turkey, Cesari demonstrates the insufficiency of contemporary theories of secularisation, which connect democracy to the expulsion of religion from the public sphere. In Egypt, Iraq, Tunisia, and Turkey, democratisation, i.e. the move from personal government of a rigidly stratified society, organised on the basis of religion, to government in the name of the people whose membership in the political community makes them in principle equal (in other words, based on national consciousness) has been accomplished by means of the politicisation, or nationalisation, of Islam. The relations between politics and religion were reversed, as, from the foundation of the secular society, religion was transformed into its instrument, and in this sense secularised indeed. But religion was not confined to the private life of the faithful, instead becoming the preferred ideology of the state. Controlled by the state and subservient to its policies, Islam came to be at the state's beck and call, irrespective of the religious inclinations of state leaders, tightly embraced or cast away by them according to political need, encouraging believers to be national patriots above all. The chief reason for the political co-option of Islam, as Noor Mian and Rosenberger explain in the cases of Pakistan and non-governmental radical Islamic organisations, respectively, again, has been the pursuit of dignified identity, whether personal (Muhammed Ali Jinnah, Osama bin-Laden) or, commonly, national. This made Islam a tremendously effective secular ideology, greatly facilitating population mobilisation for national causes.

While transforming every political process on its way, nationalism itself, in all the above cases, has not been transformed, essentially staying within the logical framework of its original principles, as these had developed by the middle of the nineteenth century. On reaching China, it did transform. For this reason, the rise of Chinese nationalism signifies a far more significant change for the world at large, bound to surprise us again and again in the future. Chinese nationalism is the subject of the three chapters that conclude this volume, by Zu Guo-xia and Wei Wan-lei, Yu Peiji, and Wong Yiu Chung. The first of these chapters, focusing on the birth of nationalism in China, confirms the crucial role of anomie among privileged educated classes, and especially the threat to their dignity, in the initial importation of the new consciousness. The two others make it clear that every political issue, movement, or event is now seen through the lens of nationalism and experienced as such, touching directly on the participants' sense of dignity: national consciousness has become the motive-force behind politics in China as well. But Chinese national consciousness appears to differ from the national consciousness that has developed in the cultures belonging to monotheistic civilisation in two important respects.

First – which is made especially visible in Wong's analysis of Hong Kong's identity in the face of increasing pressures from the PRC, but also in Yu's descriptions of today's mainland attitudes to the reunification with Taiwan – Chinese national consciousness is pragmatic, rather than ideological: opposing views are not cast in terms of good *vs.* evil (as they are even in such routine contests as regular presidential elections in the West) and compromise is not only accepted, but actively sought. The second distinguishing feature, which is, perhaps, the most remarkable aspect of the Chinese national consciousness, is strikingly evident in what all three chapters do not discuss: equality and popular sovereignty (both of which are accepted as part of the nationalism package). National dignity – which in the case of all other nationalisms in this volume is a function of these principles of nationalism, its sense waxing and waning together with the extent of their realisation – in China appears to be largely unrelated to these principles. It is the dignity of national identity that is the major attraction of nationalism, making it such a powerful force in political mobilisation; in this regard, China is no exception. But in the monotheistic civilisation, as a function of equality and popular sovereignty, it is constantly threatened by the necessarily incomplete realisation of these ideals, generating conflict and endangering the very cohesion and commitment it creates, while in China it seems not to have these disruptive effects.

These differences, unlike the differences between various nationalisms within the monotheistic civilisation go beyond the implications of the three types observed among them and the dimensions of individualism–collectivism and civic–ethnic membership which constitute these types. Instead, they may be connected to the first principles of Chinese civilisation itself (a fascinating possibility, unfortunately quite beyond the scope of this collection). Of course, it is too early to say: Chinese nationalism has been very little studied. But, with China poised to become a superpower and likely to assume the hegemonic position previously held by Great Britain and lately the United States, the specificity of the nationalism clearly responsible for its rise is something to watch and comparative political research can only benefit from the addition of the cross-civilisational layer to the cross-national one.

The contribution of this volume would have been significant even if it only succeeded in drawing attention to this question. The papers in it, however, collectively do more. They show that the most important political developments of the past twenty-five years are indeed connected through the globalisation of national consciousness. Contrary to the predictions of globalisation theory, this globalisation does not unite the world, but makes it more competitive. Animated by the same passion for dignity, communities composing it in fact become more self-centred, preoccupied with their own grievances, jealous of the dignity of others, and with little energy to spend on sympathy for their woes. Democratisation (coterminous as it is with the spread of nationalism), is as likely to contribute to bloodshed as to the development of human creative potential. But, if these conclusions are unsettling, understanding the nature of the forces at work should give us courage, for it increases our ability to control them. Knowledge, as was recognised long ago, is power.

Notes

1. The trilogy consists of *Nationalism: Five roads to modernity*, Cambridge, MA, Harvard University Press, 1992; *The Spirit of Capitalism: Nationalism and economic growth*, Cambridge, MA, Harvard University Press, 2001; and *Mind, Modernity, Madness: The impact of culture on human experience*, Cambridge, MA, Harvard University Press, 2013.

2. There were firearms in Japan in the sixteenth century, but they were prohibited and eliminated from use during the Tokugawa period and thus, for all intents and purposes, unknown in 1853.

Chapter One

Russia's Identity of Perpetual Crisis

Nina Khrushcheva

Russia is a 'revolutionary' country, advancing through negation rather than creation; it moves forward not through evolution – a slow step-by-step development when progress occurs over time – but through perpetual revolutions – a constant upheaval and crisis. This revolutionary, crisis-driven permanence is a cultural trait that Alexander Herzen encompassed in his immortal maxim, 'Disorder will always save Russia' (quoted in World Policy Institute 1992: 49).[1] The belief has been a consolation and an inspiration for generations of Russian leaders, revolutionaries and reformers alike, who in their desire to transform or preserve the state have relied on or fought against their country's traditional inertness, stagnation, and communal order that spread across its vast eleven time zones.

Often their rebellious, reforming efforts would create a rupture – from the Decembrists' uprising to the People's Will underground to the Bolshevik Revolution to the attempts at reforming the Soviet and post-Soviet state – in the 1950s under Nikita Khrushchev, during Mikhail Gorbachev's 1980s, in the 1990s of Boris Yeltsin, or even in the lengthy 2000s under Vladimir Putin, whose original intent was to modernise Russia and to create better accord with its European neighbours (Khrushcheva 2014).

However, despite these efforts, neither the late tsarist system nor communism, nor post-communism was able to generate a viable alternative to a society where changes, when they happen, always result in destructive and malfunctional developments. In all cases the replacement of the old regime has been twisted and painful beyond expectations, in the long run yielding disappointingly insufficient results.

Not that the change from monarchy to communism or post-communism was insignificant – the abolition of serfdom of the late tsarism, total access to culture and education in Soviet Russia, international travel and relative freedom of expression in recent decades ... But this was not the change that generations of tsars, Bolsheviks, reformers and revolutionaries had promised – today Russia's institutional structures of legal and civil society remain as underdeveloped as they were during the times of the seventeenth century's Peter the Great; there is little social responsibility and very limited social consciousness. One autocracy ends, but autocracies continue into the future, changing in name and, due to modern influences, in the measure of brutality – Ivan the Terrible, Joseph Stalin, Vladimir Putin, because, in the words of Isaiah Berlin, the efforts of those trying to reform Russia, be they leaders or rebels, were invariably 'the mixture of utopian faith and brutal disregard for civilized morality' (Berlin 1969: 17).

Almost two decades ago, Jeffrey Sachs, a Columbia University economist and early advisor to the first Russian president Yeltsin, suggested that Russia's geography may prove to be deterministic: it 'conditions events' and keeps 'a powerful hold even in our supposedly globalized economy ... Proximity to the West induced better policies' (Sachs 1999) throughout the post-communist region.

Indeed, Russia's geography – its position between the West and the East – can provide some answers to the country's political, social, and cultural development. Russian philosophers and foreign experts, from Pyotr Chaadaev to Mikhail Epstein to Sachs, have marvelled over the mystifying nature of this nation, whose land occupies almost the entire continent, stretching over seven million square miles from Germany to Japan: from the tsars to the terrorists, they all offered salvation but not solutions; deeds but not details.

Robert Putnam, in his book *Making Democracy Work*, once postulated something both disturbing and directly relevant to today's Russia (Putnam 1992). Putnam's study began as an experiment. In the 1970s, Italy established a slew of new regional governments. Their formal structures were virtually identical, but the regional soils in which they were planted were not. Italy's regions differed in their topographies, their educational attainments, and their levels of economic development. Putnam set out to measure the new governments' performance and, if some regions turned out to be more successful than others, to ask why.

Sure enough, some new authorities did better than others. They were innovative and well administered, and passed their budgets more or less on time. In these regions, citizen satisfaction with the new tier of government was high. In other regions, actual performance was poorer and the citizens were dissatisfied. Emilia-Romagna and Umbria came at the top of the list, Calabria and Campania at the bottom.

Why? The obvious answer was economic development: the richer the region, the more effective its regional government. But, according to Putnam, this explanation will not do. The central government skewed its grants heavily in favour of poorer regions, but often governments in those regions could not even spend the money. Moreover, in the rich north as much as in the poor south, the most successful governments turned out not to be in the most economically favoured areas. Moderately prosperous Umbria, for example, outperformed richer Lombardy, Piedmont, and Liguria.

Putnam also dismissed other possibilities, such as levels of social and political strife, educational attainment, and urbanism. Initially all seemed plausible to him; none checked out. Even the role of the Communist Party – in Italy, the party of clean government – proved marginal.

Putnam's unsettling conclusion was that regional government in modern Italy works best in regions with high levels of 'civic community' – patterns of social co-operation based on tolerance, trust and widespread norms of active citizen participation – and that the distribution of civic community among the regions in present day Italy was clearly evident as long ago as the thirteenth century. He contrasts, for example, the republicanism of medieval Florence, Bologna, and Milan with the autocratic patron–client politics of the Neapolitan and Sicilian kingdoms. Italy's past lived on, decisively, in its present. Putnam argues that economic development does not always explain political development, but it is 'civicness' that matters.

Putnam's thesis is unsettling because it suggests that political leaders in un-civic regions and countries lack the fundamental building blocks out of which a stable democracy can be built. Putnam implies, although he does not quite say so, that 'civicness' is almost impossible to create where it does not already exist. Social capital is far harder to accumulate than physical capital. Patron–client relations, with their cycles of dependence and norms of favour seeking, are very difficult to eradicate.

These implications are relevant to the study of Russia. They could also shed light onto the post-communist development of some other former Soviet states, such as Ukraine, the country that has been an intrinsic part of Russia's history. For example, could it be that the Maidan uprising of 2013–14 against Putin-supported president Victor Yanukovich to forgo an Association Agreement with the European Union in favour of Russia and the 2004 democratic Orange revolution when the Ukrainian nation decided not to accept the first rigged Yanukovich elections, were an indirect consequence of the originally democratic Kievan Russia of the 900–1000s, with its first East Slavic 'legal code' and the tradition of the *veches* (popular assemblies)? Harvard historian Richard Pipes long insisted that Russia cannot exist without Ukraine (Motyl 2011); translated as the Edge (of Russia), it is also known as *Malorossiya* or Small Russia. When threatened with a Ukrainian push for independence, the Kremlin has never hesitated to suppress it. Modern Russia, after all, derived from Kievan Russia, and the Ukrainians have contested their supremacy and independence ever since. In contrast, which, if any, parts of Russian society possess the necessary 'norms and networks of social engagement'? How does it affect our contemporaries that the people-shared governance in Kiev, or later in the fifteenth century in Nizhny Novgorod and Pskov, was completely overtaken by the despotic Muscovite princes? Should we write off Russia's chances or find a way to encourage Russians to develop civic norms?

To draw further upon Sachs' 'geographical' idea, it is the vastness of the Russian land that has long been its handicap: in order to get anything done rationally and systematically, there have to be boundaries and laws, but in Russia the only order that matters is the one that comes from the top, from the tsars or the communist apparatchiks. Russia did acquire its many times zones, but without the sense to map out borders it can manage, or to create reasonable conditions for its people's lives. We are capable of sending a man to space, of making a Sputnik or the best (and only) computer for, say, KGB monitoring, but are hardly able to arrange consumer production of decent washing machines. Like its giant land, Russia's interests are spontaneous and spread everywhere. A contemporary cultural historian Mikhail Epstein notes that Russian successes are generally due to either instructions from the top or dilettantism and inspiration – there is no method behind them: 'Our hero was the Jack of all trades: a tailor, a tiller, and a reed-player [*i shvetz, i zhnetz, i na dude igretz*]. Each hand does miracles: incredible dress designs, incredible harvests, incredible melodies – while in reality we had convicts in rags and starving millions' (Epstein 1992: 99).

Over a century before Sachs and Epstein, Pyotr Chaadaev in his *Philosophical Letters* also tried to clarify Russianness:

> We still look and act like travellers. No one has a definite sphere of engagement; we have no rules for anything; we don't even have a home. Nothing that can link us . . . nothing durable, nothing permanent; everything flows by, goes by, without leaving an imprint either within or outside us.
>
> (quoted in Taranov 1996: 553)

He suggested that 'the most important feature of our historic make-up is the absence of free initiative in our social development' (Chaadaev 1991, 527). A specific character of Russian culture, according to Chaadaev, was that it was 'brought from elsewhere, and imitative. Russians take on only absolutely ready ideas, and so do not inherit experiences related to making these ideas work in reality' (Chaadaev 1991: 326).

In simple terms, Russia can be explained as the *Un-West*: its values are not specific or original, as say, Confucianism in China; they are more of what the West is not, Western values with an opposite sign. In Russia *mercy* [*miloserdie*] stands for the Western *justice*, *truth* for *rules*, *spirituality* for *interests*, *trust* for *responsibility*, *love* for *contracts* and *personal relationship* for *state law*. Because of its oppositional nature, Russia is a culture, whose existence is best described by pendulum swings between imitation and the following negation of the earlier adopted influences.

Due to its size and the formative stance of being 'against [the West]', Russia's is a *hypothetical* culture. Lacking much of method or organising principle except for just being big and great, Russia has been run by despots for most of its history. Predominantly serfs until only a century and a half ago, Russians end up living in fiction more than reality – today it is the virtual reality Putin relies upon to keep people occupied and entertained as Russian TV is dominated by channels that are either run directly by the state or owned by companies with close links to the Kremlin (BBC, 'Russia profile – Media', 25 February 2015). But, in all ages of Russian history, one has had to invent an acceptable form of the everyday in order to justify constant oppression – and most of the justifications come from the notion that others are out to get the Russians, the victims of general injustice. In this reality the state, either tsarist or Soviet or Putin's, always comes first. Individual hard work and international competition, measured in GDP figures or quality of life, count for much less than the belief that the government would protect and secure Russia as a glorious – feared and respected – nation. For this glory, many Russians are often ready to accept their debasement and enslavement. In fact, progress in Russia is rarely seen as a means of improving people's lives, but as helping the state prove itself to be superior to other states.

Russian history has provided ample evidence of our grandiose, yet imitative nature: Peter the Great's famous Westernizing reforms manifested themselves in the 1712 creation of Saint Petersburg, a grand new capital built in just a decade and with great human sacrifice as Russia's 'window into Europe'. The Bolshevik Revolution of 1917 was yet another radical and brutal attempt to rationalize this land of the serfs, in a quick fix applying Karl Marx's dialectical materialism to a peasant communal country, with its primary and mystical belief in the Holy Ghost. Finally, post-1991, American-style devastating capitalism was proudly explained by Alfred Kokh, an official close to the privatisation chief Anatoly Chubais, as 'the time of Social Darwinism during which a process of natural selection must take place' (Interview with Alfred Kokh, *Chas Pik*, 12 October 1992). Chubais himself insisted that:

> the aim of privatisation was to build capitalism in Russia. And not just that, it was to build capitalism in just a few [*udarnykh*] shock years, meeting the norms of production which the rest of the world spent hundreds of years achieving.

> (Russian television programme 'Details', 29 June, 2014)

These and other great triumphs – Petersburg's Europeanism, Vladimir Lenin's Socialism, Joseph Stalin's Industrialisation, Boris Yeltsin's Privatisation as well as Vladimir Putin's current resurgence on the world stage – have been arrogant and revolutionary creations of 'heroes', who, constructing their grandiose realities, insisted that the only way to move their backward and enormous country forward is through fear, force, and fast. As the fifteenth-century Grand Prince of All the Russias Ivan III once pointed out to a European visitor who reproached him for cruelty: 'It is different for you with your enlightened people, with ours this is the only way' (Herberstein 1966).

Ivan, indeed, had a point. The attitudes towards the West for most Russians could be best described not by Chaadaev, who like other Westernisers believed that Russians should rationalise themselves, that is, behave and think as Europeans, but by the Slavophile Alexey Khomyakov: the West has only 'self-interest [and] no warranty in morality; material gain, a quantitative private benefit, excludes the qualitative dimensions of life centred around the service to the community' (Khomyakov 1992: 58), which sets Russia apart from the West and assures its future glory. The rational individual was considered inferior to the community, defined by the Slavophiles as *sobornost* – universality of all-encompassing Orthodox faith (*Pravoslavie* was, and now again is, seen as the only correct form of Christianity versus its other brands, condemned for their pragmatism – insufficient reverence for the human soul and support of formal social laws). Extolling the Holy Ghost, the commune is seen as representing the higher spiritual mission of the people, the perfect model for the life of the Russian *obshchina-mir* (a peasant commune, also translated as 'world', or 'peace') with such traits as religiosity, capacity for suffering, brotherly love, and cultural unity (Berlin 1978).

The nineteenth-century Slavophiles were precursors to the twentieth-century Eurasianists, whose proponents, too, believed that Russia did not belong to the Western civilisation, and instead should be the global leader of the Slavic and non-European brotherhood. For them the idea of what Russia *should appear to be* – strong and powerful – defined its identity. Today Vladimir Putin, no longer a Westerniser as he once was,[2] fully subscribes to this faith (Robinson 2012), following the teachings of Ivan Ilyin, one of the Eurasianism philosophical fathers, who popularised the views in the 1930s and 1940s while in anti-communist exile in Germany and Switzerland (Ilyin 1992). Just like Ilyin, Putin now believes in Russia's resurrection through the revival of the true Christian spirit – the love of God, the love of Russia, respect for the law, a sense of duty and honour, and devotion to the state.

To a degree, Putin's current conservative views have derived from the extremes imposed by the Westernisers of the capitalist 1990s. And yet Yeltsin, Chubais, and their colleagues, too, fell victim to the swings of the Russian pendulum: they also fought the extremes of the past that preceded them. They defined the mythical West, which was then understood primarily in terms of opposition to the Soviet Union. The reason for this absolute vision derived from the fact that, for centuries, Russia was separated from the rest of the world by physical and psychological borders, its rulers always seeing those borders as under threat. Thus the post-communist reformers, despite their liberalism, accepted the usual totalitarian formula of 'we know best' when attempting to transform the old Soviet society. Communism failed because it was a bankrupt ideology. They reasoned that the Russian society and economy would begin to work only by a quick, and miraculous, adoption of a viable ideology, the free market model. Never mind that such change could only be imposed by the autocratic techniques of 'ends justifying the means', and, as Orthodoxy or communism before, was based on the totality of faith and the ultimate negation paradigm.

Soviet dissident Andrei Sinyavsky (Abram Tertz) in his *Voice from the Chorus* has established a connection between religion, anti-rationalism, and Russia's hypothetical character:

> This religion of the Holy Spirit somehow accords with our national characteristics – a natural inclination for anarchy … fluidity, amorphousness, readiness to adopt any mould ('come and rule over us'), our gift – or vice – of thinking and living artistically, combined with an inability to manage the very serious practical side of daily life: 'Why bother? Who cares?' we ask. In this sense Russia offers a most favorable soil for the experiments and fantasies of the artist, though his lot as a human being is sometimes very terrible indeed.

(Tertz 1976: 247–8)

In the same work Tertz also commented on the consequences of Russia's spiritual obsessions as well as the extreme nature of the Russian thinking – its violent swings back and forth from absolute conservatism – the Slavophiles – to absolute radicalism – the Westernisers and the Revolutionaries, with 'liberal conservatism' of Eurasianism – now rebranded as Putinism – at times trying to fit into both extremes. Indeed, Russia, and by extension the Russian identity, follows the country's traditional pendulum pattern. It is the alternation between the periods of 'oppression' – examples include Joseph Stalin's 'Gulag socialism' or Leonid Brezhnev's Developed Socialist 'stagnation', and periods of 'remission' (which also cannot be entirely separated from the 'strong hand' politics) –Peter the Great's westernising reforms, Nikita Khrushchev's 'thaw', Mikhail Gorbachev's *perestroika*, or Boris Yeltsin's chaotic capitalism of the 1990s. At the current stage, Vladimir Putin, with his 'dictatorship of law and order', and declarations of 'managed democracy', has been trying to walk both sides of the aisle: like his chosen philosopher Ilyin, he professes to be a legalistic technocrat, who is also soulful and spiritual (Myers 2015). Of course, Ilyin and other Eurasianists imagined their perfect Russia in European exile, while Putin rules the actual country. Therefore, like other leaders before him, he wants to implement the dream of Russia created away from the Russian land.

Tertz provides a convincing explanation for this phenomenon:

> Because of the Spirit we are sensitive to the influence of all kinds of ideas – so much so that at certain moments we lose our own language and personality and become Germans, Frenchmen, or Jews, and, then, recovering our senses, rush from one spiritual servitude to the opposite extreme, freezing in a posture of narrow-minded suspicion and hostility towards everything foreign.

> We are conservatives because we are nihilists – the one turns into the other and they are interchangeable in our history. But all this because the Spirit bloweth where it listeth, and in order not to be blown away by it we turn to stone, protect ourselves with the crust of ritual, the ice of formalism, the letter of the decree or the standard formula. We cling to form because we have not enough of it; we have never had and never can have either hierarchy or structure (we are too spiritual for this), and move freely from nihilism to conservatism and back again.

(Tertz 1976: 247–8)

Surely, the Russian understanding of spirit as the essence of life is yet another imitation: it derives from the traditions of Byzantium, the original empire of the Holy Ghost, whose descendant, the Third Rome, Moscow proclaimed to be during the reign of Ivan III. In opposition to the Western structure of the suzerain and vassals, in the Byzantine East there were the ruler and the serfs – a vertical hierarchy (Vladimir Putin's 'vertical of power', or 'managed democracy' as it is otherwise known, is far from new). In such an order, the ruler does not provide guarantees or laws, needs no explanations, but like God has the right to punish or to pardon his people, whose only duty is to obey their tsar. In practice, it is arbitrariness, in theory, the tsardom of God on earth. Richard Pipes, who has spent decades studying Russia's political attitudes, not long ago reconfirmed Russian's desire for a tsar, this time in a form of Putin:

> With few lateral social ties, they relied on the state to protect them from each other. They wanted their rulers to be strong and harsh, qualities designated by the Russian word groznyi, meaning 'awesome' (incorrectly translated as

terrible) the epithet applied to Tsar Ivan IV. Experience has taught Russians to associate weak government – and democracy is seen as weak – with anarchy and lawlessness.

(Pipes 2004)

In a continuous absence of 'lateral social ties', with no viable legal institutions, the Russians even now, in the twenty-first century, hold on to a grandiose ideal of 'awesome' leadership that assures their belonging to some harmonious cosmic order.

After Yeltsin's anarchy of post-communism, when, as some critics complained, 'the country, deprived of high ideals in just a few decades has rotted to the ground' (Prudnikova 2003: 9), Putin's power centralisation for the sake of a restoration of Russia's 'glory, its faith, and above all its proper place in the world' (Schmemann 2007), had been a welcome development. Today we still lack free individuals, secure private property and all other rights the West takes for granted, but our state has given us back our pride again – Russia's oil and gas, tanks in Ukraine and plane strikes in Syria should make the world tremble as Russia 'is a great, powerful, divinely ordained state that stretches back a thousand years' (Schmemann 2007). This current state of affairs may seem to contradict a claim Anatoly Chubais made just a decade ago that it would not 'take long to implement capitalism in Russia' because 'Soviet man like every other man was nothing more than "homo economicus". That he is fully engrossed in the economic interests: interest in money, interest in property and profit' (Chubais 1999: 29), and therefore would develop a strong sense of individuality, which would temper the state demands. In fact, in order to protect their personal achievements, people would seek stronger institutional and legal support and the 'civicness' Putnam talked about.

True, in the 1990s–2000s, Russians have discovered money and comfortable life, but what stands in the way of Chubais's argument is that in the strictest of terms the 'homo economicus' has never been born quickly as 'habits die hard and mentalities change slow' (Holmes 1996: 26). The process is even slower in Russia, where, predating homo economicus:

Homo Soveticus, successor and predecessor of Homo Russicus, labored long and willingly, but his labor lacked a foundation … There was no firm, lifelong tie with the object and the product of labor. His love [for labor] was general, public and belonged to no one.

(Epstein 1992: 92, 102)

Indeed, Russians of all generations have been plagued with this kind of 'public' labour – an exploit, a deed, a sacrifice – from eradicating enemies to forging steel to herding sheep. And when labour belongs to no one, it results in 'oligarchism' – economic under Yeltsin or political under Putin – a system of big semi-nationalised businesses – where a narrow elite has been able to 'steal the state, and everything else' (Murphy and Hessel 1999). Today as in the Soviet times, the main task of the contemporary ruling elite – Putin and his former KGB associates – is to preserve their tight-knit political and economic regime, built for their own personal control and material benefit.

In this, the Russian 'economic' mind has not changed much since the times when Western businessmen coming to Russia right after the Soviet collapse experienced an unusual way of doing business. In Western-style hotels, such as the Sheraton or the Metropol, one could easily have a chance breakfast with a stranger who had on offer a large oil refinery for sale. Russia has looked with disdain at small undertakings. Although Moscow has always been 'desperate for vegetable stands, restaurants, car washes, dry cleaners, and hardware stores ... many people in business are selling oceans of natural gas, tons of gold, timber concessions the size of Michigan, or used MIG crafts' (Stevenson 1993: 501). Under Putin, it is Gazprom, the natural resource Kremlin-run giant, that controls a mammoth share in the Russian economy and also provides riches to its affiliates (Khrushcheva 2009). In recent years natural resources have comprised 70 percent of Russia's exports, and transfers from Gazprom's revenues alone account for at least 5 percent of the national budget (Khrushcheva 2015). It also helped to secure Putin's popularity and to give him the resources to reconstruct Russia's military might, now on display in Ukraine.

Understanding the Russian state-centric thinking, the Kremlin has been able to sustain the perception that the West, as always, wants to destroy Russia via economic sanctions over its annexation of the Crimean Peninsula from Ukraine. The country's economy has been badly hurt: its output is expected to shrink by almost 5 per cent in 2015 and its credit ratings have been reduced to the 'junk' status (Monaghan 2015). And Putin, along with the country's population, presents himself as a victim of this cunning plot. The 2014 Ukrainian conflict has been framed as a renewed struggle against fascism – and in defence of Russia's anti-Western identity – and heroically (even if grudgingly) enduring the sanctions is seen as renewed Russian patriotism. Russians are asked to prepare themselves for a looming disaster – hunger, poverty, inability to travel, and the supposed threat to Russia was underscored for the seventieth anniversary of the end of World War II, celebrated in May 2015, with billboards put up across Moscow to remind Russians of the anti-materialist sacrifices for a better humanity that the victory over Nazism required.

Communist Leon Trotsky insisted that this everyday heroism of self-sacrifice represents 'an improved edition of mankind' and is required for 'reforging humanity and creating an earthly paradise [which] was the raison d'etre of the communist movement' (quoted in Hellbeck 2006: 5–6). His contemporary, and arch-nemesis, religious philosopher Nikolai Berdyaev, another Eurasianist that Putin is fond of, similarly defined a *specifically* Russian messianic idea of the ethical transformation of society in favour of a purer form of community: 'The Russian people ... has no love for the ordering of this earthly city and struggles toward a city that is to come, towards the new Jerusalem' (Berdyaev 1946: 255). After the 2014 Crimean annexation, Putin declared, 'In the hearts and minds of people, Crimea has always been and remains an inseparable part of Russia' (Walker and Traynnor 2014). Because, as he explained later that year in his annual State of the Nation address, 'It was here, in Crimea, in ancient Chersonesus, or Korsun as the Russian chroniclers called it, that Prince Vladimir took baptism, before he baptised all of Rus' (Putin 2014). Thus Putin not only justified the annexation – the peninsula was as sacred to Russians as Temple Mount in Jerusalem is to Muslims and Jews, he explained – but also set up his own heritage as a descendant of the noble, divine even, Russian prince. Moreover, the president also validated the Russian psyche and its status in the world as unique: 'We are less pragmatic than other people, less calculating. But then we have a more generous heart. Perhaps this reflects the greatness of our country, its vast size' (Berry 2014). Another time he explained how this 'generous' character has been repeatedly duped:

> Russia strived to engage in dialogue with our colleagues in the West. We are constantly proposing cooperation on all key issues; we want to strengthen our level of trust and for our relations to be equal, open and fair. But we saw no reciprocal steps.

> (*Washington Post* 2014)

There is a striking similarity between all Russian thinkers, leaders, radicals, and revolutionaries – an overarching ideal of belonging to some higher, better than the West, harmonious order expressed in the communal or communist form, in which only *collective, i.e. state, values*, not *individual rights*, matter. And even those who have rejected universal *sobornost* or international communism, such as Chaadaev, are still convinced of the grandiosely messianic destiny for the Russian nation: 'We are an exception among nations. We exist in order to give a great lesson to the world' (Chaadaev 1991: 326). To be sure, rarely a country so recklessly disposes of its citizens while striving towards cosmic harmony: bleeding to save humanity but refusing to lift a finger to save a single human being, Russia counted twenty plus million people who tragically perished during Stalinism; many more millions were sacrificed to the seventy-five years of the brutal Soviet regime, and other uncounted millions vanished during many centuries of the despotic monarchic rule; not long ago many millions became (less bloody) victims of Yeltsin's unruly capitalism.

A conviction of Russia's humanistic superiority has most recently been dramatically playing out in Syria, where Russia began a bombing campaign against the Islamic State (IS) militant group. Largely, the campaign is directed towards preventing Syrian president Bashar-alAssad, Putin's ally, from losing power, which has been under threat from the rebel protesters since 2011. Assad's religion, the Alawite, is considered one of the most syncretic of brands of the Muslim faith. Although containing aspects of Christianity, it is lauded as non-fundamentalist by the Russian Orthodox Church. Along with Putin, the Russian Patriarchy declared the Russian fight with terrorism in Syria a 'holy battle', explaining that 'the fight against terrorism is a holy struggle and today our country is perhaps the most active force in the world to combat terrorism' (Torres 2015). Moreover, Russians justify their involvement by the fact that the US and the West in general are to blame for strengthening the terrorists and their allies, because of Western self-interest in the region, its striving for world domination, and obsession with exporting democracy around the world. Obsessed with toppling President Assad, the Kremlin maintains, the West paid no attention to the IS threat; moreover, they sought no common solutions because they regarded any possible cooperation with Moscow as a sign of failure.

This excursion into Russian history, politics, and psychology has already shown that Russia is hardly likely to change. In the early 1990s, when Putnam explained how to make democracy work in Italy, Russian cultural historian Yuri Lotman was sceptical regarding the prospects of democracy in Russia. In his book *Culture and Explosion*, he offered an explanation for the country's lack of moderation in swinging from one revolutionary extreme to another – from the absolutism of the Orthodox spirit to the absolutism of dialectical materialism (Lotman 1992); from the chaos of the unbridled post-communist chaotic capitalism to the contemporary 'vertical' state. Lotman suggests that Russian culture, unlike the cultures of the West, embodies an underlying binary logic of opposition: individuals and groups conceptualise social lives in terms of absolute alternatives with no neutral ground or compromise. He identifies this as a paradox of 'tyranny': a 'weak state' often functions as 'strong' by instilling a controlling government and depriving its peoples of basic liberties and legal structures, which should allow them to make their own decisions. Such a state is generally impotent to solve the fundamental problems of modern society, but it is effective in weakening alternative approaches to governance. According to Lotman, a fateful result of binary thinking is Russia's revolutionary crisis mentality – a victor after defeating an opponent tries to radically annihilate the past. The past is regarded not as the foundation for organic growth, but as a source of error that must be completely eradicated. Total destruction must precede creation, and so creation takes place in a void. Means and ends are thus separate, as the desired new world can only be constructed on the ruins of the old, which is perceived as wholly corrupt. Consequently, all Russian revolutions and regimes have felt completely justified in their never-changing motto of ends being superior to means.

Meanwhile, both the communist and post-communist claims of radically breaking with the Russian or Soviet past have been deceiving – the Russian present always becomes a certain regurgitation of that past, not a true step forward. For example, the indictment of communism is not that it was based upon Western rationalism or atheism, but that it too quickly succumbed to the Russian traditions of despotism, mysticism, and obscurantism. Despite the Soviets' supposed belief in scientific laws of development and the rationality of their existence, behind Stalin's collectivisation of agriculture and the industrial exploits lay not Marxism but the social and moral–psychological tradition of serfdom and the ancient communality of the *mir* (a type of rural community in Imperial Russia).

Russia's repeated failure to transform in an evolutionary way brings to the fore yet another paradox: tolerating the worst despots in world history, Russians have displayed an almost apocalyptic fear of change, especially change of power. People often consider the end of a certain order as the end of order altogether, as this shift tends to bring unexpected and fearful results. In the Russian experience – promises of a better future notwithstanding – things usually get worse, and rarely better. Therefore, power here is subject to inertia, which in turn creates a favourable environment for despotism. The autocratic leader embodies power and is supported by the population, regardless of the policies he implements, and often despite those policies. This in part explains the phenomenon of people's enduring devotion to harsh rulers such as Peter the Great or Joseph Stalin, as well as a secret behind Boris Yeltsin's presidential re-election in 1996. Despite the poll numbers, which showed his minimal popularity, Russians voted for him, reasoning, 'Better the devil we know'.

This phenomenon also stands behind Putin's popularity, with the president's approval rating for most of 2015 at almost 90 per cent (Levada Center 2015a). Putin's Kremlin expertly taps a deep and familiar emotion: fear. Whatever Russians may think of the country's current economic malaise, with GDP contraction and inflation nearly topping 15 per cent, they are certain that they would be much worse off without Putin. As one observer put it, he has 'an image of a tough guy who stands up to the West; and heads a supremely powerful state system that puts stability and security ahead of liberal freedoms' (Challands 2015). This support is often subconscious rather than conscious, part of the centuries-established tradition, which only time and different, i.e. positive, experience may be able to change: 'people do more easily what they are used to do than what they have never done ... Habits and expectations, which perversely constrict freedom of choice, can be handed down from generation to generation and survive for centuries by sheer inertia' (Holmes 1996). In 2009, Russian radio station Ekho Moskvy polled its listeners on the question of values: what is more important for a state official, his humanity (as understood in Russia) and high morality or his professionalism and sense of responsibility? Of the 200 on-air respondents, 79 per cent believed that humanity matters most.[3] When Russia began its military operations in Syria in September 2015, only 18 per cent of the population supported the country's involvement; by October the number had increased to almost 50 per cent. For them, this is a TV war, which fits well into Russia's hypothetical culture. It is an unreal battle in a far away land, a balancing act of sorts, which sets Russia centre-stage between the menacing West and militant East (fundamentalist Islam). But, more than anything, it serves to confirm that Russia and Putin, who speaks of Russia's global humanism in the Middle East, are paid attention to (Levada Center 2015b).

But what is this humanism in the twenty-first century anyway?

With what we know about Russian history – a vicious cycle of despotism, of unfulfilled promises and lost lives – self-righteous claims of 'service to the community, sacred notion of the Motherland, the nation's honour, and high morality' (Vishnevsky 2009) today are nothing more than just slogans. For that reason, no obvious adjective such as 'tsarist' or 'Soviet' has yet been affixed to Russia's name today. There is of course 'Putin', but with all his popularity he is still simply a person in charge. He is not yet a regime or an ideology, which historically has been a requirement for national unity and people's enthusiasm, as it was in the times of Stalin's industrialisation, for example. Stalinism worked, at least for a while, because it offered people a cause greater than themselves: they were told they were protecting humanity from the greedy clutches of imperialism through egalitarianism and personal sacrifice. Indeed, 'the power of the communist appeal, which promised that those who have been slaves could remodel themselves into the exemplary members of humanity, cannot be overestimated' (Hellbeck 2006). In the country, which used to be populated with the rural majority and a small minority of aristocrats, the democratising influence of the Bolshevik revolution, even if brutal and bloody, provided a host of opportunities – universal healthcare and education. Moreover, everybody could become a hero of the new people's regime. Putin, however, only strives to create his own all-encompassing ideology. He may yet become successful – if he stays in power until 2024, a term that is afforded to him by the Russian constitution – but, as it stands today, he is not Stalin, not only because Stalin was incomparably more brutal and deadly in his tactics, but also because his goal, unquestionably, was to create a better future. At the time, very few people realised that one cannot improve the life of humanity by killing off individual humans. In Putin's case, there is nothing visionary in his approach. It is *all* about the past. The unsustainable 'greatness' of the eleven time zones will eventually lead to pragmatic and powerful China swallowing the Far East and Siberia; a weakened Russia will then also lose the Northern Caucasus and the Volga region to their growing Muslim population, and Kaliningrad will become German Koenigsberg all over again. Russian Orthodoxy, a religion of spirit, by its very definition should not be worn on the sleeve, and once one does (like Vladimir Putin, who turns his faith into policy matters), it becomes obsolete.

These seem like the perfect conditions for starting an evolution. 'The petit bourgeois', whom the 1920s writer Andrei Platonov wanted to carry 'history forward' (quoted in McDaniel 1996: 39–40), has long been waiting his Russian turn. Even if Putin remains in the Kremlin for another decade, economic hardship may still bring an end to the virtual reality of strength that the president has been able to construct in Ukraine or Syria. Their current support for the President notwithstanding, Russians are more and more heard saying, 'They feed us with propaganda, but you can't put propaganda on your bread' (Levada Center 2015b).

Notes

1. Unless otherwise indicated, all translations from the Russian sources are the author's own.

2. Indeed, years ago, stepping into the Kremlin leadership role, Putin was full of hope for the better relations between Russia and the West. Interviewed on the BBC in March 2000, then a presidential candidate, he insisted that 'Russia is part of the European culture. And I cannot imagine my own country

in isolation from Europe and what we often call the civilised world. So it is hard for me to visualise NATO as an enemy'. ('Breakfast with Frost', BBC, 6 March 2014.)

3. See http://www.echo.msk.ru/.

References

Berdyaev, N. (1946) *The Russian Idea*, Paris: YMCA Press.

Berlin, I. (1969) 'Political ideas in the twentieth century', in I. Berlin *Four Essays on Liberty*, Oxford: Oxford University Press.

— (1978) *Russian Thinkers*, London: The Hogarth Press.

Berry, L. (2014) 'Putin's choice of words shed light on Ukraine', AP, 17 April.

Chaadaev, P. (1991) *Complete Collection of Works and Select Letters*, vol. 1, Moscow: Nauka.

— (1996) *Filosofskie pisma* [Philosophical letters], in P. S. Taranov (ed.) *Filosofskaya aforistika* [Philosophical Aphorisms], Moscow: Ostozhe.

Challands, R. (2015) 'Understanding Putin's popularity in Russia', Al Jazeera English, 22 October.

Chubais, A. (ed.) (1999) *Privatizatsiya po-rossiiski* [Privatization Russian Style] Moscow: Vagrius.

Epstein, M. (1992) 'Labor of Lust', *Common Knowledge*, 1(3) (Winter): 99.

Hellbeck, J. (2006) *Revolution on My Mind: Writing a diary under Stalin*, Cambridge, MA: Harvard University Press.

von Herberstein, S. (1966) *Description of Moscow and Moscovy, 1557*, edited by B. Picard, translated by J. B. C. Grudny, London: Dent.

Holmes, S. (1996) 'Cultural legacies or state collapse?' in *Post-Communism: Four perspectives*, edited by M. Mandelbaum, New York: Council on Foreign Relations.

Ilyin, I. (1992) *Nashi zadachi [Our tasks]* Moscow.

Khomyakov, A. S. (1992) 'O starom i novom' [On the old and the new], in *Russkaya ideya* [The Russian Idea], edited by M. A. Maslin, Moscow: Respublica.

Khrushcheva, N. (2009) 'KGB petroleum', Project Syndicate, 16 November.

— (2014) 'Inside Vladimir Putin's mind: looking back in anger', *World Affairs*, July/August.

— (2015) 'Europe versus Gazprom', Project Syndicate, 1 May.

Levada Center (2015a) 'Indexes: Approval of Putin', 31 October.

— (2015b) 'Analitika: Stranny sposob zavodit druzei' [A strange way to make friends], 12 October.

Lotman, Y. (1992) *Kultura I Vzryv* [Culture and Explosion] Moscow: Gnozis.

McDaniel, T. (1996) *The Agony of the Russian Idea*, Princeton, NJ: Princeton University Press.

Monaghan, A. (2015) 'The junk credit rating club: which countries join Russia at the bottom?' *The Guardian*, 27 January.

Motyl, A. J. (2011) 'A Russian threat to Ukraine?', *World Affairs*, 28 October.

Murphy, K. and Hessel, M. (1999) *Stealing the State and Everything Else: a Survey on corruption in the post-communist world*, Prague: Project Syndicate.

Myers, S. L. (2015) *The New Tsar: the Rise and reign of Vladimir Putin*, New York: Knopf.

Pipes, R. (2004) 'Flight from freedom: what Russians think and want', *Foreign Affairs* (May/June).

Prudnikova, Y. (2003) *Stalin. Vtoroe ubiistvo* [Stalin: The second murder] St Petersburg: Neva.

Putin, V. (2014) 'Address to the Federal Assembly', Kremlin.ru, 4 December.

Putnam, R. D. (1992) *Making Democracy Work: Civic traditions in modern Italy*, Princeton, NJ: Princeton University Press.

Robinson, P. (2012) 'Putin's philosophy', *The American Conservative*, 28 March.

Sachs, J. D. (1999) 'Eastern Europe reforms: why the outcomes differed so sharply', *Boston Globe*, 19 September.

Schmemann, S. (2007) 'A visit with Putin', *International Herald Tribune*, 16 September.

Stevenson, M. (1993) 'Dealing in Russia', *The American Scholar*, (Autumn).

Tertz, A. (Andrei Sinyavsky) (1976) *A Voice from the Chorus*, translated by K. Fitzlyon and M. Hayward, New York: Farrar, Straus, and Giroux.

Torres, H. (2015) 'Russian Orthodox Church supports Putin's 'holy war' in Syria to protect Christians', *Christian Today*, 2 October.

Vishnevsky, B. (2009) 'Lyudi bez svyatykh ponyatii' [People Without Sacred Beliefs], *Novaya Gazeta*, 3 June.

Walker, S. and Traynor, I. (2014) 'Putin confirms Crimea annexation as Ukraine soldier becomes first casualty', *The Guardian*, 18 March.

Washington Post, The (2014) 'Transcript: Putin says Russia will protect the rights of Russians abroad', 18 March.

World Policy Institute (1992) *Russkie o Russkikh: Mneniya Russkikh o samikh sebe* [Russians about Russians: Russians thinking of themselves] St Petersburg: Petro-Rif.

Chapter Two

The 'Russian Idea': A Fragment

Dmitry Bykov

The subject of my novel *Assassins* is the famous 'case of Ivannikova' – the woman who, under circumstances that remain unclear, killed an Armenian man who either tried to rape her or propositioned her, or simply reacted to her clearly suggestive behaviour.[2] In this novel, I attempted to paint the panoramic landscape of clandestine Russia – because today everyone is driven underground: liberals, nationalists, religious believers. In one of the nationalistic communities – the organisation of radical 'ruscists' (Russo-fascists) with its own training camp – the main hero of the novel finds an ideologist who is writing a treatise on the Russian character and national values. I would like to offer some fragments from this treatise, under the characteristic title of 'Russian Scum', in lieu of theses regarding the current state of 'the Russian Idea'. Leonid Leonov has already suggested to Korney Chukovsky[3] that the author's secret thoughts should be expressed through a negative character – the author remaining above suspicion; just in case, I remind the reader that the author of the treatise is unquestionably scum himself, a frequenter of one of Moscow's esoteric circles, whose prototype is the young Alexander Dugin,[4] and partly, perhaps, the mystical poet Eugene Golovin. Some of the ideas of the treatise reflect the theoretical propositions of the well-known contemporary anti-semite Konstantin Krylov.[5]

The Russian idea is not an idea: our ideology changes with the times and always entails support for the worst ideas, the bloodiest tendencies, and most revolting scoundrels, which a Russian nationalist must discover with the instinct of a bloodhound. The Russian idea is a mysterious modus operandi, and, because it is changeable and slithering, we can never be found out. This Russian modus operandi consists of us always being worse than both any possible adversary and any possible ally; the practice of Russian nationalism consists of always lowering standards, shocking the enemy into the realisation that, however cruel and unprincipled, he is never the cruellest and the most unprincipled. Russians can and must outdo any monstrosity; any evil can come to our land and meet absolute evil.

Here, of course, one could stop, because concrete examples are widely known. But this begs the question: Why? The answer may appear complicated to those who do not understand the reason for evil in life in the first place, but those few who have discovered from personal experience that true ecstasy is the ecstasy of the fall and none other – they realise that only Russia adds meaning and flavour to dull modern existence.

Every sphere of life in Russia is organised in the worst possible way: the goal of every official is to reject the greatest number of applications, finding fault in every curlicue, while every doctor, on the entrance of a patient, experiences first of all hatred and irritation, as if being torn away from something more important. The guarantee for any Russian to keep a position, indeed, is incompetence reinforced with lack of civility. Politeness in Russia is seen as a sign of weakness, honesty as cowardice, while competence is needed only to mask the innate incapacity to occupy the post. The true right to occupy it is manifested in that special haughtiness which, for Russians, takes the place of all professional virtues: we all know that the overwhelming majority of Russian bosses have fewer skills and less knowledge than their underlings – and only this justifies their superior position. Only those who cannot demonstrate such superiority have to work.

Sometimes, in patriotic publications, Russian culture is called a warrior culture, but this is incorrect: Russian culture, predominantly, is the culture of prisons. It is in prison that it reaches its highest concentration: prison is the ideal of Russia's life, and a Russian boss who has not known prison or did not have contacts with the criminal world is not a real boss. It is a mistake to attribute the prison taint of Russian culture to the criminal 1990s: these years only exposed the foundations of Russian life, because the cover of so-called 'culture' slid off actual day-to-day existence. Every Russian longs for prison, for the expectation of the inevitable arrest is a greater torment than the hell of prison itself. It deprives the food that we eat of taste, and even poisons sex. Chekhov, who felt the essence of Russian culture and our character especially acutely (because this was his character too), went to Sakhalin for the same reason that the hero of Tarkovski's *Sacrifice* burns his house: one is doomed, and waiting for the axe to fall is torture. In 'Ward No. 6' Chekhov described his own neurosis, common, however, to the majority of Russians, of the incessant expectation of arrest: one can be taken for nothing (and the clearer the innocence, the more certain the arrest), the lawyer can do nothing and makes his plea automatically, and the law can be turned any which way. Ivan Dmitrievich Gromov[6] understood this – and, others thought, went mad, while in fact becoming truly lucid. Chekhov also understood and went to Sakhalin voluntarily, in the hope that, were he to be arrested, he would at least be sent to a familiar place.

Tolstoy constantly and obsessively thought about prison, and most of his last novel takes place in one. Russians incessantly argue – not about the possibility of escaping prison as such, but about whether the experience of prison is harmful or salutary. This is precisely what Shalamov and Solzhenitsyn argue about,[7] losing from sight that their argument, happening in prison, is senseless, as is everything that happens there. Prison work is ineffective, prison ideas perverted, and everything that occurs in prison is oriented towards the greatest evil, most effective degradation, and maximum filth. The one who becomes the boss among criminals in prison is the one who has the fewest inhibitions.

Russians subconsciously attempt to create a world in which there will not be any inhibitions at all. To be Russian – as is stressed by every chansonnier, patriotic poet, and Komsomol leader who makes speeches from the podium at party meetings – usually means to be unruly, bull-headed, reckless, etc; love, he sings, must be mad, every cut – as the expression goes – from the shoulder. Russian love is traumatic: if one does not beat the woman, it is not love. When the woman is killed, which is what happens to Nastassya Filippovna at the hands of the truly Russian man Rogozhin,[8] one says that this is precisely what she needed, since nothing else would satisfy her.

Russians are ready to out monster every monster, to answer every good with a mockery, and they mask this constant readiness to up the ante for evil with freaky, tearful humility, under which always hides a bandit with a knife. Pity a crying Russian and he will immediately stab you; give a Russian beggar a coin and he will rob you, perhaps even murder you, because pity humiliates, and nobody has the right to humiliate Russians – theirs is the true, absolute grandeur. Should the Devil himself come to Russia, within moments he would lose his horns. When the devil tempter of the twentieth century Julio Jurenito[9] arrives in revolutionary Russia, he is killed for his boots. A Russian will out devil the devil, and he will simply cut into pieces anyone who laughs at him, for he does not understand humour. Russian humour consists of this cutting into pieces, because a human being cut into pieces is, above all, funny. Russians hate Jews with a particular intensity because of the abominable Jewish aspiration always to become more civilised: the Jew is incessantly hypocritical, always attempting to give form to the formless, the raw, the overcooked, the dilapidated, the rotten. The Jew would spray raw earth with perfume and try to make raw tripe look beautiful. Russians love what is raw and are raw themselves, and all this Jewish paraphernalia, this love of mothers for their children and love of children for their mothers, this reading of books and writing of poetry, all this filthy, cowardly, shaking-in-the-knees Jewishness is especially offensive for those who grow out of the land and return to it in the end. 'We lie with and become the land; that's why it belongs to us', wrote the most Russian of the Russian women-poets, unfailingly choosing the worst behaviour in the game of love. 'As is, I wish you another': suffer me as I am, as the fancy takes me. Every step in the direction of humanisation is a step down. Even Nietzsche went mad precisely because he started to act against his great demonic nature. A man, he declared, is one's ability to become a man; but this is like saying 'a billionaire is one's effort to become a billionaire'. No, a man is a step down, to an ant, to the condition of a slave; all that we call humanity is, in fact, slavery. A Russian, especially one conscious of being a Russian (and sometimes acting instinctively), is a demon, a superman, who has no obligations and spits on all rights. Humanity is precisely Jewishness, baby talk, salivation, concern for useless old people and disgusting, forever sick, constantly defecating children.

The only activity worthy of a superman is a bloody feast, the killing of all kinds of lowlife; Russians despise slave labour and do not wish to waste time on the creation of means for comforts and entertainment. Black mud, sucking swamps, heavy fog – this is the Russian landscape; the sight of valleys with cornflowers irritates a Russian, because he senses deceit. Goodness is invented for slaves and only slaves have a need of it – because any morality, every commandment and duty revolt a free man. A Russian is one who enters the tidy Western society or the filthy Eastern one and, whomever they worship there, that Russian is capable of destroying every temple and desecrating every faith. He knows no sacrilege, or, rather, sacrilege for him is what others call morality, service, and worship.

The planet must have a point of absolute contempt for everything, for this is precisely the highest point of freedom. A Russian despises everyone who works, everyone who respects rules and the law, everyone who loves or depends on others. A Russian would kill anyone who is weaker and spit in the eyes of anyone who is stronger; though one who would bow to the strong and do his every bidding is even more of a Russian, since rules of honour and nobility are also abominable. To stalk and kill from behind – this is in our nature. However, no one can be stronger than a Russian, because every strongman has to follow some rules, while a Russian follows none; one who already understand this will not be our enemy, for he would merge with our collective body.

We call someone a patriot whose behaviour is the worst and the surliest. The one who loves birch trees and languid noble maidens is not a patriot; a patriot wants to prohibit everything, and, having prohibited, openly and arrogantly transgress against every prohibition, for regulations exist only for slaves, never for the superman. A Russian wins in every struggle just by changing the rules of that struggle. Anyone might become a Russian, but only Russians can do so – perhaps, because our land is eternally damned, and this is its greatest blessing.

God looks at Russians with infinite curiosity, love, admiration – and treats them exactly as they treat others.

Notes

1. Translated by Liah Greenfeld.
2. See, among others, 'Conviction of would-be rape victim sparks uproar', www.nysun.com>foreign>conviction 24 June 2005; 'Nationalists give cash to Ivannikova', *The Moscow Times*>news>article>nat… 28 July 2005; 'Russian woman accused of killing rapist gets full acquittal', Free Republic>focus>f-news>posts 19 November 2005.
3. Leonid Leonov (1899–1994) – a Soviet writer (Stalin's Prize, 1943; Lenin's Prize, 1957). Korney Chukovsky (1882–1969) – children's poet, literary critic.
4. A Russian political thinker with close ties to the Kremlin and the Russian military; Ph.D. in Sociology; the leading organizer of the National Bolshevik Party and Eurasia Party; according to Wikipedia, 'the driving conceptual force behind Vladimir Putin's initiative for the annexation of Crimea'.
5. Editor-in-chief of *Russian March* (*Russkiy Marsh*) and of *Questions of Nationalism*; fifth most influential Russian intellectual in *Openspace* poll.
6. The hero of 'Ward No. 6'.
7. See, among others, 'Varlam Shalamov – Russiapedia Literature Prominent Russians', RT.com>russiapedia>…>Literature.
8. Reference is to protagonists of Dostoyevsky's *The Idiot*.
9. The hero of the eponymous 1922 novel by Ilya Ehrenburg.

Chapter Three

The Construction, Deconstruction and Conflict of National Identities in Moldova

Lee Cojocaru

Introduction

The idea of nation-state has become so deeply embedded in our socio-political vocabulary that it is almost impossible to conceive of other forms of socio-political organisation or expression without reference to it.

> People of new states are animated by a powerful motive: to be noticed, it is a search for identity, and a demand that identity be publicly acknowledged as having import, a social assertion of the self as 'being somebody in the world'.

> (Geertz 1963: 108)

The nation-state develops only where nationalism and a state, oriented towards a particular nationalism, converge. Although the governments of post-Soviet Moldova intended to develop a unitary national identity to serve as a foundation for the state, after more than two decades, Moldova is still not a nation-state. Not because it lacks nationalism, but because it has two competing, diverging versions of nationalism. The story of Bessarabia/Moldavia/Moldova clearly illustrates the dynamics of a disputed national identity, caused by a succession of constructed and deconstructed identities imposed on the people inhabiting this land.[1]

This chapter attempts to shed light on the way identities were constructed and deconstructed in the case of Moldova, which led to the present-day conflict between Romanian and Moldovan nationalists. The first section briefly introduces the theoretical debate on what constitutes ethnic/national identity and presents the evolution of various identities in Moldova. The second section gives an overview of the creation of Bessarabia, the Russian (and later Soviet) policies towards the formation of 'Moldavian nation' and the rise of supporters of this 'Moldovan' identity. The third section presents how Romanian ethnic nationalism emerged in Bessarabia and later in Soviet Moldavia. The fourth section examines the struggle of the Romanian and Moldovan nationalist camps in Moldova today.

National identity and its evolution in Moldova

The primordialist school claims that ethnicity constitutes a fundamental feature of society and that ethnic/national identity is natural and unalienable.[2] They see ethnic identity as 'essential' to human identity and mostly inalterable. This means that ethnicity forms slowly and, once formed, tends to be exceptionally durable and persistent. Ethnicity, therefore, is defined by cultural and biological heritage and is territorially rooted. In contrast, the instrumentalist approach emphasises the rational-choice and interest-driven character of nationalism (Bell 1975; Brass 1991). Instrumentalism focuses on elite competition for resources and suggests that the manipulation of symbols is vital for gaining the support of the masses and achieving political goals. The structuralists (also known as materialists and Marxists) identify some variation of material advancements in human history (the modern state and its needs: print, public education, a middle class) as the progenitor of nationalism (Hobsbawm 1990; Gellner 1983; Anderson 1983). Unlike structuralists, who posit the existence of deterministic structures, the cultural approach (Max Weber, Liah Greenfeld) emphasises meaning and human action (Weber 1978; Greenfeld 1992). Ethnicity does not constitute an objective group, but only 'facilitates group formation of any kind, particularly in the political sphere' (Greenfled 1992: 389). And it is this political community 'no matter how artificially organized that inspires the belief in common ethnicity' (Greenfeld 1992: 391). According to this view, identity (national, but not only) is not a reflection of the material world, but a mental process. 'It is a mental image of the social structure and one's specific place in it ... [which] orients [one's] actions' (Greenfeld and Prevelakis 2010: 2516). Therefore, nationalism must precede the nation, because it is the worldview that 'locates the source of individual identity within a people, which is seen as the bearer of sovereignty, the central object of loyalty, and the basis of collective solidarity' (Greenfeld 1992: 3).

According to Greenfeld, a nationalist vision of reality is predicated on three principles: it is an essentially secular vision, it is fundamentally egalitarian, and it assumes popular sovereignty. Nations removed sovereignty from traditional authorities, such as God or a royal lineage, and vested it within the people (Greenfeld and Prevelakis 2010).

We are presently witnessing a conflict between the 'Moldovan' identity constructed by the Russian authorities in the nineteenth century and perfected by the Soviets in the twentieth century and the Romanian national identity which emerged at the end of the nineteenth century under Russian control, developed when Moldova was united with Romania in the interwar years, and reappeared in the 1980s when Moldova was part of the Soviet Union. Today, the Romanian and Moldovan nationalisms are fighting to dictate the terms of this new, post-Soviet national identity. The two centuries of overlapping and intermittent Russian and Romanian control over this land provided plenty of ammunition for each camp.

Nationalism is attractive to large masses of people because it provides its holders with dignity. In many societies, the individuals most attuned to issues of identity and concerned about dignity are the intellectuals. Often, alienated from traditional society, the *intelligentsia* felt a disequilibrium between their perceived high self-value and their low social status. This imbalance also known as *anomie* acted as the motivating factor in the creation of a new ideology of nationalism, which propels them to a new, dignified social status (Geertz 1973: 204; see also Durkheim 1984). Not accidentally, it was the intellectuals who embraced nationalism, both in Russian Bessarabia and later in Soviet Moldavia. Moreover, Moldova, like most post–Soviet societies, experienced cultural trauma as a consequence of the unexpected, rapid, and fundamental changes brought about by the end of the Soviet Union. Insecurity and uncertainty became a normal experience of daily life for many citizens. A breakdown of social trust and a loss of a sense of agency – anomie – ensued. Suddenly, culturally shared templates were no longer appropriate for guiding behaviours in the changing socioeconomic and cultural contexts, and therefore national identity became the default identity (Sztompka 2004).

Table 3.1 summarises the historical evolution of identities in Bessarabia, Soviet Moldavia, and Moldova. Each identity was filled with various cultural elements and had its promoters. Some identities have been shared only by a minority, while others have been held by a majority of the population.

Table 3.1: Ethnic identities in Moldova 1812–2015

Identity	Period	Agents/ Interested Party	Population	Character/content
Bessarabian Moldavians	1812–1991	None	Majority (peasants)	Local, Christian, non-national identity
Assimilated Moldavians/ Russians	1840–1918 1945–1989	Tsarist Russia	Nobility, Communist members (career opportunity)	Russian nationalism, Russian culture (language and literature), xenophobia, anti-Semitism
Bessarabian Romanians	1840–1940	Romanian Nationalists both in Romania and Bessarabia	Intellectuals (with time, most of the literate population)	Romanian nationalism – Romanian language, literature, history; xenophobic and anti-Semitic as well
Moldavians (Soviet)	1924–89	USSR, Communist Party	Initially Party members;with time – majority (peasants, workers)	Class-based initially (Moldavians were the working people, Romanians were bourgeois exploiters and their administration). Transformed into ethnic identity (Cyrillic alphabet, Slavonic words)

(Continued)

Table 3.1: *(continued)*

Identity	Period	Agents/ Interested Party	Population	Character/content
Moldovans	1989-2015	Former party members, collective farm managers, politicians	Majority (peasants, workers)	Moldovan nationalism – historical claims from medieval Moldavia, admits Russian influence and avoids cultural debates as much as possible; claims of civic nationalism, 'Moldavian' language in the Constitution
Romanians	1960s –2015	Intellectuals	Minority (journalists, teachers, writers)	Romanian nationalism – cultural unity with Romania (Latin alphabet, Romanian history and literature)

Note that many in rural Moldova have developed neither a Romanian nor a Moldovan national identity, but rather have a non-national, localised ethnic identity.

The birth of Bessarabia and the construction of Moldovan identity

During the 1806–12 war with the Ottoman empire, Russia's goal was the annexation of both the principalities of Moldavia and Wallachia, but the threat of invasion from Napoleon's France forced Russia to settle for a smaller territory – Eastern Moldavia/Bessarabia (a territory in which the present-day Republic of Moldova lies). After annexation, in order to make Russian rule attractive for the Christian Orthodox people of the Balkans, Tsar Alexander I decided to leave the local laws in place and exempted the population from poll taxes and military service for three years (Postarencu 1998: 66).

At this time, the national spirit in Bessarabia was 'weak' and 'self-interest of family or class was more important [than nationality]' (Jewsbury 1976: 8).

After the Crimean War (1853–6), the rebellion in Poland (1863), and the Union of Romanian Principalities (1859), Russia focused on imposing full control over Bessarabia to prevent Romanian claims on this territory. Russian administration employed large-scale Russification policies in schools, administration, and churches. In 1892, Pompey Batyushkov, a Russian Interior Ministry employee, was sent to prove that Bessarabian Moldavians are not Romanian. A staunch Russian nationalist, Batyushkov described his role as a Russian scholar to present 'the Russian point of view and to prove Bessarabia's ancient bonds to the Slavic-Russian tribe' (Batyushkov 1892: 2). Batyushkov insisted that the Slavs had been the predominant element in Bessarabia from the sixth century onward

Figure 3.1: Moldavia in 1812 – without Bessarabia and Bukovina

and the 1812 annexation was nothing but 'a reunion of Bessarabia with Russia' (Batyushkov 1892: 5). Batyushkov openly recommended that authorities use the public education system to Russify the locals:

> If we want to save Bessarabia from being the object of Romanophile ambitions and agitations, and if we want to form an organic union with Russia, then we must hasten to utilize our schools for the purpose of changing (let us hope) half of these Moldavian peasants into Russians.

(Batyushkov 1892: 172)

Under Russian rule, Romanian-language newspapers appeared sporadically and briefly. Out of 254 periodical publications in Bessarabia in the period 1854–1916, only sixteen were in Romanian (Trubetskoi, *Периодические Печати Бессарабии* [Periodical Prints of Bessarabia], in Jewsbury 1976: 9). With trans-border traffic restricted, access to Romanian and Western books dwindled severely. Some Romanian books made their way into Bessarabia, but only if purchased in St Petersburg or Moscow and with authorisation from a censure committee in Odessa (Arbore 1898: 529). Alexei Mateevici, a Bessarabian poet, complained:

> The greatest difficulty I had was that I lacked the necessary books for guidance. I was totally isolated from literature published in *Regat* [Romanian Kingdom]. … The hunger for books in our native language is indescribable.

(Mateevici 1989: 108)

Similar language restrictions were imposed in churches. In 1871, the newly appointed Metropolitan Pavel Lebedev discovered that many of the priests spoke little, if any, Russian (Constantinescu-Iasi 1929: 5). Infuriated by this, he suppressed the Romanian version of the official newspaper of the Bessarabian Church and burned all the books in Romanian at the Chisinau Seminary.[3] All Church documents and registries were now kept only in Russian, and priests were given a six-month deadline to learn Russian (Clark 1927: 104). Metropolitan Lebedev's language policies raised a lot of resistance, as most priests kept using Romanian, not because they were ardent nationalists, but mostly because their parishioners were illiterate and resistant to the imposition of a foreign language.

Most of the new public schools had already been teaching in Russian since 1824, when Count Vorontsov instructed that 'Moldavian [Romanian] should be taught to the students who want to learn it only as a second language' (Pelivan 1919: 19). By 1912, out of 1,709 primary schools, only one third taught in Romanian (Ciobanu 1993: 260). This fact did not help combat high illiteracy among the rural population (mostly Moldavians) and ensured that Moldavians were mostly

Figure 3.2: Administrative map of Guberniya, Bessarabia, 1883

unaffected by Russian culture and Russification of the schools, churches, mass media, and administration.

After the union of Bessarabia with Romania in 1918, the new Soviet government denied it recognition and insisted that Bessarabia's majority population constituted a separate nation whose cultural distinctiveness was being obfuscated by Romania. To prove this, some historians and writers – most of whom had a Slavic and not a Romanian background – rehashed Batyushkov's old claims and began to assert the existence of a unique Moldavian nationality with a language and history distinct from that of Romania.[4] The same theory was espoused by the Soviet authorities when they regained Bessarabia after World War II and named it the Moldavian Soviet Socialist Republic (MSSR). In his 1974 book, Artem Lazarev, the head of the Soviet Moldavian Academy of Science, claimed that there were two East Romance nationalities – Moldavian and Romanian (Lazarev 1974: 530–5). A variation of this view was later embraced by many 'Moldovanists', who stated that the Bessarabian population developed into a separate nation in the nineteenth century when Bessarabians did not share the historical and cultural experiences of the unified Romanian nation.

Before the USSR regained Bessarabia from Romania in 1924, the Soviets decided to establish a Soviet autonomous republic on the eastern bank of the Nistru River, the Moldavian Autonomous Soviet Socialist Republic (MASSR) (King 2000: 52). The goal behind MASSR was either to Sovietise Romania or to annex Bessarabia, thus 'uniting the separated Moldavian nation'. Either way, the

Figure 3.3: Bessarabia, Bukovina, and Transnistria (1924–1940)

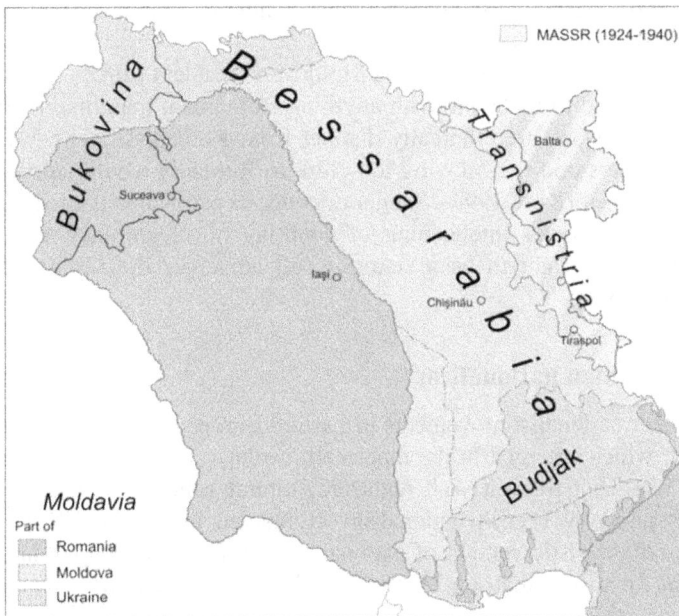

MASSR represented an element of Soviet political pressure on Romania (King 2000: 55).

To support their claims on Bessarabia, the Soviets decided to fabricate an entirely new language (King 1999: 58). To start, Cyrillic alphabet was introduced in the 'Moldavian' language in MASSR. Because the new language was based on an archaic vocabulary and lacked modern terminology, the Communists had problems using it in the press, scientific texts, or official communiqués. To address this, a whole new vocabulary of Russian words with Romanian suffixes was introduced. However, the new tongue was so removed from the actual language spoken by the population that it was incomprehensible to the masses.[5] Moreover, Soviet propaganda still used Romanian poets and personalities to build a Moldavian literature, only claiming them to be Moldavian.

Stalin's policies in the Soviet Moldavian Republic after the World War II focused on the negation of national culture and the destruction of any form of social organisation outside the Communist Party, achieved by mass killings, arrests, and deportations. Among hundreds of thousands deported were teachers, priests, policemen, holders of political and administrative positions, etc.

> The deportations, arrests, executions and deliberately induced famines were applied in Soviet Moldavia with a rigor which probably claimed the life of one Moldavian out of ten between 1945 and 1953.

> (Eyal 1990: 126)

With most of the local intellectual elite gone to Romania or deported to Siberia, the memory and the identity of 'Romanianness' diminished drastically after the war. There were only isolated incidents of anti-Soviet resistance (Grecul 1974: 158).

After independence, newly elected Moldovan president Mircea Snegur and his supporters refused to associate with anything Romanian, maintaining the Soviet view that Moldovans are ethnically distinct from Romanians. The Moldovanist politicians understood that moving too close to Romania would jeopardise their positions of power (King 1994). Snegur denounced pan-Romanianism as betrayal and accused Moldova's intellectuals of doubting 'the legitimacy and historical foundation of our right to be a state, to call ourselves the Moldovan people' (Snegur 1994: 3).

Rise of Romanian nationalism

Just like other nationalist movements in Eastern Europe, the Romanian nationalist movement, which emerged in the nineteenth century, adopted the national model from the West, but filled it with domestic cultural content. Although they were initially inspired by French nationalism, Romanian intellectuals had settled on the ethnic-collectivistic version of nationalism espoused by German intellectuals. The reason for this is that, unlike the French, but similarly to the Germans, the

Romanians built a nation and a national culture before they could have a state. Just as in Germany, the Romanian intellectuals imprinted an ethnic character on their national identity, because they had to focus on the task of creating an original literature, composing music, writing history and philosophy, publishing magazines and newspapers, establishing theatres and museums, educating teachers, and opening public schools.[6] After the 1859 union that formed Romania, Romanian intellectuals obtained their nation-state and focused on spreading that identity to the masses.

In Bessarabia, Romanian national ideas emerged a few decades later than in the Romanian principalities (Moldavia and Wallachia). Some nobles and intellectuals were connected to the cultural life of Romania and developed a Romanian national identity, despite all the efforts of the Russian authorities to prevent it. Ion Doncev's fifth edition of the ABC in 1863 no longer had the word 'Moldavian' in the title but was named *Cursul primitiv de limba rumînă* [The Primary Course of the <u>Romanian</u> Language] (Postarencu 1998: 117). Doncev's book was printed in Latin script and had content similar to the ones published in Romania.

The most prominent intellectual of his generation the historian and philosopher, Alexandru Haşdeu (1811–74), despite studying in Russia and Germany, was a staunch Romanian nationalist. On the occasion of the 1859 union of the principalities, he sent a famous letter addressed to 'our Romanian brothers':

I belong with body and bone to the same bones from which you are made; and in my veins flows the same Romanian blood as in yours. ... to live without you and outside of you, oh, my dear Fatherland is possible, but a life like this is worse than dying a thousand times and resurrecting every time just for a moment.

(Arbore 1898: 470)

As the first nationalist ideas emerged in Bessarabia throughout the nineteenth century, most of the holders of these ideas had to flee to Romania to avoid being censured or imprisoned by the Russian authorities. This is how the émigré Alecu Russo described his impression of his life in Bessarabia:

We are fugitives in the parental hut and foreigners in the land paid for with our blood! The intruders told us: 'This is our land and all who live on it belong to us, as well as the fields, the hills, the hamlets, the towns and the villages, the houses with their yards, all that moves and breaths.'

(Adauge 1990: 115)

If the flourishing cultural space of Romania attracted the Bessarabian intellectuals, the nobility found benefits (land and service careers) in remaining loyal to Russia. Romanian nationalists/intellectuals lambasted and criticised what they saw as an act of betrayal on the part of the nobility (the boyars). Because they valued their culture so much, it was inconceivable for these intellectuals that someone could renounce one's culture. Zamfir Arbore was among those who condemned the boyars for this:

Russian administration transformed Moldavian boyars into bureaucrats devoted to Russia and enemies of the Romanian people. One can rarely hear Romanian spoken in their houses and many do not know how to speak it.

(Arbore 1898: 541)

With the access to Romanian literature and media severely restricted, few pro-Romanian voices were left in Bessarabia. Only when the youth (some of them Russified) went to study in other Russian cities and encountered representatives of other national groups from the empire did national consciousness emerge in their minds. Studying in the cities of the Russian empire, young Bessarabians became active members of the political underground. One of its strongest cells was at the Dorpat University in Tartu, Estonia. The leader of the Dorpat group Ioan Pelivan had experienced an interesting life transition from a loyal Russian subject to becoming a staunch Romanian nationalist.

Like many other Bessarabian intellectuals and nationalists, Pelivan started his education at the Kishinev (Chisinau) seminary, where studies were conducted in Russian, and Romanian was considered 'the language of the *mujiks*'. At the seminary 'all our thoughts, our love and our minds were directed towards Russia,' recalled Pelivan in his memoirs (Pelivan 2006: 38). It was later, in his college years at Dorpat, when, through contagion from other national groups, Pelivan developed a sense of national identity of his own. The sight of portraits of national poets and writers in their classmates' dorm rooms (such as the Ukrainian Taras Shevchenko; the Poles – Mickiewicz and Sienkiewicz), 'left a feeling of shame

Figure 3.4: Romania with Bessarabia and Bukovina (1920)

with all of us Moldavians who knew nothing about our past and had no knowledge of a Bessarabian poet or writer' (Pelivan 2006: 38).

Pelivan and others decided to form the *Pământenia Basarabeană* [Bessarabian Compatriots] – student cultural association – at whose meetings they started reading Romanian literature and singing folk songs. They contacted cultural clubs and other Bessarabians in Romania and started smuggling Romanian literature into Russian cities where they were studying. For example, in a letter of 25 October 1901, Pelivan asked Gheorghe Madan to send some books, commenting: 'the boys are developing the taste for Romanian books and culture, and are awakening a national consciousness' (Pelivan's correspondence 1999: 6). His colleague Vasile Oatu who could barely write in Romanian, in a letter asked Madan for more books about Romanian history, saying: 'Myself a Romanian, I've been looking for a long time now to familiarise myself with Romanian culture and especially history' (Pelivan's correspondence 1999: 7). In 1902, however, most of the members of *Pământenia* were arrested and sentenced to prison on several charges: for organising an illegal and revolutionary society; for political propaganda against the regime; and for Moldavian separatism. These intellectuals were the ones who later fought and contributed to the union of Bessarabia with Romania. During the interwar years, Romanian identity was spread in Bessarabia via public education, press, and administration.

Half a century later, in Soviet Moldavia, despite the fact that whole villages and most intellectuals had been executed or deported to Siberia, Romanian nationalism persisted. In 1966, Mihai Morosanu, a student at the Polytechnic Institute in Chisinau, was condemned to three years in the Gulag for protesting about the removal of the statue of Stephen the Great from the city centre. The same year, another nationalist Gheorghe Muruziuc suffered a similar fate for raising the tricolour flag at a sugar factory in Alexandreni. In 1967, three conservatory students (Postolache, Cuciureanu, and Cemârtan) received sentences of between four and seven years for anti-Soviet propaganda and 'nationalism', because they had promoted the reunification of Moldavia and Bukovina with Romania. Many nationalists were forcibly admitted to psychiatric clinics, while many others lost their jobs and careers (Graur 1999: 8).

Russification policies failed to fully dislodge Romanian culture from the minds of the new generation of ethnic Moldavian intellectuals. Since the old guard of historians and writers educated at Tiraspol Pedagogical Institute in Transnistria had to retire, some works of Romanian writers such as Eminescu, Coşbuc and Goga were reintroduced in the school textbooks while a course on local history was introduced in some universities.[7] By the early 1970s, this new generation of Moldavian intellectuals inferred that, if the classics of their literature, with whom they identified, such as Eminescu and Alecsandri, considered themselves Romanian, they themselves were also Romanian (King 2000: 108).

Many young nationalists in Soviet Moldavia left Chisinau to escape Communist harassment. In Russian cities, young Moldavians had access to libraries and bookstores filled with Romanian literature, history, and commentary, forbidden in their home capital Chişinău. Although, they could not organise as their predecessors at Dorpat and Kiev (who formed *Pământenia Basarabeană* and

Desteparea) had done, these Moldavians would meet to sing and recite Romanian poetry. Moreover, they were encouraging their friends and acquaintances to continue their 'fight for Romanian revival'. Mircea Druc, who would later become the prime minister of Moldova from the nationalist Popular Front, wrote to his younger brother Vlad in 1962:

> You should try to open a discussion club for the improvement of language. You have to teach people around you about the necessity of studying their own language, to read Romanian literature, to pronounce correctly. First of all, do not forget that we are Moldavians, and, therefore, Romanians.

> (Patrichi 1998: 55)

Romanian nationalists such as Alexandru Şoltoianu, Gheorghe Ghimpu, Valeriu Graur, and Alexandru Usatiuc were arrested and tried in 1972 for forming a nationalist organisation – the National Front. They were fighting to establish Romanian language as a state language, to organise free and fair elections, to exit the Soviet Union and to ultimately unite with Romania. Most in the group met the fate of their Bessarabian predecessors sentenced and sent to harsh Siberian prisons.

Education and interest in high culture (literature, music, history) in both Bessarabia and Soviet Moldavia thus led inevitably to Romanian nationalism. Individuals with such interests were automatically drawn to the Romanian cultural space. Romanian nationalists did not have to write their own history and literature or reinvent their origin – all they had to do was to adopt the culture from across the Prut River (Negru, in Pelivan's correspondence 2009: 63–4). This importance of culture in the formation of Romanian nationalism imprinted on it an ethnic character. One of the Romanian nationalists Iurie Roşca described his identity in 1995:

> Like any Romanian, I was born in the midst of a church, in the midst of a kind, in the midst of a family. These are realities given to me by God, which I cannot and wish not to modify. Because these realities do not represent an act of volition, I cannot do anything else but orient all my efforts to preserve and affirm these values which I received through birth.

> (Roşca 1995)

After Gorbachev's glasnost reform in the 1980s opened up the public space for criticism and allowed opposition to the Communist Party to emerge, Romanian intellectuals in Moldavia quickly mobilised. They gained editorial control of several mass circulation newspapers (*Literatura şi Arta* [Literature and Art] and *Învăţamînt Public* [Public Education]) and began to espouse publicly the case for radical restructuring (Crowther 1991: 188). They used the newfound free speech and freedom of assembly to organise themselves into a cohesive movement – the Moldovan Popular Front. Soon it would rally thousands to gather in Chişinău to protest about the status of their native language.[8]

The Front demanded the recognition that Romanian and 'Moldavian' are one and the same tongue (Eyal 1990: 132). The intellectuals' claims to language and cultural affirmation made it increasingly clear, as in the 1900s, that Moldova's identity could not be defined without reference to Romania (Eyal 1990: 131). Latin script was soon adopted, along with the Romanian anthem *Deșteaptă-te Române* [Romanian Arise] as Moldova's anthem and the Romanian tricolour as the official flag of Moldova. The Popular Front eschewed the 'Moldavian' Soviet identity and declared:

> The historic name of our people, which we have carried for centuries – a right to which chronicles and manuscripts, historical documents from the modern and contemporary periods, and the classics of Marxism–Leninism testify – is Romanian and the name of the language is the Romanian Language.
>
> (*Documentul final al Marii Adunari Naționale* 1989: 2)

At its second congress in February 1990, the Popular Front openly called for exit from the USSR and union with Romania. However, the people were fearful of such drastic changes, especially since the Moldovanist politicians opposed the nationalists from the Front, rallying the peasants to oppose the union with Romania. In 1993, the Front split, with one group leaving to form the Congress of Intellectuals which advocated a slower, gradual integration with Romania, rather than immediate political union. The poet Grigore Vieru admitted that intellectuals would have to take up the difficult task of reawakening the sense of 'Romanianness' within the rest of the population before unification could be considered (Vieru 1991: 1, 5). In other words, to construct the Romanian identity they had to deconstruct the Soviet project of 'Moldavian' nation.

The role of Russians and Russia

Losing their high status as members of a global superpower, many Russians regretted the dissolution of the USSR. They felt betrayed by the rapid and jubilant separation of the republics from the Soviet Union and threatened by the rise of new ethnic elites to power. The pro-Russian parties often reproached Moldovans/ Romanians, accusing them of being ungrateful for Russia's civilisational role in modernising Moldova.

To redress the fall of USSR, the Russian Government proposed the creation of the Community of Independent States (CIS) as a step towards rebuilding the union. At the same time, the Russian authorities pressured the republics to preserve the socio-economic and cultural privileges which the Russian minority had enjoyed in them during Soviet times, especially resisting any policy of imposing local national languages. This helped the adoption of very lenient pro-Russian laws in Moldova and the preservation of the status of the Russian language as the language of inter-ethnic communication till today, which satisfied other ethnic minorities as well. In an attempt to create a 'civic nation', a set of inclusive citizenship laws was adopted in

1991, which still failed to prevent the secessionist movement of the minorities.[9] Like Romanian nationalists, the Russians in Transnistria and the Gagauz in the South do not believe Moldova to be a legitimate state and agitate for closer ties with Russia.

Russia's geopolitical games in the region are blamed for diverting Moldova's path from closer ties with Romania and Europe. In the early 1990s, Russia encouraged ethnic minorities to rebel and ask for autonomy and, in the case of Transnistria, for independence. The Russian army, which was stationed in Transnistria, intervened on the side of Russian separatists who had de facto won the 1992 war and declared an independent, but unrecognised, state of their own. Today, the survival of the Transnistrian regime is possible because of Russian economic help and the presence of the Russian military in Transnistria.[10] Moldova depends on energy imports from Russia and relies on the Russian market for its agricultural products.[11] Russia also actively supports the Russian-speaking media, and pro-Russian parties and organisations. The Moldovan airwaves are dominated by Russian TV channels.[12]

Just like the Romanians, who want to see Moldova as part of Romania, the Russians prefer that Moldova revert to Russian control. The lack of loyalty of many citizens towards the Moldovan state is well illustrated by the issue of dual citizenship. Although Moldovan governments have prohibited dual citizenship for a while, it failed to stop more than half a million citizens from becoming citizens of Romania and almost two hundred thousand citizens of Russia, besides several tens of thousands who became citizens of Bulgaria and Ukraine.[13]

Moldovanism versus Romanian nationalism

The first Russian census in Bessarabia was conducted in 1817 and found Moldavians (Romanians) to represent 86 per cent of the population, Ukrainians 6.5 per cent, and Jews 4.2 per cent (Nistor 1991: 103). Because of Russian colonisation, by mid-century the proportion of Moldavians (Romanians) in Bessarabia's population had decreased to 65 per cent (Nistor 1991: 103). A century later, in 1992, the census revealed that 64.5 per cent were Moldavians (Romanians), 13.8 per cent Ukrainians, 13 per cent Russians, 3.5 per cent Gagauz, and 3 per cent Bulgarians.

The identity issue has been used in every electoral campaign, socio-economic and political topics being replaced by debates about history and language. Some experts and commentators (i.e. King and Druc), believe that the rise of the Moldovanist movement was mostly interest based and prompted by the desire to hold positions of power. Although this is true, the main reason for the rejection of Romanian culture is that people such as Snegur and his allies were not ready for such a step. They were unfamiliar with Romanian culture, as they grew up immersed in Russian culture, and thought of themselves as Moldavians. Moldovanists and their electorate, formed mostly of peasants, felt awkward speaking literary Romanian. With their thick accent, Russian calques and archaic dialectal expressions, Moldovanists were embarrassed when compared with the highly educated intellectuals, just as they were embarrassed by the Russian cultural dominance under the Soviets. To escape this embarrassment, they chose a third way – neither with Romania, nor with Russia.

The isolation of the Bessarabian peasants protected them from Russification, thus helping preserve a localised and village-based identity. In fact, there were two parallel worlds coexisting in Bessarabia and Soviet Moldavia: the rural world, which was illiterate, mainly Romanian-speaking, and lacking any national identity; and the urban, which was much smaller in size, ethnically diverse, and dominated by Russian language and culture. The rural world had no national consciousness, only a folklore-based culture, which was preserved due to its isolation from the city. The urban world was dominated by other ethnic groups (usually Jews, followed by Russians and Ukrainians, and some Germans in the South). In the nineteenth century, a Romanian nationalist discourse had no audience in the cities, while in villages the message and its vectors were not adjusted to the illiterate audience. However, with time, more Moldavians moved into the cities and were exposed to education and nationalist ideas. Throughout the twentieth century, a majority of peasants kept their local ethnic identity, despite the efforts of the Soviet and Romanian authorities (Cash 2007).

Lately, Romanians have organised marches every year to celebrate the 1918 union of Bessarabia with Romania on 27 March and promote the idea of reuniting with Romania. In turn, they are accused by Moldovanists of destroying Moldova's socio-political stability and Moldova's statehood.

Figure 3.5: Evolution of ethnic identities in Moldova since the 1300s.

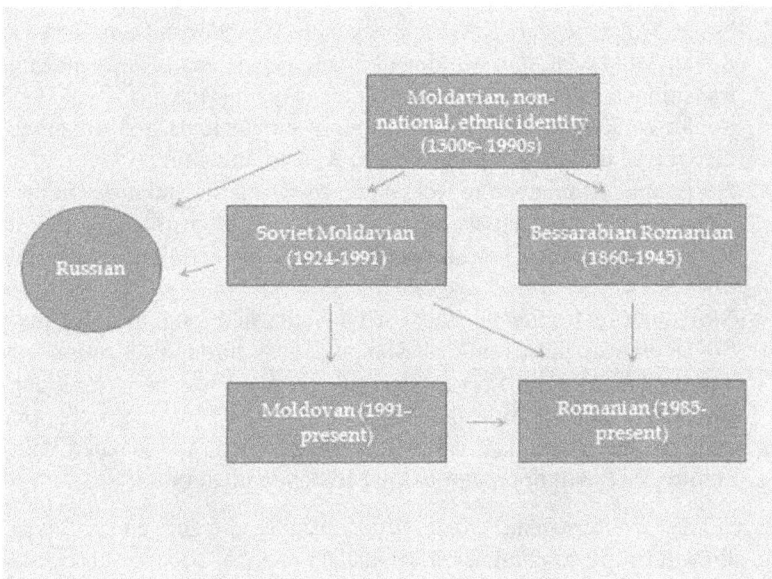

We are celebrating a historic date in the past of our people – 27 March – the union of Bessarabia with Romania. We believe that, just like those who criticise us have the right to identify as Moldovans, we also have the right to call ourselves Romanians.

(Declaratia Platformei Civice Actiuinea 2012)

Romanian nationalists also commemorate the day of the invasion of Romanian Bessarabia by the Soviets in June 1940. In contrast, the Moldovanist camp avoids mentioning the deportations and famine caused by the Soviets after the annexation of Bessarabia. In fact, they treat the Russians as liberators and celebrate Victory Day on 9 May. Christmas, too, is a subject of debate: Romanians celebrate it following the Gregorian calendar on 25 December, while Moldovanists follow the Russian Church and Julian calendar which celebrates Christmas on 7 January. Thus even this holiday serves as an identity marker in this battle of nationalisms.

The chart below is a summary of all the various identity transitions of the people in Moldova.

- Moldavian into Russian: many Moldavian nobles have assimilated into Russian culture. In fact, this was a transition from an ethnic local identity into the Russian national identity.
- Moldavian into Romanian: most intellectuals such as Haşdeu, Stere and Pelivan. This was the transition from an ethnic local identity to the Romanian national identity.
- Moldavian into Soviet Moldavian: Communist ideologues who helped build the concept of the 'Moldavian' nation. It is difficult to say whether it was a national identity, but it definitely presented elements of ethnicity.
- Soviet Moldavian into Russian: many mixed families and assimilated locals.
- Soviet Moldavian into Moldovan: many politicians such as Snegur, who transitioned effortlessly to this new identity after the fall of the USSR.
- Soviet Moldavian to Romanian: many intellectuals and urbanites who discovered that they belonged to the Romanian culture.
- Bessarabian Romanian to Romanian: Mircea Druc and many in the older generation of intellectuals, who had their identity instilled by their family in their youth after World War II, despite the efforts of the Soviets to dislodge it.
- Moldovan to Romanian: the younger educated generation of the post-Soviet era who discover their 'Romanianness' through education and high culture (literature, history). Interestingly, there was no 'transition' from Romanian identity to Moldovan. It might be a sign that, once someone acquires the Romanian national identity, which is associated with high culture, they will not revert to the Moldovan identity.

To summarise, Romanian ethnic nationalism reemerged under Soviet rule despite all the attempts to eliminate it. Romanian nationalists were strongest in the period 1988–91, when they were at the forefront of liberation and the language movement. Once independence was achieved, Moldovanists took control of power and marginalised the nationalists. Since then, Moldovanists have tried to build a separate national identity to legitimise the existence of the new state, while Romanian nationalists have strived to thwart their efforts and keep pushing for union with Romania. The Moldovanist camp has managed to maintain independence, but continues to struggle in creating a unified national identity, because Romanian nationalists (along with Russian nationalists and other minorities) challenge the legitimacy of the state itself. Romanian nationalism has historical and cultural support, but is shared mostly by a minority of educated people. In the 2004 census, 75.8 per cent declared themselves Moldavians and only 2.2 per cent of the population self-identified as Romanians.[14] However, since the census, various surveys indicate that between 5 and 28 per cent of the population self-identified as Romanians.[15]

The Romanian nationalists maintain their claim that Moldovans are nothing but ethnic Romanians who were late to develop a Romanian consciousness because of the Russification policies applied in Moldova over the last two centuries. They show disdain for Moldovan identity, because they see it as an artificial Soviet construct or at most a low culture based on folk art. On the other side, the Moldovanists claim that Moldovans are a distinct nation, because it formed separately from Romania and under the impact of Russian culture. They accept that Moldovans share some aspects of culture with Romanians; nevertheless, they claim that a separate historical experience caused Moldovans to develop a distinct identity.

Unlike the more linear cases of emergence of nationalism, Moldova has seen a rather angular trajectory of nationalism: Romanian nationalism (late nineteenth century and early twentieth century), followed by a Moldavian nationalism (constructed by the Soviets); the rise of Romanian nationalism under the Soviets; and finally the battle of the two ethnic nationalisms today.

Notes

1. Note that the terms 'Moldavia/Moldavians' designate the medieval state and the population residing in it while it was under Russian and Soviet control and the population which had no national identity or ethnic Moldovan identity. The name 'Bessarabia' was introduced when the Eastern part of the principality of Moldavia (present day Moldova) was annexed in 1812 by Russia. This name has been used as a synonym for Eastern Moldavia ever since. The modern name 'Moldova' was (re)introduced by the nationalist movement in the 1980s and has been used since then to designate the modern Republic of Moldova.

2. This theory is also called essentialist, ethnonationalist, or ethnosymbolist. (Connor 1994; Geertz 1973; Smith, 1986).

3. This happened in the same year that Bessarabia lost its privileged status and became a gubernya.

4. This is also the period when the Transnistria was artificially created, carved up out of Ukrainian territory in order to claim unification with Moldova. See Jelavich 1983.

5. All modern scientific terms were replaced with ones that existed in the vocabulary of the peasants at the time. This led to some hilarious results. For instance, the term 'uric acid' was replaced with 'oţet chişălnic' [piss-vinegar]!

6. Signs of Romanian national consciousness appeared much earlier in the seventeenth century. First, it was Moldavian humanists, who under the influence of the Polish Catholic schools discovered the common Latin/Roman origin of Moldavians, Wallachians, and Transylvanians. Later, the union between the Catholic and the Orthodox Churches in Transylvania gave rise first to a cogent nationalist programme espoused by the Uniate bishop, Inochentie Micu-Klein. The rebellion of Tudor Vladimirescu in Wallachia (1821) spread nationalist ideas from the clergy to the lower nobility and the military. Only a decade later, after the opening of trade with Western Europe when young boyars travelled to Western Europe and were exposed to nationalist ideas, Romanian nationalism emerged.

7. Until then only the history of the USSR and the Communist Party were studied.

8. The leaders of the Front were mainly writers and journalists such as Grigore Vieru, Leonida Lari, Dumitru Matcovschi, Nicolae Daija, Valentin Mandacanu, Nicolae Matcas, Constantin Tanase, and Vasile Bahnaru.

9. Compared with the Baltic Republics, which mandated that anyone who wanted to obtain citizenship had to be a resident for a certain amount of time, speak the state language fluently, etc., Moldova offered citizenship to all residents of Moldova at the time of declaring independence with no conditions.

10. The Russian government supplies the natural gas for which Transnistria did not pay and accrued billions of dollars of debt, and also funds the pensions for Transnistrian retirees.

11. In 2014, after the Moldovan government signed the Association Agreement with the European Union, Russia imposed restrictions on imports of agricultural products from Moldova, which seriously hurt local farmers who lost their traditional customers. The EU provided some relief funds to reimburse the losses caused by the Russian embargo.

12. By my own calculations conducted in 2013, out of 54 TV channels, 32 were in Russian, 8 were in Romanian and the rest were transmitting programmes in both languages or in other languages.

13. Many assume that Moldovans want Romanian citizenship only to have free access to European Union (no visa requirement), but a 2007 IMAS-IPP survey (November) showed that 48.5 per cent wanted Romanian citizenship so that they could travel to Romania, 32 per cent because they felt Romanian, and only ten per cent because they wanted to travel freely to the European Union.

14. Many sociologists and pollsters suspect that there was a lot of interviewer error and bias in the way the questions in the census were designed. This suspicion was confirmed to me in a private conversation by Doru Petruţi, the director of the IMAS polling institute.

15. The survey with the highest numbers was conducted in 2005 by a Moldovan polling agency 'ABC X'.

References

Adauge, M. (1990) 'Istoria şi faptele' [History and Facts], *Dnestr*, Chisinau 4.

Anderson, B. (1992) *Imagined Communities: Reflections on the origin and spread of nationalism*, New York: Verso.

Arbore, C. Z. (1898) *Basarabia în secolul XIX [Besarabia in the XIXth century]*, Bucharest: Institutul de Arte Grafice Carol Göbl.

Avramescu, T. (ed.) (1996) *Scrisori din Basarabia. 1880–1883 [Letters from Bessarabia]*, Chisinau: Ştiinţa.

Batyushkov, P. (1892) *Бессарабия. Историческое Описание [Bessarabia: A Historical Description]*, St Petersburg: Edition of the Ministry of the Interior.

Bell, D. (1975) 'Ethnicity and social change', in *Ethnicity: Theory and experience*, edited by N. Glazer and D. P. Moynihan, Cambridge, MA: Harvard University Press.

Berejan, S. (1985) *Literatura si Arta*, 24 August.

Brass, P. (1991) *Ethnicity and Nationalism*, New Delhi: Sage Publications.

Bruchis, M. (1996) *The Republic of Moldavia: From the collapse of Soviet Empire to the restoration of the Russian Empire*, Boulder, CO: East European Monographs.

Cash, J. (2007) 'Origins, memory, and identity: 'Villages' and the politics of nationalism in the Republic of Moldova', *East European Politics and Societies* 21.

Chicu, G. (1936) 'Pamântenia basarabeană din Dorpat', *Viaţa Basarabiei* 7–8.

Ciobanu, Ş. (1993) *Unirea Basarabiei [The Union of Bessarabia]*, Chişinau: Universitas.

Clark, C. U. (1927) *Bessarabia: Russia and Roumania on the Black Sea*, New York: Dodd, Mead and Company.

Connor, W. (1994) *Ethnonationalism: The quest to understanding*, Princeton, NJ: Princeton University Press.

Constantin, I., Negrei, I., and Gheorghe, N. (2012) *Ioan Pelivan, Părinte al Mişcarii Naţionale din Basarabia [Ioan Pelivan, The Parent of National Movement in Bessarabia]*, Chisinau: Notograf Prim.

Constantinescu-Iasi, P. (1929) *Circulaţia vechilor cărţi bisericeşti româneşti în Basarabia sub ruşi [The Circulation of Romanian Old Church Books under the Russians]*, Chisinau: Notograf Prim.

Crowther, W. (1991) 'The politics of ethno-national mobilization: nationalism and reform in Soviet Moldova', *The Russian Review* 50.

Dima, N. (1991) *From Moldavia to Moldova: the Soviet–Romanian territorial dispute*, Boulder, CO: East European Monographs.

Durkheim, E. (1984) *The Division of Labor in Society*, New York: Free Press.

Ețco, D. (2008) 'The Chisinau seminary', *Revista de Istorie a Moldovei* 1.

Eyal, J. (1990) 'Moldavians', in *The Nationalities Question in the Soviet Union*, edited by Graham Smith, London: Longman.

Feldmans, W. (1975) 'The theoretical basis for the definition of Moldavian nationality', in *The Soviet West: Interplay between nationality and social organization*, edited by R. Clem, New York: Praeger.

Fischer-Galati, S. (1973) 'Moldavia and Moldavians', In *Attitudes of Major Soviet Nationalities*. Cambridge, MA: Center for International Studies, MIT.

Geertz, C. (1963) *Old Societies and New States*, New York: Free Press.

— (1973) *The Interpretation of Cultures*, New York: Basic Books.

Gellner, E. (1983) *Nations and Nationalism*, Ithaca, NY: Cornell University Press.

Graur, V. (1999) *De te voi uita Basarabie [If I Forget You, Bessarabia]*, Chisinau.

Greenfeld, L. (1992) *Nationalism: Five roads to modernity*, Cambridge, MA: Harvard University Press.

— (2001) 'Etymology, definitions and types', in *The Encyclopedia of Nationalism*, edited by Alexander Motyl, 1, San Diego: The Academic Press.

Grecul, I (1974) *Расцвет Молдавской Социалистической Нации. [The Flourishing of Moldavian Socialist Nation]*, Chisinau: Cartea Moldovenească.

Hobsbawm, E. (1990) *Nations and Nationalism Since 1780: Programme, myth, reality*, New York: Cambridge University Press.

Holban, M. (ed.) Călători străini despre Țările Române [Foreign Travelers about Romanian Countries], *Academia Română*, Vol. X.

Iorga, N. (1940) *Adevărul asupra trecutului și prezentului Basarabiei [The truth about Bessarabia's Past and Present]*, Bucharest: Institutul Cultural Roman (Romanian Cultural Institute)

— (1917) *Histoire de Relations Russo-Roumaines*. Iasi.

— (1979) *O lupta literara*, Bucharest: Minerva.

— (1983) *Istoria literaturii române în veacul al XIX-lea [History of Romanian Literature in the XIXth Century]*, Bucharest.

Jelavich, B. (1995) *History of the Balkans: Twentieth century*, New York: Cambridge University Press.

Jewsbury, F. G. (1976) *The Russian Annexation of Bessarabia 1774–1828: a Study of imperial expansion*, Boulder, CO: East European Monographs.

King, C. (1994) 'Moldovan identity and the politics of pan-Romanianism', *Slavic Review* 53.

— (1995) 'Moldova with a Russian face', *Foreign Policy* 97.

— (1999) 'The ambivalence of authenticity, or how the Moldovan language was made', *Slavic Review* 58.

— (2000) *The Moldovans: Romania, Russia, and the politics of culture*, Stanford, CA: Hoover Institution Press.

Lazarev, A. (1974) *Молдавская Советская Государственность и Бессарабский Вопрос [Soviet Moldavian Statehood and Bessarabian Question]*, Chisinau: Cartea Moldoveneasca.

Mateevici, A. (1989) *Scrieri [Writings]*, Iasi: Editura Junimea.

Mircea, S. (1994) 'Republica Moldova este ţara tuturor cetaţenilor săi' [Moldova is the country of all its citizens], *Pamînt şi Oameni*, 12 February, 3.

Negru, G. (2000) *Politica etnolingvistica in R.S.S. Moldoveneasca* [Ethnolinguistic politics in Moldavian S.S.R], Chisinau: Prut International.

Nistor, I. (1991) *Istoria Basarabiei*, Bucharest: Humanitas.

Ornea, Z. (1989) 'Ştiinţa spre a străbate la adevăr', *Magazin istoric* 8.

Patrichi, V. (1998) *Mircea Druc sau Lupta cu Ultimul Imperiu [Mircea Druc and the Battle with the Last Empire]*, Bucharest: Zamolxe.

Pelivan, G. I. (1919/2006) *La Bessarabie sous le régime russe*, Paris: Minard.

Pelivan, I. (2006) 'Basarabia cea diferită de Rusia', *Magazin istoric* 3.

'Pelivan's correspondence', (2009) *Destin Românesc* 5–6.

Pelivan, I. Romanian Central Archives, Bucharest, Personal File 1908–45.

— Romanian Central Archives, Bucharest, Personal File 1876–1944.

— Romanian Central Archives, Bucharest, Personal File 1842–1943.

Postarencu, D. (1998) *O istorie a Basarabiei in date si documente, 1812–1940 [A history of Bessarabia in dates and documents]*, Chisinau: Cartier.

Roşca, I. (1995) 'După Exerciţii de luciditate', *Contrafort*, August.

Scurtu, I. (1998) *Istoria Basarabiei*, Iasi: Polirom.

Seton-Watson, R. W. (1963) *A History of the Roumanians*, second edition, Hamden, CT: Archon Books.

Smith, A. D. (1971) *Theories of Nationalism*, New York: Harper & Row.

Sztompka, P. (2004) 'The trauma of social change: a case of post-communist societies', in J. Alexander et al. (eds) *Cultural Trauma and Collective Identity*. Berkeley, CA: University of California Press.

Van Meurs, P. W. (1994) *The Bessarabian Question in Communist Historiography*, Boulder, CO: *East European Monographs*.

Vieru, G. 'Unirea nu se proclama la mitinguri', *Dimineata*, 27 November 1991, 1.

Weber, M. (1978) *Economy and Society: An outline of interpretive sociology*, edited by G. Roth and C. Wittich, Berkeley, CA: California University Press.

Zavtur, A. (1972) *Formarea si dezvolatrea structurii sociale socialiste in Moldova [The Formation and Development of Socialist Social Structure in Moldavia]*, Chisinau.

Archival documents in *Destin Românesc*, 2008, (XV) No. 5–6, Institutul Cultural Român, Chisinau.

'Declaratia Platformei Civice Actiunea 2012', *Jurnal MD*, 26 March 2012.

Documentul final al Marii Adunari Naţionale [The Final Document of The Great National Meeting] in *Literatura si Arta*, 31 August 1989.

Programul Frontului Popular Crestin Democrat [Political Platform of Christian Popular Front], Chisinau, 1992.

Totalurile recensămîntului unional al populaţiei din RSSM din anul 1989 [Collection of Census Data of MSSR 1989] Chisinau, 1990.

Chapter Four

A Partnership of Equals or Equal Membership? Equality and Difference in Multinational States

Emmanuel Dalle Mulle

Introduction

In his Tanner Lecture on 'Dignity, rank and rights', Jeremy Waldron reported the story of Isabel, Countess of Rutland, who, in 1606, was arrested in London by two sergeants and put in prison for a week, until she paid a long-overdue debt of £1,000. Yet, the Star Chamber later found the imprisonment unlawful and meted out a harsh punishment against the creditor – a commoner who had sued the Countess – and the two sergeants. The court argued that:

> the person of one who is ... a countess by marriage, or by descent, is not to be arrested for debt or trespass; for although in respect of her sex she cannot sit in Parliament, yet she is a peer of the realm, and shall be tried by her peers.

> (quoted in Waldron 2009: 241)

Pointing out that the privilege granted to Countess Isabel in 1606 is today bestowed upon every citizen,[1] Waldron suggested that the last centuries have witnessed a historical transformation: the attribution of the dignity recognised for Countess Isabel to every member of society, or, in other words: 'an upwards equalization of rank, so that we now try to accord to every human being something of the dignity, rank, and expectation of respect that was formerly accorded to nobility' (Waldron 2009: 229).

A similar insight lies at the core of Liah Greenfeld's conception of nationalism. According to Greenfeld (1992: 1)

> the specificity of nationalism, that which distinguishes nationality from other types of identity, derives from the fact that nationalism locates the source of individual identity within a 'people', which is seen as the bearer of sovereignty, the central object of loyalty, and the basis of collective solidarity.

The novelty of nationalism consisted in the coincidence of the concepts of the people, which in the pre-modern era mainly referred to the plebs, and the nation, which instead indicated an elite. From such a coincidence derived one of the pillars of modern nationalism: the belief in the fundamental equality of all members of the national community (Greenfeld 1992: 1–10).[2]

Both Waldron's and Greenfeld's accounts relate to the progressive expansion of the idea of the equality of men, which has become a mainstay of liberal democracy (Beitz 1989: 217; Cristiano 2008: 2–3; Dahl 1986: 9; Dworkin 2007: 43; McGann 2006: 5; Sadurski 2008: 19). Yet, while Waldron's considerations are framed in universalist terms, Greenfeld clearly points to equality within a bounded group: the national sovereign community. Most theoretical works on democracy take it for granted that such community is endowed with its own state institutions, thus forming a nation-state where equality is ensured by means of equal citizenship. But, what if there are alternative and conflicting definitions of the relevant national community within the same political system? In other words, how is equality to be understood in the context of a plurinational state? Is there a clash between different understandings of equality, in particular between individual and group equality?

This chapter tries to answer these questions by looking at the arguments for independence and self-determination formulated in recent years by two separatist parties (the Scottish National Party and the Republican Left of Catalonia) in two plurinational states (the UK and Spain) and by analysing the idea of equality that they have defended and/or implicitly assumed. It first provides an introduction on the interrelation between the concepts of equality, nationalism, and democracy. Yet it does not aim at a theoretical or a normative contribution to the literature on the subject, but – in the second and third sections – rather offers empirical materials that are often missing in such theoretical treatments. The fourth section then examines whether and to what extent their demands have triggered competitive dynamics among other regions of the parent state. In the conclusion, I briefly address the question of whether the deepening of democracy is likely to stimulate nationalist conflict.

Equality, nationalism and democracy

As argued by Charles Beitz (1989: 217), 'political equality is the central organizing idea of modern democratic belief'. Yet, equality is an ambiguous concept. Jonathan Still (1981) singled out six meanings of political equality, while Douglas Rae *et al.* (1981) concluded that, counting all possible permutations, one might obtain 108 senses. The ambivalence of equality goes much beyond a mere lack of clarity and constitutes a fundamental ambiguity. Opposing prescriptions can be defended in good faith on the basis of the principle of equality because of a fundamental disagreement about the meaning of the concept. A good example is provided by the principle of affirmative action, which replaces the idea of formal equality (embodied by the maxims of 'equality before the law' and of 'one man one vote') with that of substantive equality (requiring positive action to redress the marginalisation of specific groups). Both supporters and detractors have resorted to the concept of equality to underpin their arguments (Sadurski 2008: 100). Such a fundamental disagreement also has to do with the recognition of morally relevant differences within the populations in question, such as to justify differential treatment (Cristiano 2008: 24–5), or with a belief in the possibility of an agreement on what differences would be relevant for this purpose (McGann 2006: 13).

Furthermore, much of the theoretical debate about equality and democracy has been conducted from an individualist perspective. Yet, equality is enforced by government institutions that refer to a specific body politic – the *demos* – and, therefore, to varying extents discriminate against outsiders. In this way, despite being conducted in individualist terms, discussions about equality and democracy often effectively refer to a form of group equality in disguise (Tamir 1993: 139). This raises the question of 'what group?' As sharply stressed by Robert Dahl (1982: 98), the question of who is the *demos* 'is in fact an embarrassment to all normative theories of democracy, or would be were it not ignored'. The boundaries of the political community can come under attack from two sources. First, as suggested above, the *demos* can be contested from the outside. Although democracy is a system in which the rulers and the ruled coincide (Abizadeh 2012: 867), exceptions exist. While some, based on functional considerations (children, criminals), are relatively unchallenged, others (long-term residents of foreign nationality) are contested on moral grounds – equality underlying democracy is an eminently moral principle – and their legitimacy ultimately rests on the importance attributed to collective cultural membership for individual freedom, welfare and self-respect (Kymlicka 1995: 75–106; Margalit and Raz 1990; Miller 1995; Tamir 1993: 72–7; Taylor 1994).[3] Second, and more importantly, the *demos* can be contested from 'within'. This is the case with national minorities who see themselves as a distinct political community endowed with a right to self-determination. As insightfully captured by Will Kymlicka (1995: 10–33), while immigrants might ask for the recognition of some cultural specificities, their primary interest is integration into the new society. Autochthonous national minorities, on the other hand, do not like to be portrayed as a 'sub-category' of the wider society, but rather prefer to be considered as a distinct demos on a par with the other demoi inhabiting the state. The scope of the group rights demanded in the second case is much bigger, because they not only involve the recognition and accommodation of different cultural practices, but openly call for sovereignty, understood as self-determination.[4] Equality is thus to be evaluated on an individual level within each demos and on a collective one between demoi, therefore entailing inequality on an individual level across demoi. In the second to fourth sections, these theoretical considerations will be applied to the claims of equality made by the Scottish National Party (SNP) and the Catalan *Esquerra Republicana de Catalunya* (Republican Left of Catalonia – ERC).

Before proceeding we must briefly discuss the relationship between democracy and nationalism. Democracy being a self-referential system – 'the principle of legitimacy refers right back to the very persons over whom political power is exercised' (Abizadeh 2012: 867) – there is nothing inherent in democratic theory that can, by itself, help us derive any criteria to determine the boundaries of the self-ruling community. Such a function is performed by nationalism (Calhoun 1993; Canovan 1996: 1–4; 2000).[5] This does not mean that nationalism is always democratic, but modern democracies did develop in the bosom of nationalism

(Greenfeld 1992: 10). A quick perusal of the constitutional texts of most democracies shows that states ground their legitimacy in the will of the people – understood as the nation. Yet, in a context in which more peoples inhabit the same state, such a claim fundamentally undermines their legitimacy, since it is indubitably contradictory to claim self-determination as the main source of political legitimacy and, at the same time, deny the very same self-determination to another national community (Requejo 2011: 16). This contradiction in the normative structure of plurinational states accounts for numerous nationalist conflicts. It is with this insight in mind that in the conclusion I shall deal with the question of whether 'more democracy' – and notably a stronger stress on popular sovereignty – puts under stress the cohesion of plurinational polities.

The SNP, Scotland and the democratic deficit

In its 1978 booklet *Return to Nationhood*, the SNP made it very clear that 'Scotland has never been regarded by British Governments as a free and equal partner in the Union with England but as a lesser province with reservoirs of manpower, ability, space and wealth which could be tapped as required' (SNP 1978: 11–12). This sentence contains an element of the party's rhetoric that has persisted throughout its recent history, i.e. the denunciation of Scotland's marginalisation – often referred to as provincialisation – within a Union that was formally intended as a 'partnership of equals'. Hence, equality in the UK has been primarily conceived of by the party as equality among the constituent nations (England, Northern Ireland, Scotland and Wales), violated by the dominance of England and justifying differential treatment for the members of each unit. As argued by Stephen Maxwell (1981: 5–6), one of the most influential intellectuals within the SNP in the early 1980s:

> unlike Wales and Ireland, Scotland had had the strength to withstand the military challenge to her statehood. But she had neither the population nor the wealth to share the British Isles with England as a political and cultural equal. In an unequal compromise with her powerful neighbour she sacrificed her political independence to her economic prosperity (see also Wilson 1988: 6).

The clearest example of this understanding of the Union as a partnership of equal collective units – and equality as group equality – is embodied by one of the mainstays of the party's discourse: the argument of the 'democratic deficit', developed during the 1980s, especially the second half of that decade, under the successive Conservative governments of Margaret Thatcher. The core of this narrative lay in the point that Scotland had to withstand painful economic policies inflicted by the Tories, who were a political minority in the region (Mitchell 1996: 221–43). As a leaflet distributed ahead of the 1987 election asserted, the Labour Party was dominant in Scotland but could not govern in London because of the Tory preponderance in England. Hence – it concluded – 'it's as if the general election counted for nothing in Scotland' and the Scots had to choose between 'either suffering decades of Tory rule from England, OR helping the SNP fight for our own Independent Scottish Parliament' (SNP 1987, emphasis in the original). The 'imposition' of Tory rule over Scotland was considered even more illegitimate because Scotland 'had consistently rejected the ethical, social and political values entailed in Thatcherism which Britain as a whole has endorsed' (Wilson 1988: 11; See also McIlvanney 1987: 8).

Why was Thatcher's rule considered illegitimate in Scotland and not in other areas of the UK where the Tories were not in a majority? The north of England, for instance, experienced higher unemployment and continued supporting Labour to a similar extent as Scotland did throughout the 1980s (Martin 1988). Yet, no serious argument of democratic deficit developed there. Furthermore, on a simple arithmetical basis, in 1981, with 9.2 per cent of the UK population, Scotland was entitled to 10.9 per cent of seats in the House of Commons, being therefore overrepresented on a per capita basis with regard to other parts of the country. The idea that Conservative rule during the 1980s was illegitimate therefore stemmed from Scotland's identity as a constituent unit of the Union, endowed with a special status that made the detrimental policies of a party holding a minority in the region unacceptable. This is also confirmed by Thatcher's reasons for rejecting Scottish devolution. Thatcher's staunch opposition to any transfers of powers to Edinburgh derived from her belief in the free market and a strong state (Gamble 1988) which required privatisation, centralisation and the erosion of intermediary structures between atomised individual citizens and the state. Given this, Thatcher conceived of the Scottish Office as an 'added layer of bureaucracy, standing in the way of reforms' and Scottish autonomy, in general, as a vested interest 'overburdening the British state' (Bennie *et al*. 1997: 12). She wanted to rule the UK as a unitary country – a 'nation of property owners' (Evans 2009) – with a strong majority enjoying the democratic legitimacy to implement its own will across the country. But her new kind of 'One Nation Policy' was divisive, because conflating unionism and unitarianism (Finlay 2012: 168) in Scotland sounded like an English violation of the partnership of equals formally underlying the Union.

The importance of the Thatcher years and the narrative of the democratic deficit that arose towards their end could hardly be exaggerated. The argument reverberated in the SNP's propaganda (see Salmond 1993a: 58; SNP 1997: 7, 2003: para. 19), its use escalating with the austerity measures imposed by Cameron's administration during the recent economic crisis and the 2014 independence referendum campaign (SNP 2011: 28; 2013: 41 and 331–7; Sturgeon 2013). But its impact was much larger. Thatcherism provided Scottish anti-Unionists with material to craft the narrative of victimisation that had been lacking, or was weak, until then, a narrative that enabled the 'nation' to clearly identify a force responsible for all that was wrong with it (Hassan 2012: 85). It thus breathed new life into the struggle for the establishment of a Scottish Parliament, which had vanished from sight after the 1979 referendum (Hassan 2009: 153–5; Lynch 2002: 166–85). The 1980s also brought about a change in the meaning of Britishness and an increase in the distinctive character of Scottishness. Specifically, Britishness was repackaged as Scottish: 'the Scots, it was claimed, had different values of political culture from the English. They were more in favour of state intervention and the social institutions of the state' (Finlay 2005: 375). Accordingly, British institutions such as the NHS were increasingly depicted as Scottish ones.

Being Scottish came to be increasingly associated with being more egalitarian than being English – and thus British, since in this perspective Britain would be dominated by England. Such a view has been potently exploited by the SNP – whose propaganda obviously contributed to further spreading it. Independence became portrayed as a means to ensure greater equality, better democracy and more social justice for the Scottish population. According to the party, this improved egalitarianism would take two forms. First, an independent Scotland would be based on the 'Scottish' doctrine of popular sovereignty, as opposed to the British principle of the Crown-in-Parliament. This would entail more direct citizen participation in the democratic process, through referenda and public committee hearings (Salmond 1993a: 58–61). The 1997 manifesto made clear:

> citizens of Scotland, wherever they have come from, will be full participants in a twenty-first century democracy, not subjects of an outmoded and decaying eighteenth-century state ... An independent Scotland will have a written constitution and Bill of Rights ... they will be protected from the type of arbitrary interference that is the hallmark of Westminster government, and they will be able to force the state to honour its commitments to them.

> (SNP 1997: 7)

At the same time, equality will also mean social equality. Given the (purportedly) higher 'compassionate ethos' of the Scottish population, independence will mean a more redistributive social policy and a fairer economic model than those pursued by successive UK governments. For instance, in 2005, the party argued that

> in modern Europe, social justice and economic prosperity go hand in hand, and the most successful small nations are those that give equal weight to both. All of the Nordic countries are more competitive than the UK. And they also give greater priority to social justice and equality than the UK. An independent Scotland will follow their example.

> (SNP 2005: para. 5.2)

Similarly, during the 2014 independence referendum campaign, the SNP consistently suggested that an independent Scotland would be a fairer democracy simply because:

> it will be the people who live in Scotland who will be in charge ... we will be able to take the right decisions for our future, based on our shared values and priorities and using our wealth of resources and talent.

> (SNP 2012: 11)

Again, this relies on the representation, stressed above, of the Scottish population as inherently more egalitarian than the English one. The achievement of more equality among Scottish individuals therefore requires getting rid of British (in)equality in order to ensure a truly equal partnership between the English and the Scottish nations:

> we believe the 300-year old political Union is no longer fit for purpose. It was never designed for the 21st-century world. It's time for a new partnership on our isles – a social union that ensures Scotland and England are equal nations – friends and partners – both free to make our own choices.
>
> (SNP 2010: 17)

Economic policy – according to the SNP – is probably the area in which such a need is clearest. A key argument in this respect has been that formal equality between economic actors in the UK substantially favours London and the south-east of England, where most of the government and economic activity is already concentrated. This means that:

> Scotland already competes with England. And the competition is an unfair one. Westminster has dictated a so-called level playing field for all regions and countries of the UK. This means that a business trying to decide between locating in London or Glasgow has the same monetary policy in place, the same interest rates, and the same levels of corporation tax but set at their current levels, none of them favour Scottish cities and towns. This further supports the south east of England as the centre of power, business, and transport and London as the wealthy epicentre drawing talents, profits and growth ... we need to reverse this gravitational pull, put Scotland at a competitive advantage and deliver the growth we so badly need.
>
> (SNP 2002)

These economic considerations are related to the theme of social equality. In the party's mind, a strong economy is necessary for achieving more social justice, since prosperity and growth lie at the core of any effective redistribution. In this connection, the SNP also accused the south-east of England of being made up of 'subsidy junkies' (Salmond 1993b: 18) and successive Westminster governments of having wasted much of Scotland's North Sea oil revenues, which, if used by an independent country, would have contributed to building a 'social-democratic utopia'[6] on the Norwegian model (SNP 1984, 2003: para. 6.1, 2011: 40). Yet, when compared to ERC (as we will see below), the party has not played so strongly on the theme of Scotland's excessive solidarity burden with the rest of UK, because of its ambiguous fiscal position within the British system. Hence, it is dubious whether the demand for more equality for Scotland, through keeping and redistribution within Scotland of a higher share of the resources produced there, implies a rejection of solidarity with the rest of Britain, since, in practical terms, it is impossible to clearly establish whether Scotland has been damaged by British redistribution or not – the most reliable estimates actually suggest that the balance is roughly even, if not to Scotland's advantage (Clive 1995; McCrone 2013). Yet the decision of the SNP Scottish Government, in 2012-2013, to exclude pupils domiciled in the rest of the UK from the abolition of university tuition fees in force in Scotland – which means that they will pay an amount established by Scottish universities but in any case similar to what they will face in England, Wales or Northern Ireland – can be interpreted as expressing rejection of solidarity with the rest of the UK. While the policy was justified by the need to 'shelter' students domiciled in Scotland from the unprecedented level of competition that would naturally stem from the differential in tuition costs (SNP 2013: 197–200), it clearly suggests that the protection of the equal opportunities of Scotland's residents requires discrimination against students from the rest of the UK. Although such a policy was certainly motivated by the limits of the then funding agreement with Westminster, it was intended by the SNP to remain in place after independence, when Scotland would be arguably free of the budget strictures imposed by Westminster.

ERC, the Catalan nation and asymmetric federalism

The relationship between Spain and Catalonia as portrayed in the propaganda of ERC after the process of rejuvenation between 1987 and 1989 – which turned it into an unambiguously separatist party (Rubiralta 2004: 200–3) – has been characterised by much stronger claims of oppression and subordination than those of 'provincialisation' with regard to Scotland and the United Kingdom. Thus, for instance, in the early 1990s, the party denounced the failure of Spain's democratic transition, complaining that Catalonia had remained 'a nation separated into two states, economically plundered, culturally subjugated and, what is most important and determines the rest: politically subordinated' (ERC 1992: 13).[7]

The main policy areas in which the (Spanish) mononational and the (*Esquerra*'s) plurinational conceptions of Spain have openly clashed – with all the implications for understandings of equality – are the constitutional reform of the country into a federal entity and the fiscal transfers between Catalonia and the central state.

With regard to the first, in the years immediately after the 'rejuvenation', and arguably up until the mid-1990s, the idea that the democratic transition had failed and that Spain had not fundamentally changed after the end of the dictatorship featured high in the party's propaganda (see, for instance, Colom 1989, 1995: 51; ERC 1990, 1993a: 11). When such claims are examined in detail, one finds that *Esquerra*'s criticism boils down to the non-recognition of Catalonia as a sovereign constituent unit of Spain endowed with a right to self-determination (ERC 1989: 21, 1992: 12; Carod-Rovira 1991: 4; Colom 1995: 19). The party argued that democracy was more than a theory of the legitimate power of the majority and in fact entailed limits to its power. But the reasoning went further: true democracy should allow for the possibility that the relationship between minorities and majorities be redefined. Minorities should be able to deal on a par with majorities and set up their own state institutions if they so wish. According to this understanding, Spain would not be a democracy because the Spanish constitution does not recognise the plurinational character of the state (ERC 1989: 20–2, 1992: 23–5, 1993c: 20; Colom 1995: 38–41), thus imposing individual equality across the country, instead of recognising the group equality of its constituent units. The party also deplored the low level of citizens' participation in the democratic process and – like the SNP – called for setting up mechanisms to increase their involvement in public decisions.

Towards the end of the 1990s, the party began campaigning for a modification of the statute of autonomy of Catalonia, approved in 1978 (Culla 2013: 502–05). This debate became increasingly important after, in 2000, the Popular Party (PP) won an absolute majority in the Spanish Parliament, which enabled it to stop the process of devolution of powers that had taken place throughout the 1990s (Colino 2009; Guibernau 2013: 380–81).[8] In this context, *Esquerra* vocally deplored the PP's attempts at recentralisation and the persistence of the so-called '*mentalitat radial*', whereby every political decision should be taken in Madrid and from there uniformly applied everywhere in the country (ERC 2000b, 2001b, 2002, 2003b: 6). The party made clear in 2000: 'the PP unleashed again a clear reactionary offensive, based on the claims of the stalest Spanish-centred mentality and the return to the unitary state, thus stigmatising democratic peripheral nationalism and rejecting any proposals of a plurinational structure' (ERC 2000a: 7). *Esquerra* further accused the PP of using the pretext of 'equality' between the different Spanish autonomous communities in order to stop the democratic process of devolution of powers to Catalonia (ERC 2004: 6). Once again, the principles of group equality among demoi and individual equality within a single demos conflicted.

In the Spanish context, such a conflict traces back – to limit ourselves to the recent democratic period – to the Constitution adopted in 1978: a full description of the process is beyond the scope of this chapter. Suffice it to say that the major fault-line pitted the most important state-wide parties – the PSOE and the Union of the Democratic Centre (UCD)[9] – against peripheral nationalist parties, especially the Basque and Catalan ones. The former were keen on limiting the degree of powers transferred to the autonomous communities – the UDC to a larger extent than the PSOE – and, in any case, supported a symmetric federal model based on the equalisation of the powers transferred to the regions[10] (known in Spanish as *café para todos*, i.e. coffee for everybody). The peripheral parties, on the other hand, asked for a special status based on the recognition of their national difference (*hecho diferencial*) (Keating and Wilson 2009: 540). A compromise was found in an ambiguous constitutional formulation whereby the national groups that had been granted, or had voted for, autonomy before the Civil War in the 1930s – the Basque Country, Catalonia and Galicia – obtained the status of historic nationalities and were allowed to initiate the transfer of powers immediately, while the other communities had to wait longer and to follow a different procedure. In the long run, however, all communities were allowed to obtain similar degrees of autonomy (Colomer 1998: 40–42).

After more than twenty years of overall successful, although not easy, accommodation, the conflict between 'federal equalisation' and the Catalan demand for a special status broke out in force during the reform of the Community's statute of autonomy. Such reform was one of the major items on the agenda of the government coalition formed by ERC, the Catalan Socialist Party (PSC) and the Greens after the 2003 Catalan elections (Orte and Wilson 2009: 424–5). According to the gradualist strategy favoured by the new leadership of Josep-Lluis Carod-Rovira, *Esquerra* envisioned the reform as a necessary intermediate step in the transition to full independence. The main aim of the party was to reach a new constitutional agreement recognising Catalonia as a nation on a par with Spain and endowed with a right of self-determination (ERC 1999b, 2003a, 2003b: 6). Carod-Rovira argued during the negotiations of the statute,

> it is time for a second transition and this has to lead to plurinationality, to plurinational federalism. Because in the Spanish state, democracy either is plurinational or is not full democracy … our project is not anti-Spanish, we are not anti-Spanish, we do not go against Spain. On the contrary, we want to get on together, but with mutual respect, not with subordination.

> (ERC 2005)

When the Spanish Parliament heavily amended the statute approved by the Catalan Parliament, the ERC defined the occurrence as 'an authentic democratic scandal' (ERC 2006b) and concluded that 'the non-recognition of Catalonia as a nation means the perpetuation of the contempt for the country [Catalonia EDM] on the part of Spanish nationalism' (ERC 2006a).

Contrary to Scotland, the demand for recognition of Catalan national difference has entailed a strong linguistic component. The *Generalitat* (autonomous government) of Catalonia enacted a policy of 'linguistic normalisation' aimed at making Catalan the 'proper language' (*llengua propria*) of the region – its language of common use.[11] Catalan was introduced as the main language of instruction in schools (from 1998 through a system of linguistic immersion), civil servants were asked to be proficient in both Catalan and Spanish, and from 1998 onwards Catalan became the standard language of use in the administration – citizens can ask to be addressed in Spanish though (Woolard and Gahng 1990: 314–15; Costa 2003: 416–20). According to *Esquerra*, the policy of normalisation was warranted by the history of oppression of the Catalan language and culture in Spain and by the unequal power of the two nations. In this context, bilingualism has been rejected because, in the long run, formal equality would privilege the stronger language (Spanish), thus jeopardising the preservation of Catalan (Llopart 1989: 4; ERC 1998). In this connection, and especially from 2000 onwards, the party has campaigned for the recognition of Catalan as an official language at the state level and as a preferential language in the region. This would lead to the transformation of Spain into a true plurinational state with linguistic territorialisation in each community ensuring the primacy of the local language, while personal linguistic rights for Spanish speakers would be guaranteed (ERC 2000a: 63–4; Sever 2003; Bofill 2006). The entrenched constitutional equality of Spanish and Catalan demanded by the party would therefore reflect the equality of rights of the Catalan and Spanish nations, allowing for discrimination to the advantage of the members of either within the respective territories.

As regards fiscal transfers between the central administration and the autonomous community (the second policy area mentioned above), the central argument made by the party since the late 1980s has been that Catalonia suffers fiscal plundering (*espoli fiscal*) whereby the region contributes substantially more to the central Spanish administration than it receives (see ERC 1989: 4–5, 1992: 47, 1996: 13, 2001b: 4, 2012b: 12.). As stated in the 2003 manifesto, 'we [the Catalan population EDM] pay taxes as a social-democratic and receive public spending as an ultraliberal country' (ERC 2003b: 5). On the one hand, this imbalance mainly derives from the higher revenue per capita of Catalonia's residents compared to the Spanish average (Uriel and Barberan 2007: 412); on the other, it is due to insufficient levels of investment in the region, especially in infrastructures (De la Fuente 2001: 25, 2005: 36–45). While the latter would result from specific choices made by central governments, the former would be affected by overcompensation effects whereby, after redistribution, autonomous communities making a lower per capita contribution to the system of national solidarity will end up enjoying a higher per capita fiscal capacity (both in relation to the national average) (Espasa and Bosch 2010).

ERC has not limited its demands to a more equitable system of redistribution, with each community paying proportionally to its income and receiving roughly equal levels of spending. Instead, it has called for the establishment of a special fiscal relationship on the model of that in force between the Spanish central administration and the Autonomous Community of the Basque Country and the Chartered Community of Navarre (*concierto economico*) (Camps Boy 1990; ERC 1996: 13, 2001a, 2008: 13; Capella 2012). There, the community collects all taxes raised on its territory, paying a fee to the central administration for the services offered. This agreement not only provides a clearer recognition of the special character of the autonomous communities to which it applies; it constitutes a very advantageous deal, since, despite enjoying some of the highest average per capita revenues of the country, both the Basque Country and Navarre are net recipients of the system of fiscal redistribution (Uriel and Barberan 2007: 412–15; De la Fuente 2005: 22–3). Such inequality – in individual terms – can only be justified by the existence of a different *demos* in the territories where this regime applies.

Because of its questioning of the Spanish system of social solidarity, *Esquerra* has often been accused of selfishness. The main answer provided by the party has been that Spanish redistribution would not be true solidarity, but rather a means to prop up clientelist networks and dependence in poorer regions to the advantage of the major parties, while Catalan citizens would suffer from social services of lower quality than those that they could afford if they managed a higher share of their revenues (Colom 1995: 21; ERC 1993b, 2000a: 17). Therefore, Spain's solidarity is deemed to be damaging for the welfare and social equality of the Catalan population, while independence would be a means to improve them on the model of the Scandinavian social-democracies – here one can see a clear parallel with SNP arguments on the matter. Especially in the context of the recent economic crisis and budget cuts imposed by the Spanish government, ERC has made a clear link between *l'espoli fiscal* and *l'espoli social* (social plundering), whereby without the burden of Spanish solidarity, the Catalan *Generalitat* could ensure much higher levels of welfare and social equality for its citizens (Aragones 2012; ERC 2012a, 2012b: 111). Hence, solidarity should be directly managed by the Catalan autonomous community instead of being automatic and compulsory; it should target endogenous growth, and be limited in time and amount. More important, in the longer term, it should progressively decrease until becoming no different from the development cooperation contributions made by most independent states. Carod-Rovira made clear in 1999: 'we want to exercise solidarity, but not in a compulsory and unjust form. Not with the Andalusian gentry or the Madrid bourgeois who travel by high-speed train, but rather with Central America and the countries of the Sahara' (ERC 1999a: 1).

Competitive dynamics?

As shown above, demands for differential treatment and group equality can trigger negative reactions from majority constituencies and central governments. Let us now look at the possibility that other groups within the parent state put forth claims similar to those made by the SNP and ERC, thus generating competitive centrifugal dynamics (Giordano and Roller 2004). In this respect, there is a difference between the UK and Spain.

In the UK, competitive dynamics have not been as strong as in Spain. Although, to some extent, far-reaching demands for devolution in Scotland have had a 'pulling-effect' in Wales (Jeffery 2009), this has not led to a 'race to the top' with constituent nations competing in a cycle of attempts to outbid and catch up with the powers obtained by each. In other words, there have been few concerns with the asymmetric nature of the system. Especially surprising is the weakness of calls for a specific form of English autonomy. Vernon Bogdanor (2010: 158) argues:

> asymmetrical devolution seems to breach the principle of equal rights for all citizens of the UK. Those in the non-English parts of the UK enjoy devolution, while the English do not. Scotland receives, as she did before devolution, around 20 per cent more per head in public spending than England. Wales is over-represented at Westminster, returning 40 MPs, whereas on a comparable basis to England, she should return only 32. Scotland, Wales and Northern Ireland still have Secretaries of State to represent their interests in the Cabinet, while England does not. Perhaps the most important institutional expression of the inequality of rights, however, is that MPs from the non-English parts of the UK can vote on all English matters, while English MPs cannot vote on Scottish or Northern Irish domestic matters, or on Welsh secondary legislation.

The last 'expression of inequality' mentioned by Bogdanor has been a recurrent issue – under the name of the 'West Lothian Question' – since the late 1970s, when plans for the establishment of Scottish and Welsh Parliaments were debated at Westminster. The question resurfaced at the turn of the twenty-first century, as a consequence of the creation of the Scottish and Welsh Parliaments (Gay *et al.* 2011), and was brought up again by Prime Minister Cameron in the aftermath of the 2014 independence referendum in Scotland (*Financial Times* 2014). Three main solutions have been envisaged to solve it: the dissolution of the UK; the creation of an English parliament and the transformation of Westminster into a truly federal assembly; the introduction of a provision whereby non-English MPs at Westminster could not vote on English-only matters – often referred to as 'English Votes for English Laws', or EVEL. The first has not been seriously taken into account in English political debates and enjoys no grassroots support. The creation of an English Parliament has formally been demanded by an official campaign, established in 1998, and supported by some small political formations such as the English Democrats. Despite signs of growing sympathy with the idea among the population, the issue has remained at the margin of English politics (Bryant 2008: 670; Hazel 2006: 9). EVEL does receive the support of a consistent and substantial majority in England, as well as in other parts of the UK. Yet, it involves major technical difficulties – first of all clearly identifying English-only matters – and it might end up collapsing into the previous option of creating an English Parliament within the UK one. It might also lead to a 'bifurcation' of the UK government, whereby this would command a UK majority, by means of decisive votes in the devolved areas of the country, but only a minority in England. It would finally officially create two classes of MPs,[12] thus undermining any unionist message outside of England (Bogdanor 2010: 157–65; Hazel 2006: 11).

There are many reasons why, in the UK, asymmetry has not become as much of an issue as in Spain. The first is that the country has always been characterised by asymmetric agreements between its constituent units, which are the norm rather than an exception. The UK has never been a true unitary state with an unambiguous single *demos* and a homogeneous administration throughout the country, but rather a union state in which different territorial arrangements reflecting the plural composition of the country had been preserved without leading to a clear federal structure (Gamble and Wright 2009: 1–2; Hassan 2007: 81; Mitchell 1996: 38; Rokkan and Urwin 1982: 11). For instance, Scotland preserved its own legal and education system, along with its national Church, thus enjoying 'informal' autonomy since the very foundation of the UK, which later continued in the form of administrative autonomy within a kind of Scottish welfare state (Devine 2008: 13–14; Paterson 1994: 103–31). Also, asymmetry has been tolerated because it is a way of compensating the UK minority nations – Northern Ireland, Scotland and Wales – for England's dominance, since England accounts for 84 per cent of the total population of the UK and 82 per cent of Westminster seats. Hence, 'the English remain the dominant nation in the UK, and this dominance has hardly been affected by the establishment of devolved bodies in Scotland and Wales' (Bogdanor 2010: 168). On the contrary, a formal federation of four such constituent units would probably be so unbalanced as to be unworkable. Thus, in the end, as Lord Falconer once suggested, the West Lothian question might simply be 'an anomaly which is much more tolerable than any of the means of rectifying it' (quoted in Bryant 2008: 680).

In Spain, in contrast, asymmetry and competitive dynamics have been a problematic issue. The main feature of the Spanish process of devolution of power in the post-dictatorship period has been its 'openness'. The dictatorship discredited state centralisation to such an extent that after its end 'decentralisation' became associated with 'democratisation' (Balfour and Quiroga 2007: 41–4). Yet, there was no widespread consensus on how far decentralisation should go. The constitution left the matter deliberately undefined and introduced a principle – the *principio dispositivo* – whereby the autonomous communities were left free to claim their powers from the centre. Simultaneously, as mentioned above, a differentiation was introduced between regions and historical nationalities, with the latter being granted a 'fast-track' procedure to devolution. This differentiation was made in order to accommodate the demands for differential treatment and recognition of the peripheral nations, but such distinction was later blurred, as the other communities were given the opportunity to catch up (Colomer 1998; Fossas 1999: 6). Hence, the Spanish context has been marked by 'the coexistence of nationalities with a very strong political personality with regions where the main goal is to reach an efficient system of government with wide political decentralisation' (Fossas 1999: 5).

This has led to a clash between the demands for recognition of their national difference by the historical nationalities – notably the Basque Country and Catalonia – with what Luis Moreno (2001: 97) has named the principle of 'comparative grievance', according to which 'the exercise of the right to autonomy legitimately practiced by the regions compels them to claim the same degree of autonomy as the "historical nationalities"'. In other words, the Spanish 'ordinary' regions have aimed at equalising their levels of autonomy with those obtained by the Basque Country and Catalonia. This in turn has triggered further demands on the part of these latter, since they have consistently sought precisely a special status. This process was started by Andalusia's mobilisation at the very beginning of the devolution process, in early 1980, and ended with the region's accession to the fast-track procedure. Andalusia's behaviour was then replicated by other regions through a process of 'ethnoterritorial mimesis' whose result has been a self-reinforcing centrifugal competitive cycle (Moreno 2001: 95–8). As a result:

> without a single reform of Chapter VIII of the Constitution, the system has gradually transformed itself from an asymmetric decentralized system toward a largely symmetric federation, defined by the dominance of legislative concurrent powers and revenue sharing as the main funding model and may be transforming itself again into a more decentralized and asymmetric federation.
>
> (Colino 2009: 264)

The history of Spanish devolution can thus be read as a series of waves of historical nationalities' advances along the path of devolution and 'ordinary' communities catching up. 'Rounds of equalisation' were carried out by either the PSOE or the PP-led governments in 1982, 1992, 1997 and 2009. These exercises in equalisation, however, should not be confused with attempts at recentralising powers. They rather were efforts to bring an asymmetric system back to symmetry, as a consequence of the demands for an equal share of devolved powers for all coming from 'ordinary' communities (Moreno 2001: 97–8). The fundamental difference between the calls for autonomy of political forces in the Basque Country and Catalonia and those in the other autonomous communities, however, should be borne in mind: while nationalist parties in the former case have stressed their *hecho differencial*, that is, their representing different demoi from the Spanish one, the demands for federal equalisation of the other regions have been predicated upon the inequality introduced by granting special status to the historical nationalities. Hence, it is a call for equal degrees of decentralisation that does not call into question the fundamental homogeneity and identity of the Spanish demos. It cannot therefore be considered as a call for group equality in a plurinational context, but rather a rejection of the group equality demanded by the historical nationalities on account of the individual inequality – within the perspective of a single Spanish demos – brought about by the latter's special status.

Again a clear example of the historical nationalities' demands for differential treatment provoking the hostility of political leaders in other Spanish autonomous communities is provided by the reform of the Catalan statute of autonomy. One of the main reasons why the PSOE could not accept the text approved by the Catalan Parliament lay in the backlash threatened by Socialist leaders in other Spanish autonomous communities, such as the president of Extremadura José Rodriguez Ibarra, who, during the discussion of the text in the Spanish Parliament, asserted:

the final text will be radically different from the one adopted in Catalonia. If the basic points remained the same, there would not be a statute. If that is the minimum of the game, a Treasury Agency and the concept of nation, I tell you no and I am the member of the PSOE's Executive Committee.

(quoted in Orte and Wilson 2009: 427)

The reasons why asymmetry has been much more of a problem in Spain than in the United Kingdom are multiple. One might simply have to do with size. The Basque Country and Catalonia – to take only the historical nationalities that have experienced the highest levels of mobilisation in favour of autonomy – together account for about 21 per cent of the total Spanish population. More importantly, their economic weight is equal to about a quarter of the Spanish GDP.[13] Also, as far as Catalonia is concerned, it is one of the most importance sources of tax revenues for the central administration, as well as one of the first contributors to the system of interregional solidarity. Since any reduction of Catalonia's payments to the common purse will certainly affect the resources available to the recipient regions, these have opposed Catalan demands for a better fiscal treatment on account of the constitutional principles of individual and interregional solidarity (Moreno 2001: 99). Yet, while demographic and economic size can explain anxiety with asymmetry, as governing parties might fear that granting historical nationalities increased degrees of autonomy might embolden them to ask for even more powers, this is not a convincing answer because rejecting demands for special treatment can equally lead to calls for more self-government and even independence – as shown by the grassroots mobilisation realised in Catalonia since 2010–12. Another reason probably lies in that, contrary to in the UK, asymmetry has not been a constitutional habit in Spain. While the Crown of Aragon enjoyed autonomy within the Kingdom of Spain for a few centuries, Catalonia was later annexed through military conquest at the end of the War of Spanish succession in 1714 (Linz 1973: 38–47; Culla 1999: 36). Hence, Spain evolved from a dynastic union into a unitary state to a much larger extent than the UK. This was especially the case during the nineteenth century, when Spanish nationalism evolved along the Jacobin idea of the homogeneous centralised state inherited from the French Revolution and with a conservative organicist conception of the nation (De Riquer 2000: 14).[14]A limited version of this understanding, in the form of the *estado integral* (the integral state) was proposed for a short period in the 1930s, but was later replaced by the unitary and fascist conception of the Falangist movement (Fusi 2000: 37–41). In the post-dictatorship period, the conservative organicist conception has lived on in the discourse on the nation developed – since the end of the 'pact of silence' in early 2000 – by the Popular Party. The Socialists, on the other hand, have subscribed to a more open interpretation that looks favourably at regional autonomy, but, simultaneously, they have given priority to the political and social equality of all Spaniards, which requires symmetry and federal equalisation. Despite the formal adherence of both to an inclusive 'constitutional patriotism', they have failed to craft a narrative capable of accommodating peripheral nationalisms and their claim to recognition of national difference (Balfour and Quiroga 2007: 84).

Does democracy stimulate nationalist conflict? A conclusion

In an article explaining the recent rise of grassroots separatism in Catalonia, Montserrat Guibernau argued that this stemmed from the consolidation of democracy in Spain and the contemporary refusal of the central government to recognise Catalonia as a nation, and to accept its demands for further devolution. She wrote:

> the consolidation of democracy has allowed people to express their political aspirations without fear – this is new to a society that endured almost 40 years of dictatorship – while regarding them as legitimate. New generations brought up within democratic Spain are convinced of the legitimacy of their claims, among them, the right to decide upon their political future by means of a referendum, as will be the case in other European democracies, for example in Scotland. To a significant extent this accounts for the Catalans' eagerness to engage in grass-roots mobilization to express their discontent with the status quo.

(2013: 390–1)

This raises the question of whether the deepening of democracy in a plurinational context favours the intensification of nationalist conflicts. This is especially relevant in coincidence with two related phenomena experienced by most European democracies in recent decades: a general questioning of representative democracy (Ignazi 2005); and a generalised process of devolution of powers to sub-state levels of government (Hooghe *et al.* 2009). Both relate directly to the question of which relevant political community has the right to decide. Regarding the former, calls for restoring popular sovereignty and promoting popular participation in the decision-making process – as made by the SNP and ERC – inevitably involve advocacy of empowering the people. Where the definition of the sovereign people is contested, this can exacerbate relationships between national communities within the same state. Concerning the latter, territorial devolution requires a determination of the unit to which power is devolved, also directly touching upon the definition of the demos. Furthermore, the attribution of such powers entails not only issues of political efficiency, but also of representation, recognition, and status.

As seen in the previous sections, different conceptions of equality play a critical role in fuelling confrontation between communities within the state. Specifically, the inherent contradiction between individual equality within a single demos and group equality among demoi, entailing individual inequality across demoi, can lead to principled conflicts and centrifugal dynamics that threaten the unity and integrity of existing states. Yet, one need not conclude that increasing democratisation necessarily increases conflict in a plurinational context. The question is, rather, what kind of democracy is implemented. The Scottish and Catalan cases show that constitutional traditions of flexibility and asymmetry recognising the sovereignty of the state's constituent units might help reduce competitive dynamics as well as to frame debates in less confrontational ways. They might also work as a nation-building tool, since recognising the identity of minority nations might create a feeling of loyalty to the wider union among its members. In Scotland, for instance, it was precisely a unitarist interpretation of the Kingdom in the 1980s that set the ground for the later major reinterpretation of the British and Scottish identities and that fuelled grassroots mobilisation for devolution. The rejection of such recognition, on the other hand, is likely to nourish alienation and radicalise support for independence and separation (Parekh 2009: 33–4). This does not mean that respecting calls of national minorities for self-determination is a panacea. Separatist parties can use the autonomous institutions set up as a result of such recognition as a platform to frame debates around national cleavages and pursue pro-independence agenda, as has happened in both Scotland and Catalonia. Yet, despite the success of the SNP in organising the independence referendum and its landslide victory at the 2015 general elections, neither support for independence – when evaluated as one constitutional option among a range of others including devolution and the status quo – nor levels of exclusive or predominantly Scottish national identification[15] have substantially increased in the region since at least the late 1990s (ScotCen 2016; Eichhorn 2015). In contrast, grassroots support for independence – when calculated in the same way – and exclusive and predominantly Catalan national identification have increased dramatically since the onset of the constitutional crisis arisen around the revision of the Catalan statute of autonomy and, especially, since the 2010 ruling of the Constitutional Tribunal (Guibernau 2013: 285–393). The recognition of plurinationality and the ensuing acceptance of group equality within the same political union cannot eliminate conflict, but may make it manageable and curb radicalisation.

Notes

1. He asserted 'now we apply this whole presumption to all debtors: no one's body is allowed to be seized; no one can be held or imprisoned for debt' (Waldron 2009: 241).
2. This fundamental point is shared also by Benedict Anderson (1983: 16), Ernest Gellner (1983: 73) and Rogers Brubaker (1996: 85).
3. A good illustration of the tension between a purely universalist and a 'communitarian' understanding of equality and justice is Will Kymlicka (1995: 93) in regard to the debate on open borders in contemporary democracies:

   few people favour a system of open borders, where people could freely cross borders and settle, work, and vote in whatever country they desired. Such a system would dramatically increase the domain within which people would be treated as free and equal citizens. Yet open borders would also make it more likely that people's own national community would be overrun by settlers from other cultures, and that they would be unable to ensure their survival as a distinct national culture. So we have a choice between, on the one hand, increased mobility and an expanded domain within which people are free and equal individuals, and, on the other, decreased mobility but greater assurance that people can continue to be free and equal members of their own national culture.

4. On sovereignty conceived of as a right to self-determination, i.e. the opportunity to choose one's destiny rather than the actual choice made, see Keating 2001: 15.
5. It should be noted that nationalism, too, is self-referential, since it is based on the principle of national self-determination. Yet, while democracy focuses on the procedures ensuring that each citizen is treated with equal concern (Dworkin 2007: 43), nationalism is all about the definition of the self-governing community.
6. The expression comes from *The Economist* (1976).
7. Henceforth, and unless stated otherwise, the quotes reported here are my translation.
8. Between 1989 and 2000, the PSOE, first, and the PP, later, needed the backing of the Catalan moderate nationalist party Convergence and Union (CiU) to secure an absolute majority in the Spanish Parliament. This enabled CiU to

obtain substantial improvements in the autonomy granted to the region (Chari 2000: 210–12).

9. This was a self-styled centrist party that included many members of the former Francoist establishment. It dissolved quickly after the 1982 elections. Many of its former members then joined the Popular Alliance, predecessor of the PP.

10. Although strictly speaking there are no regions, but autonomous communities in Spain, for matters of expediency the two terms are used as synonyms in this chapter.

11. Although other languages can be declared official in the various autonomous communities, the Constitution recognises only Spanish as the official language of the state. The 'official' character of Spanish means that all citizens have not only a right to use it, but also a duty to know it. The official nature of the languages recognised in the autonomous communities entails only the former.

12. Although this is already the case de facto – as proved by the existence of the West Lothian Question – the Westminster Parliament remains officially sovereign and can potentially overrule the devolved Parliaments, which it does not do by convention.

13. Data for 2009 from the Spanish National Statistics Institute.

14. De Riquer notably stressed the failure of the Spanish liberals to craft a solid alternative to such conservative understanding.

15. With the expression 'exclusive Scottish/Catalan national identity', we refer to the answer 'exclusively Scottish/Catalan' to the standard Moreno question about subjective national identification used in most opinion polls. With 'predominantly Scottish/Catalan' identity, we refer to the sum of the 'exclusive Scottish/Catalan' and 'more Scottish/Catalan than British/Spanish' answers.

References

Abizadeh, A. (2012) 'On the demos and its kin: nationalism, democracy, and the boundary problem', *American Political Science Review*, 106(4): 867–82.

Anderson, B. (1983) *Imagined Communities. Reflections on the origins and spread of nationalism*, London: Verso.

Aragonès, P. (2011) 'Execucions hipotecàries', *Esquerra Nacional*, 198, August: 6–10.

Balfour, S. and Quiroga, A. (2007) *The Reinvention of Spain: Nation and identity since democracy*, Oxford: Oxford University Press.

Beitz, C. (1989) *Political Equality: an Essay in democratic theory*, Princeton, NJ: Princeton University Press.

Bennie, L., Brand, J., and Mitchell, J. (1997) *How Scotland Votes: Scottish parties and elections*, Manchester: Manchester University Press.

Bogdanor, V. (2010) 'The West Lothian Question', *Parliamentary Affairs*, 63(1): 156–72.

Bofill, M. (2006) 'Plurilingüisme, dret democratic', *Esquerra Nacional*, 73, August–September: 18.

Brubaker, R. (1996) *Nationalism Reframed: Nationhood and the national question in the new Europe*, Cambridge: Cambridge University Press.

Bryant, C. G. A. (2008) 'Devolution, equity and the English question', *Nations and Nationalism*, 14(4): 664–83.

Calhoun, C. (1993) 'Nationalism and civil society: democracy, diversity and self-determination', *International Sociology*, 8(4): 387–411.

Camps Boy, J. (1990) 'El sistema de finançament autonomic ara (2)', *La Republica*, 9, November–December: 6–8.

Canovan, M. (1996) *Nationhood and Political Theory*, Cheltenham: Edward Elgar.

Capella, E. (2012) 'L'etern espoli fiscal', *Esquerra Nacional*, 204, February: 3.

Carod-Rovira, J.-P. (1991) *La via democratica a la independencia nacional*, Barcelona.

Chari, R. S. (2000) 'The March 2000 Spanish election: a critical election?', *West European Politics*, 23(3): 207–14.

Clive, L. (1995) *Scotland and the United Kingdom: the Economy and the union in the twentieth century*, Manchester: Manchester University Press.

Colino, C. (2009) 'Constitutional change without constitutional reform: Spanish federalism and the revision of Catalonia's statute of autonomy', *Publius*, 39(2): 262–88.

Colom, A. (1989) 'Per la llibertat del presos Catalans', *La Republica*, 4, July: 3.

— (1995) *Contracte amb Catalunya*, Barcelona: Columna.

Colomer, J. (1998) 'The Spanish state of autonomies: non institutional federalism', *West European Politics*, 21(4): 40–52.

Costa, J. (2003) 'Catalan linguistic policy: liberal or illiberal?', *Nations and Nationalism*, 9(3): 416–26.

Culla i Clara, J. (1999) 'La Catalogne: histoire, identité, contradictions, *Herodote*, 91: 35–46.

— (2013) *Esquerra Republicana de Catalunya 1931–2012: una història politica*, Barcelona: La Campana.

Cristiano, T. (2008) *The Constitution of Equality: Democratic authority and its limits*, Oxford: Oxford University Press.

Dahl, R. (1982) *Dilemmas of Pluralist Democracy*, New Haven, CT: Yale University Press.

— (1986) *Democracy, Liberty and Equality*, Oslo: Norwegian University Press.

De la Fuente, A. (2001) 'Un poco de aritmetica territorial: anatomia de una balanza fiscal para las regiones espanolas', *Studies on the Spanish Economy*, n. 91, FEDEA.

— (2005) *Los mecanismos de cohesion territorial en Espana: un analisis y alguanas propuestas*, Fundacion Alternativas, working document n. 62/2005.

De Riquer i Permaner, B. (2000) *Identitats contemporanies: Catalunya i Espanya*, Vic: Eumo Editorial.

Devine, T. M. (2008) 'Three hundred years of Anglo-Scottish union', in T. M. Devine (ed.) *Scotland and the Union 1707–2007*, Edinburgh: Edinburgh University Press 1–23.

Dworkin, R. (2007) *La vertu souveraine*, Brussels: Bruylant.

Eichhorn, J. (2015) 'There was no rise in Scottish nationalism: understanding the SNP victory', *LSE Blogs*, 14 May, http://blogs.lse.ac.uk/politicsandpolicy/there-was-no-rise-in-scottish-nationalism-understanding-the-snp-victory/ (accessed on 8 August 2015).

ERC (Esquerra Republicana da Catalunya) (1989) *L'Esquerra, la nova frontera, vota Esquerra Republicana de Catalunya*, Spanish election manifesto.

— (1990) 'Espai entrevista: Heribert Barrera i Costa', *La Republica*, 6, May–June: 16.

— (1992) *Cap a la independència*, Catalan Parliament election manifesto.

— (1993a) *Cap a la independència*, Catalan Parliament election manifesto.

— (1993b) 'Editorial: Nord-Sud', *La Republica*, 17, December: 2.

— (1993c) *Ideological Declaration of the Esquerra Republicana of Catalonia*, Diliname, CAT0005, http://diliname.eu/index.php/catalonia/item/42-ideological-declaration-of-the-esquerra-republicana-of-catalonia.html (accessed on 1 August 2015).

— (1996) *La teva veu, cap a la independencia*, Spanish Parliament election manifesto, 13.

— (1998) 'La intervencio de Josep-Lluis Carod-Rovira', *Esquerra Nacional*, 1, January, p. 2.

— (1999a) 'ERC presenta Josep-Lluis Carod-Rovira com a candidat a la presidència de la Generalitat de Catalunya', 11, *Esquerra Nacional*, January: 1.

— (1999b) 'ERC presenta l'Avantprojecte d'Estatut Nacional de Catalunya', *Esquerra Nacional*, 14, May: 9.

— (2000a) *Programa marc*, Spanish election manifesto.

— (2000b) 'Puigcercos evidencia les discriminacions de l'Estat cap a Catalunya', *Esquerra Nacional*, 20, May–June: 7.

— (2001a) 'ERC torna a portar al carrer la reivindicacio d'un finançament just', *Esquerra Nacional*, 26, May-June, p. 4;

— (2001b) 'Pacte nacional per Catalunya', *Esquerra Nacional*, 28, September–October: 5.

— (2002) 'Espanya: un estat, una nacio, una capital', *Esquerra Nacional*, 30, January–February: 4.

— (2003a) 'Una constitucio per a Catalunya', *Esquerra Nacional*, 43, April: 5.

— (2003b) *Un pais actiu i equilibrat, eleccions al parlement de Catalunya 2003*, Catalan Parliament election manifesto.

— (2004) *Parlant la gent s'entén*, Spanish Parliament election manifesto.

— (2005) 'Federalisme, la propera estacio cap a la independència', *Esquerra Nacional*, 62, May: 4.

— (2006a) *Ara toca no, Catalunya Mereix Més*, campaign brochure.

—   (2006b) *Preguntes entor a l'estatut*, campaign flyer.
—   (2008) *Objectiu: un pais de 1a (per aixo volem la independència)*, Spanish Parliament election manifesto.
—   (2012a) 'Ni espoli fiscal, ni espoli social', *Esquerra Nacional*, 204, February: 13. See also the infographic in *Esquerra Nacional*, 208, October 2012: 6.
—   (2012b) *Un nou pais per a tothom*, Catalan Parliament elections manifesto.
Espasa, M. and Bosch, N. (2010) 'Inter-regional fiscal flows: methodologies, results and their determinant factors for Spain', in N. Bosch, M. Espasa, and A. Solé Ollé, (eds) *The Political Economy of Inter-Regional Fiscal Flows*, Cheltenham: Edward Elgar 15–172.
Evans, S. (2009) 'The not so odd couple: Margaret Thatcher and One Nation Conservatism', *Contemporary British History*, 23(1): 101–21.
The Economist (1976) 'Decline and fall', 3 January.
Financial Times (2014) 'David Cameron's statement on the Scottish result', 19 September.
Finlay, R. J. (2005) *Modern Scotland, 1914–2000*, London: Profile Books.
—   (2012) 'Thatcherism, unionism and nationalism: a comparative study of Scotland and Wales', in B. Jackson, and R. Saunders (eds) *Making Thatcher's Britain*, Cambridge: Cambridge University Press 165–79.
Fossas, E. (1999) *Asymmetry and Plurinationality in Spain*, Working Paper 167, Institut de Ciènces Politiques i Socials, Universitat Autonoma de Barcelona.
Fusi Aizpurua, J. P. (2000) 'Los nacionalismos y el Estado espanol: el siglo XX', *Cuadernos de historia contemporanea*, 22: 21–52.
Gamble, A. (1988) *The free economy and the strong state. The politics of Thatcherism*, London: MacMillan.
Gamble, A. and Wright, T. (2009) 'Introduction: the Britishness question', in A. Gamble and T. Wright (eds) *Britishness, Perspectives on the British Question*, Chichester: John Wiley & Sons 1–10.
Gay, O., Holden, H., and Bowers, P. (2011) *The West Lothian Question*, Standard Note SN/PC/02586, House of Commons Library, 23 March.
Gellner, E. (1983) *Nations and Nationalism*, Ithaca, NY: Cornell University Press.
Giordano, B. and Roller, E. (2004) 'Te´ para todos? A comparison of the processes of devolution in Spain and the UK', *Environment and Planning*, A(36): 2163–81.
Greenfeld, L. (1992) *Nationalism: Five roads to modernity*, Cambridge, MA: Harvard University Press.
Guibernau, M. (2013) 'Secessionism in Catalonia: After democracy', *Ethnopolitics*, 12(4): 368–93.
Hassan, G. (2007) 'Labour, Britishness and the concepts of "nation" and "state"', in G. Hassan (ed.) *After Blair: Politics after the New Labour decade*, London: Lawrence & Wishart, 75–93.
—   (2009) 'The auld enemies: Scottish nationalism and Scottish Labour', in G. Hassan (ed.) *The Modern SNP: From protest to power*, Edinburgh: Edinburgh University Press, 147–59.

—   (2012) "'It's only a northern song": The constant smirr of anti-Thatcherism and anti-Toryism', in D. Torrance (ed.) *Whatever Happened to Tory Scotland*, Edinburgh: Edinburgh University Press 76–92.

Hazel, R. (2006) *The English Question*, London: The Constitutional Unit.

Hooghe, L., Marks, G., and Schakel, A. H. (2009) *The Rise of Regional Authority: a Comparative study of 42 democracies*, pre-published version, available at: http://www.unc.edu/~gwmarks/assets/doc/The%20Rise%20of%20 Regional%20Authority.pdf (accessed on 8 August 2015).

Ignazi, P. (2005) 'L'evoluzione dei partiti contemporanei fra delegittimazione e centralità', *Polis*, 2: 265–78.

Jeffery, C. (2009) 'Devolution in the United Kingdom: problems of a piecemeal approach to constitutional change', *Publius: The Journal of Federalism*, 39(2): 289–313.

Keating, M. (2001) *Plurinational Democracy: Stateless nations in a post-sovereignty era*, Oxford: Oxford University Press.

Keating, M. and Wilson, A. (2009) 'Renegotiating the state of autonomies: statute reform and multilevel politics in Spain', *West European Politics*, 32(3): 536–58.

Kymlicka, W. (1995) *Multicultural Citizenship*, Oxford: Oxford University Press.

Linz, J. (1973) 'Early state-building and late peripheral nationalism against the state: the case of Spain', in S. N. Eisenstadt and S. Rokkan (eds) *Building States and Nations*, Vol. 2, Beverly Hills: Sage Publication 32–116.

Llopart, F. (1989) 'Que vol dir...Normalitzacio Lingüistica', *La Humanitat*, 1, May, p. 6.

Lynch, P. (2002) *SNP. The History of the Scottish National Party*, Cardiff: Welsh Academic Press.

Margalit, A. and Raz, J. (1990) 'National self-determination', *The Journal of Philosophy*, 87(9): 439–61.

Martin, R. (1988) 'The political economy of Britain's north-south divide', *Transactions of the Institute of British Geographers*, 13(4): 389–418.

McCrone, G. (2013) *Scottish Independence: Weighing up the economics*, Edinburgh: Birlinn, Kindle edition.

McGann, A. (2006) *The Logic of Democracy: Reconciling, equality, deliberation, and minority protection*, Ann Arbor, MI: University of Michigan Press.

McIlvanney, W. (1987) *Stands Scotland Where it Did?*, Second lecture chaired by Gordon Wilson, SNP's Annual National Conference, Dundee.

Miller, D. (1995) *On Nationality*, Oxford: Oxford University Press.

Mitchell, J. (1996) *Strategies for Self-Government*, Edinburgh: Polygon.

Moreno, L. (2001) *The Federalization of Spain*, London: Frank Cass.

Orte, A. and Wilson, A. (2009) 'Multi-level coalitions and status reform in Spain', *Regional and Federal Studies*, 19(3): 415–36.

Parekh, B. (2009) 'Liberal democracy and national minorities', in F. Requejo and M. Caminal (eds) *Political Liberalism and Plurinational Democracies*, London: Routledge 31–43.

Paterson, L. (1994) *The Autonomy of Modern Scotland*, Edinburgh: Edinburgh University Press.

Rae, D. W., Yates, D., Hochschild, J., Morone, J., and Fessler, C. (1981) *Equalities*, Cambridge, MA: Harvard University Press.

Requejo, F. (2011) 'Shadows of the Enlightenment: Refining pluralism in liberal democracies', in F. Requejo and M. Caminal (eds) *Political Liberalism and Plurinational Democracies*, London: Routledge, 11–30.

Rokkan, S. and Urwin, D. (1982) *The Politics of Territorial Identity: Studies in European regionalism*, London: Sage.

Rubiralta, F. (2004) *Una història de l'independentisme politic català. De Francesc Macià a Josep Lluis Carod Rovira*, Lleida: Pagès.

Salmond, A. (1993a) 'Independence and Scottish democracy', in *Horizon Without Bars: the Future of Scotland. A series of speeches*, Edinburgh: SNP 55–64.

— (1993b) 'Towards a prosperous Scotland', in *Horizon Without Bars: the Future of Scotland. A series of speeches*, Edinburgh: SNP 8–21.

ScotCen (2016) *How should Scotland be governed (five response categories collapsed to three)*, http://whatscotlandthinks.org/questions/how-should-scotland-be-governed-five-response-categories-collapsed-to-three#line (accessed on 7 August 2016).

Sever, S. (2003) 'Cinc anys de la Llei de Politica Linguïstica: una valoracio', *Esquerra Nacional*, 41, February: 13.

SNP (Scottish National Party) (1978) *Return to Nationhood*, Edinburgh: SNP.

— (1984) 'Nats Expose Watford Gap', *Free Scot*, autumn, Acc. 13099/50 National Library of Scotland (NLS).

— (1987) *The Feeble Fifty*, SNP campaign leaflet, Acc. 13099/51 NLS.

— (1997) *Yes We Can Win the Best for Scotland*, General Election Manifesto.

— (2002) 'The Scottish economy – your top ten questions answered', *Snapshot*, Summer: 16–17.

— (2003) *Talking Independence*, Edinburgh: SNP.

— (2005) *If Scotland Matters to You Make it Matter in May*, UK general election manifesto.

— (2011) *Re-Elect. A Scottish government working for Scotland*, Scottish Parliament election manifesto.

— (2012) *Choice. An historic opportunity for our nation*, Edinburgh: SNP.

— (2013) *Scotland's Future: Your guide to an independent Scotland*, Edinburgh: The Scottish Government.

Still, Jonathan (1981) 'Political equality and elections system', *Ethics*, 91(3): 375–94.

Sturgeon, N. (2013) 'No more "what ifs"', in *Scotland on Sunday*, 'Scotland decides, the case for independence, and the case for the UK' March 17, p. 2..

Tamir, Y. (1993) *Liberal Nationalism*, Princeton, NJ: Princeton University Press.

Taylor, C. (1994) 'The politics of recognition', in A. Gutmann (ed.) *Multiculturalism: Examining the politics of recognition*, Princeton, NJ: Princeton University Press 25–74.

Uriel Jimenez, E. and Barberan Orti, R. (2007) *Las balanzas fiscales de las comunidades autonomas con la Administracion Publica Central*, Bilbao: Fudacion BBVA.

Waldron, J. 'Dignity, ranks and rights', the Tanner Lectures on Human Values, University of California, Berkeley, April 2009.

Wilson, G. (1988) 'The Scottish paradox', Andrew Lang Lecture delivered at the University of St. Andrews and published by the SNP.

Woolard, K. and Gahng, T.-J. (1990) 'Changing language policies and attitudes in autonomous Catalonia', *Language in Society*, 19(3): 314–15.

Chapter Five

Political Union Without Territory? Space Representation and Identity Deficit in the EU

Axel Marion

The political geography of Europe has always been at the centre of vivid debates among intellectuals and politicians. The major discussions usually concerned the definition and scope of the European territory. Since the seventeenth century, the geographical frontiers of the continent and especially the place of Russia and the Ottoman Empire in the 'Concert of Europe' have been extensively interrogated. No definitive answer – of course – has ever been given to these questions, which continue to frequently occupy newspaper tribunes, as the debate about the accession of Turkey in the EU or, more recently, the Ukrainian crisis, have showed.

Does this explain why the geographical dimension is missing to such a point in the European Union discourse? Few words have been said, since the beginning of the Community in the 1950s, on the crucial question of the common territory. At the core of this ambiguity remains the famous article 237 of the Treaty of Rome, declaring that 'any European State may apply to become a member of the Community' – a line that survived all the following treaties until today. No definition was ever given to what exactly is this 'European' area, what it comprises, and who should decide it. Furthermore the subject was constantly avoided by the authorities – national governments as well as the EU Commission – even in the different periods of enlargement. This topic remains taboo in the EU political agenda.

This taboo is amplified by the internal policies of the EU. The progressive disappearance of interstate borders and the development of multi-scale territories inside the EU (the Schengen area and the Eurozone for example) have created new paradigms for the Europeans. Contrary to the 'external borders' debate, this dimension has direct implications for the role of the state in Europe and for the everyday life of Europe's inhabitants. It embodies the ambition of the EU to create functional spaces inside Europe beyond the states, and to forge ultimately a new, 'continental' citizen.

However, borders are coming back in popular consciousness. There are many signs pointing in that direction. The success of nationalist and Europhobic parties questions the European integration process. Amid economic difficulties, with an increasing deficit of political legitimacy (see Schmidt 2006), a growing number of European citizens are considering that the 'old Nation State' is the protector they need. If they recognise themselves in national symbols such as flags, anthems, or football teams, they also want a stronger role for national borders. Nationalists on the far right and protectionists on the far left are indeed asking for better border control, and refer more and more to the national territory as a 'sanctuary'.[1]

This gap between the lack of territorial representation in Europe and the expectations of the citizens for a return of borders should be better studied.[2] The fundamental question here is the link between geography and identity. And we assume that this link is only possible with a constructed narrative about the European territory, like those created over time by the nation-state. In fact, if an important amount of research has been done these last years about the political geography of Europe, few studies have concentrated on the discourse about European geography and the significance of this topic in the EU's political agenda. The questions should be the following: How does one speak about the territory of Europe? Is Europe a territorial unit? What geographical representations are suggested by the EU authorities? And what does it all say about our (European) common self-identification?

This chapter approaches these questions by focusing on the importance of the representation of the common territory in the process of political self-identification, and the ways to achieve it. First, we examine the question of the European (non) representation of the territory, and then suggest some reasons which explain why the geographical question has been generally avoided in the process of building the EU. Second, the chapter explains why the link between territory and identity is important in the creation of popular identification. Third, it makes three theoretical propositions that could be used to better understand the challenges and options that face the EU in creating its territorial narrative.

In search of a narrative

A distinctive characteristic of the European Union as a political entity is that it has no real 'territorial narrative' proposed by its authorities. For many years and still today, the Union was only conceived – in terms of geography – as the assemblage of nation states with their particular features, or as functional areas dedicated to specific policies, such as the Eurozone or the Schengen agreement. In these conditions, no discourse could really emerge about the definition and, in a sense, the 'ontology' of the EU territorial destiny. As a demonstration of this reality, one might invoke the difficulty the EU has in representing itself on a simple map.[3]

In fact, the only geographical narrative that seems to exist in the European Union is related to the notion of 'continent'. From the beginning, the common ambition was to unify the countries from Portugal to the East. This vision is obvious in the declarations of the early leaders of the Community such as Walter Hallstein, who stated:

Now, these communities have six members only. This is a historical accident which is due to the fact that only these six states were prepared to embark upon the adventure involved in this first attempt at unification ... It has again been evident – and this has always been part of our political design – that Community policy is not just a policy for six states but that it is the campaign of a unit which deems itself to be the vanguard of a greater Europe ... The success or failure of the communities is therefore a matter that concerns the whole of Europe.[4]

This vision gained more weight after 1989, in the effort to unify the former Eastern bloc with the European Community. In that period, the European Union could become – theoretically – the European continent and vice-versa. But the Commission saw the problem coming and declared quite frankly that there was no 'geographical clue' to the Enlargement:

> Article 237 of the Rome Treaty, and article O of the Maastricht Treaty, say that 'any European State may apply to become a member'. The term 'European' has not been officially defined. It combines geographical, historical and cultural elements which all contribute to the European identity. The shared experience of proximity, ideas, values, and historical interaction cannot be condensed into a simple formula, and is subject to review by each succeeding generation. The Commission believes that it is neither possible nor opportune to establish now the frontiers of the European Union, whose contours will be shaped over many years to come.[5]

As we see, the Commission (and after it the Council) considered that it was too hot a potato to have a clear statement about Turkey and other interested countries.[6] In fact, EU officials began to use terms such as 'Wider Europe' to identify possible new members, or create neighbourhood policies toward the East and the South, an indirect way to determine who should be 'in the club' and who not.

It is then obvious that the EU has difficulties in identifying its own territory. To be precise, this is not an institutional problem – the EU territory is the sum of the territories of its Members, easily identified[7] – but a symbolic one. A true narrative about what defines the European territory – thus the European demos – and whom it encompasses remains absent from the official discourse. Put differently, the conceptualisation of its external borders is taboo in the European Union. The most interesting thing here is the fact that the leaders are becoming aware of this situation and the risks it carries, but cannot face it convincingly.[8]

A deterritorialised ambition

What explains this situation? Of course, there are conjectural aspects, such as the geopolitical agenda or economic challenges, that create good reasons for not rejecting any potential members and keeping the door open. But there are also signs that suggest that the problem lies deeper. I propose here five related hypotheses for explaining this taboo about external and internal borders in the EU.

The first is linked to the opposition between European integration and the nation-state. Committed to preserving peace on the continent after World War II, the founding fathers targeted the old state model as the nest of nationalism and thus of irreducible rivalries between countries. As François Mitterrand later declared: 'Le nationalisme, c'est la guerre!' (discourse in Luxembourg, 17 January 1995). In this context, the borders represent the very expression of the harmfulness of the nation-state. The deconstruction of the separations inside Europe thus appeared as a legitimate and noble mission for the newborn Community. As symbols of military threat, of separated families, of the geographical enclosure of the citizen's liberty, the concept of borders was to be overthrown and, in a sense, abandoned.

The second reason is closely linked to the first. It refers to the next ambition of the new Europe after peace: the creation of prosperity. For the liberal makers of the Community, the borders were the symbol of economic protectionism and restriction of free trade. In contrast, European integration had from the beginning the objective of creating a vast open market, soon called 'internal'. This clearly suggests than the interstate borders, with their tariff barriers and other obstacles, had no place within the Community, and therefore should be abolished. This was the second consideration behind discrediting the concept of borders on the eve of the construction of Europe.

The third hypothesis has to do with the universalistic values of the EU. The founding texts of the Community and almost all that has been written and said since then refer to European integration as an expression of democracy, liberal values, and human rights. These values are by definition not related to a specific territory, although they are seen as typical of the historical development of Europe. In particular, they are hardly distinguishable from those of the US (see Fukuyama 1992; Lucarelli 2008) and the rest of the Western world. In this sense, it would be contradictory for the EU to present itself as the incarnation of universalistic values, and to claim at the same time a (de)finite territory. Geography and borders appear here once again as obsolete and counterproductive concepts.

The fourth hypothesis is directly related to the Enlargement policy. Since the beginning, the Community invited other 'European' countries to join, and indeed it has succeeded in integrating 28 members to date. In fact, the Enlargement process appears as the most successful foreign affairs policy for the EU, permitting a peaceful expansion. In these conditions, it would be counterproductive for the EU to indicate where the external borders are, because this would diminish its appeal for the neighbouring countries.

The fifth and final hypothesis concerns the internal dynamics of the EU. It has to do with the inherent complexity of European sectorial and thematic geography. Several policies developed in the Community created specific spaces which included some of the countries but not all (for example the Eurozone). Meanwhile, non-member states could join some of these 'internal territories' (e.g. the Schengen area). In these conditions, it is difficult or even impossible to offer a 'legibility' to the EU territory. In contrast to the old nation-state, the link between territory and policy is no longer easily definable and understandable.[9] Several European maps become simultaneously legitimate, depending on what dimension is represented. The collective geographical representation of 'Europe' as a political agent is blurred.

In my view, these five hypotheses may explain why the geographical issue is so thorny for the EU. Having identified borders as the opposite of its own *raison d'être*, the EU cannot easily conceive of a definite and predictable territory. As a consequence, a coherent narrative about the significance of the European geography can hardly be imagined. Indeed, the utilisation of the concepts of territory and geography in internal or external discourse could only be interpreted as a renunciation of either the ideals underlying the Union, or some of its most successful policies. Any discourse or narrative of this sort would therefore be seen as counterproductive by the EU authorities, or at least difficult to create. As Moisio stated, 'a number of differentiated and overlapping geopolitical imaginations have been, and currently are, at play in Europe' (Moisio et al. 2012: 745). There are few attempts to merge these imaginations in a coherent vision.

On the importance of geography in identity processes

But is this 'territorial discourse' really important? In particular, does it have a role to play in the construction of a European identity? One way to answer this is to explore the general link between territory and identity. In the EU, for the reasons tentatively described above, this articulation is thin, as Vivien Schmidt summarised:

> The EU has political, economic and social boundaries rather than the usual geographical ones; it lacks the strong identity found at national level since it is a community created by fate meaning a community that emerges from the experience of the interdependence of people – it is a created identity, not a given one.

> (Schmidt 2006: 18)

The problem is that this 'created identity' is therefore merely intellectual and thus makes sense for a part of the European population – let us say simply the educated and internationalised citizens – but not all the people. Boundaries seem indeed necessary for the self-recognition of political groups. To quote Zielonka, 'identity is basically about belonging to a certain kind of community that lives on a certain territory and cherishes certain types of norms' (2001: 527).

Let us examine three relevant positions on this topic. The political analyst Stein Rokkan, who worked intensively on nation-building processes, insisted on the link between territory and identity. He argued that 'the history of the structuring of human societies can be fruitfully analyzed in terms of the interaction between geographical spaces and membership spaces' (Flora 1999: 104). In the past, social boundaries were dominant in human groups. But 'the nation-state gradually merged the concept of citizenship with that of territorial identity' (Flora 1999: 106). Therefore, according to Rokkan, the notion of identity cannot be separated from geography in modern western societies. This is likely to be a message for the contemporary EU also. Even if one believes in 'post-national' behaviour in twenty-first-century Europe, there is a need to accept that territory, which is merely a product of nationalist discourse, is still at stake. We have therefore to integrate it in the definition of EU policies.

Sonia Lucarelli offers another interesting insight. Questioning the EU's identity process, she insists on the image of the 'Other' in defining the self-representation of the community. Foreign relations are essential in this context, because they offer a 'mirror in which the group can view itself and its values' (2008: 36). She concludes that 'relationship between foreign policy and self-awareness is particularly important in cases of less consolidated political identities, such as the one developing among Europeans' (2008: 36). The external borders appear therefore as an essential tool for communities to distinguish themselves from 'other' societies – a constitutive act of existence. One can argue that this is also true for the European Union.

Finally Benedict Anderson, in his masterpiece *Imagined Communities*, recognised the importance of geographical representation for human societies. He insisted on the fact that the map is not merely the 'flat' representation of a territory, but the expression of a collective project. In some cases, it precedes rather than follows the reality of the territory it should represent. The map, as an expression of the territorial representation of the community, therefore becomes a logo and 'instantly recognizable, everywhere visible, [it penetrates] deep into the popular imagination' (Anderson 1983: 170–8).

This selective overview of the literature demonstrates the importance of the territory in the creation and self-representation of any community, and thus the appeal of a common imagination of this territory. Is the EU an exception? One might argue that its post-national/post-modern profile exempts it from this contingency. However, one might also consider that EU citizens are still shaped by standards of the nation-state and thus attribute a greater importance to that 'particularistic' dimension than to the 'universalistic' one. If this is true, it appears advisable that the European Union develops a geographical definition and constructs a narrative of its territory. But how could it do that? In order to define a coherent strategy, we should better understand the different conceptual views at stake about the European territory. In my view, three main approaches are recognisable.

Three approaches to the European territory

In his major book, Luuk Van Middelaar describes the three strategies of the EU: 'German', 'Roman' and 'Greek' (Middelaar 2013). The first refers to the ambition to create a popular identification with the EU. The European flag, the European Anthem, the Euro money – these are tools inspired by the nation-state, designed to establish a sentiment of common identity between European citizens. The Community was conscious of the importance of this 'popular' approach when inaugurating the European identity process in the 1970s. As suggested above, a coherent narrative about the territory of the EU would also be an important tool in the creation of this sentiment. Similarly to Middelaar, I distinguish here three conceptual approaches which could help to shape a territorial discourse in Europe: the French, the American, and the Imperial.

The French approach lies in the narrative of a 'strong and stable' geography, established in the historical *longue durée*. It is founded on typical concepts of the nation-state. The first is the reference to the 'natural borders', which assertively closes every French border with the help of the sea, the Pyrenees, the Alps, Jura, Rhine and Bulge – the Flemish plains being the only 'non-natural border'. Presented as geographical evidence, independent of social choices, these frontiers embody the idea of security and long-term stability. The second one is the code of nationality, relying on the *droit du sol*: the territory appears here as the main determinant for designating who is and who is not in the community. Finally, it embodies a clear narrative of self-representation and collective 'mind-mapping' with the frequent use of the word 'hexagon' as well as its graphical representation (for example in commercial labels). Briefly stated, this strategy refers to the classical nation-state representation, which uses 'hard borders' and distinctive symbols when speaking about the national territory. It creates a clear delimitation between 'us' and 'the others'. As such, it is an integral part of the French national imagination.

Of course, one may object that the French imagination of the territory is far more complex than that. That France conceives itself – like the US as we will see just below – as a 'shining nation', a civilisational lighthouse whose influence goes much farther than its frontiers. It is surely true, but this does not contradict the fact that France has a strong feeling of its own territory, and thus a clear understanding and image of it.

The American approach is completely different. It could refer to the 'Frontier thesis' promoted by Frederick Jackson Turner in 1893, or the 'manifest destiny' theory. The main idea here is that the territory has a dynamic character and that its expansion serves the ideals and objectives of the community. There are no natural borders to consider: mountains and river have to be crossed; only the ocean is perhaps the limit. In this model the national territory is not an inheritance of the past, but an expression of the values and ambitions of the community. The national imagination thus considers the territory as a 'work in progress', always in construction. The links between citizens, communities, and territories are not dictated by the soil or the blood, but by the willingness to build a (better) place together.

Of course, once again, one may object that the US territory is now finite. It is true that the 'Frontier' is more a historical relic than a contemporary reality. However it is also true that it remains firmly anchored in the American psyche. In one sense, Americans have never given up their ambition to convert the rest of the word to their model, as they did with the 'wild west' – although not perhaps with the same methods.

I call the third strategy the 'Imperial' one, because it refers to the typical empire model which is proposed mainly by Jan Zielonka in the EU context (Zielonka 2001). In this model, there are no fixed external borders for delimiting the territory. The community is composed of several autonomous entities which can join or leave, and therefore its geographical scope can evolve with the times. Inside the community, many different spaces can coexist, because there is no strong link between policies – or polities – and territories. In this model, the identities themselves are more connected to communities than to geographical spaces. In opposition to the French strategy, it is the *droit du sang* that predominates. These multi-scale territories are oriented toward functional efficiency and mutual prosperity rather than political (ideological) objectives. Concerning the external borders, the geographical changes are neither irreversible nor dictated by values only, as in the American strategy: the 'Empire' has an ambition to extend, but this movement is political or economic rather than inspired by 'destiny'.

In my view, as far as the territory narrative is concerned, the European Union is torn between these three different models. In short, one could affirm that the Enlargement policy is inspired by the American model, the multi-scale internal space by the Imperial, and the external borders securitisation policies by the French. Of course it is too simple to present reality in this way, but these concepts offer an interesting basis for a better understanding of the tensions at stake. The Turkish debate is a good example. The promoters of the accession defend the fact that it should be natural for the EU to extend to Turkey, because of the values of openness and inclusion of the Union – a typical 'American' conception. Others consider that the entry of Turkey is an economic as well as geopolitical opportunity, and should be secured as such – an 'Imperial' conception. Opponents mostly state that Turkey does not share the same cultural background as the other European countries, or that the internal borders should not include a country so close to the Middle East – a 'French' vision. A coherent discourse about the European territory could certainly be elaborated through these stereotypical standards, in order to gain popular attention and, we should say, 'emotion'.

Conclusion

The European Union is still in search of its territorial narrative. This challenge should be taken into consideration in discussions aiming to construct the European identity. While not saying that territory is the central issue in this context, it is clearly most important and should not be neglected by leaders of both the Member States and the EU organs.

At least three acute European contemporary problems are, indirectly at least, linked to this challenge. The first is Ukraine. The ambivalent discourse of the EU about the 'Europeanness' of Ukraine and its capacity to join the Union 'one day' gave rise to numerous expectations that are today disputed in a bloody war. The second one is the tragedy of the migrants in the Mediterranean. The strengthening of the external borders is not only a practical challenge, but a moral challenge as well. It reinforces the 'us' versus 'them' dynamics and thus contradicts the universalistic ambition of the EU. The third one is the strengthening of nationalisms inside Europe. The (perceived) weakness of internal and external borders contributes to the distrust of a growing number of EU inhabitants towards European integration. In an increasingly insecure environment, they feel that the nation-state is more capable of answering their needs for protection and control than the European Union. The fact that the latter did not really define its territorial ambition and scope does not help to create a strong feeling of 'being part of it in my skin'.

Of course, there is no intention of explaining these problematic situations in their entirety by the lack of a territorial narrative. But this surely contributes to the general embarrassment about the EU today. Studying the three approaches described above could help to distinguish the scope and finality of the external borders, at the same time articulating an understanding of the internal territories. The Enlargements since 1989 were certainly missed opportunities in this respect; perhaps the difficulties and approaching crises of the current situation will oblige the Commission and Member States to clarify their views before it is too late.

Notes

1. This discourse is visible not only in such parties as the *Front national* in France or UKIP in Great Britain, but also *Syriza* in Greece or *Podemos* in Spain. For example, see *Libération*, 26 January 2015.

2. Few publications have indeed focused on this subject. There is a gap between the numerous and often brilliant studies on European identity and citizenship (for example, the works of Lucarelli, Cerutti or Moro) and the research on the geographical dimension of the European Construction (for example Anderson, Bort or Moisio).

3. A specific example of this situation is that there is no common representation of the European map in the official documents of the EU (including the coins and banknotes of the Euro). Some represent the EU in the broader context – with Russia, Turkey, North Africa, and the Caucasus. Some represent 'just' the European countries, as an island in the ocean. Finally some fewer represent only the EU countries, without Norway and with Switzerland as a 'black hole' in the middle of the continent.

4. Speech delivered by Professor Walter Hallstein to the Federal Council of the European Movement on the occasion of his election as President of the European Movement, Rome, 20 January 1968. Retrieved from the Archives of the European Integration, Pittsburgh University, Fund 420.7.

5. *Europe and the Challenge of Enlargement*, 24 June 1992. Prepared for the European Council, Lisbon, 26–27 June 1992. Bulletin of the European Communities, Supplement 3/92.

6. A clear line with Africa was drawn, however, by the rejection of the Moroccan candidacy to the (then) European Communities in 1987.

7. Even this point is not so evident, considering that many European overseas territories (particularly British and French) remain outside the Community or have a special status in it.

8. In a weekly newsletter about the Enlargement, Romano Prodi, President of the Commission, 'recognised that the EU must be able to answer people in the present member states who are already starting to ask "Where does Europe stop?"'. Weekly Newsletter, 10 December 2002: *Ensuring links with new neighbours*. Retrieved from the Archives of the European Integration, Pittsburgh University, Fund 441.215A.

9. As Jan Zielonka recalls: 'Next to a central government, citizenship and the legitimacy to collect taxes and use violence, borders are the pre-requisites of any state-like organization' (Zielonka 2001: 508).

References

Aksoy, S. Z. (2009) 'The prospect of Turkey's EU membership as represented in the British newspapers *The Times* and *The Guardian*, 2002–2005', *Journal of European Studies*, 39(4): 469–506.

Anderson, B. (1983) *Imagined Communities: Reflection of the origin and spread of nationalism*, London: Verso.

Anderson, M. and Bort, E. (2001) *The Frontiers of the European Union*, New York: Palgrave.

Azrout, R., Van Spanje, J. and de Vreese, C. (2011) 'Talking Turkey: Anti-immigrant attitudes and their effect on support for Turkish membership of the EU', *European Union Politics*, 12(3): 3–19.

Berglund, S. (ed.) (2009) *Where Does Europe End? Borders, limits and direction of the EU*, Cheltenham (UK): Edward Elgar.

Bialasiewicz, L. (ed.) (2011) *Europe in the World: EU geopolitics and the making of European Space*, Farnham: Ashgate.

Buckingham, L. (2013) 'Mixed messages of solidarity in the Mediterranean: Turkey, the EU and the Spanish press', *Discourse Society*, 24(2): 186–207.

Burdy, J. P. (2004) *La Turquie est-elle européenne?* Paris: Turquoise.

Cederman, L. E. (2001) *Constructing Europe's Identity: the External dimension*, Boulder: Lynne Riener.

Cerutti, F. and Lucarelli, S. (eds) (2008) *The Search for a European Identity: Values, policies and legitimacy of the European Union*, London: Routledge.

De Vreese, C. H., Boomgaarden, H. G. and Semetko, H. A. (2008) 'Hard and soft: public support for Turkish membership in the EU', *European Union Politics* 9(4): 511–30.

Diez, T. (2001) 'Europe as a discursive battleground: discourse analysis and European integration studies', *Cooperation and Conflict*, 31(1): 5–38.

Flora, P. (ed.) (1999) *State Formation, Nation-Building, and Mass Politics in Europe: the Theory of Stein Rokkan*, Oxford: Oxford University Press.

Fukuyama, F. (1992) *The End of History and the Last Man*, New York: Free Press.

Hughes, K. (2004) 'Turkey and the European Union: just another enlargement?', *A Friends of Europe Report*.

— (2006) 'Turkey and the EU: four scenarios from train crash to full steam ahead', *A Friends of Europe Report*.

Kuus, M. (2004) 'Europe's eastern expansion and the reinscription of otherness in East-Central Europe', *Progress in Human Geography*, 28(4): 472–89.

— (2005) 'Multiple Europes: boundaries and margins in European Union enlargement', *Geopolitics*, 10: 567–70.

Lucarelli, S. (2008) 'European political identity, foreign policy and the Other's image: an underexplored relationship', in F. Cerutti and S. Lucarelli (eds) *The Search for a European Identity: Values, policies and legitimacy of the European Union*, Abingdon, UK: Routledge pp. 23–42.

Maier, J. and Rittberger, B. (2008) 'Shifting Europe's boundaries: mass media, public opinion and the enlargement of the EU', *European Union Politics*, 9(2): 243–67.

McLaren, L. M. (2007) 'Explaining opposition to Turkish membership of the EU', *European Union Politics*, 8(2): 251–78.

Van Middelaar, L. (2013) *The Passage to Europe: How a continent became a union*, New Haven, CT: Yale University Press.

Moisio, S., Bachmann, V., Bialasiewicz, L., dell'Agnese, E., Dittmer, J., and Mamadouh, V. (2013) 'Mapping the political geographies of Europeanization: National discourses, external perceptions and the question of popular culture', *Progress in Human Geography*, 37(6): 737–61.

Negrine, R. (2008) 'Imagining Turkey: British press coverage of Turkey's bid for accession to the European Union in 2004', *Journalism*, 9(5): 624–45.

Negrine, R., Kejanlioglu, B., Aissaoui, R. and Papathanassopoulos, S. (2008) 'Turkey and the European Union: an analysis of how the press in four countries covered Turkey's bid for accession in 2004', *European Journal of Communication*, 23(1): 47–68.

Paksoy, A. F. (2013) 'Turkey and the issue of European identity: an analysis of the media representation of Turkey's EU bid within the framework of religion and culture', *Romanian Journal of Communication and Public Relations*, 15(1): 29.

Parker, N. (ed.) (2008) *The Geopolitics of Europe's identity: Centers, boundaries and margins*, New York: Palgrave Macmillan.

Schmidt, V. A. (2006) *Democracy in Europe: the EU and the national polities*, Oxford: Oxford University Press.

— (2008) 'Discursive institutionalism: the explanatory power of ideas and discourse', *Annual Review of Political Science*, 11: 303–26.

Schneeberger, A. I. (2009) 'Constructing European identity through mediated difference: a content analysis of Turkey's EU accession process in the British press', *Journal of Media and Communication*, 1: 83–102.

Scott, J. and Van Houtum, H. (2009) 'Reflections on EU territoriality and the "bordering" of Europe', *Political Geography*, 28: 271–73.

Silberman, M. (ed.) (2012) *Walls, Borders, Boundaries: Spatial and cultural practices in Europe*, New York: Berghahn Books.

Tekin, B. C. (2008) 'The construction of Turkey's possible EU membership in French political discourse', *Discourse & Society*, 19(6): 727–63.

Waever, O. (2009) 'Discursive approaches', in A. Wiener and T. Diez (eds) *European Integration Theory* (2nd ed.), Oxford: Oxford University Press pp. 197–217.

Walter, J. and Albert, M. (2009) 'Turkey on the European doorstep: British and German debates about Turkey in the European Communities', *Journal of International Relations and Development*, 12: 223–50.

Walters, W. (2004) 'The frontiers of the European Union: a geo-strategic perspective', *Geopolitics*, 9: 674–98.

Wimmel, A. (2006) *Beyond the Bosphorus? Comparing German, French and British discourses on Turkey's application to join the European Union.* IHS Political Science Series Paper no. 111, December. Vienna: IHS.

Wintle, M. (2009) *The Image of Europe: Visualizing Europe in cartography and iconography throughout the ages*, Cambridge: Cambridge University Press.

Wodak, R. (2011) *The Discourse of Politics in Action: Politics as usual* (2nd rev. edn), Basingstoke: Palgrave.

— (2013) 'Dis-citizenship and migration: a critical discourse–analytical perspective', *Journal of Language, Identity & Education*, 12(3): 173–8.

Wodak, R. and Fairclough, N. (1997) 'Critical discourse analysis', in T. A. van Dijk, (ed.) *Discourse as Social Interaction*, London: Sage, pp. 258–84.

Zielonka, J. (2001) 'How new enlarged borders will reshape the European Union', *Journal of Common Market Studies*, 39(3): 507–36.

Chapter Six

Identity Technologies and the 'Nationalism Lite' of the European Union

Ireneusz Pawel Karolewski

Introduction

Nationalism studies focus mainly on nation-states or nationalising regionalisms for the obvious reason that nationalism has been and still is associated with the activities of nation-states or separatist tendencies within them. In this context, the European Union (EU) has frequently been viewed as a circumvention of nationalism, rather than its saviour or copy at a higher level. Scholars of nationalism have been rather sceptical about the EU's ability to reproduce national identity at a higher level. For instance, Anthony D. Smith (1993, 1995) argued that the search for European identity arises from flawed assumptions about the end of nation-states, ignoring the persistence of nation-states as long-term historical phenomena and therefore the rootedness of national identities. Smith pointed out that the EU lacks a common ethnic base with a reliable set of common historical memories, myths, symbols, and values, which would function as nationalising instruments, forging a strong and stable collective identity. Another sceptic David Miller rejected the idea of euro-nationalism on the grounds that citizens in Europe lacked mutual trust. According to Miller, the EU would need to justify material redistribution beyond the self-interest of the member-states, moving towards direct obligations between compatriots. Yet, such obligations are justifiable only against a background of reciprocity and trust, which in turn can be provided only by a national community which symbolises continuity between generations and reflects the virtues of the ancestors by encouraging citizens to live up to them (Miller 1995: 36). Such reciprocity and trust between compatriots, he claimed, are still invisible in today's EU.

Nationalism, traditional or otherwise, has to be maintained, reinforced, and transferred to new generations by the usage of various social technologies: national remembrance days, national flags, anthems, discourses on national greatness, images of a given nation's role in the region or the world, images of superiority, scenarios of threats from 'others' (Billig 1995; Teachout 2006; Guibernau 2013). National identity as 'a collective sentiment based on the belief of belonging to the same nation and sharing most of the attributes' (Guibernau 2013: 39) must be constantly reconstructed with reference to collective representations, emotions, and evaluations regarding a given nation, its distinctiveness, and its precious nature worthy of preserving at any cost – including, ultimately, sacrifice of one's life. Carolyn Marvin and David W. Ingle (1999) argue that nationalism shares this power to make individuals sacrifice their lives in the name of an 'imagined community' (Anderson 1991) only with organised religions. Nationalism has a huge impact on people's thinking, the organisation of their economic activities, and even the development of mental illnesses among them (Greenfeld 2001, 2013). Nationalism is a powerful force which does not only generate the feeling of dignity among the citizens (Greenfeld 1992) but also legitimises political elites as representatives of the people. In this sense, modern majoritarian polyarchies (Dahl 1972) can only claim to be democracies as the result of their fusion with a national community (Greenfeld 1992). Otherwise, there would be no reason for citizens to believe that majoritarian elections, majoritarian governments, and majoritarian decisions reflect anything more than just the tyranny of the majority.

The idea of forging an EU nationalism of sorts is surprising at first glance, as the Union is not a fully fledged state (even less a nation-state), given the central role that member states still play in Brussels. Yet, it shares many prominent features of the state, regulating a growing number of economic, political, and social issues of European societies and engaging in redistribution of financial resources through majoritarian decisions (Hix and Høyland 2011). The EU might fall short of traditional statehood but it has become a political authority which requires general legitimacy (or diffuse support, to use David Easton's term) beyond the short-term effectiveness of its governance (e.g. direct payments to the farmers, investments in the infrastructure of less developed member states, support for countries in economic crisis, etc.). In addition, the EU has been promoting a sort of euro-national civil religion of European integration. It glorifies its own founding fathers Robert Schumann and Jean Monnet as heroes and champions of an ideology of peace-making, which links the peaceful period in European history after World War II to the effects of European integration. In addition, the EU has developed a set of symbols, rituals, and practices regarding its own history, destiny, and the collective 'self' that are similar to the identity technologies of nationalism. Some students of the European Union have even begun using quasi-religiopolitical terminology in their analyses of the EU. For instance, Ian Manners (2013) introduced the term 'European Communion' to highlight the growing core of references to the EU's 'sacred' nature, while Viatcheslav Morozov and Bahar Rumelili (2012) point to conversion strategies of the EU regarding potential membership of neighbouring countries, which resemble the expansionist strategies of some nationalisms of the nineteenth and twentieth century.

I argue in this chapter that the EU has for some time been trying to establish a collective identity and promote social and political cohesion, beyond the utilitarian belief of citizens in its political and economic usefulness. This can be interpreted as the intentional development of euro-nationalism. This has two reasons. First, given the growing heterogeneity of the EU (currently twenty-eight member states) as a result of several enlargement waves, the Union has become increasingly conflicted. The financial and sovereign debt crisis (since 2010), the Russia–Ukraine war (since 2014), and the migration crisis (since 2015) demonstrate how diverse the interests within the EU are and how fragile is the legitimacy of its decisions. The EU is having increasingly serious difficulties in managing internal heterogeneity.

Second, until the early 1990s, the EU (then still the European Community) enjoyed a so-called 'permissive consensus' (Lindberg and Scheingold 1970), from the European citizens' benign neglect of the decisions of its political elites, as long as the marginal utility of unification was visible. However, with the transformation of the EU project from a single market into a political Union, with common citizenship and the Europeanisation of new policy fields, it entered a phase of 'constraining dissensus' as proved by numerous failed referenda and growing euroscepticism (Hooghe and Marks 2006). These failures of the EU as a polity (in particular the rejection of the grand project of the European constitution in 2005) led to increasing questioning of the Union's value. Against this background, the development of a euro-nationalism that would weaken centrifugal forces, smooth internal conflicts, and legitimise collectively binding decisions appears necessary to keep the EU from falling apart, this being more than a hypothetical possibility today, given, for instance, the so-called 'Brexit' or renationalisation trends in the migration policies leading to reaffirmation of internal EU borders in the course of the 2015 crisis. Some authors discerned the instrumental dimension of the EU's quest for greater legitimacy earlier. For instance, Bo Stråth (2002) argues that it could be already seen at the Copenhagen summit of the European Commission in 1973. The then challenge was to find instruments to consolidate the European Community, since the global oil price crisis and its impact on the welfare state undermined belief in its political effectiveness. This and other challenges to the European Union (e.g. German reunification of 1990 and the EU Eastern enlargement in 2004) moved it to apply social technologies borrowed from nationalism and aimed in a top-down manner at EU citizens. This imitation by the EU of certain aspects of nationalism in turn brings it back within the realm of modern, rather than post-modern or post-national, polity.

Regardless of the scepticism of nationalism scholars as referred to above, the EU does attempt to construct a collective European identity on the national model with the help of identity technologies, albeit using them differently from EU member states when they revert to nationalism. The EU's 'nationalism lite' distinguishes itself from the nationalisms of nation states by three characteristics. First, it highlights 'diversity' as a frame of reference for European identity making. Peter Kraus (2008) explored this issue in great depth in his seminal work on EU culture and language policies. There are limitations to 'achiev[ing] "integration in diversity" in conjunction with forms of a collective experience based upon large-scale horizontal communication and interaction among Union citizens' (Kraus 2008: 196). Second, the EU's 'nationalism lite' does not target the national identities of the member states directly; it promotes regional and local identities through a set of instruments, including regional policy or rotating cultural events at the city level. Monica Sassatelli argues that the EU has been trying to establish European identity as a cultural layer of more complex identities. By strengthening Europeans' multiple identities, the EU encourages a regulatory idea, in which 'diversity is encouraged within the European frame as this promotes an approach where no single content can try to impose itself as hegemonic' (Sassatelli 2009: 198). This multiple and content-rotating European identity does not question national identities directly but makes collective identities in Europe more complex and thus embeds the nationalisms of the member states into a larger identity context. Third, the 'nationalism lite' uses selected identity technologies of nationalism and at a subtler level, since the EU cannot be as aggressive and demanding of sacrifice as traditional nation-states. The EU cannot expect its citizens to lay down their lives for Europe, or react in a consistent way to external threats such as the Russian–Ukraine war or the migration crisis, and thus it is bound to stay heterogeneous. In the following, I will focus on four aspects related to the EU's identity technologies: (1) collective symbols and ritualistic practices, (2) foundational mythology, (3) self-images of superiority, and (4) European citizenship. By exploring these four aspects of nascent euro-nationalism, the chapter attempts to answer tentatively three main questions: (1) Is there a coherent euro-national ideology regarding the symbolic, ritual and myth-orientated practices in the EU? (2) To what extent does the EU mimic the techniques of traditional nationalism? (3) What are the expectations concerning the 'effectiveness' of identity technologies vis-à-vis the citizens in the EU?

Collective symbols and ritualistic practices

Belonging to a national community is reinforced through rituals of attachment and symbols with collective appeal. Symbols highlight the unique character of a nation and stand for 'things that matter' to it (Guibernau 2013: 92). However, they are only effective as identity technology to the degree that they are recognized for what they stand for and become internalised by the citizens. That is why symbols must carry a cognitive meaning before they develop an emotional one (Guibernau 2013: 99).

The EU has consistently generated and promoted collective totems and rituals, similar to those of traditional nationalism, in particular after the ratification of the Maastricht Treaty which involved a deepening of the EU as a response to the first Eastern enlargement, following German reunification and the incorporation of Eastern Germany into the EU. The totems are tangible manifestations of the EU and include the flag, the anthem, the motto ('united in diversity'), and the so-called EU passport (Manners 2011). François Foret (2009: 315) argues that the blue of the European flag can be viewed as an evocation of 'the blue of the Western sky' and 'stars figuring peoples of Europe form the circle as a sign of union. They are invariably twelve, symbol of perfection and completeness'. The flag seems to be the most recognisable totem of the EU, both for citizens and non-citizens. The functional expectation of totems is that they transcend linguistic boundaries due to their non-oral content. Other totems, such as the EU passport and driver's licence, fulfil mainly symbolic functions vis-à-vis EU citizens, as they enhance the perceived tangibility of the EU. One of the reasons why the EU passport has had a limited symbolic impact is probably the fact that there is no EU passport per se but only member states' national passports with an additional inscription 'The European Union' and harmonised burgundy-coloured cover, while the iconographic form, state symbolism, language, and even the material the cover is made of remain distinctly national. In contrast to the flag and to some extent the passport, the anthem, and the motto of the EU have no cognitive resonance, remaining unrecognisable to most EU citizens.

The most effective collective symbol of the EU until now is the common currency (Hymans 2004). The establishment of a palpable symbol of the euro and its specific iconography certainly raises the salience of the EU and may be significant for the development of a 'we-feeling' in the European Union (Risse *et al.* 1999: 147). Some scholars suggest that the power of the euro lies in its everyday presence and its iconographic diversity, allowing for representation of national motifs on the European notes and coins. Thus, on the one hand, the euro enhances the 'realness' of Europe by providing a tangible connection between the EU and citizens' daily lives (Risse 2003; Cerulo 1995). On the other hand, the EU cannot use such nation-like symbolism as directly as nation-states did in the nineteenth and twentieth centuries. The EU promotes commonality via symbolic diffusion into everyday life, but without relinquishing the symbolic ambiguity of these 'identity techniques' (Sassatelli 2002: 435–51). This certainly differentiates this type of practice from that of the nations, which has a stronger homogenising effect. Even though the financial and sovereign debt crisis in the EU has weakened the attractiveness of the euro (public support fell by 12 per cent and numerous voices were raised in favour of the return to national currency, for instance in Germany by the Alternative for Germany party), the euro still remains the most recognisable collective symbol of the EU. Moreover, the support for the common currency is on the rise again. While it fell between 2007 and 2013 from 63 to 51 per cent, it has since increased gradually to 57 per cent in 2015 (Eurobarometer 83/2015).

In addition, the EU supports and carries out ritualistic practices. According to Ian Manners (2011), one such ritual addresses Franco-German reconciliation, portrayed as closely connected to the 'birth' of the European Community/ Union. Regardless of the political differences between Germany and France, the celebrations of the Elysée Treaty include choreographed practices of joint acts of remembrance and hand holding at war memorials. These practices, however, are limited to Germany, France, and some other Western EU member states, and are not much shared by Great Britain or Eastern European members of the EU. In today's European Union of twenty-eight countries and high diversity of political and historical experience it is difficult to explain why the Franco-German reconciliation should take precedence over, say, the Polish–German or the Dutch–German ones.

The EU has attempted to establish several other remembrance days: the European Holocaust Memorial Day (marking the liberation of Auschwitz on 27 January 1945), the European Day of Remembrance for Victims of Stalinism and Nazism (observed on 23 August, marking the Ribbentrop–Molotov Pact of 23 August 1939), the European Day for the Victims of Terrorism (marking the Madrid train bombings on 11 March 2004), and Europe Day (marking Robert Schuman's declaration of the European Coal and Steel Community on 9 May 1950) (Manners 2011). These commemorative practices have had limited dramatising effect on the wider public and are quite ineffective. They remain communicative events, rather than proper political celebrations, which would be more typical for national celebrations (Foret 2010). Also, the weight and outreach of these events varies: the European Holocaust Memorial Day is global and more dramatic by definition, while that of Schuman's declaration is limited both in context and dramatic impact. This not only creates an uneven symbolic calendar but is also dependent on the member nations' publics for the transmission of the message. As a result, these European rituals are virtually unknown to the wider public in EU societies and remain ineffective as identity technologies.

Ian Manners (2011) stresses that the EU has been successful at establishing so-called 'symbolic taboos' throughout recent decades, that is, concepts or phrases immediately identifiable as central to the unification discourse and rarely questioned in the context of European integration. They include 'Schengen', 'common high authority', 'pooling of sovereignty', and 'acquis communautaire'. These symbolic taboos have become increasingly 'sanctified' as essential for the rationale of European integration. Others were added more recently – 'four freedoms', 'single currency', 'Copenhagen criteria', 'environmental imperative' – phrases repeated in EU discourses and contributing to the construction of the EU political reality. In line with Shore (2006), this list of symbolic taboos could be extended to include concepts such as 'multi-level polity', 'civil tolerance', and 'governance without government'. However, the existence of such symbolic taboos has to be regarded with a certain reservation. In most cases, they figure in elite discourse at the EU level and reflect the way in which political, economic, and social issues are communicated within its institutional set-up. Only a few of the 'symbolic taboos' find their way into the national publics, and this only briefly and to a limited extent. For instance, the concept of 'pooling sovereignty' was used in 2011 in a speech by Poland's foreign minister in Berlin, evidently to the big surprise and confusion of Polish public intellectuals and pundits (Sikorski 2011). Thus, while symbolic taboos may very well be a feature of elite euro-talk, they do not seem to be an effective identity technology, not being able to permeate and affect the thinking of national publics.

There is a twofold way in which the creation of totems, rituals, and symbols by EU elites works at cross-purposes to EU legitimacy. First, these practices (resembling practices of nationalism) aim at enhancing EU legitimacy by producing or strengthening the European 'we-feeling'. The visibility of the EU in the community, which these identity technologies may increase, does not necessarily translate into greater legitimacy and stronger identity. As the concept of 'constraining dissensus' suggests, the higher visibility and politicisation of the EU can instead exacerbate controversies and lead to further rejection of European projects and institutions.

Second, the EU attempts to create a collective identity that is not derived from popular sovereignty. Since the EU is not a democratic polity (in the traditional sense at least), identity technologies pose a challenge to the Union's legitimacy, as they might be difficult to distinguish from indoctrination by EU elites (and practices of authoritarian regimes), thus contradicting the EU's democratic aspirations.

Foundational mythology

In addition to such symbolic and ritual practices, the EU has for some time been developing a foundational mythology. In nationalism studies, constitutive myths or 'mythomoteurs' have often been the focus (Smith 1987: 24, 2015; Motyl 2002; Hobsbawm 1992). Foundational mythology, that is, narratives creating normative and cognitive fundamentals for a national community, are a key aspect of nationalism, helping to establish intergenerational continuity and construct a nation as an 'immortal' community that can be resurrected, should it temporarily vanish from the political map. Foundational myths are different from ordinary political and economic narratives. Erik Jones (2010: 93) argued convincingly in response to Berger und Luckmann that myths should be distinguished from ideology, as 'myth-makers have a weaker motivation and a lower regard for consistency while ideologists are much more rigidly determined and religious proponents give harsh treatment to dissenters or heretics'. This is the reason why political and economic ideological constructs are usually ineffective as sources of legitimation. Foundational myths, if stable and convincing (see also Hansen and Williams 1999), construct a 'glorious past' (or a past based on suffering – leading to a messianic self-image) and appeal to new generations that cannot remember the origins of the polity. They forge collective identity through creating a feeling of continuity between generations, using fateful points in the past with which one finds it easy to identify individually.

For the EU, the major 'mythomoteur' has for decades been the narrative of the integration responsible for peace, prosperity, and democracy in Europe. Vincent della Sala argues that the narrative of peace, prosperity, and democracy went through all stages of successful national mythologising: diffusion, ritual, and sacralisation (Della Sala 2010: 11, also Della Sala 2013). This foundational myth has become deeply embedded in the political discourse of united Europe, being activated mainly prior to important decisions involving EU citizens – national referenda on EU issues or the establishment of European institutions to deal with crises such as the recent financial and sovereign debt one. The image of the EU as the ultimate peace-making, peace-keeping force in Europe as well as the saviour of common welfare is triggered when the danger of 'constraining dissensus' lurks behind. In recent years, this foundational myth of the European Union as the vehicle for peace, stability and economic growth has continuously been losing its appeal, in particular for younger Europeans, as the idea of military conflict between EU countries becomes increasingly abstract for them. As a consequence, the EU has been at pains to find new 'mythomoteurs'. One such makes fundamental rights an inherent part of the European project, and based on a common European heritage, albeit fundamental rights were not part of the initial project of the European integration. The narrative of the EU as a guardian of fundamental rights is based on the Union's adoption of the fundamental rights credentials of its member states and the Council of Europe (Simismans 2010: 62). Though fundamental rights were not in the Rome Treaty, the EU has gradually generated the fundamental rights myth, now acted upon by both institutional myth-makers and civil society actors. The latter target the EU as a new ally and thus construct this myth actively throughout the EU at the discursive level. The new myth became particularly prominent during the debates on the Charter of Fundamental Rights in 2001 and its ratification around 2007. In addition, there have been suggestions that the Holocaust remembrance could also be viewed as a symbolic foundation for European integration and reference for European identity (Probst 2003). The disorientation of the EU regarding its foundational myth became quite visible with the migration crisis of 2015, when renationalisation tendencies in the member states came to dominate public discourse.

Positive self-images

Alongside ritual practices and foundational myth-making, the European Union engages in the promotion of positive self-images or even images of superiority. These images strongly resemble the national images of being the best country in the world (US), the progressive power for a just and classless society (Soviet Union) or a civilising force (Great Britain or France). The images promoted by the EU must be recognised and reacted to by other actors. They rely on constant articulation and repetition, otherwise they would lose their identity-making power and might disappear. In contrast, even the rejection of self-images by others may strengthen them, since any reaction makes them relevant. For instance, Neve Gordon and Sharon Pardo have demonstrated that the very publication of the EU Guidelines prohibiting the allocation of funds to Israeli entities in the Occupied Territories in 2013 reinforced the EU's self-image as a power for good, simply by making it visible in the international discourse. 'Without Israel's furious reaction, hardly anyone would have heard of the Guidelines and they would have had little, if any, impact on the political arena' (Gordon and Pardo 2015: 424).

All self-images of the EU are based on a meta-narrative of 'ideal power Europe'. This meta-narrative is created not only by European institutions and actors advocating specific measures in international politics but also by academics discussing European issues (Cebeci 2012: 583). In both political action and academic discourse, the meta-narrative is stabilised and contributes to the self-understanding of the EU. The meta-narrative of 'ideal power Europe' is based on the universalistic interpretation of the EU's community values and institutional or ethical supremacy vis-à-vis countries outside it. The EU sees itself and is seen by a number of academics as a force for good, bearing universal responsibility for the civilising process in non-EU countries. Three main types of self-image promoted by the EU can be discerned: the image of cosmopolitan Europe, civilian power Europe and normative power Europe. All these self-images highlight the EU's civilisational progress and thus supremacy in relation to other polities, not only undemocratic ones but also vis-à-vis other contenders to the title of the ideal power, notably the US.

The first type of positive self-image refers to the EU as the embodiment of cosmopolitan values. This self-image depicts the European Union as based on a set of universalistic principles such as human rights that congeal into a sort of

European constitutional patriotism. This self-image is cosmopolitan, as the EU represents a 'post-national constellation', in which European citizens are likely to develop a sense of loyalty and solidarity 'among strangers' by abstracting from their particular national identities (Habermas 2001). Such cosmopolitan Europe is embedded in a shared culture of universal and liberal values (Rosmond 2014; Shabani 2006: 699–718, Lacroix 2002: 944–58) and relates to the modified concept of power, according to which the EU promotes the rule of law, democracy, and human rights worldwide. In this view, the EU subordinates its external policies to the constraints of a higher-ranking universal law (Eriksen 2006: 252–69). Thus, the EU is superior to many other polities in international politics, as it acts based on a sense of justice or ethical duty pertaining to human rights, rather than material interests. According to this image, the EU identifies and problematises infringements of human rights worldwide, fulfilling the role of the harbinger of a more civilised international order. The catalogue of the European criteria of superiority has been famously compiled by Jürgen Habermas and Jacques Derrida in the plea for a normative Europe, including secularisation, priority of the state over the market, primacy of social solidarity over achievement, scepticism concerning technology, rejection of the law of the stronger, and commitment to peace (Habermas and Derrida 2003, also Habermas 2003). Clearly aimed at the US, Habermas and Derrida focused their normative position on the so-called 'core of Europe', rejecting the normative added value of the Eastern European newcomers to the EU and assigning to this core (called the 'old Europe') a civilising role within the EU itself also.

Another positive self-image in the meta-narrative 'ideal power Europe' pertains to the notion of the EU as a civilian power. The notion of civilian power refers to the methods of international politics rather than their substance (Orbie 2006: 123f; Telò 2005). The EU is believed to apply methods of civilian change rather than military force. The civilian power Europe acts principally in accordance with ideas and values, not military or economic strength. As a result, the EU's actions are believed to be not only civilian but also more civilising, which reinforces the vision of the EU as an ethically superior polity and more advanced political system as compared to nation-states (see Sjursen 2006). One of the main creeds of 'civilian power Europe' is multilateralism, which is a form of self-binding by law. In this context, the EU's objective is to promote the advancement of a rule-based international order, the power of international institutions and regional organisations, all of which allows for the extensive coordination and cooperation of actors in international politics (Youngs 2004). Simultaneously, the EU advocates deliberative and institutionalised cooperation mechanisms of conflict resolution, rather than the military power preferred by other international actors, including the US, China and Russia (Mitzen 2006). By using civilian means of power, the EU can cope with problematic issues in international politics such as the nuclear negotiations with Iran much more efficiently, as it enjoys a better reputation in the international arena than, for instance, the US.

The third self-image of European identity is that of the EU as a normative power. In this case, the EU stresses its progressive stance, for instance in rejecting the death sentence or in promoting and implementing progressive environmental policies. By so doing, the EU not only shows its moral superiority but also asserts its leading role and depicts the US as a laggard. Thus, the EU promotes its positive image as the vanguard of the fight against climate change and refers to environmental diplomacy and bio-safety regulations as a reflection of the distinctive societal values of European societies. Therefore, the 'green' normative power defines itself through the difference from other less environment-friendly countries, such as the US or China (Falkner 2007: 507–26; also Lenschow and Sprungk 2010; Scheipers and Sicurelli 2007). A further issue connected to this is sustainable development, which the EU has been trying to put on the agenda during major international negotiations. For instance, during the 2002 World Summit on Sustainable Development, the EU played a leading role while trying to convince other participants, mainly the US, to promote sustainability and policy goals connected with it (Lightfoot and Burchell 2005).

Unfortunately, the positive self-images generated by the EU exhibit serious cracks in consistency and coherence. For instance, the image of green normative power can be quite easily challenged at the empirical level. Robert Falkner (2007: 521) argues that the EU's distinctive stance in environmental politics is not simply the product of a deep-rooted normative orientation but frequently the result of domestic conflicts over biotechnology, in which some enterprises are able to lobby successfully in favour of their technological solutions, presented later as the EU common good and best practices at international level. Also, the positive view of the EU as a foreign policy actor guided by the common good does not accurately depict the Union's international behaviour (Pardo 2012). This is well documented in the case of the EU arms trade policy, as countries with poor human rights records are still frequent receivers of European weapons and military technology (Erickson 2011). A particularly instructive case is the China weapons embargo debate, in which pressures to lift the embargo rose considerably after China, on the condition that the embargo ended, became a willing supporter in the European sovereign debt crises (Erickson 2011: 12).

The ongoing conflicts between the leading EU member states show the difficulty of upholding a consistently normative position within the EU. These findings are particularly striking when compared with the EU's official discourse on European security, in which the cosmopolitan, civilian and normative images are not only pervasive but also closely connected to the roles the EU claims in international relations (see Ferreira Nunes 2011). In addition, there are studies strongly suggesting that the normative power practices of the EU serve primarily the security and economic interests of the EU and its member states. Against this backdrop, the norm-based behaviour of the EU can be viewed as a utility-maximising strategy. Raffaella A. Del Sarto has suggested, regarding the EU's governance of the Arab Spring (2015: 13), that, even though the normative power image suggests a quasi-benevolent export of democracy and human rights, the EU has been involved in international governance of trade, economic regulations, border controls and administrative practice, all of which serve primarily the interests of the EU member states or the EU itself.

This lack of consistency and even the awareness of the European elites that the notion of 'ideal power Europe' is utopian do not necessarily undermine the effectiveness of positive self-images as identity technologies. Scheipers and Sicurelli argue regarding the EU's role in negotiations on the International Criminal Court and the Kyoto Protocol: 'the EU's identity is taking shape regardless of its actual consistency and awareness of its utopian stands' (Scheipers and Sicurelli 2007: 453), as the self-representation of the EU becomes crystallised through international law.

European citizenship as identity technology

Citizenship ascribes rights and duties of membership in a community. However, it also defines who is allowed to belong to the community and who is excluded. Rogers Brubaker argues that even democratic citizenship is a device of social closure and exclusion, as it necessarily discriminates between citizens and non-citizens and excludes the non-citizens from the polity (Brubaker 1994, 1999).

In the context of EU scholarship, the 'Union citizenship' is sometimes viewed as a fundamental institution pertaining to the rule of law, fundamental freedoms and human rights, and democracy (Wiener 2006, 2007: 1–7). The integrating function of Union citizenship is expected to be particularly important, as the EU is not only a complex organisation, but also encompasses highly diverse European societies. In this context, Andreas Føllesdal (2001: 315) regards European citizenship as a central measure for increasing reciprocity and trust among Europeans, because it is a special institution likely to socialise individuals into citizens by redirecting their interests and perceptions towards the polity. In this sense, we could identify the Union citizenship as a technology of identity, which is supposed to cement the EU societies.

Yet, there is a growing doubt regarding the impact of Union citizenship on ordinary citizens (see Besson and Utzinger 2008; Koopmans 2012; Schmidtke 2012); research on its relevance paints a bleak picture. Since Union citizenship bestows mainly transnational mobility rights, and political rights in the Union, the question remains how far citizenship leads to identification with the EU. While 50 to 88 per cent of Europeans feel European citizens (Eurobarometer 83, 2015: 28) – in the majority of member states it is more than 60 per cent – qualitative research suggests not far. For instance, Adrian Favell (2008) argues that the educated and highly skilled 'free movers' living in different cities of the EU largely retain their national attachment, which points to the resilience of the national identity with its exclusionary social mechanisms. Paradoxically, the political rights guaranteed by the Maastricht Treaty do not seem to play any role in the lives of mobile European citizens, as they rarely vote in their cities of residence. They remain concerned with the national politics of their home countries or are apolitical. They predominantly use European citizenship to benefit from mobility in Europe as employees, consumers, neighbours, and public service users. Their political identities stay national.

The boundary-making mechanism of modern citizenship appears to be necessary, since citizenship integrates individuals within a community, excluding those outside it. Even European citizenship can stress exclusion, leading to exclusionary euro-nationalism. In the EU this becomes increasingly visible in the case of immigration policies, where images of threat from 'bogus asylum seekers' are increasingly presented by EU agencies as a danger to the social integration and cohesion of European societies (Karolewski 2012). Biometric technologies, detention facilities, and new methods of surveillance are employed to establish exclusionary and restrictive immigration policies by the EU. Instead of generating trust and reciprocity, these exclusionary practices tend to stimulate or reinforce collective feelings of insecurity, and are likely to promote a 'culture of fear' that makes citizens overreact to risks, rather than resolve security problems. This came into full view in the migration crisis in 2015, with new highly exclusionary discourses on who was eligible to enter the EU and who should be removed dominating policy-making.

In this context, immigrants are frequently 'constructed' as 'others' and depicted as a threat to the community's survival in its current social and cultural form. Didier Bigo (2008) uses in this context the term 'banopticon', which discriminates between those with access and those to be monitored for possible detention and removal. This banopticon supersedes the nation-state, as national governments of the EU collaborate in excluding immigrants as suspected 'others'. In particular, the European Union uses banopticon technologies in its government of external borders and in surveillance of the population within them (Amiraux 2010). The new wave of immigrants in 2015 will certainly contribute to further securitisation of immigration in the EU, as already happens in some of the member states including Hungary, the Czech Republic and Austria.

The member states of the EU collaborate closely in setting up institutions, funds, and surveillance instruments which separate the neurotic European citizens (Isin 2004) from the dangers of the outside world, represented by the 'others'. By constructing and implementing practices of exclusion, banopticon reassures the neurotic citizens and deters the 'others'. Border controls are supported by a number of monitoring institutions, data banks, screening devices and surveillance mechanisms, including Frontex, Europol, the Schengen Information System, and Eurodac. Together, these banopticon institutions and technologies strengthen the confidence of the EU citizens that they should remain among themselves and separated from the dangers of the outside world. Border controls are shifted from member states to the external borders of the EU. However, the migration crisis of 2015 has revealed that the European banoptican does not work efficiently and cannot guarantee security. Therefore, more investments in monitoring, surveillance and other banopticon technologies are very likely.

Against this backdrop, European citizenship is not only associated with transnational rights and mobility but also becomes linked to 'politics of insecurity' (Huysmans 2005) and the demarcation between the citizen and the suspect. If these trends become dominant, this would exacerbate the existing democratic deficit of the EU through the expansion of executive powers, escape from democratic accountability and overall secrecy surrounding security issues.

Conclusions

The EU represents both a system of supranational governance and a novel form of polity. It is still a fragile construction that remains a 'community in making' with an ambiguous sense of identity. Despite the use of identity technologies, the EU has not yet developed a coherent euro-nationalistic ideology. Even though certain aspects of euro-nationalism – including symbolic, ritual, and myth-orientated practices – are recognizable in the EU, they do not combine into a viable consciousness.

The financial and sovereign debt and the migration crises demonstrate plainly how feeble the European consciousness is and how easily crises and stress can provoke nationalist reactions of various kinds. Even the obvious success of the euro as a global currency has proven to be short lived, and the euro has become the target of attacks by a growing number of political groups in the EU since 2010. The foundational myth-making remains volatile and the EU is trying to invent new myths. Self-images of superiority show cracks in their consistency and rely on the utopia of an 'ideal power Europe', promoted as such by European elites. The EU mimics some technologies of nationalism but fosters euro-nationalism in a subtler manner than nation-states. Having considerably fewer institutional resources than nation-states at its disposal, it promotes 'nationalism lite'. It lacks an integrated and homogenising educational system as well as integrated public space that would allow for an effective diffusion of nationalism from the elites to the citizens. That is why the EU has to rely on national publics to stage European commemorations, which virtually does not happen. The EU has to compete with the nationalisms of member nations, being cautious not to incite conflicts between these nationalisms and euro-nationalism. However, the main challenge to euro-nationalism remains the profound indifference of ordinary citizens in the EU societies, their political apathy, and their ambivalence towards the EU. The more critical literature on the EU (White 2010a, 2010b) shows how little Europeanisation takes place in the everyday lives of ordinary Europeans. Under these conditions, the 'nationalism lite' of the European Union is likely to remain very 'lite' indeed and be confined within European elites.

References

Amiraux, V. (2010) 'Suspicion publique et gouvernance de l'intime: contrôle et surveillance des populations musulmanes dans l'Union Européenne', in A. Scherrer, E.-P. Guitet and D. Bigo (eds) *Mobilité(s) sous surveillance: Perspectives croisées*, UE-Canada, Outrement: Athena Editions, 73–87.

Anderson, B. (1991) *Imagined Communities: Reflections on the origin and spread of nationalism*, London: Verso.

Besson, S. and Utzinger, A. (2008) 'Towards European citizenship', *Journal of Social Philosophy*, 39(2): 185–208.

Bigo, D. (2008) 'Globalized (in)security: the field and the Ban-Opticon', in D. Bigo and A. Tsoukala (eds) *Terror, Insecurity and Liberty: Illiberal practices of liberal regimes after 9/11*, Abingdon: Routledge pp. 10–48.

Billig, M. (1995) *Banal Nationalism*, London: Sage.

Brubaker, R. (1994) *Citizenship and Nationhood in France and Germany*, Cambridge, MA: Harvard University Press.

— (1999) 'The Manichean myth: rethinking the distinction between civic and ethnic nationalism', in H. Kriesi et al. (eds) *Nation and national identity: The European experience in perspective*, Zürich: Rüegger, 55–71.

Cebeci, M. (2012) 'European foreign policy research reconsidered: constructing an "ideal power Europe" through theory?', *Millennium: Journal of International Studies*, 40(3): 563–83.

Cerulo, K. A. (1995) *Identity Designs: The sights and sounds of a nation*, New Brunswick, NJ: Rutgers University Press.

Dahl, R. A. (1972) *Polyarchy: Participation and opposition*, New Haven, CT: Yale University Press.

Del Sarto, R. A. (2015) 'Normative Empire Europe: the European Union, its borderlands, and the "Arab Spring"', *Journal of Common Market Studies*, first published online, 1–18, DOI: 10.1111/jcms.12282.

Della Sala, V. (2010) 'Political myth, mythology and the European Union', *Journal of Common Market Studies*, 48(1): 1–19.

— (2013) 'Myth and the post-national polity: the case of the European Union', in G. Bouchard (ed.) *Whither National Myths? Reflections on the present and future of national myths*, London: Routledge 157–72.

Eurbarometer 83 (2015) 'Public opinion in the European Union', http://ec.europa.eu/public_opinion/archives/eb/eb83/eb83_first_en.pdf, accessed on 1 November 2015.

Erickson, J. L. (2011) 'Market imperative meets normative power: human rights and European arms transfer policy', *European Journal of International Relations*, 1–26, online first 27 October 2011.

Eriksen, E. O. (2006) 'The EU: a cosmopolitan polity?', *Journal of European Public Policy*, 13(2): 252–69.

Falkner, R. (2007) 'The political economy of normative power Europe: EU environmental leadership in international biotechnology regulation', *Journal of European Public Policy*, 14(4): 507–26.

Favell, A. (2008) *Eurostars and Eurocities: Free movement and mobility in an integrating Europe*, Malden, MA: Blackwell.

Ferreira Nunes, I. (2011) 'Civilian, normative, and ethical power Europe: role claims and EU discourses', *European Foreign Affairs Review*, 16: 1–20.

Føllesdal, A. (2001) 'Union citizenship: unpacking the beast of burden', *Law and Philosophy*, 20(3): 313–43.

Foret, F. (2009) 'Symbolic dimensions of EU legitimization', *Media, Culture and Society* 31 (2): 313–324.

—   (2010) 'European political rituals: a challenging tradition in the making', *International Political Anthropology*, 3(1), 55–77.

Gordon, N. and Pardo, S. (2015) 'Normative power Europe and the power of the local', *Journal of Common Market Studies*, 53(2): 416–27.

Greenfeld, L. (1992) *Nationalism: Five roads to modernity*, Cambridge, MA: Harvard University Press.

—   (2001) *The Spirit of Capitalism: Nationalism and economic growth*, Cambridge, MA: Harvard University Press.

—   (2013) *Mind, Modernity, Madness: the Impact of culture on human experience*, Cambridge, MA: Harvard University Press.

Guibernau, M. (2013) *Belonging: Solidarity and division in modern societies*, London: Polity.

Habermas, J. (2001) *The Post-National Constellation*, Cambridge: Polity Press.

—   (2003) 'Making sense of the EU: towards a cosmopolitan Europe', *Journal of Democracy*, 14(4): 86–100.

Habermas, J. and Derrida, J. (2003) 'February 15, or what binds Europeans together: a plea for a Common Foreign Policy, beginning in the core of Europe', *Constellations*, 10(3): 291–7.

Hansen, L. and Williams, M. C. (1999) 'The myths of Europe: legitimacy, community and the "crisis" of the EU', *Journal of Common Market Studies*, 37(2): 233–49.

Huysmans, J. (2005) *The Politics of Insecurity: Security, migration and asylum in the EU*, London: Routledge.

Hobsbawm, E. (1992) *Nations and Nationalism since 1780: Programme, myth, reality*, Cambridge: Cambridge University Press.

Hix, S. and Høyland, B. (2011) *The Political System of the European Union*, third edition, Basingstoke: Palgrave Macmillan.

Hooghe, L. and Marks, G. (2006) 'Europe's blues: theoretical soul-searching after the rejection of the European constitution', *PS: Political Science & Politics*, 39(2): 247–50.

Hymans, J. E. C. (2004) 'The changing colour of money: European currency iconography and collective identity', *European Journal of International Relations*, 10(1): 5–31.

Isin, E. F. (2004) 'The neurotic citizen', *Citizenship Studies*, 8(3): 217–35.

Jones, E. (2010) 'The economic mythodology of European integration', *Journal of Common Market Studies*, 48(1): 89–109.

Karolewski, I. P. (2012) 'Caesarean citizenship and its anti-civil potential in the European Union', in V. Kaina and I. P. Karolewski (eds) *Civil Resources and the Future of the European Union*, London: Routledge.

Koopmans, R. (2012) 'The post-nationalisation of immigration rights: a theory in search of evidence', *British Journal of Sociology*, 63(1): 22–30.

Lacroix, J. (2002) 'For a European constitutional patriotism', *Political Studies*, 50(5): 944–58.

Lenschow, A. and Sprungk, C. (2010) 'The myth of a green Europe', *Journal of Common Market Studies*, 48(1): 133–54.

Lindberg, L. N. and Scheingold, S. A. (1970) *Europe's Would-Be Polity: Patterns of change in the European Community*, Englewood Cliffs, NJ: Prentice-Hall.

Lightfoot, S. and Burchell, J. (2005) 'The European Union and the World Summit on Sustainable Development: normative power Europe in action?', *Journal of Common Market Studies*, 43(1): 75–95.

Manners, I. (2011) 'Symbolism in European integration', *Comparative European Politics*, 9, 243–68.

— (2013) 'European communion: political theory of European Union', *Journal of European Public Policy*, 20(4): 473–94.

Marvin, C. and Ingle, D. W. (1999) *Blood Sacrifice and the Nation: Totem rituals and the American flag*, Cambridge: Cambridge University Press.

Miller, D. (1995) *On Nationality*, Oxford: Oxford University Press.

Mitzen, J. (2006) 'Anchoring Europe's civilizing identity: habits, capabilities and ontological security', *Journal of European Public Policy*, 13(2): 270–85.

Morozov, V. and Rumelili, B. (2012) 'The external constitution of European identity: Russia and Turkey as Europe-makers', *Cooperation and Conflict*, 47(1): 28–48.

Motyl, A. J. (2002) 'Imagined communities, rational choosers, invented ethnies, *Comparative Politics*, 43(2): 233–50.

Orbie, J. (2006) 'Civilian power Europe: review of the original and current debates', *Cooperation and Conflict*, 41(1): 123–8.

Pardo, P. R. (2012) 'Normal Power Europe: Non-Proliferation and the Normalization of EU's Foreign Policy', *Journal of European Integration 34* (1): 1–18.

Probst, L. (2003) 'Founding myths in Europe and the role of the Holocaust', *New German Critique* 90, 'Taboo, Trauma, Holocaust', 45–58.

Risse, T. (2003) 'The Euro between national and European identity', *Journal of European Public Policy*, 10(4): 487–505.

Risse, T., Engelmann-Martin, D., Knope, H-J. and Roscher, K. (1999) 'To Euro or not to Euro? The EMU and identity politics in the European Union', *European Journal of International Relations*, 5(2): 147–87.

Rosmond, B. (2014) 'Three ways of speaking Europe to the world: markets, peace, cosmopolitan duty and the EU's normative power, *British Journal of Politics and International Relations*, 16(1): 133–48.

Sassatelli, M. (2002) 'Imagined Europe: the shaping of a European cultural identity through EU cultural policy', *European Journal of Social Theory*, 5(4): 435–51.

— (2009) *Becoming Europeans: Cultural identity and cultural policies*, Basingstoke: Palgrave Macmillan.

Scheipers, S. and Sicurelli, D. (2007) 'Normative power Europe: a credible utopia?', *Journal of Common Market Studies*, 45(2): 435–57.

Schmidtke, O. (2012) 'Commodifying migration: excluding migrants in Europe's emerging social model', *British Journal of Sociology*, 63(1): 31–8.

Shabani, P. O. (2006) 'Constitutional patriotism as a model of postnational political association: the case of the EU', *Philosophy and Social Criticism*, 32(6): 699–718.

Shore, C. (2006) 'Government without statehood? Anthropological perspectives on governance and sovereignty in the European Union', *European Law Journal* 12(6): 709–24.

Sikorski, R. (2011) 'Poland and the future of the European Union', speech at DGPA in Berlin on 28 November 2011, http://www.mfa.gov.pl/resource/33ce6061-ec12-4da1-a145-01e2995c6302:JCR, accessed on 1 November 2015.

Sjursen, H. (2006) 'What kind of power?', *Journal of European Public Policy*, 13(2): 169–81.

Simismans, S. (2010) 'The European Union's fundamental rights myth', *Journal of Common Market Studies*, 48 (1): 45–66.

Smith, A. D. (1987) *The Ethnic Origins of Nations*, Malden. MA: Blackwell.

— (1993) 'A Europe of nations or the nation of Europe?', *Journal of Peace Research*, 30(2): 129–35.

— (1995) *Nations and Nationalism in a Global Era*, Cambridge: Polity Press.

Stråth, B. (2002) 'A European identity: to the historical limits of a concept', *European Journal of Social Theory* 5(4): 387–401.

Teachout, W. (2006) *Capture the Flag: a Political history of American patriotism*, New York: Basic Books.

Telò, M. (2005) *Europe: a Civilian power. European Union, global governance, world order*, Basingstoke: Palgrave Macmillan.

Wiener, A. (2007) 'Contested meanings of norms: a research framework', Comparative European Politics 5: 1–17.

White, J. (2010a) 'Europe and the common', *Political Studies*, 58: 104–22.

— (2010b) 'Europe in the political imagination', *Journal of Common Market Studies*, 48(4): 1015–38.

Wiener, A. (2006) 'Comment: fact or artefact? Analysing core constitutional norms in beyond-the-state contexts', *Journal of European Public Policy*, 13(8): 1308–13.

Youngs, R. (2004) 'Normative dynamics and strategic interests in the EU's external identity', *Journal of Common Market Studies*, 42(2): 415–35.

Chapter Seven

Dignity for All: Nationalism in Tanzania

Katrina Demulling

Tanzania, the country on the east coast of Africa that formed when Tanganyika and Zanzibar united in 1964, rarely attracts world attention. No hostilities keep it in international news as in neighbouring Congo, Rwanda, Zambia, Kenya, and Mozambique. Despite this difference, it has much in common with other African polities. Tanzania is an illuminating case study of nationalism's spread into Africa.

In Tanzania, the creation of a shared sense of national identity began after independence: the independent state was not a nation. Prior to independence, a few Tanzanian intellectuals and politically motivated individuals began creating its national image. Their narratives shaped the wider social world and the identities of those they influenced. At the time, it was not clear which would emerge as the dominant vision. As in much of Africa, the first Tanzanian nationalists were first-generation intellectuals, educated in Western institutions, but this alone does not explain why they turned nationalists (Odhiambo 1981: 103). Encouraged to aspire, yet systematically denied outlets for fulfilment, these individuals came to see it as their duty to guide and transform their societies. They consciously and purposefully articulated the ideals of nationalism to solve the psychologically difficult situation they found themselves in (Geiger 1997:5).[1]

The introduction of nationalism cannot be isolated from other Western influences in eastern Africa; initially, it came packaged with other ideas. The colonisers' religious beliefs, justice system, economic orientation, administrative structure, etc. were all imprinted with the nationalist view of reality. Yet, something more than this availability is needed to explain why nationalism became important for people in what is now Tanzania. A close examination of this area's history shows that countless actions undermined the traditional sources of authority and power, which drove some people to seek out new sources of meaning. The dignity brought by nationalism appealed to these seekers, who created their own vision of a nation.

During the late nineteenth and early twentieth centuries, missionaries and colonial governments cultivated select native individuals, placing them educationally and in terms of aspirations and sensitivities on a par with foreign personnel. Yet, channels of advancement to a status equal to that of their foreign counterparts remained closed to these people. Disgruntled by this status inconsistency, they attempted to rationalise their dissatisfaction and did so with the help of national consciousness. As late as the early 1950s, few had a clear sense of the nation to which they belonged. By the late 1950s, appeals to a nation, calls for equality and even independence reverberated throughout the territories of

Tanganyika and Zanzibar. The 1960s and 1970s were the time when the national sentiment crystallised, spread, and focused on the Tanzanian nation.

The entire East African coast and outlying islands had been subject to trading ventures and colonisation from Persia, Arabia, India, Somaliland, and indirectly from China and the Mediterranean. These earlier episodes of cultural contact differed from the foreign influences of the middle to late 1800s, which coincided with dramatic changes experienced in this region and led to alterations in the social and political structures and relations. A series of wars and famines, combined with an increase in porterage and the slave trade, served to undermine traditional sources of legitimacy. The caravan trade, Omani rule, and the presence of missionaries also contributed to the changing social dynamics. These transformations were not, however, clear-cut replacements of an older order by a new one.

Missionaries carrying the word of God to 'dark Africa' made a conscious effort to remake men in a new mould. Bishop Steere called others 'to join in the work of making a Christian nation out of what is now degraded Africa' (Steere 1871: 181). But, while the most explicit of all the foreigners attempting social change, missionaries did not and could not impose their views anywhere by force. While most purposefully avoiding 'Europeanising' their converts, missionaries brought Western ideas to the people among whom they worked, women as well as men (Hassing 1970: 387). Nationalism pervaded their translations of biblical texts and even compilations of local vernaculars. The missionaries' most receptive audiences were found in societies whose old order and ways of life had fallen apart and not yet been replaced. Their ideas and activities offered people of very low status, such as former slaves, respectable identities and had an immediate and lasting impact beyond religious conversion.

The German and British colonial presence in what is now Tanzania also helped usher in important changes in social and political structures, as well as transform the locals' attitudes and beliefs. Colonisers' biases and predilections concerning the ways of governing and conducting business were institutionalised in the course of their rule. They championed 'modernisation' of the economy: increased agricultural production, commercialisation, and the idea that success meant ever increasing profits and growth. One of the most significant imports – because of its reach and transformative influence – was the administrative bureaucracy of office-holders. Leadership as a *role* rather than a *right* undermined the legitimacy of countless chiefs and headmen, as one could be replaced at the administration's wish. Both German and British colonial governments were instrumental in creating and solidifying 'tribes' out of coexisting local populations. Their actions hardened previously transitory political divisions into groups seen as ethnic.

In 1890, Zanzibar's Sultan, as a result of mounting threats to his empire, agreed to make his territory a British Protectorate. The British intended to maintain the Sultanate by developing Zanzibar as an Arab state. Although they were wary of policies that made them look like a full-fledged colonial administration, their intrusions were nevertheless far reaching. Over the first half of the 1900s, the Sultan became a puppet figurehead whose influence waned, as the British protectors took over managing and leading the sultanate. British attitudes to slavery and race transformed the nature of society. Before this transformation, Zanzibar's economy rested on the slave trade and cloves. The British prohibited the export of slaves in 1873, ending the slave trade altogether in 1897 (though all slaves in the region were not freed until after Tanganyika became a British trust territory following World War I).

British notions of race shaped administrative policies. The British saw Zanzibari society as divided along racial lines, with the Arabs at the top. Since this was not the case in fact, the British had trouble clearly defining 'Arabs'. In practice, ethnic categories were relatively fluid and the distinctions between 'Arab', 'Shirazi', and 'African' also reflected one's economic status. Though initially social status was determined by descent, it could be achieved through wealth, adopting Arab dress and manners, or being a patron of the less fortunate (Fair 2001: 43). As former slaves sought to recast themselves as freeborn islanders to enjoy the social and economic benefits of free status, the indigenous population tried to increase the distance between themselves and former slaves by appropriating Arab or Shirazi identity. This earlier system with its cultural markers changed as the British assumed that the social hierarchy reflected ethnic stratification. Though earlier views persisted, Zanzibaris could do little to thwart the institutionalisation of British ideas. British policies reinforced and rigidified racial distinctions, leaving no room for the grey area between African and Arab. What mattered most during the first half of the twentieth century was one's official status, not traditional status symbols. British ethnic categories reified the loosely defined hierarchy marked as Arab at the top, and Indian, Shirazi, and African below. All were lumped into one of these four ethnic groups, although the British hierarchy often reduced this division further into three classes of people – Arabs, Indians, and Africans. British economic policies aimed to preserve the Omani Arabs as the landlord caste. Administrative and educational policies cemented this ruling political position. Most educational and employment opportunities went to Arabs and Indians (de Saissy 1981: 30; Glassmann 2000: 398).

Tanganyika came under German colonial rule in the 1880s. This rule ended less than thirty years later, in 1916, after the British seized it from the Germans during World War I. The German colonisers did not have an easy time in Tanganyika: hardly a year passed between 1886 and 1898 without an uprising (Sunseri 2000: 584). Ultimately, however, none of the existing polities was strong enough to resist the imposition of German overrule. The Abushiri and Maji Maji rebellions highlight key issues of social and political discord. The overriding goal of Abushiri and the chiefs who supported him was to restore the former economic and political order. They wanted strangers, such as the Germans, as business partners but barred from the control or interference with the Arab-dominated trade (De Jong 2002: 66). The rebels failed to protect their interests from German encroachment. By the time the Maji Maji rebellion began, the area had been a German colony for around fifteen years. Participants did not join together to defend a greater nation and fight for its freedom. At the outbreak of Maji Maji, inter-tribal boundaries were fluid, with the pre-colonial authority structures in a state of disintegration (Gwassa 2005; Monson 1998).[2] The goal of the rebellion was to preserve the status quo against the new cultural intrusions that were undermining it.

The Western-style bureaucratic administration of office-holders introduced to Tanganyika under German rule was not a democratic system. The power and status of the local elites were reduced, but the Germans saw themselves as 'lords and masters' to the natives of the colony. Treating them as inferior, colonisers often compared the inhabitants to children (Poeschel 1919: 30).[3] The Germans wished to facilitate trade: they invested in railway and road infrastructure, brought new economic enterprises, and promoted cash crop production. Their operations were supported by taxes and forced labour, both unpopular. German administrators were aware that many of their initiatives brought no positive changes. 'Up till now our system of plantations and our railway construction have caused great upheavals among the black population, have upset ancient social customs, uprooted in part the new generation and depopulated whole districts', Emil Zimmerman wrote in 1917 (Zimmerman 1918: 43).

At the end of World War I, Germany lost its colonial possessions and Tanganyika became a British-mandated trust territory. The British, like the Germans before them, found it difficult to govern such a large and heterogeneous territory: 'the Territory is so vast in extent and its tribes are so different in language, customs, and characteristics, that it is difficult to give a description of administration which is of general application'. Typically, administrative officers supervised administration carried out by the sultans, chiefs, and other native authorities. The native authorities served judicial functions and had some executive power over the native population. Administrative officers laboured for the 'improvement of the position of the native population' and attempted to nudge influential sultans and chiefs to coax their adherents into compliance with these government schemes (League of Nations 1925: 6–7).

The British wished to respect local ruling systems, but assumed that an ethnic government, with a native chief ruling over his own people, was ideal. Indirect rule became the hallmark of Britain's colonial rule. Donald Cameron, the colonial governor who oversaw its implementation, stated that British administrators would 'do everything in our power to develop the native on lines which will not Westernise him and turn him into a bad imitation of a European' (quoted in Iliffe 1979: 321). Yet, the colonial administration continuously sought to 'improve' and develop the native. The policy of indirect rule clashed with the desire for effective and efficient district administration. This resulted in creating 'tribal' groups where none existed before. In some areas, a distinction emerged between established authorities and the newly created ones, such as among the Gogo with a *mutemi wa serikali* (government chief) and *mutemi wa mvula* (rain chief) (Jackson and Maddox 1993: 280). In the 1930s, the British considered descent a primary determinant of the right to rule. The exception of course was Zanzibar; it was not origin, but pre-existing rule structure. The British collected official tribal histories, but made assumptions about African social structure, tribal groupings, and the 'proper' system of governance for them, which they reinforced in their writings. Their policies reflected their ethnic bias, ignoring or downplaying religious differences and other specific features of native power structures. But, at the same time as the British enforced an ethnic, lineage-based right to rule, they were defining office holding as a position and not a right. Limitations of the British tribal view soon became apparent. Differentiation of the indigenous inhabitants into tribes or races or even into religious interest blocks, all reflecting Western perspectives, did not capture important points of fission in Africa.

Biographies of Martin Kayamba and Shaaban Robert – observers and social commentators who felt the pulse of local culture – help to elucidate broader trends of the 1920–50s. They paint a picture of a society which is by no means unified, yet is characterised by an emerging sense that all Africans are kinsmen and should have certain communal feelings. Before independence, the group of individuals with some Western education within what is now Tanzania was very small. Out of this small indigenous group, only perhaps 1 per cent advocated far-going social change. In this group, nationalist ideas appealed to an even smaller handful. (For example, two of the first president Julius Nyerere's siblings do not appear in the annals of 'nationalist history' although they received a similar 'Western' education.)

Generally respected in their society, these individuals typically came from the former elite but began to push against prevailing norms and customs. They admired the foreign culture to which their education had exposed them, some even considering themselves carriers of this culture. Kayamba (1891–1939), born to Christian parents in Mbweni Zanzibar, obtained a missionary education, travelled to England, and entered the civil service, following a path forged by his father. His educational achievements and merits opened some doors, but he found others closed to him as an African. He had the opportunity to hold government positions traditionally reserved for Europeans, such as acting sub-storekeeper for six months following the deaths of two European sub-storekeepers. Despite his superior education and qualifications, the salary Kayamba received as a civil servant was lower than a person of a different ethnicity would have been paid. But a German District Commissioner expected him to pay higher transit fees, since intellectually (with his command of English) he was on level with Indians (Kayamba 1963: 185).

Kayamba helped found the African Civil Servants' Association (later transformed into the Tanganyika Africa Association, and then TANU). The association, focused on sports and socialising, was not a politically motivated organisation, but served to bring like-minded Africans together. At this time, socialising between different religions was new and Kayamba fondly remembered 'Christians and Mohammedans, Africans and Arabs joining together' at his club. He was among the first to call for African unity irrespective of religion:

Religion is the matter for the heart and must come first, but it does not prevent members of one religious community from combining with members of another religious community. I firmly believe that Africans will never progress unless they realize the necessity for unity. A great deal of our progress rests with us. We cannot move if we do not wish to move together.

(Kayamba 1963: 198)

In 1931, Kayamba was appointed as one of Tanganyika's representatives to the Joint Parliamentary Committee on East Africa, sent to England to discuss a 'closer union' between the British East African territories of Kenya, Uganda, Tanganyika, and Zanzibar. He stressed how important this was:

> Up till now the African has not been given a chance or an opportunity to speak for himself or to air his feelings. Many people think the African is so childish that he cannot even open his mouth and say whether he is well or not. To some of us it seems that even a child can speak and parents are always anxious to hear his voice and his requests. Those gentlemen who wisely planned to get Africans to England to speak before the Joint Committee have done the most noble service to the African community. The African cannot claim as yet that he can champion his cause as efficiently as the best Europeans, but he can justly claim the privilege for an opportunity for his voice to be heard and his views to be sought where matters concern his vital interests. Nobody knows the African's requirements better than himself. His mode of living, his customs and habits are peculiar to himself and require a thorough study. In order to understand an African as he actually is, one needs to live like him, with him, and be intimate with him, which is very difficult.

(Kayamba 1963: 232)

The trip impressed upon Kayamba the differences between Africa and England. While he admired the English, he believed Africans would forever remain different, writing in 1936:

> No wise African can be spoilt by traveling in Europe nor can he be Europeanized. An African knows quite well that he is an African and is always proud of his colour and nationality. He has a valuable place among his own people and if he can help them it is to his credit and to the benefit of the people.

Yet still, he saw Africans as 'the most backward race in the world' (Kayamba 1963: 261).

Kayamba identified as African and writes as an authority on African native life and customs, even though his upbringing and concerns clearly differed from those of most people around him. He was born to Western-educated parents and lived within the elite sphere of educated Africans and government officials. He knew that Africans were not united but wished that they would come together. He never spoke of *Tanganyikans* as a group. He wanted to improve his society but not to transform its fundamental nature. Moreover, while dissatisfied with the limited opportunities open to him, he felt that the English were culturally superior. He was most upset when not treated in accordance with his abilities, but believed he had opportunities unimaginable a generation before. He wanted to be judged on merit and valued fairly, as his co-workers were, not based on his ethnic heritage, which he calls 'nationality'. His was a confusing position to be in.

Robert is lauded as the first Swahili novelist and modern writer. His life (1909–62) was begun under German colonial rule and he saw Tanganyika transform into a British colonial trust territory, but he died years before Tanzania came into being. Still, he is revered as a *Tanzanian nationalist* poet (Mulokozi 1976). Naturally, Robert never described himself as such, but he also never described himself as a nationalist. Robert lived on the cusp of two worlds. His life and thought mark the beginning of a turn in Tanzania's history.[4] He lived under a colonial yoke that, for the most part, was not questioned by those around him. Even Nyerere, born over ten years later than Robert, would say: 'When I was born, there was not a single person who questioned why we were being ruled' (*Africa News Online*, 8 November 1999). During Robert's formative years, there were no political parties or even African-based associations. The concept of nation itself was hardly in circulation, though used by foreigners in reference to their societies.

Poetry and prose fiction was a vehicle for Robert's life philosophy, and observations of society and its discontents. He used familiar forms to discuss new themes. His focus was no longer on being a good Muslim or a good wife, but on being a good citizen. He had a universalistic understanding of humanity unknown to previous generations of Swahili poets: 'The created world repeats itself within the nations of human beings in order to show their common origin and their great unity' (Harries 1962: 275). Robert wrote on women's rights and place in society, and on the relationship between citizens and government. He believed citizens had an obligation to work with the government to help their country, to civilise Tanganyika (Mulokozi 2002: 212). He attempted to adjust the Swahili language to the emerging national sentiment, adding glossaries to his publications to express new ideas.

Robert's admiration of the English was open. He wrote often on the darkness that engulfed Africans before their coming, which had brought civilisation and light to the continent (Mulokozi 2002: 192). He lauded the English 'spirit of generosity, compassion, kindness' and their intention to raise the level of civilisation in Africa to put it on an equal plane with Europe. In a letter to the editor in *Mambo Leo* he wrote:

> On behalf of Africa, I thank the European rulers. They have extraordinary faith, spirit of generosity, sympathy, kindness, and the chief intention of equalising all countries' levels of civilisation and development. I am sure that perhaps after many years we will succeed in being able to say 'like Europe, like Africa' [*Kama Ulaya Kama Afrika*]. The poor continent was in darkness for a long time, until the Europeans arrived people were blinded, everywhere there was a shameful [slave] trade market. Now the light of civilisation is lit, its radiance can be seen in every region.

> (Mulokozi 2002: 192)

This light, Robert argued, however, was unlike the eternal sun, but required cleaning and maintenance to burn bright (Topan 2006: 108).[5] Without care and effort on the part of Africans, it could be extinguished. But he remained grateful to the English, in much the same way as Kayamba, for bringing it in the first place.

As Robert's thought developed, his localised, personal concerns shifted to questions about the continent and humanity as a whole. In 'Whispers from my Heart', 'Like the Rainbow', and 'Our Colours', he wrote on colour discrimination, racism, and social equality. These themes became important elements in the nationalist discourse in Tanzania. Robert was also one of the first to have a sense of Tanganyika as a unique cultural entity. In his collection *Pambo la Lugha* (1947), several of his poems used the words *taifa* or *mataifa* (nation) and *Mtanganyika*, as in one, published in 1932 in *Mambo Leo*, where he talks about 'My Tribe Tanganyika'. He never identified himself ethnically (as Yao) and was one of the earliest to call himself Swahili. When he joined the African Association, it was still more a social club than a political group advocating social change. Still, in his poem on it, 'Chama cha Waafrika', he called for the people to 'rise up', admonishing 'kila Mtanganyika' (every Tanganyikan) to take responsibility, to 'do his turn', as he wrote in English in the final stanza (Robert 1966: 10).

Kayamba and Robert represent a small group of exceptional individuals who occupied a cultural sphere outside their surrounding society as much as they were a part of it; it is such a perspective, straddling different viewpoints, that their social commentary reflects. Robert saw himself as a Swahili and as a loyal British subject. He was not a nationalist, but was appropriated later by nationalists. He wanted to change his society, but did not question British rule. Despite similar admiration for English customs, Robert avoided being called a colonial stooge ('kibaraka wa wakoloni') or 'Mzungu Mweusi' (Black European) as Kayamba was (Mulokozi 2002: 195). By the 1940s, intellectuals expressed their frustrations and worked through social problems in fiction, though many of these Swahili authors supported themselves with government jobs. Kayamba began to identify as an African but did not envision Africans as a nation endowed with certain qualities. Like Kayamba, Robert found his experiences inconsistent with what his education led him to expect. He saw himself as part of a larger community – but not a nation. He helped create a vocabulary and give voice to some of the feelings and frustrations that he and those around him experienced because of the inconsistencies in the British colonial system. But neither of the two men realised what a lever in their hands the new ideas brought by the British could become.

The colonisers introduced into Africa a system that encouraged aspirations and merit-based opportunities – which implied related frustrations – that did not exist before colonialism. Frustrations grew among 'Africans who had been brought up in Western civilization, yet never allowed to blend in a natural and normal way with that civilization' (Chachage 1986: 55). By the 1920s, a few people, who internalised national ideas of equality and popular sovereignty, saw themselves as equal to the colonisers and able to rule. Petro Njau of Kilimanjaro lamented, 'I wish I could tear off this black skin of mine. We are every whit as good as the white man and as fit to control the country' (Iliffe 1979: 334). By the 1930s, a broader change of attitude to the colonial system was visible. In 1943, Medical Officer

Mwaisela said: 'The general outlook at present as far as my life is concerned, is very gloomy. I have been brought up to such a level in life that I can neither cope with my own people's life, nor that of a civilized man' (Chacage 1986: 8).

Discrimination based on race became problematic. Frustrations mounted at every level. In 1938, a letter to the *Tanganyika Herald and Tanganyika Opinion* on the sale of sweepstakes tickets lamented:

> We are tired of being treated as babies in everything. If lotteries are bad for natives, are they good for Europeans and Indians? Or is it God's will that a man of white or brown colour alone can indulge in sweepstakes either to satisfy his gambling instincts or worship the Goddess of luck, hoping therefore to make good use of windfall if it does come.

The conclusion was that:

> We, black people, today want to enjoy the same privileges as white people, we want good stone houses, motorcars, aeroplanes, etc., what is good for the whites is also good for the blacks: color makes no difference. Everything in the world has got its own color and cannot be regarded as useless on account of non-white or non-brown colour, provided it was made by the Almighty. Furthermore, we want to send our sons to colleges in Europe, America and India, etc., we want to open big Dukas [shops] too.

> (Chachage 1986: 22)

The 'colour bar,' the institutionalised racial segregation based on skin colour, had come under attack by the 1940s (Chachage 1986: 23). A. K. Juma wrote to the newspaper *Venture* in 1949, upset over British settlers who were trying to halt 'African political progress and blunting our political aspirations' (26 October 1949).

In Tanganyika and Zanzibar, the frustrated ambitions of the upwardly mobile boiled into discontent, while previously privileged groups grew weary of the erosion of their dominant position. Among the educated, the sense of inferiority gave way to the articulation of pride in Africans' skin colour and the insistence that Africa had its own civilisation and contributed to the general one: Egypt, after all, was part of Africa. Nevertheless, there was a continuity between many of the ideas of colonial indirect rule and theirs. They did not want to return Africans to the type of government characteristic of their former societies.

Press outlets, founded by the missionaries and colonial governments, became important venues for sharing ideas and venting frustrations. After World War II, community newspapers emerged in places such as Dar es Salaam, Tabora, Bukoba, and Mwanza. Concerned mainly with local, territorial interests, these papers spread the notion of an independent Tanganyika under an African leader, with Swahili as the territorial language. Many more appeared in the 1950s. Erica Fiah established the first independent newspaper *Kwetu* in 1937 as a 'means whereby it may be able to spread knowledge among the sons of the soil who could read and write' (Chachage 1986: 21). Over two-dozen politically oriented newspapers existed in Zanzibar after World War II.

Various associations developed in the early 1900s, reflecting the emergence of new communities with common interests, to protect these interests. The Arab Association formed in the early 1900s to fight for fair compensation of Arab slave owners affected by the abolition of slavery. Initially representing the interests of the wealthiest and longest established Arab families in Zanzibar, it grew to represent Arabs in general. Civil servants founded the African Association in 1929. It was concerned with the 'whole nation' of African inhabitants, using the word *taifa* in opposition to *kabila* (tribe) or *ukoo* (clan). Its main purpose was to promote civilisation and to 'help our government' (*Mambo Leo* 1931: 105). Fiah established The Tanganyika African Welfare and Commercial Association in 1934 to safeguard 'African interests', mainly those of shop and stall keepers. Its motto was 'Educated Africans are the agents of African civilisation' (Chachage 1986: 23). The Shirazi Association, rather inactive until the 1950s, formed in 1939. Different political parties developed out of these largely racial organisations in anticipation of the Legislative Council elections in 1957. In the struggle for political voice, competing political and social visions emerged. The biggest divide was between race-based conceptions and civic conceptions of the polity. But all this was before the polity in question was thought of as an independent nation.

While still insisting on loyalty to the sultan, newspapers such as *Mwongozi* and *Alflaq* began to argue that the overarching Zanzibar national identity was inherent in the 'mixture of blood' of the people. *Mwongozi* sought to define as enemies of the nation anyone who was not loyal to the sultan and to Islamic Middle Eastern culture. Such were mainlanders with only a shallow experience of coastal society, as well as Christians, whom *Mwongozi* writers considered *washenzi* (savages or barbarians). Two of *Mwongozi*'s slogans were 'Politics is not ethnicity' (*Siasa si kabila*) and 'Politics is not drumming and dancing' (*Siasa si ngoma*) (Glassman 2000: 406). Civilisation was distinctly Arab and Islam centred.

Africa Kwetu, as the mouthpiece of oppressed Africans, aired grievances against the Arab elite. This paper sought to convince Zanzibaris that their interests and identities were defined by descent. It responded to the debates launched by the Arab intellectuals of *Mwongozi*. On 25 September 1952, the paper asserted:

> Our interests have for long been represented by the alien races and the result is … the alien races have become the masters and the real natives of the island and we, the Africans in these islands, have become the alien races denied all justice and all the rights that a native should have.

> (Hamdani 1981: 34)

To the Zanzibar Nationalist Party's (ZNP) advocacy of a multiracial government, *Africa Kwetu* responded by attacking those who did not define the nation in racial terms, declaring on 5 May 1955:

We wish to assure all the so called Zanzibaris ... that anything short of an African state will never be accepted when self-government is achieved in this protectorate ... we are also opposed to multiracial government in these islands.

(Hamdani 1981: 34)

From early 1952, the African Association stressed that only Africans could claim to be indigenous to the islands. One can easily see who was a true African: 'if the person's skin is black or reddish brown, and if the hair is kinky. If you see a person with these traits, well then, he's a pure African' (Glassman 2000: 413).

There is a prevalent idea in local sources at the time that people without national consciousness were slumbering and needed to be 'awakened'.[6] For nationalists this was already a natural phenomenon. In 1941, *Kwetu* announced: '[the] African is awakening from his long slumber' (Chachage 1986: 48). Peter Mtambao wrote, 'Civilization started in Africa long before the other countries of the world were awake, but Africa's progress was retarded by the awakening of other countries ... Now she is awakening from her long siesta' (Ilife 1979: 379). By 1947, the dominant argument was that 'Africans should regain their former glory' by waking up those who slumbered, oblivious to Tanzania's strength as a nation and not yet passionately enough committed to the opposition to the colonial presence.

On 9 December 1961, Tanganyika became independent, with Nyerere the first prime minister. Nyerere had earlier proclaimed:

We the people of Tanganyika would like to light a candle and put it on top of Mount Kilimanjaro, which would shine beyond our borders giving hope where there was despair, love where there was hate and dignity where before there was only humiliation.

(Tanganyika Legislative Council 1959: 1)

On the night of independence, a team of climbers did just that. The Zanzibar Revolution on 12 January 1964 resulted in the overthrow of the Sultan's government. It occurred only a few months after the ZNP/Zanzibar and Pemba People's Party (ZNPP) alliance won the election over the Afro-Shirazi Party (ASP). Many land and property owners, mainly of Arab descent, were killed or fled the island. This alienated supporters of the ZNP/ZPPP; many supporters in Pemba were publicly humiliated – men had their beards and heads shaved and were subjected to public floggings. Several months later, in April 1964, Zanzibar united with Tanganyika.

Small or isolated pockets of people may espouse nationalist views and orient their life by them without any lasting impact. A certain body of people now converted to and was inspired by nationalism, which, for these people, replaced other worldviews. While a sovereign geopolitical entity was created and gained international recognition, it would be premature to call this entity a nation (though, of course, it was so called officially). By independence, without a doubt, it was nationalism that drove the leaders Nyerere and Karume. What this entailed beyond the belief that Tanzania was a nation (a dignified self-governing community), however, was not clear. Nyerere and Karume professed to share the same idea of Tanzania as a nation, but their policies and pronouncements show deep divisions in understanding. The goal of independence was to make Africans sovereign in politics, economic activity, and culture, thus conferring on them dignity and self-respect. The core philosophy was socialist, stressing national self-reliance. The variation in interpretation of this core philosophy, its goals and values, however, was great.

Nyerere is described as *the* Tanzanian nationalist. Those who disagree with this assessment insist he was foremost an *African* nationalist. This man, seen both as a superior human and the quintessential common man, was believed to represent all of Tanzania, embodying its values. Nyerere was so influential that even those who disagreed did not contest him: Mwakikagile states, 'few people – anywhere across the country – wanted to be seen as uncaring, betraying the masses' (Mwakikagile 2007: 347). Many among the educated elite evidently practised self-censorship in order to identify themselves with the majority, the poor peasants and workers who 'were the nation' (Mwakikagile 2007: 347).

Nyerere, one of the most influential African intellectuals and political figures, began articulating his socio-political vision around 1960. At first, it was clearly pan-African, but already, by 1967, in the Arusha Declaration, he presented the image of the Tanzanian nation. This declaration served as a policy roadmap. Tanzanian citizenship was defined as independent from race and based solely upon loyalty to country. Nyerere's ideal vision refracted the liberal civic English national model, replacing its individualism, expressed in capitalism, with the socialism that, for him, was the most perfect realisation of the core values of nationalism: 'The people's will must be sovereign; but it will only lead them to the equalities and dignities of socialism if they exert that sovereignty with the understanding of socialism' (Nyerere 1968: 26). His writings in *Uhuru na Ujamaa/Freedom and Socialism* clearly demonstrate that he equated socialism and nationalism. It is a state of mind, fundamentally secular in orientation, in which people are seen as free and equal sovereign members of a society, imbued with dignity. All men, while not created physically equal, are and should be treated as equal:

> The word 'man' to a socialist, means all men – all human beings. Male and female, black, white, brown, yellow; long-nosed and short-nosed; educated and uneducated; wise and stupid; strong and weak; all these, and all other distinctions between human beings, are irrelevant to the fact that all members of the society – all the human beings who are its purpose – are equal.

> (Nyerere 1968: 4)

This equality above all implied equal human dignity: 'A socialist society would seek to uphold human dignity everywhere' (Nyerere 1968: 5). Such a society is also necessarily democratic as the people are sovereign:

Democracy is another essential characteristic of a socialist society. For the people's equality must be reflected in the political organization; everyone must be an equal participant in the government of his society. Whatever devices are used to implement this principle, the people (meaning all the members of the society equally) must be sovereign, and they must be able to exert their sovereignty without causing a breakdown of the law and order, or of the administration of their society.

(Nyerere 1968: 50)

Nyerere's nationalism was fundamentally secular: 'Socialism is concerned with man's life in this society. A man's relationship with his God is a personal matter for him and him alone; his beliefs about the hereafter are his own affair' (Nyerere 1968: 12).

The governments in Zanzibar and on the Tanzania mainland used propaganda to spread the vision of the nation and construct its history. In Zanzibar, for instance, the ASP disseminated *A Short History of Zanzibar*, rationalising and justifying the party platform. Published in 1974, it argued that others made differences between African tribes appear greater than they were, while '[T]he plain and indisputable truth is that Africans are people of the same origin and this can be clearly seen in our dignity, humanity, generosity, and patience, which are some of the remains of our ancient culture' (p. 6). This was proven by the 'humanitarian and socialist way of life' of Africans, to which they wished to return, now that power has been restored to its rightful owners (p. 9). Zanzibar revolutionaries were represented as rural folk, although actually many were urban dwellers, 'embittered by the oppressive class system of the Sultanate' (Cameron 2004: 106). Their reason for the revolution was the insufferable exploitation by foreigners. The Sultanate was blamed for all ills.

The ASP terminology and the manner in which the former society is characterised betrays Marxist derivation. After the revolution, there were efforts to Africanise institutions and cultural practices, and Arabic-sounding names were Africanised. These policies alienated many of the Zanzibari elite. Arab and European intellectuals who were not terrorised into leaving often left of their own accord, dissatisfied with the political and economic situation in which they now found themselves (Saleh 2004: 153; Glassman 2000: 399).

From the outset, in both Tanganyika and Zanzibar, all momentum was behind collectivistic conceptions of the body politic. As in many other cases, this led to the emergence of an authoritarian regime, critical and suspicious of differing opinions. There was low tolerance of dissent. After independence, shoring up the majority opinion entailed ostracising, imprisoning, and discounting those whose views were marginal. Persons once held in great respect, such as Oscar Kambona, Abdulrahman Mohamed Babu, and Bibi Titi Mohammed, were imprisoned or sought political exile. Tanzania mainland and Zanzibar became single party states. Union movements, once seen as useful participants in building a nation, became possible sponsors of dissent; those not officially sanctioned by the government were shut down. Pan-Africanism and Marxist socialist ideals faded to the sidelines of discourse, as intellectuals and those in political power concentrated attention on what it meant to be part of the Tanzanian nation.

Major rallying cries during the 1960s and 1970s concerned preventing, rejecting, and fighting the Western domination of Tanzania (and of Africa as a whole). Upholding the dignity of the Tanzanian nation was at the heart of the speech Nyerere gave in 1978, 'Tanzania rejects Western domination of Africa'. The struggle was over rights, freedom, and expectations of how to comport themselves in the world:

> Tanzania is not the only nationalist country in Africa. There are nationalists everywhere. Sooner or later, and for as long as necessary, Africa will fight against neo-colonialism as it has fought against colonialism. And eventually it will win.

> (Ministry of Information and Broadcasting 1978: 10)

Basic 'facts of power in the world' made the independent governments justifiably suspicious that, without care, they would become 'the instruments through which foreign domination is maintained in a new form'. Nyerere opposed foreign involvement as contrary to Africa's right for self-determination (Ministry of Information and Broadcasting 1978: 14).

Nyerere, Tanzania's first president and most influential nationalist, left an indelible imprint on the country and helped to create in it a collectivistic civic nation. His ideology transformed over his lifetime. One of the small group of nationalists awakened over the 1950s and 1960s, he sought for a vision of a nation that most resonated for himself and those around him. His initial, distinctly pan-African ideal evolved into an African socialist vision, encapsulated in *ujamaa ('socialism', literally 'familyhood')*, which became a core aspect of Tanzanian identity and differentiated Tanzania from other African nations. He wanted Tanzania to be the truest embodiment of national ideals. It was to be a society without oppression, discrimination, or exploitation; not divided into races, ethnicities, masters and slaves, or even classes. Throughout his presidency, Nyerere felt that Tanzania was engaged in an urgent battle to modernise. His modernisation objectives were not achieved during his presidency or even afterwards. Despite advances in education, health services, and other sectors, Tanzania continues to be one of the poorest countries in the world. And yet, he succeeded in creating a nation which grew and, albeit slowly, developed.

At independence, political leaders led an urgent effort to 'catch up' and 'catch up quickly'. Development is still cited as an ultimate goal. It was not enough to advance for the sake of Tanzanians; the leaders wanted Tanzania to be measured favourably against other nations. The task Nyerere set forth before his successors was to ensure dignity for all. The independent governments of

Africa 'must be the instruments through which the peoples of Africa develop themselves and their countries, and enlarge their freedom until it means a life of dignity for every individual African' (Ministry of Information and broadcasting 1978: 16).

Notes

1. Other scholars note the role of status anxiety and the desire for dignity in the emergence of nationalist sentiment in Tanzania. Susan Geiger describes the symbolic force of first Tanzanian president Julius Nyerere standing next to Bibi Titi Mohammed, the leader of the women's TANU league, as 'a moment of "truth" regarding Tanzanian nationalism as an historical process in which people drew on their social experience to construct a "nation" in which they might experience freedom from colonial overrule and dignity as human beings' (Geiger 1997: 5).

2. Both texts mention its occurrence but do not explicitly treat violence's role in recruitment.

3. Poeschel, who served for several years in German East Africa, mentions how 'According to my experience it is true that the negro possesses, like most children, an incorruptible feeling for right and wrong and a simple-hearted admiration for the great, the manly and the heroic.'

4. Most of the details regarding Robert's life come from his autobiographical text, *Maisha Yangu na Baada Ya Miaka Hamsini* (My Life and After Fifty Years), Dar es Salaam: Mkuki na Nyota, 2003. Additional biographical details are contained in *The Barua za Shaaban Robert, 1931–1958*, edited by M. M. Mulokozi, Dar es Salaam: Chuo Kikuu cha Dar es Salaam, 2002 which contains sixty-nine letters addressed by Shaaban Robert to his younger brother Yusuf Ulenge, and twenty-six various documents, mainly letters to the editor of Mambo Leo that Robert wrote.

5. Scholar Farouk Topan contends that Robert's admiration masked his true opinions, which he suppressed for fear of repercussions. I disagree that Robert feigned admiration since it is evident in his letters to his brother, in his letters to the editor of *Mambo Leo*, as well as in poems such as 'Vitabu'. He also wrote several poems concerning British involvement in the war that were positive, supportive, and expressed the wish for the British victory over the Germans. In January 1942, he published the short poem, 'Waingereza Watashinda' (the British will prevail), in *Mambo Leo*.

6. It is inherent even within much of the theoretical literature on the subject; but this stems from the actors assumptions that nationalism is somehow a natural, biological, racial, mode and so, of course, it is there at all times, waiting for the right conditions to be activated.

References

Cameron, G. (2004) 'Political Violence, Ethnicity and the Agrarian Question in Zanzibar,' in P. Caplan and F. Topan (eds) *Swahili Modernities*, Trenton: Africa World Press.

Chachage, C. S. (1986) 'Socialist ideology and the reality of Tanzania', PhD thesis, University of Glasgow.

De Jong, A. (2002) 'Church, colonialism and nationalism in Tanzania', in F. Wijsen and P. Nissen (eds) *'Mission is a Must': Church and theology in context*, New York: Rodopi BV.

de Saissy, E. M. (1981) *The Role of the Ethnic Factor in the Politics of Pre-Revolutionary Zanzibar*, Uppsala, Sweden: Uppsala University.

Fair, L. (2001) *Pastimes and Politics*, Athens, Ohio: Ohio University Press.

Geiger, S. (1997) *TANU Women*, Portsmouth, NH: Heinemann.

Glassman, J. (2000) 'Sorting out the tribes', *The Journal of African History*, 41(3).

Gwassa, G. (2005) in W. Apelt (ed.) *The Outbreak and Development of the Maji Maji War 1905–1907*, Koln: Rudiger Koppe Verlag.

Hamdani, M. M. (1981) 'Zanzibar newspapers', Diploma Thesis, Dar es Salaam: Tanzania School of Journalism.

Harries, L. (1962) *Swahili Poetry*, Oxford: Clarendon Press.

Hassing, P. (1970) 'German missionaries and the Maji Maji rising', *African Historical Studies*, 3.

Iliffe, J. (1979) *Modern History of Tanganyika*, Cambridge: Cambridge University Press.

Jackson, R. and Maddox, G. (1993) 'The creation of identity: colonial society in Bolivia and Tanzania', *Comparative Studies in Society and History*, 35.

Kayamba, M. (1963) 'The story of Martin Kayamba', in M. Perham (ed.) *Ten Africans*, 2nd edition, Evanston, IL: Northwestern University Press, pp. 173–272.

League of Nations (1925) 'Report by His Britannic Majesty's Government on the administration under mandate of Tanganyika Territory for the year 1924', Geneva, 3 September, 6.

Ministry of Information and Broadcasting (1978) 'Tanzania rejects Western domination of Africa/La Tanzanie rejete la domination Occidentale en Afriqu', Dar es Salaam: Information Services Division, Ministry of Information and Broadcasting.

Monson, J. (1998) 'Relocating Maji Maji: the politics of alliance and authority in the southern highlands of Tanzania, 1870–1918', *The Journal of African History*, 39(1): 95–120.

Mulokozi, M. M. (1976) 'Revolution and reaction in Swahili poetry', *Utafiti* 1: 127–48.

—— (ed.) (2002) *The Barua za Shaaban Robert, 1931–1958*, Dar es Salaam: Chuo Kikuu cha Dar es Salaam.

Mwakikagile, G. (2007) *Nyerere and Africa*, Dar es Salaam: New Africa Press.

Nyerere, J. (1968) *Ujamaa*, London: Oxford University Press.

Odhiambo, A. (1981) *Siasa: Politics and nationalism in E. A. 1905–1939*, Nairobi: Kenya Literature Bureau.

Poeschel, H. (1919) *Voice of German East Africa*, Berlin: August Scherl.

Robert, S. (1966) 'Chama cha Waafrika', *Pambo la Lugha*, Kenya: Oxford University Press.

——— (2003) *Maisha Yangu na Baada Ya Miaka Hamsini* (My Life and After Fifty Years), Dar es Salaam: Mkuki na Nyota.

Saleh, M. A. (2004) '"Going with the Times": Conflicting Swahili Norms and Values Today,' in P. Caplan and F. Topan (eds) *Swahili Modernities*, Trenton: Africa World Press.

Steere, E., Rev. (1871) *Report of the Proceedings, Church Congress, Authorized Report of the Church [of England] Congress Held at Nottingham, Oct 10, 11, 12, 13, 1871*, London: W. Wells Gardner.

Sunseri, T. (2000) 'Statis narratives and Maji Maji ellipses', *The International Journal of African Historical Studies*, 33.

Tanganyika Legislative Council (1959) Council Debates: Official Report, Volume 1, Thirty Fifth Session, South Africa: Government Printer. Pg 111.

Topan, F. (2006) 'Why does a Swahili writer write?', *Research in African Literatures* 27.

Zimmerman, E. (1918) *German Empire of Central Africa*, trans. E. R. Bevan, London: Longmans, Green and Co.

Chapter Eight

Quebec and French–Canadian Nationalisms

Marc-Olivier Gagné

This paper aims to outline the history of, and offer arguments *for*, post-1960 Quebec nationalism. To do so, it specifies how the concepts of nation and nationalism are used, then presents the chronology of the development of *Canadian* nationalism, distinguishing within it five periods, each defined by its dominant emphasis, namely: (1) Canadian nationalism of origin; (2) traditional Canadian nationalism of survival; (3) Canadian nationalism of liberation; (4) French-Canadian nationalism of conservation and finally (5) modern Quebec nationalism emerging with the *Révolution tranquille* (Quiet Revolution) in 1960, punctuated by autonomist and even separatist struggles. It then proceeds with an analysis of Quebec's economic nationalism since the Quiet Revolution, stressing certain strengths and weaknesses in it and drawing attention to the ambivalence of Quebec's identity, which is based both on the remains of French-Canadian nationalism and a reaction to British (mostly economic) nationalism. The chapter argues that Quebec's identity was consolidated after the Quiet Revolution, as French-Canadian identity tended to disappear, except in the few Canadian French-speaking communities outside Quebec. Since the second referendum on Quebec independence (1995), the importance of identity issues in Quebec nationalism decreased. This analysis leads to some hypotheses concerning the future of Quebec and French-Canadian nationalisms.

Several definitions of 'nation' and 'nationalism'

I use the normative definition of 'nation', which enjoys broad currency in modern Canada. It is based on the ideas of the socio-political philosopher, professor at the Université de Montréal, Michel Seymour, who argues: a 'nation is a cultural group, possibly but not necessarily united by a common descent, endowed with civic ties' (Seymour 2000) or 'a sort of political community that requires the existence of a national majority in a recognized territory' (Seymour 1999: 25). By 'national majority', Seymour means 'a community that, across the planet, is the most important sample of people with a certain language, culture and history' (Seymour 1999: 25).

In this normative framework, 'nationalism' refers to the 'national conscience and common will [of a national group] to exist as a nation'. The particularly interesting aspect of these definitions is that they by no means exclude individuals from belonging to minorities (ethnic, linguistic, recent immigrant, etc.) who do not share the characteristics of individuals forming the national majority. On the contrary, they are also considered members of the nation, which is historically based on a majority, but encompasses the entire population partaking in the same sociopolitical institutions. This normative framework is therefore both ethnocultural and civic: ethnocultural because of an essential reference to the historic majority, civic because it includes all individuals living in the territory and sharing national sociopolitical institutions. Using it, we avoid the reified conception of the nation, considering that this majority can change over time and events, in addition to proposing a solution to the tired debate between civic nationalism and ethnocultural nationalism.

The origins of the name 'Canada'

Canadians today often forget that the word 'Canada' is the name given to the first French colony in North America. In 1535, Jacques Cartier, considered the founder of Canada, uses the 'Kanata' path, so named by Native Americans and leading to the Iroquoian village of Stadacona (later becoming Quebec City).[1] The name 'Canada' (a modified version of 'Kanata') becomes the name of the territory discovered by Cartier. From 1550 onwards, one can see the word 'Canada' on the French explorers' maps.[2] Then it becomes the name of the main French colony, permanently established from the early seventeenth century on the banks of the St. Lawrence River, after several failed attempts at colonisation in the sixteenth century.

It is important to differentiate Canada from Acadia, another French colony, located on the coast of today's provinces of New Brunswick and Nova Scotia and of the US State of Maine. Until its destruction in 1755, French Acadia is distinct from Canada, although together they form the 'New France'. It is not until 1791 that the word 'Canada' is officially used to name the two territories formed by the separation of the 'province of Quebec' that becomes Upper Canada (corresponding approximately to the territory of the province of Ontario of today) and Lower Canada (corresponding approximately to the territory of today's Quebec).[3]

Nationalism of origin (1534–1759)

From the first years after the establishment of the French colony in America, the first inhabitants (who already call themselves 'Canadiens') develop a different national consciousness from that of the mother country (France) (Gougeon 1993: 6). Their language acquires a unique accent, very different from the French spoken in France. The society is also much less stratified than it is in contemporary France. Thereafter, a distinct Canadian identity grows rapidly (Gougeon 1993: 6). The 'natural' rivalry between French and English colonists and the war between the French colonists and the Iroquois reinforce this identity. So, we originally have a Canadian nation whose identity is based on the French language, the Catholic religion, and the experience of a harsh territory, surrounded by hostile neighbours, and a long cold winter. Nationalism is therefore present in New France because

Canadians already have a national consciousness and a common will to exist as a distinct nation.

Traditional nationalism (1759–1791)

Canadian identity faces a sudden shock in the conquest of Canada by the British during the Seven Years War (1756–63), an event known in the literature as 'the conquest' (la Conquête). The Battle of the Plains of Abraham in Quebec City (1759) is the decisive engagement of the conquest, which ends with the surrender of Montreal in 1760. A military regime is established until 1763. The conquest is brutal: besides the many fallen soldiers, one civilian in six die, almost all farms are burned, Quebec City is completely destroyed, etc.

At this point, we already observe a glaring divide between the majority of poor French-speaking Catholics (95 per cent), mostly farmers, and the English minority that manages the entire new 'Province of Quebec'. Following this shock, the Canadian nation folds in upon itself and loses confidence, guided by a survival type of nationalism. Canadian identity then tightens around the two traditional pillars present since the very beginning, the French language and the Catholic religion, despite the official language now being English and the imposition of the Test Acts.[4]

Canadian nationalism of liberation (expression used in Monière 2001) (1791–1840)

After the American War of Independence (1776), many loyalists from the United States migrate to territories which remain British and many come to settle in the Province of Quebec. Anglophones, still a minority but increasingly present, see their proportion grow from 4 to 9 per cent in just six years (1778–84) (Quellet 1980: 25). Given this demographic change, we witness the rise of two nationalisms: Canadian and British. Canadians sense that the British attempt to assimilate them, despite some concessions since 1763, notably in the Quebec Act (1774), which gives Canadians more freedoms, among others rejecting the Test Acts. Nevertheless, the Constitutional Act of 1791, primarily intended to satisfy the minority of loyalists now installed in the province, pours oil onto the fire. The province is divided into two territories: Lower Canada and Upper Canada. The British become the majority in the vast Upper Canada and completely control its institutions.

Despite the attempt to assimilate Canadians, Canadian nationalism does not disappear (Balthazar 2013: 69). However, because the British deliberately choose mostly English-speaking immigrants, the French-speaking majority remains suspicious and defensive (Balthazar 2013: 69). In addition, Canadian nationalism resists British immigrants, notably because they reject the name 'Canadians' but perceive themselves as North American representatives of the 'empire on which the sun never sets'.

From the early nineteenth century, Canadian nationalism becomes rather liberal and 'modern'. The nationalists of the time are concentrated in the *Parti canadien* (Canadian Party), later renamed the *Parti patriote* (Patriot Party). They mostly come from the liberal petite bourgeoisie of Lower Canada. They want a responsible, tolerant government concerning language and religion issues, separation of Church and State, and a more democratic and egalitarian political system. This implies truly popular sovereignty, no more privileges for a 'higher class' (judges, some people of the Executive Council, etc.) and, above all, the abolition of the Legislative Council (unelected Upper House) composed of a few 'enlightened' British aristocrats (Balthazar 2013: 62). Canadian nationalism still retains its traditional focus on the French language and the Catholic religion. The modern doctrine of economic liberalism is rejected, because it would give more power to the British and, in addition, threaten the traditional order of the Canadian nation. In sum, the nationalism of the period opens to modernity, while preserving the fundamental pillars of its original structure necessary for the survival of the nation. This may be explained by the fact that the fundamental national character is constantly threatened. Canadians are thus advocating the establishment of a modern political system, but exhibit a form of cultural conservatism. Because French speakers are not the main players in economic and political spheres, a modern Canadian nation, paradoxically, can only emerge within the framework of traditional values (Balthazar 2013: 64).

The Canadian nationalist movement, liberal and modern, however, takes form vis-à-vis a British nationalism defended by the political and economic forces in place and perceived as imperial encroachment.[5] Faced with the intransigence of the British authorities, the Canadian nationalist movement radicalises. In 1837–8, a patriotic rebellion culminates in a defeat and the Union Act (1840) turns Canadians into a minority, uniting Lower and Upper Canada, the latter having become more populous than the former since the Constitutional Act (1791). The liberal emancipation movement having failed, the Canadian nation once again becomes isolationist. Since the main political democratic levers are lost and the economy since 1760 is mainly managed by the British, Canadian nationalism focuses on what it has left: its ethnocultural component. Meanwhile the name 'Canada' is appropriated and extended to the entire territory of Upper Canada (English-speaking majority) and Lower Canada (French-speaking majority). Canadian nationalism thus bifurcates into French-Canadian nationalism and English-Canadian nationalism, English Canadians perceiving themselves as members of the British nation living in Canada.

French–Canadian nationalism of conservation (1840–1960)

A long period follows in which the traditional conceptions within French-Canadian nationalism predominate, although there are exceptions, for example the opposition of the Rouges (1848–58) who try in vain to re-politicise the definition of the French-Canadian nation. This is a phase of ultramontanism and national survival, centred on language and ethnicity.

In 1867, the first Canadian constitution is signed and unites four provinces (Quebec, Ontario, New Brunswick and Nova Scotia) as Canada. Two distinctive types of nationalism coexist at this time. First, a conservative cultural nationalism oriented to traditional values is still very powerful among both Francophones and Anglophones. Second, there is French–Canadian nationalism associated with Henri Bourassa, the journalist, politician and French-Canadian intellectual (1868–1952), which advocates openness to the rest of Canada, with many French-Canadians, conservative and liberal, advocating a bicultural, bilingual nation, a collaboration between English speakers and French speakers. To Bourassa a federation appears the best option for the French-Canadian nation and Canada in general.

Honoré Mercier, Liberal Prime Minister of Quebec from 1887 to 1891, questions the usefulness of the federation in its contemporary form for French-Canadians. He is among the first politicians to demand more cultural and political autonomy for the French-Canadian nation within the federation: his nationalism is autonomist. Like Bourassa, he defends a bicultural, bilingual community, insisting on the full equality of French speakers alongside an English-speaking majority that must respect their autonomy: 'The nation that we want to develop is the Canadian nation, made up of French-Canadians and English-Canadians' (Wade 1966: 554). At this moment of history, the independence of French-Canada is not considered an option.[6]

However, it is the conservative type of nationalism that rules the day in the early twentieth century, when the Boer War of 1905 eliminates any chance for a bicultural Canada to materialise. This event categorically opposes the French and English in Canada, with Anglophones, who see themselves as British subjects, overwhelmingly in favour of Canada's involvement in the conflict, and Francophones, who have no such attachment to the British Empire, mostly unfavourable. The Anglophone support is so strong that Wilfrid Laurier, then Prime Minister of Canada and a French speaker, defending in fact bicultural nationalism like Bourassa, sides with the English majority, as he often did. Canada is involved in the Boer War and many French speakers feel that their opinion does not count. The issue of conscription during World War I also accentuates the contrast between the 'two Canadas,' with English-Canadians supporting conscription and French-Canadians opposing it.

In French-Canada, we thus enter an era of conservative nationalism that is naturally associated with Lionel Groulx (1878–1967), a Catholic priest, teacher, historian and French-Canadian nationalist writer. The latter conceives the nation as a historical community based on culture, language, and religion.[7] The mission of French-Canadians should be to protect and propagate Catholicism and the French language. Very influential among young intellectuals, Groulx encourages entrepreneurship and an increase in State power culturally and economically (while categorically rejecting socialism). Today he is severely criticised for his attitudes toward the Jews.[8]

Nationalism is revised after the Great Depression of 1929 when economic liberalism is questioned. Most nationalists support the anti-trust *Action nationale* ('National Action'). For a short time, there is even a minority of extreme right-wing nationalists, separatists, sympathetic to fascism. This sympathy is, however, not exclusive to French-Canadians but also present in English-Canada. It is in this era dominated by the French-Canadian conservative nationalism that Duplessis, leader of *Union nationale* (National Union party), becomes Prime Minister of Quebec from 1936 until 1939 and from 1944 to 1959. On the social and political levels, Duplessis is a conservative who defends traditionalism. He is close to the Church and maintains its role and influence, especially in the health and education sectors. In economic matters, he is clearly anti-unionist and anti-statist.

Quebec nationalism of modernisation (since 1960)

During the Duplessis period the *Révolution tranquille* prepares itself. It is 'quiet' on account of being bloodless, and a 'revolution', because, at this moment of history, Quebec starts embracing modernity.

In the early 1960s, Quebec at several levels appears backward compared to the rest of Canada. Many see it as an *Ancien Régime* surrounded by modern societies. The central role of religion in society and the State is questioned first and foremost. Initially, nationalists are following the example of the federal government which is more interventionist and seen as more 'progressive' at that time. The Quebec government then takes over several powers previously entrusted to civil society, the private sector, and, of course, the Church. As Quebec society is secularised, the State increases its influence, especially in the education and health sectors.[9]

The State also becomes the main economic tool used by Quebec nationalists, empowering French speakers who cannot at the time by any means compete economically with British, English-Canadian and American companies. So, the bigger the government, the greater is the transfer of economic power from Anglophones to Francophones. Electricity, for example, is nationalised in 1962, this strategic sector being previously controlled by a majority of English, English-Canadian and American interests.

It is also by means of the State that Quebec nationalists attempt to protect the French language, which spreads as the State (mostly governed by the French majority) grows. Closely linked to the Quebec government, this nationalism is now restricted to the Province of Quebec, and thus defined territorially. From now on we talk of 'Quebec nationalism', 'French-Canadian nationalism' becoming gradually less present. Very different from the conservative nationalism of the early century, it prompts some analysts to call it 'Quebec neonationalism' (Balthazar 2013: 148).

Marginal far left violent and radical Quebec nationalism

For some, the process of reconquest of the main economic and political levers of Quebec by Francophones is not happening fast enough. Such nationalists unfortunately choose the path of radicalism and violence. In the early 1960s, the FLQ (*Front de Libération du Québec*) is formed. This group of militants is inspired by Marxist–Leninist ideas and advocates the 'decolonisation' and independence of Quebec, following the example of the far left revolutionary movements in Africa and Europe of the time. Although the movement claims to represent the poor and oppressed people of Quebec, it is in fact formed of a very small number of activists (barely a few dozens) and their ideas are not popular. They attract attention not by their number, but by their radical actions. From 1963 to 1972, the FLQ organises several terrorist acts against targets accused of maintaining the 'system of oppression' of the mass of French-speaking Quebecers: the Canadian army, McGill University, Montreal Exchange, Westmount (a rich town west of Montreal with a strong English-speaking majority), etc. The events of October 1970, when FLQ terrorism spikes, are known as the 'October Crisis'. On 5 October, members of the FLQ kidnap James Richard Cross, the British trade commissioner who is visiting the country. Cross is released after negotiations. On 10 October, the FLQ kidnaps the Deputy Prime Minister and Minister of Employment of Quebec, Pierre Laporte. Laporte is killed on 17 October.[10]

Following the abductions, the then Prime Minister of Canada Pierre Elliott Trudeau invokes the War Measures Act that allows the government to suspend the Canadian Bill of Rights and gives to authorities wide powers including preventive detentions. Several hundred of people are arrested, many unfairly. Except for a few exceptional events, the October Crisis puts an end to the actions of the FLQ, which no longer has any legitimacy. The separatist movement dissociates itself once and for all from any extremist group which uses violence.[11]

It is, however, important to note that Trudeau profits politically from the October Crisis, which allows him to present himself as the main opponent of Quebec nationalism, in accordance with his anti-nationalist philosophy as expressed in *Cité libre* (Trudeau 1961: 3–5). Although the FLQ is composed of only a few dozen activists, anti-nationalists such as Trudeau willingly exaggerate the importance of the movement, trying – in vain – to discredit Quebec nationalism, actually a moderate and democratic nationalism for the great majority of people. Even if the threat of the FLQ is real, the means of countering it seem disproportionate.[12] Trudeau's rejection of nationalism is also contradictory, as he strengthens Canadian nationalism, by giving more power to the federal government and trying to create a real bicultural Canadian identity in Canada. In doing so, Trudeau seems to privilege the nation-state as the only acceptable political model. Nationalism, in this context, is defined in strictly individualistic terms, and the recognition of any other nation or community within the nation-state is impossible. Interpreted in this narrow way, nationalism becomes a tool of the government, and therefore a handful of leaders, for maintaining the loyalty of a majority of the population to the State, while dissolving the other internal nationalist movements. A dialectical relationship between the federal State and minority nationalisms becomes the norm. On one hand, Lévesque – Prime Minister of Quebec from 1976 to 1985 and certainly the most emblematic figure of the Quebec independence movement – argues that the sovereignty-association for Quebec is necessary to prevent the dissolution of the Quebec nation within a federation which does not recognize its existence. On the other, Trudeau claims that Quebec nationalism is harmful for Quebecers themselves, both because it shows signs of becoming ethnic (the FLQ being an example), and because it fuels the independence movement which may eventually deprive them of the privilege of being Canadians.

Majority 'progressive' nationalism

Although some nationalists remain conservative and there is a radical far left minority, Quebec nationalism in its general character is 'progressive' – democratic and moderate. This explains close links since 1960 between major unions and the nationalist sovereigntist movement. Even today, at every provincial election, most unions continue to support the Parti Quebecois (PQ), which emerged as the main political representative of nationalism during the Quiet Revolution.[13] Both the party and the unions advocate universality of services, with programmes constructed and defended on the 1960 'wall-to-wall' model, sometimes with a lack of nuance.

Since 1960, defence of French is also justified by reference to progressive ideas: the State must allow the 'emancipation' of Francophones who believe themselves to be imprisoned within a system that excludes them systematically, especially in economic matters. This type of nationalism is modelled on other 'liberation movements', economic and political, occurring elsewhere in the world (decolonisation of Africa, the civil rights movement in the US, Northern Ireland, etc.). Law 101 of 1977 is the strongest – some say too radical – identity affirmation of the Francophone national majority. The law ensures that French is recognised as the only official language of the Quebec State. Services in English (including education) remain available for the historical Anglophone minority only. This policy is justified by historical and sociological considerations. For example, prior to 1977, immigrants who settled in Quebec almost all joined Quebec's English-speaking minority. Bill 101 allows Quebec to maintain high immigration rates (higher than in the US per person), while protecting the future of French in Quebec. The majority of English speakers obviously oppose this new law (e.g. Myles 2000: A1) that they sometimes describe as 'Anglophobe' or even racist. Many of them fought in the courts, but failed, Bill 101 being considered constitutional: the court held that the Quebec government has the right to promote French, if it does not prohibit English, which is the case since nothing prevents individuals from attending unsubsidised institutions. Some Anglophone Quebeckers accept the bill and even support it. Nevertheless, the policy tends to oppose Francophones and Anglophones in Quebec, as well as to damage the reputation of Quebeckers as perceived by the rest of Canada.

Separatist nationalism

Quebec nationalism reaches its climax during the two referendums of 1980 and 1995, whose ultimate goal is Quebec sovereignty. For some nationalists, independence must be the final goal of the Quiet Revolution, since the federal State refuses to recognise the Quebec nation as a nation or even as a '*société distincte*' (distinct society).

After the unexpected win of the Parti Québécois in the 1976 elections, Lévesque offers Quebeckers a form of sovereignty-association through a referendum in 1980. If 'yes' wins, PQ says, the Quebec government would no longer be subject to federal government policies, while retaining some privileged links with Canada.[14] 60 per cent vote 'no'. A good loser, Lévesque promises Quebeckers that there will be a 'next time'.[15] In 1995, Jacques Parizeau, now leader of the Parti Québécois, surprises everyone by keeping this promise, despite unfavourable polls. This time only 50.58 per cent vote against sovereignty, the 'Yes' vote surging by the end of campaign to 49.42 per cent. Accepting defeat, Parizeau uses words that will mark Quebec nationalism for decades, blaming the 'ethnic vote' and 'money' as responsible.[16] Regarding 'money', Parizeau refers to economic forces behind the 'No' vote. As to 'ethnic responsibility', Parizeau's statements, unfortunately, help to present the entire Quebec nationalist movement as ethnic (not civic). Parizeau attempts to walk back, insisting that he did not mean the non-French population, but simply pointed to some community leaders who voted and encouraged others to vote 'No'. In fact, Parizeau, speaks perfect English, has a Ph.D. from the London School of Economics, and is 'Anglophile', saying for example: 'Mon Dieu, je botterais le derrière de quiconque au Québec qui ne saurait parler l'anglais. En effet, à notre époque, un petit peuple comme nous se doit de le parler.'[17] Parizeau's true sentiments (whatever they are) notwithstanding, his statements still embarrass the sovereigntist movement.

Getting away from Quebec 'identity nationalism', since 1995

Following Parizeau's declarations, many sovereignty supporters among intellectuals attempt to separate the project from the identity component of the conservative form of nationalism. They present Quebec independence as a modern political project, open to the world. Its ultimate goal is the emancipation of the Quebec people. Because it is not recognised as a nation by the federal State, Quebec should exist as a sovereign country.

A minority of Quebec intellectuals, however, are trying to revive the moribund identity-based nationalism. The problem of Quebec nationalism, they say, is that it turned its back on its identity dimension. Following Parizeau's controversial concession speech in 1995, the independence movement has fallen into the trap of 'political correctness', completely denying its identity and culture for fear of being judged negatively, and forced to support an essentially civic nationalism. In the view of these intellectuals, nationalists should listen to the 'real representatives of the nation': the French-speaking majority.

Such ethnocultural definition of the nation is out of favour in today's Quebec, especially among young people.[18] Even when politicians use the 'identity strategy' successfully, such success is short-lived. This does not mean that we witness a 'de-nationalisation' as these conservative nationalists claim,[19] but that Quebec nationalism, still very present, has transformed itself into a more political and economic consciousness. The identity-based strategy of these intellectual separatists is doomed in the long run in a modern Quebec, year after year, becoming more multi-ethnic, multi-linguistic and multicultural. Multiculturalism, the policy of refusing to define a nation or collectivity in cultural terms, is more promising for Quebec nationalism, if Quebec handles immigration policies ethically (acceptable rate of immigration, assistance and integration of immigrants by the State, better recognition of studies of newcomers, etc.). In a multicultural framework, members of the community, especially newcomers, have different cultural attachments, but tend (mathematically, through individual interactions) to adopt the culture of the majority while also enriching it. Some people in Quebec prefer to talk of 'interculturalism', stressing the fact that there is something like a basic empirical 'culture of the majority' which is there to integrate other cultures and be shaped by them. These two terms (which are, for some, synonyms) are more useful than the discourse-polarising Quebec society between 'natives' who feel threatened and 'neo' who feel excluded. A minority of Quebec intellectuals, however, fan this polarisation to serve their careers. But, contrary to what they say, this type of nationalism is not popular, but populist and rather elitist.[20]

Despite the abandonment of identity-based definition of Quebec nation, the defence of French remains a concern for the majority of Quebeckers, language not being considered as an ethnic characteristic, but as a social institution. In legislating to protect French, the majority of the population does not seek to deny non-French Quebec nationality or individual freedoms. Instead, most Quebeckers seek with the help of such legislation to maintain social cohesion and the 'context of choice', in the words of Will Kymlicka, which is necessary for any form of liberalism (Kymlicka 2001). How, indeed, can we speak of true individual freedom in a society where the absence of minimum cultural and linguistic commonality prevents most social interactions, and individuals, limited in their choice, are prisoners in a Babel tower? Language, in this perspective, appears much more like an institution required to hold a nation together, a necessary condition for progress, social cohesion, and stability, than like an ascriptive characteristic to be defended in the name of a certain conservative nationalism. The common language(s) can of course change through time, but we need to consider the reality of a specific society at a certain moment of its history.

The Quebec economic nationalism (since 1960)

The idealised presentation of the Quiet Revolution must be qualified. Of course, in the early 1960s, the economy is mostly controlled by the English-speaking minority. The intervention of the Quebec State at this moment may indeed have been needed to rebalance forces, to the greater benefit of Francophones. To this linguistic collectivity, the revolution was clearly helpful. But did it benefit individuals or was this simply a transfer from one elite to another?

In his book *Du Grand Rattrapage au Déclin Tranquille* (2013), Vincent Geloso argues that Quebec nationalists are wrong to believe that Quebec's economic growth and power was caused by State actions aiming to liberated the province from British hegemony. The real 'Grand Rattrapage' (Great Comeback) of the

Quebec economy, he shows, takes place under Duplessis, more specifically from 1945 to 1960, in the era of conservative nationalism. Geloso notes the improvement in the Quebeckers' situation during that period according to several indicators. For example, in these fifteen years, the gap between the average wages of Quebeckers and other Canadians is greatly reduced, which benefits Francophone workers, proving that the growth of the national wealth was not at the cost of the 'French-speaking proletariat' becoming poorer.[21] Geloso shows that growth continued after 1960 (during the Quiet Revolution), but was inferior to that observed in the rest of Canada. The author thus maintains that the Revolution slowed economic growth: the improvements observed during it were not caused by the multitude of State reforms, but by the mere extension of the Great Comeback of 1945–60. These interesting observations clash with most intellectuals' conception of Duplessis, regularly described as a reactionary refusing to modernise Quebec's economy, bringing the era of 'Grande Noirceur' (Great Darkness). Geloso suggests the interesting hypothesis that, by nationalising too quickly certain services previously provided by the private sector and by the Church, Quebeckers squandered much of their 'social capital', allowing their 'relationships [to] develop[ed] freely to facilitate economic exchanges'.[22] The Quiet Revolution helped to restore much of the economic levers to Francophones, but, in return, hurt Quebec's economic growth by damaging the social capital built by Francophone and Anglophone Quebeckers together.

Most Quebeckers, especially intellectuals, nevertheless continue to consider the Quiet Revolution as positive. In the modern age, with the economy often playing an important role in a people's identity, this identity can suffer when the national majority is under-represented in it. It may also suggest that, in the long term, collective productivity suffers if the majority does not invest in key sectors. Crises can occur if nothing is changed. A possible – and undesirable – reaction could amplify differences between a minority and the national majority, redefining the nation along ethnic lines, with the majority showing increased distrust toward certain minorities. This is, perhaps, what explains in part the ethnic nationalism of Groulx in the early twentieth century. To assure, with or without State intervention, the place of the national majority in the economy is a better way to deal with its low participation.

In this case, State intervention is justified – rightly or wrongly – as 'affirmative action' necessary for social peace and genuine equality between different groups within the nation. Its advocates claim that 'formal equality' is not 'real equality', pointing out that classical liberalism is incomplete, because based on strictly individualistic presuppositions that cannot explain all the political considerations of individuals who also identify with groups, especially linguistic groups. In the absence of State intervention, the attitudes of the majority towards the economy must be modified. Entrepreneurship, for example, should be encouraged. Alliances and concessions must be negotiated with the minority. The process can be very difficult and sometimes impossible, especially for a group that has few economic models and little experience. But, with or without intervention, frictions between social groups are inevitable and, through the process, social peace is tried.

To summarise, Geloso is right that the Quiet Revolution prevented the Quebec economy from growing at the speed observed in other provinces. This may be one of the factors that explain, for example, that the average GDP per capita in Quebec is lower than those in Canada and the United States.[23] Nevertheless, the *Modèle québécois* does well, sometimes better, according to many indicators.[24] It is indeed possible to argue that, while creating less economic wealth overall, it distributes it in a much more egalitarian way than is done in the rest of Canada and the United States. A telling statistic is presented by political scientist Jean-François Lisée, demonstrating that, despite an average GDP per capita that is much smaller than in the US, 99 per cent of Quebeckers have a higher purchasing power than 99 per cent of Americans! (Lisée 2012: 31). In other words, to create more economic wealth, the US population must put up with great economic inequalities and a lower standard of living than the people of Quebec. Considering only aggregated statistics (average wage, average GDP per capita, etc.) and disregarding the distribution of wealth may confuse the interests of a country and interests of the individuals actually forming it.

'Quebec progressivism' vs. 'English liberalism'

The Quiet Revolution orients Quebec in an economically 'progressive' direction important for the identity of, especially, the artisan generation and 'baby boomers'. This orientation is reinforced by the idea that, forming a 'distinct' nation, Quebeckers must be distinct in economic respects as well, following a model different from the English, less interventionist, one. A decrease in state economic intervention is thus often viewed as a direct threat to Quebec identity. Conversely, discussing Quebec identity seems inseparable from questioning Quebec's economic model.

The identification of many Quebeckers with their economic model has the effect of polarising the debate between a liberal right and a nationalist left. In some cases, however, there is an alliance of interests between nationalists and liberals. The North American Free Trade Agreement (NAFTA), for example, signed in 1992 by the Progressive Conservative Party and federally supported by Quebec nationalists, demonstrates that the free market is not incompatible with nationalism. Instead, it may simply be a more subtle form of nationalism, expressed in a belief a nation can conquer outside markets in addition to achieving greater efficiency inside through international competition.[25] Far from dissolving nations economically, globalisation might benefit each of them, from the smallest to the largest (Alezina and Spolaore 2005). As a general rule, however, Quebec nationalists seem to favour interventionism in the economy. The polarisation between liberal right and nationalist left is reinforced by some obvious psychosocial consequences of interventionism. When one feels deprived of opportunities one might have enjoyed in another province with a less present state, one tends to reject the nation and nationalism supporting this economic model. Conversely, when one has opportunities thanks to state intervention, one tends to defend this model and focus on the culture associated with it.

For the same reason, there is a generational divide on this issue, the Quebec model being defended by artisans and primary beneficiaries of the Quiet Revolution, and increasingly attacked by today's youth, facing economics problems. Although Quebec is performing rather well overall, young people pay the costs of the ideological struggle between union corporatism and certain state policies. Politicians at the provincial and federal levels are facing huge debts and deficits, which they usually pay for by privatising public services, increasing taxes, or cutting budgets. But unions of the public and broader private sector defend seniority and protect the interests of their members. This means that many young people are the first to be fired and some can hardly find employment in these sectors. Furthermore, with a smaller GDP, it would appear that Quebec province creates fewer opportunities. Therefore, young people consider – rightly or wrongly – the Quebec model to be mainly responsible for their economic misfortunes, and, although they identify as Quebeckers more than their parents (68 per cent),[26] they increasingly separate their national identity from the economic model their parents established.

Ambivalence of Quebeckers' national identity

The modernisation of Quebec since the 1960s is inseparable from a certain nationalist spirit.[27] This should not be interpreted as suggesting that contemporary Quebec identity is a result of the Quiet Revolution only. This new national consciousness, rather, was produced by a complex development, skirting and being influenced by many Canadian nationalisms. Thus, although we should not over-emphasise the relationship between the (French–)Canadian and British nationalisms, one must consider both as constitutive of contemporary Quebec identity.

After the transformation of political and economic conditions in Quebec, as a consequence of (mainly economic) British nationalism, French-Canadians (who became Quebeckers) who mostly defined their nation for 200 years on the basis of identity, transformed this definition during the Quiet Revolution. Thus, we must recognise, paradoxically, that it is the upheaval wrought by the British in Canada, especially in the economy, that later enabled this specific Quebec nationalism to emerge, with the Francophone majority realising the potential of its people and the richness of the territory.

Quebec *neo-nationalism* is then based both on the remains of the old French-Canadian nationalism (part modern, part traditional) and on a reaction to the old British (economic) nationalism. This is probably why, added to other cultural factors, including the influence of Catholicism,[28] Francophone nationalists have been slow to invest in the economic sphere, resisting the integration in their national identity of this rather 'British' dimension and opting for a different economic model. It is also important to note that, because today's Quebec identity stems from a complex historical process, it is futile to speculate on the power (economically and politically) that a Quebec nation could have had the French pushed back the English in 1759 or later. Similarly, it is absurd to equate today's Quebec nation with the Canadian nation of New France period.

French-Canadian and Quebec identities

In Quebec, the Quiet Revolution led to the 'provincialisaton' of French-Canadian identity. But is it a uniform identity shared by all Quebeckers? And what can we say about Francophone collectivities in Canada outside Quebec?

In the most recent polls, about 70 per cent of Quebeckers say they have a 'Quebecker' identity, against only 15 per cent who identify as 'French-Canadian' and 15 per cent as 'Canadian' (Lisée 2012: 117). Since 1970, Quebecker identity is clearly going up (+48 per cent), while both French-Canadian (–30 per cent) and Canadian (–18 per cent) identities decline. Thus, although the majority of Quebeckers are federalists (according to one of the latest surveys, 59 per cent (Croteau 2015)) and the separatist movement has never exceeded the 50 per cent mark, the attachment of most Quebeckers to Canada seems secondary or utilitarian.

A distinction is increasingly visible between Quebeckers and French-Canadians outside Quebec: they share a common language and country, but have two separate identities. This cleavage is amplified by the 1980 and 1995 referendums and the PQ efforts to divide the country: many French-Canadians outside Quebec feel forgotten or sacrificed in the name of the ideal of independence. For the survival of French-Canadian identity outside Quebec, Canadian federalism remains necessary, especially since the repatriation of the Canadian Constitution (1982) following the first referendum. This constitution makes French and English the two official languages from coast to coast, allowing Francophone minorities to have public services and schools in French where there are enough people to justify this.[29] Before 1982, the rate of assimilation of French-speakers outside Quebec was very high, by simple force of numbers, but also because of provincial assimilationist policies in the past.[30] The trend has since been contained and stabilised: though the proportion of Francophones outside Quebec continues to decline somewhat, the number of individuals slightly increases (O'Keefe 2001). Some privileges help such minorities, for example the right to select certain French-speaking immigrants (1001 vies 2015).

However, most Quebeckers, especially sovereigntists, are rather hostile to the new Canadian constitution. According to it, Quebeckers' entitlement to services in French may be attributed not to the federal government's recognition of the 'Quebec nation' or Quebec's specificity, but simply to the sufficient number of Francophones living in the province. This in some way diminishes the Quebec nation, drowning it in Canada. The 1982 constitution thus opposes the interests of Francophones in Quebec to those of Francophones in the rest of Canada, an opposition that may be used by federalists. French–Canadians are in fact satisfied with their status of 'surviving' minority. Quebeckers, in distinction, seek recognition and reject such status. It is frustrating for most of them to define Quebec exclusively on territorial and political bases, while originally Canadian identity itself was built around the Francophone, Catholic majority. Some Anglo-Canadians, mostly conservatives, also criticise the purely civic and individualistic definition of the Canadian nation, because it excludes any reference to the obvious British heritage. Considering these facts, the members of the National Assembly of Quebec unanimously refused to sign the constitution of 1982. Subsequent administrations that have tried to resolve the impasse have instead created a climate of crisis (Meech Lake Accord in 1987, Charlottetown referendum in 1992). Since Meech, the status quo strategy has been dominant, a situation only possible because the federal government stands in an asymmetric power relationship to Quebec nation, allowing Canada to impose on it a 'social pact' not endorsed by Quebec politicians.

Future of Quebec and French-Canadian nationalisms

Quebec identity today is the one inherited from the Quiet Revolution, with the difference that today's youth is increasingly open to the world and questions of identity do not preoccupy it much. This does not mean that nationalism disappears or that the young call themselves citizens of the world 'rather than' Quebeckers – on the contrary. However, unlike their parents, young Quebec adults (Franco-, Anglo- and Allophones) find their identity unproblematic. They are born in a society with the same opportunities as their counterparts in the rest of Canada, an improvement that Francophones owe in large part to the Quiet Revolution, although many do not realise it. The individualism of the time and globalisation also seem to decrease the interest among youth in identity questions. A recent survey shows that the most popular party among young people is the Liberal Party, which is federalist and rather individualistic (Gagnon 2014a). The majority of young people seem to accept the idea that they can belong to the Quebec and Canadian nations at once, whether or not Quebec is recognised as a nation by the federal state.

The idea of Quebec independence is always present among the youth, but for somewhat different reasons than those mentioned by their parents. For most young sovereigntists, independence is a means – not an end – that would allow Quebeckers to build a more just, egalitarian, and environmentally friendly country than they have today (Gagnon 2014b). This project appears to them more easily achievable within a sovereign Quebec, first, because it seems impossible to them to reform the whole of Canada, often considered more conservative and attached to the 'American way of life', and, second, because the provincial powers of Quebec would not be enough, they say, to ensure the sustainability of such a different society inside Canada. For these reasons, a good proportion of young people are independentist, but do not support the sovereigntist Parti Québécois whose argumentation is mostly based on cultural issues. Although the project of independence unites a good proportion of Quebeckers, many factors play against it. First, many young people simply do not have a position on the topic. After two referendum defeats, many are resigned to or accepted the decision of the majority. Finally, demography is not favourable to the movement. The majority of boomers, who massively supported the sovereignty project, have reached retirement age and many, probably afraid of losing what they have built throughout their lives, turn their back on their 'old youth' project. In addition, new Quebeckers who receive Canadian citizenship are naturally inclined to choose Canada, although many support independence (see Bélanger, E. and Perrella, A. (2007)). The fear of the 'great economic upheaval' that would follow a victory for 'yes' also discourages commitment.

Given this decline of interest in the national question (renewed federalism respecting Quebec's autonomy more or the independence of Quebec), some might be tempted to say that Quebec nationalism is about to disappear or that it has been absorbed by Canadian nationalism. This would be a misinterpretation. Instead, Quebec nationalism continues to modernise and goes global: Quebeckers, rightly or wrongly, no longer feel threatened – they are now proud ambassadors of the Quebec nation throughout Canada and the world. Similarly to the patriotic revolt (1837–38) and the movement of the Rouges (1848–58) which were based on the ideals of freedom, democracy, and equality, Quebec nationalism today is healthy and increasingly open to the rest of the world (see Bélanger, E. and Perrella, A. (2007)).

Notes

1. For some people, the founder of Canada is the Venetian explorer in the service of England, John Cabot (Italian: Giovanni Caboto) who explored eastern Canada as early as 1497. Yet it is Jacques Cartier, the French explorer, from 1534 to 1542, who will take possession of the territories on behalf of the King of France, naming the new territory 'Canada'. Source : Government of Canada. http://www.cic.gc.ca/francais/ressources/publications/decouvrir/section-06.asp.

2. Source : Government of Canada. http://www.cic.gc.ca/francais/ressources/publications/decouvrir/section-06.asp.

3. Source : Government of Canada. http://www.cic.gc.ca/francais/ressources/publications/decouvrir/section-06.asp.

4. The Test Acts (1673–1828) consisted of oaths that all the English officers and officials had to take, intended to exclude Catholics from all administrative positions. Thus, those who professed the religion of Rome could not be involved in the government or official bodies and could not be members of a jury.

5. 'In 1810, in the context of revolutionary and imperial wars, perpetual tension with the US and current ideas about colonial autonomy, these reformist plans seemed so radical that the suspicious Governor James Henry Craig had the editors of Le Canadien arrested, suppressed this nationalist party organ and dissolved the legislative assembly.' Historica Canada : http://thecanadianencyclopedia.ca/en/article/lower-canada/.

6. Except for a few people, such as Tardivel (1851–1905), a journalist and novelist advocating ultramontanism. He is one of the first in Quebec to call

for the independence of the French-Canadian nation and the establishment of a French republic in North America.

7. 'Notre doctrine, elle peut tenir tout entière en cette brève formule : nous voulons reconstituer la plénitude de notre vie française. Nous voulons retrouver, ressaisir, dans son intégrité, le type ethnique qu'avait laissé ici la France et qu'avaient modelé cent cinquante ans d'histoire' (Groulx 1836: 702–3).

8. However, one must insist, in defence of Groulx, that many non-French intellectuals outside Québec espouse similar anti-Jewish sentiments. The period is contaminated by growing anti-Semitism not exclusive to Québec.

9. A telling fact: between 1961 and 1971, church attendance rate decreased from 61 to 30 per cent, to 15 per cent among young people (Laperrière 2007 : 10–13).

10. According to the official version, it is a murder. According to the FLQ, Pierre Laporte died trying to escape by jumping through a window.

11. Actually, this happens before the events of October 1970. René Lévesque, for example, has always refused to embrace violence. But since the October Crisis, the dissociation occurs in the *mind* of every independentist, since violence is both unacceptable in a modern society and harmful for the independence movement itself.

12. This law was only applied twice before the October Crisis, in World War I and II, in 1914 and 1941.

13. Interestingly, Quebec is the most unionised State in North America (39.5 per cent). Radio-Canada website: http://ici.radio-canada.ca/nouvelles/Economie/2012/06/21/010-taux-presence-syndicale-quebec.shtml.

14. Lévesque's perspective is of course disputed by many people inside and outside Quebec.

15. Lévesque, René, 20 mai 1980, Centre Paul-Sauvé, Montréal, Québec, Canada, dans La Réponse (média télévision de Radio-Canada).

16. '*C'est vrai, c'est vrai qu'on a été battus, au fond, par quoi? Par l'argent, puis des votes ethniques, essentiellement.*' Parizeau concession speech, 1995 referendum.

17. Declaration of Jacques Parizeau, *Time Magazine* (Monday, Apr. 13, 1992).

18. The identity strategy (based on ethnic nationalism) is sometimes used in the recent history of Quebec. In 2007, the ADQ (Action Démocratique du Québec), an economic centre-right and socially conservative party, lists many cases of 'religious accommodations' in order to present themselves as the party that defends the identity of Quebec. The strategy works in the short term, the ADQ becoming the official opposition (getting 31 per cent of the votes). An identity crisis happens subsequently in Quebec (called the 'crise des accomodements raisonnables'), fanned by the mass media. Despite that, the ADQ at the next elections in 2008 gets only 16 per cent of the votes.

19. This is 'denationalisation' for Bock-Côté, according to his explicitly ethnocultural and conservative conception of the nation. (Bock-Côté 2007).

20. The thesis of some theorists (notably Eric Hobsbawm) is that nationalism is a construction of the bourgeois elite of a people who receives in this way some benefits from the community, economically and socially. Nationalism would be used, for example, in order to maintain a capitalist system of exploitation of the masses. This argument is partially true, but incomplete. By placing the emphasis on a certain component of nationalism only, namely its symbolic manifestations, some elites do position themselves as official representatives of the nation and receive benefits from that, as Hobsbawm asserts. Nevertheless, the author fails to mention the positive contribution of nationalism to individuals vis-à-vis elites. In fact, if guided by a national consciousness, individuals ask for more equality, popular sovereignty, and freedom; nationalism is not the tool of a manipulative elite, but, rather, the way common people avoid falling into an unequal and undemocratic relationship. Hobsbawm's analysis condemning nationalism is therefore incomplete.

21. Hourly wage: (1) In 1946, in Montreal, 81 cents/h, in Toronto, 86 cents/h. (2) In 1960, 1,15$/h in Montreal, 1,20$ in Toronto. (Geloso 2013)

22. Le 'capital social' est un 'concept fort simple voulant que les liens de communauté que nous développons librement facilitent les échanges économiques' (Geloso 2013)

23. Site of Centre interuniversitaire de recherche en analyse des organisations (CIRANO) : http://qe.cirano.qc.ca/theme/activite_economique/pib_et_ croissance_economique.

24. Some performance indicators in which Quebec surpasses the Ontario and Canadian average: median income of single parents, the level of relative poverty, rate of low-income inhabitants according to the Market Basket Measure consumption, tax burden of families, etc. See Lisée (2012).

25. Liah Greenfeld points out that economic nationalism can lead to several economic models, including both globalised and individualised economy. In the case of the United States, for example, an individualistic type of nationalism has motivated many great entrepreneurs to open up to all individuals on the planet. Moved by a certain kind of nationalism that could certainly be described as individualistic, these entrepreneurs were ready to compete with contractors of any nation, not to subject other economies to US control, but to prove to themselves that they could do very well as American individuals. This type of nationalism (economic) may therefore be a universalist carrier of equality, since economic activity can be beneficial to all, through healthy competition open to all people of the world. There is no indication that there is a contradiction between economic globalisation and nationalism (economic), or between individualism and some type of nationalism. See Greenfeld (2001).

26. '*Or, chez les 18–24 ans, cette auto-identification québécoise atteint 68%. Pour le reste, 13% se disent également Canadiens et Québécois et seulement 14% se disent "Canadiens d'abord" ou "Canadiens seulement"*'. (Lisée 2012)

27. My view follows Greenfeld's conception of nationalism as the basis of modernity and not an epiphenomenon. See Greenfeld (2001).

28. Historically, Protestantism seems to be more compatible with economic considerations, as we can see in England and the United States.

29. Government of Canada : http://laws-lois.justice.gc.ca/fra/lois/o-3.01/page-6.html.

30. For example: (1) In 1890 in Manitoba, with the adoption of the Official Language Act that made English the only language of records, minutes and laws. English also became the only language permitted in all judicial activities. (2) In 1909, the School Act in Saskatchewan. (3) In 1905 the Alberta School Act. (4) In 1864, the Education Act in Nova Scotia. Several other historical cases exist in the other provinces and territories.

References

1001 vies. *Une langue commune, deux identités* (2015) Documentary from Radio-Canada: Réalisation: Marc Bastarache. Maison de production: Connections Productions.

Alezina, A. and Spolaore, E. (2005) *The Size of Nations*, Cambridge, MA: MIT Press.

Balthazar, L. (2013) *Nouveau bilan du nationalisme au Québec.* Québec: VLB Éditeur.

Bélanger, E. and Perrella, A. (2007) 'Facteurs d'appui à la souveraineté du Québec chez les jeunes: une comparaison entre Francophones, anglophones et allophones', Montreal: McGill University.

Bock-Côté, M. (2007) *La dénationalisation tranquille. Mémoire, identité et multiculturalisme dans le Québec postréférendaire*, Montréal: Boréal.

Croteau, M. (2015) 'Sondage CROP-La Presse: un résultat "curieux" selon Péladeau', *Journal La Presse*, 23 avril.

Gagnon, K. (2014a) 'Les jeunes et la souveraineté: la génération "Non"', *Journal La Presse*, 2 juin.

—   (2014b) 'Portrait de génération: quatre archétypes', *Journal La Presse*, 2 juin.

Geloso, V. (2013) *Du Grand Rattrapage au Déclin Tranquille*, Montréal: Éditions Accent Grave.

Gougeon, G. (1993) *A History of Quebec Nationalism* (trans. in 1994 by L. Blair, R. Chodos and J. Ubertino, Québec: VLB Éditeur and Société Radio-Canada.

Greenfeld, L. (2001) *The Spirit of Capitalism: Nationalism and economic growth*, Cambridge, MA: Harvard University Press.

— (2009) 'Transcending the nation's worth', in *The Worth of Nations* collection of the Boston, Melbourne, Oxford Conversazioni on Culture and Society, Boston University.

Groulx, L. (1836) 'Notre doctrine', *L'Action nationale*, mars.

Kymlicka, W. (2001) *La Citoyenneté multiculturelle*, Montréal: Boréal.

Laperrière, G. (2007) 'L'Église du Québec et les années 1960: l'ère de tous les changements', *Cap-aux-Diamants: la revue d'histoire du Québec*.

Lisée, J. (2012) *Comment mettre la droite K.-O. en 15 arguments*, Québec: Stanké.

Monière, D. (2001) *Pour comprendre le nationalisme au Québec et ailleurs*, Montreal: Les Presses de l'Université de Montréal.

Myles, B. (2000) 'Échec au libre choix', *Le Devoir*, 15 novembre.

O'Keefe, M. (2001) *Nouvelles Perspectives Canadiennes. Minorités francophones: assimilation et vitalité des communautés*, Québec: Ministère du Patrimoine canadien.

Ouellet, F. (1980) *Le Bas-Canada, 1791–1840*, Ottawa: Les Éditions de l'Université d'Ottawa.

Seymour, M. (1999) *La nation en question*, Montréal: Les Éditions de l'Hexagone.

— (2000) 'On redefining the nation', in Miscevic, N. (ed.) *Nationalism and Ethnic Conflict: Philosophical perspectives*, Open Court: La Salle and Chicago, IL.

Trudeau, P. E. (1961) 'L'aliénation nationaliste', *Cité libre*, 35.

Wade, M. (1966) *Les Canadiens français de 1760 à nos jours*, Montréal: Cercle du livre de France.

Chapter Nine

Nationalism in Brazil's Street Demonstrations of June 2013

Leone Campos de Sousa

During the month of June 2013, millions of people took to the streets of more than a hundred Brazilian cities to protest against federal and state authorities over a variety of social problems, especially the deterioration of basic public services such as transportation and health. This wave of large-scale demonstrations, which became known as the *Jornadas de Junho* [Journeys of June] was a surprising political phenomenon in Brazil, puzzling both the political and academic worlds.

Mass protests in Brazil have always been organised by political parties or social movements and led by recognised political leaders. The June 2013 demonstrations, however, were organised by anonymous groups, through social networks, and deliberately avoided the participation of the political parties' activists. As a matter of fact, these protests also targeted Brazil's current political institutions, particularly political parties. For their uniqueness and intensity, the June 2013 demonstrations attracted a great deal of attention from social scientists who have analysed the phenomenon through a variety of approaches.

This chapter focuses on an additional singular aspect of the June 2013 protests that has been largely ignored by Brazilian analysts: the widespread manifestation of nationalist feelings during those demonstrations. Instead of the usual leftist symbols such as red banners and flags with the hammer and sickle, the June 2013 demonstrators preferred to carry Brazilian national flags, replacing the red of the traditional banners with the yellow and green that symbolise the nation's colours. Protest songs gave way to the recurrent singing of the national anthem (see Sorj 2014).

In order to analyse the 2013 demonstrations in Brazil through the prism of nationalism, this work bases its arguments on Liah Greenfeld's concept of *ressentiment*.[1] Following her approach, the chapter argues that the nationalistic display exhibited in the demonstrations was a response to the sense of the country's historical failure to achieve first-world status, not only in regards to efficient public services but also in overall world affairs.

The protests and the meaning of the demands

The 2013 demonstrations began in the city of São Paulo after the announcement of an increase of about 8 per cent – $0.20 BRL ($0.07 US) – in bus, subway and train fares. In Rio de Janeiro, the rate hike was about 13 per cent. A small group of young activists, *Movimento Passe Livre* [Free Passage Movement], which advocates free public transportation for all Brazilian students, convened through social networks a political 'flash-mob' demonstration that brought mostly college undergraduates to the streets. The march, which started peacefully, turned into a violent insurgence due to police brutality against the protesters. A few days later, an expanding series of mass demonstrations took place not only in the other seven cities that had enacted fare increases, but also in many other cities and towns not affected by the policy.

Surprisingly, more than one hundred Brazilian cities and towns held street demonstrations during that month of June, in which more than 1.5 million people publicly expressed their dissatisfaction with a variety of social issues besides the inefficiency of Brazil's urban transportation system. Those included the decaying condition of the health-care and educational systems, the massive corruption in public administration, and the enormous costs for the construction of new soccer stadiums for the Soccer World Cup, scheduled to take place the following year.

One demand heard during all demonstrations was the insistence on 'first-world' public services, the absence of which, as is clear to all Brazilians, indicates the country's failure to reach the status of a developed nation. As will be argued in more detail later, historically, Brazil has always pursued entry into the privileged club of powerful nations, and has developed a deep frustration at not being able to fulfil this aspiration.

The protesters did not allow the participation of the political parties' activists, even those affiliated with the Leftist parties traditionally associated with the student movement. By the same token, social movements and trade unions also faced the animosity of demonstrators. It seemed that everything that in one way or another resembled the established way of doing politics was not welcome in the demonstrations.

The June 2013 phenomenon took Brazilian political actors, social scientists, and media analysts by surprise. To begin with, Brazil had not experienced huge mass demonstrations since 1992, when Leftist political parties and their associated student organisations led a successful political movement aimed at the impeachment and removal from office of President Fernando Collor de Mello (1990–2), for his involvement in a corruption scandal. Moreover, because the Left-leaning Workers Party has won the presidential elections since 2003, Brazil's social movements, especially the student movement, have deliberately avoided protests. The view of Spanish sociologist Manuel Castells, who was visiting São Paulo at the time of the demonstrations, epitomises the intellectual reception of the *Jornadas de Junho* among Brazilian social scientists. An authoritative thinker in the fields of social movements and the use of the internet for political mobilisation and participation, Castells interpreted the demonstrations as a Brazilian version of the new type of social movements that had emerged in Europe and the United States, such as the *Indignados* in Spain or 'Occupy Wall Street' in the United States (Fontes 2015).

In these two cases, as in Brazil, 'anonymous' activists using the internet galvanised protesters to flock to the streets to demonstrate their dissatisfaction with traditional political institutions, especially political parties. Brazilian social scientists also agreed that the June 2013 protests were mainly motivated by the legitimacy crisis facing Brazil's political institutions: an artificial party system, confusing electoral legislation and widespread corruption among politicians had caused profound discontent with Brazil's existing democracy (Ricci and Arley 2014: 63).

In sum, the *Jornadas de Junho* indicated that Brazilian citizens do not feel that the existing political parties and governments represent them. Indeed, a poll released on 19 June 2013 by public opinion research institute Datafolha showed that, since March 2013, the population's confidence in political parties had declined from 21 to 16 per cent and in Congress from 20 to 12 per cent.[2] Another poll, taken by the survey agency *Data Popular* and published on 21 June 2013, revealed that 75 per cent of respondents did not trust politicians or parties.[3]

While discontent with traditional politics and demands for more political participation of the population played an important role in the demonstrations, manifestations of nationalism and nationalist symbols were a constant. Yet, this unusual outburst of nationalist feeling during the *Jornadas de Junho* attracted little attention among Brazilian social scientists. The few analysts who did comment on this phenomenon interpreted it as proof that 'right-wing groups' were behind the organisation of such protests. According to these commentators, mostly Leftist activists, the Brazilian Right was 'manipulating youth's consciousness' (de Andrade Prado 2013), aiming at the discrediting of the leftist government in Brazil. There were even those who interpreted such expressions of nationalism as a sign that a coup d'état was being planned to implement a dictatorship in Brazil. For example, Brazilian philosopher Marilena Chauí, affiliated with the Workers Party, claimed that:

some protesters are adopting an ideological position typical of the middle-class … aspiring to a government with no institutional mediation, therefore, a dictatorship. This is why many protesters, wrapped in the national flag, claim that 'my party is my country', maybe ignoring that this was one of the fundamental arguments used by the Nazis against political parties [my translation].[4]

Such an interpretation of the 2013 protests, however, does not agree with reality. The participation of right-wing groups in the demonstrations was largely peripheral, and the nationalist feelings manifested by protesters were not linked to any conspiracy or right-wing movement (Ricci and Arley 2014: 25). The fact is that the outburst of nationalism in the 2013 demonstrations found no sound explanation from Brazilian political analysts.

The importance of nationalism and its types

Why did Brazilian social scientists ignore the nationalist component of the 2013 demonstrations so completely? Part of the answer can be found in the belief that nationalism is an out-dated political phenomenon, incompatible with a globalised world in which nation-states themselves are supposedly withering. Thus, such an outburst of nationalism could be seen as atavistic and therefore disregarded. Much more trendy and worthy of attention were other characteristics of the demonstrations, such as demands for direct democracy and political participation and issues linked to gender and the environment.

Moreover, nationalism in Brazil has been traditionally associated with authoritarian regimes, which used it as a tool to gain popular support. This was the case, for example, with the military dictatorship that ruled the country from 1964 to 1985, when the soccer games of the Brazilian national team were purposely used to foment nationalist feelings among the population.

Also, Brazilian academics are unfamiliar with the literature and the debates on nationalism which take place in the epistemic communities dedicated to this theme. Few of the 'classic' works on nationalism have been translated into Portuguese, and those available are not widely read or debated in Brazilian academic circles. Despite the revival of ethnic and national identities in several regions of the world, especially in the post-Soviet Union states, Brazilians saw it as a curiosity, different from the reality of their country, which has never experienced ethnic conflicts.

Nationalism, however, is very important to understanding Brazil's socioeconomic and political reality. As Greenfeld puts it, every nation's internal political structure reflects the type of national identity it has adopted. Nationalism influences political culture, the formation of social hierarchies and the image of the nation vis-à-vis other nations (Greenfeld 1992: 488). In this sense, key to understanding the manifestations of nationalism during the 2013 demonstrations is the type of 'resentful' national identity that exists in Brazil.

Ressentiment

Before relating *ressentiment* to nationalism, which is an important contribution made by Greenfeld to the studies of nationality, we should clarify the origin of the concept, which was coined by Friedrich Nietzsche and later reformulated by German sociologist Max Scheler. This is helpful if we wish to understand its usefulness in analysing the case of nationalism in Brazil and its manifestation in the *Jornadas de Junho*.

It is in *On the Genealogy of Morals* that Nietzsche puts forward the concept of *ressentiment* as a persistent 'self-poisoning' of the soul, a kind of imaginary vengeance, which, while impossible to accomplish in reality, lives on forever in the minds of the resentful.

Ressentiment, for Nietzsche, on the one hand, also creates values. Through the 'transvaluation of values', the common men or slaves – who are resentful by their very nature – give a positive connotation to their own values while demeaning those of whom they resent – the noble men. For Nietzsche, slave morality is therefore always a reaction to the values of the noble (Nietzsche 2003: 19). Furthermore, Nietzsche associates resentment with the ascension of Judeo-Christian morality, a historical process which, according to him, coincides with the development of Western civilization, as well as with the advancement of equality (Nietzsche 2003: 27–33).

On the other hand, some students of Nietzsche, such as Robert Solomon, suggest that, while *ressentiment* may have a negative origin, related as it is to inferiority and impotency, Nietzsche seems to value creativity as one of human beings' greatest virtues, and in this sense the creative power of *ressentiment* has a positive side (Solomon 1994: 104).

If Nietzsche is somewhat ambiguous in his definition of *ressentiment*, Scheler, on the contrary, dedicated a specific work to it, defining *ressentiment* with great precision and clarity. Scheler agrees with Nietzsche's analogy of *ressentiment* as a 'self-poisoning of the soul', although he does not think that Judeo-Christian morality, which emphasises the human capacity to love, could be related to the negative psychology of *ressentiment*. More importantly, however, Scheler, following Nietzsche, stresses the fact that those whose souls are captivated by *ressentiment* – the common men – develop their values in a distorted relationship with the values of the noble men (Scheler 1961: 53–6).

Ressentiment, for Scheler, finds the appropriate soil in which to flourish in the modern era. In traditional societies, social hierarchies and economic inequalities are perceived as natural. Thus, in a social context in which individuals belong to different estates by virtue of their birth, *ressentiment* is confined to members of the same estate. There can be no comparability – and therefore no *ressentiment* – between individuals of different social statuses and classes. In feudal Europe, for example, it was inconceivable that a peasant could be resentful of a nobleman.

Modern society, however, is characterised by an ethos of universal values, free competition, and social mobility that makes all individuals formally equal. The persistence, however, of social, economic, and power inequalities contradicts the modern ethos of equality, fostering *ressentiment* (Scheler 1961: 56–7).

Following Nietzsche and Scheler, Greenfeld defines *ressentiment* as a 'psychological state resulting from suppressed feelings of envy and hatred (existential envy) and the impossibility of satisfying these feelings' (Greenfeld 1992: 15). But she goes beyond individuals and social groups and applies *ressentiment* to the formation of national identities. In this sense, resentful nations are those which, very much in the fashion of Scheler's argument, have a sense of inferiority towards a model, or reference, nation they seek to imitate, but cannot.

Reference nations vary across time. According to Greenfeld, the first of them, where sovereignty came to be exercised by the people as a nation, was sixteenth-century England. It was there that the idea of 'nation' was born, in which citizenship met Greenfeld's criteria for the original type of nationalism (discussed below), and nationality became synonymous with democracy. As this idea of nation spread across the world, it underwent significant changes as most communities that adopted the idea of nation lacked the social, political, and cultural conditions which made the English type of nation possible.

Other groups suffered from 'status inconsistency', that is, an identity crisis due to their contradictory positions in terms of their class and power vis-à-vis their status within their own societies. Their uncertainty led them to import nationalism (in particular, from the eighteenth century on, into continental Europe). As Greenfeld points out:

Every society importing the foreign idea of nation inevitably focused on the source of importation – an object of imitation by definition – and reacted to it. Because the model was superior to the imitator in the latter's own perception (its being a model implied that), and the contact itself more often than not served to emphasize the latter's inferiority, the reaction commonly assumed the form of *ressentiment*.

(Greenfeld 1992)

Once *ressentiment* takes over the minds of the elite groups who import the idea of nation, a transvaluation of values takes place. The values of the reference nation are denigrated and replaced by indigenous values – sometimes based on ethnic characteristics. In this process, democratic and civic aspects belonging to the original experience of nationalism may be abandoned.

From this argument, Greenfeld draws a typology of nationalism: Type I – civic individualist–libertarian nationalism, originating from the English experience and successfully reproduced in the United States; Type II – civic collectivist–authoritarian as in France; and Type III – ethnic collectivist–authoritarian nationalism cases of which, as she points out, are Russia and Germany (Greenfeld 1992: 11). Collectivistic identities tend to be authoritarian, as they are embedded in *ressentiment* and lack the individualistic ethos, but the ethnic collectivist–authoritarian type is the most prone to xenophobia and exclusion of other ethnicities that may exist as minorities in the national realm.

These are, however, ideal types in the Weberian sense. In reality, most cases of nationalism are mixed ones, but tending to one type or another. Moreover, Greenfeld analyses the *formation* of the national identity of the above-mentioned types of nations not their further social, economic, and political development.

The importance of Greenfeld's approach to the study of nationalities, therefore, is twofold. First, she offers a broad and rich explanation for the advent of nationalism, involving the role of ideas, the symbolic dimension of reality, and the psychology of social groups, all factors largely disregarded by mainstream studies of nationalism, which tend to view it as a tool, an instrument used by elites for modernisation purposes or simply to take or maintain power (for a good example of the 'instrumentalist' view of nationalism, see Snyder 1999). Secondly, *ressentiment* and the transvaluation of values that come out of it allow the student of nationalism to comprehend the ideology and agenda of nationalist movements, especially their anti-Western stances.

Furthermore, we can trace some parallels between Greenfeld's approach to *ressentiment* and the insights of some other students of nationalism and social action, such as Benedict Anderson's explanation of the nationalist rebellion of the Creole elite in the Spanish colonies of the New World in the nineteenth century. Although Anderson does not use the term *ressentiment*, it is clear that this was the feeling towards Spain among independence leaders such as Bolívar and San Martín (Anderson 1983: chapter 4). Also, Charles Taylor's and Axel Honneth's works on the struggle of minority groups for recognition share similarities with the search for dignity that, according to Greenfeld, is intimately linked to the status that national identity confers on people (Taylor 1992: Honneth 1996: 48).

Brazil's national identity

We are now able to examine Brazil's national identity through the prism of *ressentiment* and thus gain a fuller comprehension of the meaning of the *Jornadas de Junho* in Brazil.

Once we look into the history of Brazil, it becomes clear that the country took a long time to forge a national identity. In the first place, it was a historical contingency that allowed the Portuguese provinces in South America to become a single independent nation, in contrast to what occurred in the Spanish–American Empire, where each colonial administrative unit generated a distinct nation-state.[5] The process of integration among the provinces began in 1808, when the King of Portugal and his court, fleeing from Napoleon's troops, moved from Lisbon to Rio de Janeiro, conferring upon Brazil the status of a kingdom, actually the centre of the Portuguese United Kingdom.[6] Thirteen years later, the King returned to Portugal to fight against a liberal revolution there, leaving Brazil with a structured central state apparatus run by his son, Prince Pedro.

Reacting against Portugal's plans to re-establish colonial rule in Brazil, the monarchist elites of Brazil's southern provinces persuaded Prince Pedro to proclaim the country's independence from Portugal. In 1822, the Portuguese prince declared Brazil a sovereign constitutional monarchy,[7] with the status of an empire, and named himself Emperor Dom Pedro I.[8] The provinces thus formed a new country under the rule of a centralised state, against the aspirations of independence-movement leaders and most of the regional elites. Indeed, the peculiar and conservative solution of a monarchic Brazil, still linked to Portugal by dynastic ties, faced great resistance from the regional elites.[9]

We find in this period of Brazilian history some facts which forged the country's national identity and helped foster *ressentiment*. Independence from Portugal was not an outcome typical of struggles for independence in Latin America, nor did it signify an 'elevation of the people to the status of an elite', which, as Greenfeld points out, was the case with England's national formation. It was more of a resentful reaction to the King's return to Portugal. The proclamation of Brazil as an 'empire', a visible exaggeration, confirms the aspiration of frustrated Brazilian elites to an important place in world affairs.

At the time of independence from Portugal, there was no strong sense, either among the elites or the people, of a Brazilian national identity. Rather, people attached loyalty either to Portugal or to their own provinces (Jancsó and Pimenta 1999: 127–75). Moreover, after the proclamation of the Republic in 1889, the country lost its most important symbol of unity – the monarch – and political power was the object of dispute among the elites of the most important regions.

Regional disputes for power over the central government, the general frustration with the failure of the Republic to modernise the country and the economic crisis related to the fall of coffee prices – the main Brazilian export commodity on the world market – threw the country into a deep crisis that lasted until the 1930s, when a new government, headed by a charismatic politician from the South Getúlio Vargas came to power through a coup. He centralised power, eliminated the autonomy of the provinces, and, through a massive nationalistic propaganda campaign, which included the singing of the national anthem in every Brazilian school and the prohibition of provincial flags, consolidated the idea of a unified Brazilian nation (for a good overview of Vargas's nationalist policies, see Lauerhasse 1986).

From that point on, Brazil was able to develop a great deal of its potential, very much along the lines of traditional state-building processes: it launched comprehensive industrialisation policies, expanded its internal market, underwent a widespread process of urbanisation and, despite several periods of authoritarianism, the country succeeded in establishing a democratic regime in the last two decades of the twentieth century, becoming an 'emerging democracy' and a member of the 'BRICS' club of rising economic powers, together with Russia, India, China and South Africa.

Brazilian national identity, however, remained insecure and resentful. If economic development brought about an immense growth of the middle classes, expanding the links of the country's economy with the globalised world, Brazil remained socially very unequal, with large sectors of its population living in miserable conditions. Also, the overall modernisation of the country and the establishment of a democratic regime did not curb rampant corruption, bureaucracy, backwardness in large areas of the country, inefficient public services, and an unstable federative system (for a critique of Brazil's federative system and electoral rules, see Paes Leme 2015: 15).

However, *ressentiment* festers in Brazil mainly because of its weak international position. Notwithstanding the newly acquired status of a 'rising power', the country has no voice in world affairs, and suffers from a deep *ressentiment* towards the first-world nations, especially its closest neighbour the United States. This *ressentiment* more often than not expresses itself in 'anti-imperialist' stances embraced by nationalist groups and the Left.

The middle classes and the Brazilian *intelligentsia* are the social groups most inclined to feel *ressentiment*. They are those in Brazil who, in terms of education, patterns of consumption, culture, and information are closest to a Western way of life. But it is exactly this proximity to Western values and culture that makes comparison inevitable and painful for Brazilians, for it shows the persistent distance between Brazil and the first-world nations on the most important social and economic indicators, as well as in influence on world affairs.

Conclusion: the demonstrations and changes in Brazil's national identity

It is this overall frustration with their country's status in the world that was ignited by the increase in transportation fares, leading to the 2013 demonstrations. Much of the protest targeted the Confederations Cup, a smaller soccer event also hosted by Brazil in 2013, which served as an organisational rehearsal for the Soccer World Cup of 2014. Brazilians were especially irritated by the Football International Federation's (FIFA) meddling in the country's affairs, imposing, for example, special rules over some parts of Brazilian territory during the Soccer World Cup, which was seen as a violation of Brazil's sovereignty.

Also, Brazilians felt particularly disrespected by FIFA's general secretary Jérôme Valcke who, irritated with the slow pace of the construction of the new soccer stadiums, declared in public that 'Brazil should get a kick in the ass' in order to speed up their construction (Lobo 2013). Further discontent was fuelled by the lack of transparency about the huge costs of the new soccer stadiums at a time when hospitals, roads, and other public services were in dire need of maintenance. Thus, much of the protest was directed against both the Confederations Cup and the Soccer World Cup.

Despite many incidents and some violence on the part of vandals and anarchists[10] – a factor that contributed to the gradual waning of the demonstrations during the months of June and July 2013 – the great majority of demonstrators were peaceful and intended to use the presence of the media at the Soccer World Cup to publicise their demands and denounce the country's social and economic problems.

In 2013, the rampant corruption inside FIFA was not yet known to the outside world, and so it could still present itself as an example of an efficient and modern organisation. But for the demonstrators, what Brazil really needed was not modern, costly stadiums and other sports facilities, but political, social, and economic reforms. A banner carried during the demonstrations epitomised Brazilians' concerns: 'We want first-world services, not first-world soccer stadiums' (Sport TV 2013). Another popular banner during the *Jornadas de Junho* criticised the fantasy of a Brazil perpetually in love with soccer: 'We don't live in FIFA land' (Ricci and Arley 2014: 120).

Interviews conducted by public opinion research institutes with the participants in the demonstrations show an enormous variety of demands, many of them contradicting each other (Tardáguila 2015: 11). Low appraisal of government, congress, political parties, and politicians in general was unanimous among demonstrators, as well as criticism of the costs associated with the Soccer World Cup. Nevertheless, the demands put forward by the demonstrators were all framed in the language of nationalism and backed by nationalist symbols.

This outburst of nationalism contained, however, an important if nearly imperceptible novelty. Soccer has traditionally been the sport that made Brazilians proud of their country and helped them, as Nelson Rodrigues, a Brazilian journalist and playwright once remarked, to overcome the country's 'stray dog complex'.[11] Indeed, the conquest of five World Cups in the last five decades, and the international admiration that came with it, made Brazilians feel, perhaps for the first time in the country's history, equal or even superior to the developed nations. Rodrigues, famous for his aphorisms about Brazilian culture, once remarked that the Brazilian national soccer team represented 'the fatherland in soccer shoes' (Rodrigues 2013). Governments in Brazil have traditionally used soccer as a tool to gain support from the masses; in 2013, however, soccer became insufficient to satisfy Brazil's sense of pride. The country was more developed, its society had become more sophisticated, democracy had finally taken root, and the young Brazilian middle class was tightly connected with the rest of the world. It is also important to note that Brazilian national identity, in Greenfeld's typology, is of the civic collectivist–authoritarian type (Type II). The lack of ethnic elements in its formation as a nation-state makes it more inclusive and open towards the world.

Ressentiment continues to fuel Brazil's national identity, since the comparison with the reference nations of the first world remains unfavourable to Brazil. However, the traditional transvaluation of values – replacing 'foreign' values with indigenous ones (soccer, in the case of Brazil) – visibly lost its strength. The 2013 demonstrations did not achieve any concrete results, despite the promises from various authorities and Congress, but they seem to have demonstrated that Brazilian society desires the same standard of living as that of the developed nations, as well as their political and cultural values.

Notes

1. Greenfeld, following Scheler, uses the French word *ressentiment*, instead of the English 'resentment'. Scheler explains his opting for the French word:

   we do not use the word 'ressentiment' because of a special predilection for the French language, but because we did not succeed in translating it into German. Moreover, Nietzsche has made it a *terminus technicus*. In the natural meaning of the French word I detect two elements. First of all, *ressentiment* is the repeated experiencing and reliving of a particular emotional response reaction against someone else. The continual reliving of the emotion sinks it more deeply into the center of the personality, but concomitantly removes it from the person's zone of action and expression. It is not a mere intellectual recollection of the emotion and of the events to which it 'responded' – it is a re-experiencing of the emotion itself, a renewal of the original feeling. Secondly, the word implies that the quality of this emotion is negative, i.e., that it contains a movement of hostility.

   (Scheler 1961: 39)

2. The sample had 77 per cent in favour of the protest movement, and 51 per cent said that the police used more violence than necessary against the protesters. Datafolha, accessed 12 June 2013, http://datafolha.folha.uol. com.br/opiniaopublica/2013/06/1297630-rede-social-e-imprensa-tem-maior-prestigio-e-poder-na-sociedade-brasileira-dizem-paulistanos.shtml.

3. 1,502 people between 18 and 30 years old were interviewed in 100 Brazilian cities. 59 per cent of them also distrusted Brazil's justice system (British Broadcasting Company 2013).

4. Marilena Chauí's words: 'parte dos manifestantes está adotando a posição ideológica típica da clase média, que aspira por governos sem mediações institucionais, e, portanto, ditatoriais. Eis porque surge a afirmação de muitos manifestantes, enrolados na bandeira nacional, de que "meu partido é meu país", ignorando, talvez, que essa foi uma das afirmações fundamentais do nazismo contra os partidos políticos…'. (Chauí 2013: 1).
5. At the beginning of the nineteenth century, the Spanish colony was divided administratively into four viceroyalties and four captaincies-general that gave way to seventeen different countries.
6. See, for example, Sunkel and Paz 1970: 275–43. With the arrival of the Portuguese Royal family in Rio, and the subsequent build up of the Brazilian state, the provinces lost part of their administrative autonomy but, in turn, were granted freedom to engage in direct trade with the Atlantic world.
7. Portugal accepted the independence of the former colony in exchange for an indemnity of two million British pounds.
8. For José Murilo de Carvalho, D. Pedro believed he had fulfilled the prophecy according to which one of the descendants of Portugal's founding father Prince Afonso Henriques would build a great empire in Christ's honour.
9. The Portuguese liberal rulers, at the same time that they restored Brazil's colonial status, also re-established provincial autonomy in all provinces outside Rio. New juntas, formed by local notables, held decision-making power in internal affairs, which deepened the elites' identification with the local *pátrias* and the resistance to the centralised government of D. Pedro I (Barman 1988: 75).
10. A group of several hundred militants tried to invade the stadium to disrupt the opening game on 15 June in Brasília – but the police beat them back and blocked their access to the stadium. In Rio, the protests succeeded in occupying the Avenida Rio Branco where many historic Brazilian icons were the targets of destructive violence. On 17 June, the historic Palácio Tiradentes – which houses the state legislature – was attacked and disfigured. Also, on 17 June, a large group of militants tried to invade the Mineirão soccer stadium in the city of Belo Horizonte, to disrupt the Nigeria vs. Tahiti game. On 19 June, in the city of Fortaleza, where the Brazilian soccer team played against Mexico, a group of some 15,000 people tried to storm the stadium with the intent of disrupting the game, but were driven off by the police.
11. Nelson Rodrigues, who invented the expression, gave the following definition: 'by stray dog complex I mean the inferiority that Brazilians feel towards the rest of the world' (Rodrigues 2012: 26).

References

Anderson, B. (1983) *Imagined Communities*, New York: Verso.

Barman, R. (1988) *Brazil: the Forging of a nation 1798–1852*, Stanford, CA: Stanford University Press.

British Broadcasting Company, 'Jovem confia mais na família, em Deus e em si mesmo do que no Estado, diz pesquisa', accessed 13 June 2013, British Broadcasting Company, http://www.bbc.com/portuguese/noticias/2013/06/130621_protestos_pesquisa_mdb_tp.

Chauí, M. (2013) 'As manifestações de junho de 2013 na cidade de São Paulo', accessed 21 June 2013, Teoria e Debate, http://www.teoriaedebate.org.br/materias/nacional/manifestacoes-de-junho-de-2013-na-cidade-de-sao-paulo?page=full#sthash.PEpvt1d7.dpuf.

Datafolha, accessed 12 June 2013, http://datafolha.folha.uol.com.br/opiniaopublica/2013/06/1297630-rede-social-e-imprensa-tem-maior-prestigio-e-poder-na-sociedade-brasileira-dizem-paulistanos.shtml.

de Andrade Prado, P. C. (2013) 'O perigoso "nacionalismo" tomou conta das manifestações', accessed 21 June 2013, Word Press, http://blogdopaulinho.wordpress.com/2013/06/21/o-perigoso-nacionalismo-tomou-conta-das-manifestacoes/.

Fontes, M. 'Manuel Castells: "a comunicacao em rede está revitalizando a democracia"', accessed 11 May 2015, *Fronteiras do Pensamento*, http://www.fronteiras.com/entrevistas/manuel-castells-a-comunicacao-em-rede-esta-revitalizando-a-democracia.

Greenfeld, L. (1992) *Nationalism: Five roads to modernity*, Cambridge, MA: Harvard University Press.

Honneth, A. (1996) *The Struggle for Recognition: the Moral grammar of social conflicts*, Cambridge, MA: MIT Press.

Jancsó, I. and Pimenta, J. P. (1999) 'Peças de um mosaico (ou apontamentos para o estudo da emergência da identidade nacional brasileira', in *Viagem Incompleta: A experiência brasileira*, C. G. Mota (ed.), São Paulo: Senac, pp 127–176.

Lauerhasse, L. (1986) *Getulio Vargas e o triunfo do nacionalismo brasileiro*, Belo Horizonte, Sao Paulo: Itatiaia, USP.

Lobo, T. (2013) 'Valke falou sobre "pontapé no traseiro" em inglês, não em francês', accessed 21 June 2013, *Globo*, http://oglobo.globo.com/esportes/valcke-falou-sobre-pontape-no-traseiro-em-ingles-nao-em-frances-4246844.

Nietzsche, F. (2003) *On the Genealogy of Morals*, Mineola, NY: Dover Thrift Editions.

Paes Leme, N. (2015) 'Reforma federativa urgente', *O Globo*, accessed 6 June 2015.

Ricci, R. and Arley, P. (2014) *Nas Ruas: a outra política que emergiu em junho de 2013*, Belo Horizonte: Editora Letramento.

Rodrigues, N. (2012) 'O Brasil vacila entre o pessimismo mais obtuso e a esperança mais frenética', in S. Rodrigues (ed.) *Nelson Rodrigues, Brasil em campo*, Rio de Janeiro: Editora Nova Fronteira Participação S.A.

—— (2013) *Nelson Rodrigues: a Pátria de chuteiras*, Rio de Janeiro: Editora Nova Fronteira Participação S.A.

Scheler, M. (1961) *Ressentiment*, New York: The Free Press of Glencoe.

Snyder, J. (1999) *From Voting to Violence: Democratization and nationalist conflicts*, New York: W.W. Norton Company.

Solomon, R. (1994) 'One hundred years of ressentiment: Nietzsche's genealogy of morals', in Schacht, R. (ed.) *Nietzsche, Genealogy, Morality: Essays on Nietzsche's genealogy of morals*, Berkeley, CA: University of California Press.

Sorj, B. (2014) 'Entre o local e o global', in *Junho de 2013 – A sociedade enfrenta o Estado*, Figueiredo, R. (ed.) São Paulo: Summus Editorial.

Sport TV, 'Valcke desconversa, mas explica o que é padrão FIFA: "pedimos o melhor"', accessed 21 June 2013, *Globo*, http://sportv.globo.com/site/programas/selecao-sportv/noticia/2013/06/valcke-desconversa-mas-explica-o-que-e-padrao-fifa-pedimos-o-melhor.html.

Sunkel, O. and Paz, P. (1970) *El Subdesarrollo Latino-Americano y la Teoria del Desarrollo*, Mexico City: Siglo XXI.

Tardáguila, C. Interview with Anthony Pereira, 'Governar ficou mais difícil', in. In *O Globo*, Rio de Janeiro, 8 June 2015.

Taylor, C. (1992) 'The politics of recognition', in Taylor, C. and Guttmann, A. (eds) *Multiculturalism and the Politics of Recognition*, Princeton, NJ: Princeton University Press.

Chapter Ten

Beyond Nationalism? Reflections on Political Legitimacy and Contemporary Left-Leaning Regimes in Latin America

Jonathan Eastwood

This chapter is divided into two parts. The first part considers the question of whether and to what extent left-leaning Latin American regimes in recent years have escaped, or have the potential to escape, from nationalism. In other words, do these regimes legitimate themselves through nationalism or through some novel, alternative way of representing the social world? This question is motivated both by this volume's broader agenda and by the fact that the regimes in question declare themselves to be revolutionary, not only with respect to economic and social matters but also with respect to ideas and identities. My answer to the question, in a nutshell, is that nationalism remains central in the region and that at present there are no discernible threats to its hegemony, at least in the public proclamations of the main leaders of key regimes.

The second part of the chapter moves beyond Latin America to consider *why* regimes' use of nationalism and national identity are so durable across the globe. I argue that (a) identities are conventions (Laitin 2007); (b) that, as such, it is their establishment, not their endurance, that is hard to explain; and that (c) any individual, group, or regime that would like to propose a truly novel framework has to solve a very difficult and risky coordination problem. As such, even if any given regime would prefer an alternative framework of legitimation, building one is under normal circumstances too costly. I close this section of the chapter with some notes for a theory of the persistence and change of regimes' use of national identity.. Along the way, I try to show that paradigms in the study of nationalism often thought of as incompatible – specifically the culturalist argument of Greenfeld and the more rationalist theory common among political scientists and economists – can be reconciled. This is due to the fact that Greenfeld's theory is almost alone among those produced by comparative–historical scholars in having clear, identifiable, and plausible micro-foundations (though see also Wimmer 2013).

Brief notes on concepts

Before proceeding, I will clarify my use of several terms. By 'nationalism', I mean a set of representations of the social world that takes nations to be the key political units, and which understands those nations to be sovereign and their members fundamentally equal in some respect (Greenfeld 1992). By 'legitimation', I mean the Weberian idea that regimes depend for ultimate survival not only on force, but also on public accounts of their rightness (Weber 1978), and I understand legitimation to be the process through which regimes build and maintain those accounts. By 'framework of legitimation', I simply mean the agreed upon rules in any given social context concerning *how* a regime may establish its legitimacy. For example, in some times and places the basic 'framework of legitimation' is religious. Many have argued that in modernity it is rooted in secular nationalism.

By 'identity', I mean a durable representation of some subject, a representation in which the subject participates or shares (Greenfeld and Eastwood 2007). Individuals have personal identities. They can also impute identities to groups, and national identity is obviously of the latter sort. It is worth noting that nationalism legitimates regimes in part through bestowing national identity: through giving people a shared account of who they are and linking their political rights and duties to that identity. It may be that all enduring frameworks of legitimation bestow identities and gain power through doing so, but I will only go so far as to say that nationalism clearly does so.

By 'convention', I mean a sustained coordination equilibrium (Elster 2007: 357–8). In other words, a convention persists because anyone who chooses to defect (i.e. to violate the convention) becomes worse off by doing so. Conventions can take many forms. I will argue below that identity is a type of convention,[1] and that understanding this helps us to better understand how identities persist and change.

Before moving to the cases at hand, I should note two theoretical assumptions upon which my argument rests. The first is that regimes, like individuals, can be expected typically to behave rationally in the minimal sense defined by Gintis (2011). All this means is that (1) regimes (or, rather, the individuals who lead them) have preferences, (2) that these preferences are transitively ordered, and (3) that people behave strategically as they try to achieve their preferred outcomes. It does *not* imply that people seek only 'material' payoffs. For regimes, we can assume that under ordinary circumstances regime survival is high on the list of preferences, but we need not even assume, as many rational choice theories of politics do, that it is always the over-riding preference of regimes.

The second theoretical assumption is that people get intrinsic utility from their identities (Akerloff and Kranton 2010). While a good deal of literature on nationalism and national identity has embraced at least weak instrumentalism (e.g. Hechter 2000; Bates 2008; *arguably* Laitin 2007), strong versions of instrumentalism are not plausible. Some people may indeed behave instrumentally with respect to national identity, but others are willing to sacrifice a great deal for the *sake* of their identity. It is my belief that the best analytical strategy is to recognise that people value their identities both for their own sake *and* for how those identities impact their ability to access other goods. Furthermore, while there is undoubtedly interpersonal variation in how 'needy' people are with respect to identities, all of us are dependent on our cultural environment to provide us with identity resources (Greenfeld 2013). I will assume that, all else equal, people on average prefer identities that are (a) highly ranked and (b) clear and stable. I elaborate on some of these ideas and their implications below.

Do contemporary Latin American leftist regimes move beyond nationalism?

The short answer to the question of whether contemporary leftist regimes in Latin America have moved beyond nationalism is *no*. By this I mean that in all of these regimes we see considerable use of nationalism in official rhetoric, and that I find no evidence of any serious rival to nationalism in the public proclamations of these regimes. In this brief discussion I focus on two cases: Venezuela under the Chavista regime (including the presidencies of both Hugo Chávez and Nicolás Maduro), and Bolivia under the Evo Morales regime. I include Venezuela but discuss it only briefly because (a) many consider it the 'leader' of the leftist pole in contemporary Latin America; and (b) scholars widely recognise the Chavista regime's use of nationalism. I then focus on the Morales regime because, of all contemporary Latin American regimes, it could be expected to be the most likely to transcend nationalism, precisely because the regime is innovative in many ways.[2] Indeed, some regime supporters claim that it has done so, arguing that Bolivia has created a 'pluri-national state', as it officially declares. Its current vice president, the sociologist and intellectual Álvaro García Linera, claims that the Bolivian state aims to achieve 'an alternative form of modernity' (quoted in Harten 2011: 210).

In neither case do I extensively consider the rhetoric of non-regime actors. This is not because such actors are unimportant. Moreover, there very well may be non-regime actors in either society that have developed truly nationalism-transcending frameworks for conceiving of political legitimation. The identification and analysis of any such developments would be a worthy project. They are not discussed here in any detail because (a) the systematic search for them lies beyond the scope of this chapter; and (b) this chapter focuses heavily on the strategic situation of regimes and their use of nationalism and national identity, in part because I believe that those regimes face a very different strategic situation with respect to political identities than do non-regime actors.

The Venezuelan case is relatively straightforward. Nationalism has been a key framework of Venezuelan political culture since the nineteenth century (Coronil 1997; Carrera Damas 2006; Eastwood 2006). This does not mean that everyone residing in Venezuelan territory has always been *included* in the nation, and, as in many cases, the formal implication of nationalism that all citizens are somehow equal has been violated in practice for much of the country's history. But, throughout the twentieth century, all major Venezuelan political movements were nationalist. The right-wing dictatorships of Gómez and Pérez Jimenez claimed to govern in the name of the sovereign people, as did the major political parties (AD, COPEI, and URD) of the late twentieth century (Dávila 1993). Both the Venezuelan left and right were (and are) nationalistic.

Numerous analysts (e.g. Eastwood 2007; Hawkins 2010; Smilde 2012) have documented the Chávez regime's use of national imagery and language. Chávez's populist discourse was clearly rooted in the nationalist idea of popular sovereignty, and he tended to depict his adversaries as 'oligarchs' who were 'traitors' to the 'pueblo soberano'. The regime has also rhetorically linked this 'oligarchy' to the

United States, and frequently uses the United States as a foil, claiming to have uncovered US-hatched coup plots and insisting that the United States 'respect' Venezuela and its national integrity. Chávez made great use of these rhetorical strategies, and Maduro has done so as well. Both have integrated nationalist language with socialist rhetoric, and the 'oligarchy' and the 'bourgeoisie' have been used almost interchangeably. The implicit idea is that there is no contradiction between seeing society in nationalist and socialist terms.

The Venezuelan opposition, for its part, has made extensive use of nationalism as well. They appropriated the national flag as their chief symbol (as opposed to the socialist 'red' that came to identify the government and its supporters), and claim to represent the nation's true interests. Indeed, some extreme elements have attempted to argue for Maduro's illegitimacy on the grounds that he was allegedly born in Colombia and is thus not truly Venezuelan. For at least some members of the opposition, the great external threat is not the United States but Cuba. They claim that the Cuban regime has fully infiltrated the Venezuelan government and that Raúl Castro (and before him, Fidel) truly calls the shots. Some have even claimed that Cuban doctors providing care through the Misión Barrio Adentro are actually spies. As the late Fernando Coronil observed (2011), in some respects Chavista and opposition visions of the world are mirror images of each other.

In short, the conflict that has gripped Venezuela since early in Chávez's first term has taken place within the framework of nationalism. It is the nation on whose behalf everyone claims to be working, the nation whose interests they claim to be defending, and the nation's enemies for whom they claim to be on the watch. To be clear, my argument is not that nothing has changed as a result of the so-called 'Bolivarian Revolution.' There is considerable evidence that a great deal of social mobilisation has taken place during the Chavista years,[3] and many have the impression that various social sectors feel more empowered, and perhaps fuller participants in national life, than they were before. Some of the regime's experiments in the social policy arena were novel. Additionally, there is little doubt that the regime has contributed to the ongoing polarisation of Venezuelan society (Corrales 2011). Finally, the policies of the Chávez and Maduro regimes have clearly had a major impact on the Venezuelan economy, and in my view largely for the worse. But in other, more fundamental, respects, the regime's novelty seems exaggerated. Venezuela remains oil-dependent and its regime clientelistic, and the regime's legitimating framework has changed much less than official pronouncements suggest, more a rebranding of Venezuelan nationalism – with attention to being more deliberately inclusive of subaltern groups, combined with a fairly traditional kind of socialist rhetoric – than a new framework of legitimation.

The case of Bolivia seems, at first glance, more promising for those seeking evidence of a regime that has transcended nationalism. The polity has re-named itself a 'plurinational state', and a number of intellectuals have argued that this marks a break from the traditional 'one-state, one-nation' relationship taken to be characteristic of many modern societies. Traditional identities and practices are not to be replaced or subjugated, and even traditional legal codes are to be incorporated into the state (Harten 2011: 218–21). Perhaps most strikingly, in 2010 the state passed a law for the rights of Mother Earth which recognizes Mother Earth as 'a living, dynamic system formed by the indivisible community of all life systems and living beings, which are interrelated, interdependent, and complementary, sharing a common destiny', and attributing to Mother Earth 'the character of a collective subject of public interest' (reprinted in Ari 2014). These ideas, reflective of what Ari (2014), calls the 'Earth politics' of Bolivian indigenous intellectuals and activists, may indeed signal a potential alternative to conventional nationalism as a legitimating framework for politics.

This raises the question of how widespread these revolutionary ideas are. In particular, given the focus of this chapter, I am interested in the extent to which the regime draws on these ideas, rather than traditional nationalist populism, in presenting itself to the public. For this reason, I conducted a basic content analysis of speeches by Bolivia's president Evo Morales. I focused on the speeches posted on the website of the Bolivian Government's Office of Communications, reading and coding all speeches included there that took place during the 2013 calendar year.[4] The vast majority were given by Morales himself, though several were given by Álvaro García Linera, Bolivia's vice president. The coverage of speeches is sparse for the first half of the year, with most taking place between August and December. The sample totalled 268 official speeches. Many were directed to local communities within Bolivia, though several were international speeches and it is clear from context that Morales is often simultaneously speaking to multiple audiences.

The content analysis was simple and focused somewhat narrowly on the question of this chapter. I coded the speeches for reference to or discussion of the 'Bolivian people'; of other (sub-polity) 'peoples'; of 'nations'; of explicit reference to indigenous groups; of discussion of Bolivian 'culture' or 'identity' and particularistic (sub-polity) 'culture' or 'identity'; of social/economic classes or sectors (looking for both positive and negative references); of non-traditional forms of legitimacy; of 'revolution'; of socialism; of pan-Americanism (defined broadly so as to include sub-regional cooperation, as in ALBA); of 'sovereignty'; and of unity. Here I will just summarise my main conclusions.

First, nowhere did I find any apparent rival to traditional forms of legitimation. Morales – at least in his public speeches in this period – tends to rely heavily on nationalist populism, anti-imperialism, and rhetoric that emphasises sovereignty and (to a lesser extent) unity while recognising regional and cultural differences within the polity. Nationalism is present throughout. Most speeches make reference to 'el pueblo boliviano' to garner legitimacy, often repeatedly. Bolivia is seldom described as a 'nación', but the broader worldview of nationalism (equality and popular sovereignty) is clearly the main framework assumed by the speaker.

This is accompanied by a frequent focus on imperialism, linking the twenty-first-century position of the United States to that of the earliest European colonisers. Colonialism, 'neo-liberalism', capitalism, and empire are roughly equated in the speeches. Morales depicts the regime's attempts at social change as continuous with indigenous rebellions of centuries past and the Wars of Independence. These themes are repeated frequently: since the European invasion of the region in the sixteenth century, there has been indigenous resistance. The nineteenth-century independence movement began largely with indigenous people and was an extension of this resistance. Late twentieth-century social movements that resisted 'neoliberalism' were another chapter in this history and the Morales government itself is the realisation of this longstanding historical process. The Morales government, though, is the expression of the Bolivian people, the long history really the story of that people's 'lucha' (struggle). This basic story is repeatedly told and reinforced.

The word 'pueblo', though, does have multiple referents, perhaps owing to the marked regional/local differences in Bolivian society. Regional and city 'peoples' are acknowledged ('pueblo' in Spanish means people but can also mean 'town'): he refers to 'el pueblo cochambino' (as on 6 August 2013) as well as 'el pueblo potosino' (as on 7 August 2013) and 'el pueblo paceño' (27 August 2013). However, these pueblos do not seem to be mutually exclusive, but rather 'nested'. In other words, 'el pueblo cochambino' is nested in 'el pueblo boliviano', and so forth. When he mentions a smaller 'pueblo', he sometimes soon thereafter mentions 'el pueblo boliviano', as if he is conscious of the potential divisiveness of local identities. And yet when push comes to shove he makes it clear that Bolivia is the key reference. As he reminds his audience (on 4 October 2013), 'La lucha desde aimaras, quechuas, guaranís, nunca ha sido solamente por ellos sino por Bolivia.'

Morales sometimes refers to the Bolivian government as the 'gobierno nacional' but always carefully refers to the polity as the 'Estado Plurinacional'. Generally he does not use 'nación' very often, but when he does it seems usually to be connected to indigenous groups.[5] Interestingly, he engages in very little discussion of 'plurinationalism', other than its being mentioned as part of the name of the state or institutions connected to the state. Yet the tendency not to refer to Bolivia explicitly as a nation, but rather as 'el pueblo Boliviano' undoubtedly has the strategic benefit of maintaining consistency both with preferences of Bolivian nationalists and with any in his target audience who have a more truly 'plurinational' conception of the Bolivian state and the populations subject to it.

Morales speaks of 'our culture' and 'our identity' in ways that suggest he is referring to Bolivia as a whole, but inclusive of differences across Bolivia, especially indigenous groups. He speaks of the need to 'recover our identity'. Educational institutions, including those that teach traditional languages, are extolled on the grounds that they will aid in this recovery of identity. And yet the identity to be recovered is 'our identity' (not 'our identities'): the over-riding emphasis seems to be on a Bolivian identity informed by many roots and one involving respect for and recognition of differences.

While there is a strong leftist tilt to the speeches, they include relatively little explicit discussion of socialism, and less traditional Marxist rhetoric than one sees in the post-2005 speeches of Chávez or Maduro. The other major contrast with Chavismo that I noticed is that Morales's speeches tend to be far less polarising, at least with respect to actors within Bolivian society (he very frequently speaks about the United States in highly polarising terms). Whereas Chávez's speeches abounded with references to 'oligarchs', 'the bourgeoisie', and 'escualidos', among other derogatory terms for his opponents, Morales relies less on such rhetorical strategies and tends to emphasise the need for within-polity unity, at least during the time period under study here.[6]

In short, after reviewing approximately 268 speeches, my main conclusion is that, despite what one might expect based on the hype, Morales's rhetoric is fairly conventional by the standards of Latin American nationalist populism. There are obviously more rhetorically radical actors in Bolivian society (and within the Bolivian regime), but the regime's most important voice often uses what seems a fairly traditional nationalist legitimating strategy. Some of the regime's policies may be revolutionary but by and large the rhetoric of its central figure is not. If we assume that many actors affiliated with the regime would like to move beyond traditional nationalism and populism, this is somewhat puzzling.

Why do regimes so seldom move beyond nationalism?

Greenfeld (1993) has argued that it is almost impossible for us to imagine a post-national world. Just as the idea of a sovereign community of equals might have seemed absurd to those who lived through alternative frameworks, whatever might follow nationalism and national identity would likewise be difficult for us to grasp. I find this convincing. The barriers to the rise of some new form of political legitimation, though, are not limited to this. Here I will make a complementary argument that focuses on the difficulties facing those who seek to transform or replace well-established political identities.

For the sake of discussion, let us assume that some regime has internally developed a novel framework of legitimation. The characteristic features of this imagined alternative framework need not concern us. Let us also assume that for whatever reason – they truly believe in this new framework, say, or because they believe its widespread adoption would give them some strategic advantage – they hope to persuade their citizens that they should adopt it. To really approximate the case at hand, this hypothetical regime would need to be seeking something more than just to refine or add onto some existing identity. As noted with respect to the case of Venezuela, encouraging citizens to see themselves as socialist revolutionaries is not an alternative to national identity if the regime goes on making use of nationalism and treats the socialist revolution as a national project. So for a regime to meet our threshold it would really have to favour creating a rival to national identity.

Why do they so seldom do so? Why, once established, are collective identities so durable?

One reason is that, as noted at the outset of this chapter, identities are conventional. As such, it is costly to ignore them, as Laitin (2007: 34) notes with respect to efforts to promote language change. Those individuals who for whatever reason cannot or do not wish to accept the collective identity labels that society stereotypically bestows on them routinely experience these costs. In a highly racialised society, an individual may choose not to identify his or herself with respect to race, and yet be repeatedly told that he or she does have such and such a racial identity. Similar issues are observed with respect to gender identity. These problems are not insurmountable, but they often require patience and resilience on the part of the individuals concerned. The point here is that classification systems get established as conventional and thus become hard to escape, even in those cases where people *wish* to escape them. Indeed, a collective identity's grip could be sustained indefinitely by pluralistic ignorance.

Imagine that our regime decides to propose its alternative, and recall that this alternative must be in zero-sum competition with national identity in order to truly *be* an alternative. There are two problems the regime must address. First, it must defy the old convention. Second, it must establish the new one.

Thus there are actually two sets of costs for regimes that forgo the use of conventional identities. The first is simply the 'inconvenience' deriving from loss of use of the existing convention. Though this may seem trivial, in most cases it is probably not. Conventional identities are precious resources for regimes. They are tools for the construction of legitimating frameworks. Consider the example of Chavista populism discussed briefly above. At the time of writing, the Maduro regime faces myriad problems, including major economic difficulties, food scarcities, poorly functioning institutions, an ongoing crime epidemic, and very low approval ratings. In this context, the temptation to use existing identity conventions to shore up popular support is undoubtedly great (on this strategy in general, see Solt 2011).

Another example concerns coalitional politics. Regimes typically have to hold together coalitions of groups that differ markedly in their preferences. Often, a shared national identity – shared participation in the convention – may be one of the few things that unite members of a coalition (beyond the strategic gains each group gets from cooperating). As such, forgoing the use of nationalism would be very costly for those regimes hoping to maintain fragile coalitions. This may help to explain the ubiquity of references to the 'Bolivian people' in the political rhetoric of Evo Morales, as well as his emphasis on unity. Another way to say this would be to say that established identities constitute 'common knowledge' in Chwe's (2001, see especially pp. 91–2; see also Laitin 2007: 64–5) sense, a precious resource for a regime interested in coordinating the actions of their subject population.

The second cost such a regime can expect to face is resistance. If a conventional identity is at equilibrium, we can expect people – in this case, citizens – to actively defend it. In other words, if I like my current identity, and if what you propose would either (a) reduce its status, or (b) perhaps more importantly, problematise it, rendering it unclear or unstable, then I will be inclined to resist your efforts to change it. Resistance to efforts to change collective identities can take many forms, both democratic and non-democratic. We might expect them to vary in intensity as well, as a function of how much people believe they have to lose. As Greenfeld (1993) has stressed, any rival to national identity would likely be unsuccessful if it could not provide its bearers with the same sort of dignity they get from nationalism.

So ceasing to make use of an existing conventional identity can bring two types of costs to a regime: loss of the use of the existing convention and the risk of active resistance. Yet establishing a new convention may be the more difficult problem here. Indeed, social scientists do not understand very well where conventions (including norms, which constitute a subtype) come from (Elster 2007). The reason is that most conventions evolve in a highly decentralised way, and we have little data that allow us to empirically track conventions from their origins through to their establishment. Functionalist explanations have failed, and seem bound to do so, due to logical problems. Historical accounts emphasising contingency fail because, under most circumstances, they cannot empirically identify the convention's origins.

On the one hand, it would seem as if regimes have an advantage here when compared to others interested in identity change. Their structural position might render them more able to solve coordination problems than some weaker or less central actor would be. A regime in a state with reasonable capacity should be able to communicate new ideas about identity to its populace and to structure incentives in ways that would encourage people to participate in the new identity.

On the other hand, in terms of impact on the probability of any given actor being the 'originator' of identity change, states' advantages as coordinators of collective action may be outweighed by their interests in maintaining established identities, due to their conventional status, as discussed above. To advance our understanding of these issues, we need to step back and think about identity issues from the perspective of all relevant actors, before turning back to the specific strategic interests of political regimes.

Towards a theory of persistence and change of regimes' use of national identity

At this point, we have only speculative theory, which builds especially on Greenfeld (1992, 2001) and Laitin (2007), but in the future this theory might be formalised and tested. I hope that the following are reasonable starting points.

1. Identities (not just national identities, but all collective identities) are themselves forms of ongoing coordination, as some existing theories argue. That is, they do not exist independently of the coordinated efforts of individuals to believe in them, express them symbolically, and act through them.
2. Since identities are forms of ongoing coordination, to explain them we need to account for their emergence but also for how they are maintained. We have very good accounts of the emergence of national identity (e.g. Greenfeld 1992), but at present its persistence is under-theorised, often being described by the Durkheimian metaphor of their 'crystallisation'. This is not incorrect, but we can advance our knowledge by developing a more specific account of what 'crystallisation' means in this context. Persistence can be thought of as the non-emergence of alternative forms: in other words, as an identity equilibrium (as in Laitin 2007; Shayo 2009; Wimmer 2013)

3. Identities almost always develop out of some other identities (i.e. there is, except in the most unusual of circumstances, no pre-identity-state from which any given case of collective identity develops).
4. Payoffs for identities are both political/strategic and psychological. In other words, one can become better or worse off with respect to an identity, both by virtue of how that identity impacts one's political strategy and by virtue of how that identity makes one feel (Greenfeld 1992; Laitin 2007: 54-56; Shayo 2009; Akerlof and Kranton 2010).
5. In general, given the structure of modern polities ('nation-states'), in those societies where national identity has been consolidated it is in the political–strategic interest of most groups to identity with the 'nation'. All else equal, this should be expected to reinforce national identity equilibria where these exist. In other words, in many circumstances political–strategic interests exert a sort of centripetal effect. However, this will not *always* be the case.
6. It may or may not be in the *psychological* interest of key actors in such circumstances to identity with the nation. Under certain conditions we might expect psychological interests to exert a kind of centrifugal effect. These would be circumstances in which existing identities are stigmatised or otherwise 'spoiled' (Goffman 1963) or in which some other identity could be envisioned that would be conducive to increased status for the relevant group. These are situations ripe for identity change.

This would allow us to make several general predictions with respect to political identities (and regimes' attempts to shape them), assuming a range of situations in which political–strategic and group identity variables differ.

1. All else equal, established identities will tend to endure.
2. To the extent that any given actor's identity yields (a) consistent status and (b) high status (i.e. higher status than can realistically be envisioned through some seemingly achievable alternative identity system), that actor will continue to hold the identity (i.e. uphold and believe in it, act in accordance with its implications, and exert social control on those who challenge it).
3. To the extent that any given actor's identity yields better political and economic payoffs than some other identity (again, one that can realistically be envisioned through some seemingly achievable alternative identity system[7]), that actor will continue to hold the identity.
4. These general rules will hold for both individual actors and for organisations with clearly defined interests, (e.g. regimes).
5. In general, regimes have an interest in generating or maintaining identities that encourage populations to behave as they would wish them to do. This often means national identities that take the states controlled by those regimes as their geo-political referents.
6. Under ordinary circumstances, therefore, we should expect regimes to work to maintain (a) existing identities that (b) reinforce the authority of the regimes – and the states they control – themselves.

7. If such regimes, for whatever reason, *desire* identity change, we should expect them (a) to continue to make use of the existing convention in the short term while (b) attempting to sew the seeds of identity change for the longer term.

8. A society with a 'crystallised' national identity is likely to be one in which (a) the prevailing regime's interests are largely served by the prevailing equilibrium; and (b) no major group or organisation (i) could unilaterally benefit in terms of political or economic competition through attempting some macro-level identity change, and/or (ii) could unilaterally benefit in terms of status interests from attempting some macro-level identity change.

9. If a society has a crystallised national identity, we should expect it to be maintained indefinitely in the absence of some exogenous shock. However, exogenous shocks do happen, and can take at least the following forms: a dramatic change in the status of the identity in question (perhaps especially a dramatic decline); demographic shifts that change the strategic position of groups within societies; an increase or decrease in the power of the state (or other key actors); inter-state conflict; or the emergence of some new form of identity that yields better payoffs than the existing one.

To be developed further, these speculative propositions need elaboration, perhaps some formalisation, and empirical testing. Complicating this task is that they generate predictions about future events, but not retroactive predictions about historical events. National identity remains the most important political identity in our world. Therefore, it would seem that the propositions could not yet be tested. However, we might fruitfully consider whether their observable implications are consistent with major cases of identity change that we know of from the past. The most obvious question is whether the observable implications of these claims are consistent with that process of identity change that led to the emergence of nationalism and national identity itself.

This chapter is not the place for a full consideration of that question, but it is worth noting that the theory is very consistent with previous findings that status-inconsistency is a precursor to the emergence of national identity in many cases, as a variety of studies have found (Greenfeld 1992; Eastwood 2006; Benoit 2007). Status-inconsistent identities could be thought of as 'spoiled', yielding pressure for identity change via social–psychological mechanisms that are reasonably well understood.[8] Whether the theory can be modelled and then systematically tested against historical evidence is a question for future research.

The approach sketched here has two additional advantages. First, it may help to resolve some false dichotomies in the existing literature on nationalism and national identity, such as debates about whether nationalism is fundamentally the product of the state or of 'society'. Bell (2001) for example, criticises Greenfeld's account of nationalism in the case of France by suggesting that nationalism was a product of the state (growing out of 'royal patriotism') rather than of status-inconsistent aristocrats whose position in the ancien regime had been problematised. This perspective has parallels among many who have taken a 'state-centred' view of nationalism and national identity (e.g. Weber 1976; Breuilly 1993; Tilly 1994; Herbst 2000; Centeno 2002; Vom Hau 2009; Wimmer and Feinstein 2010). Yet as my approach makes clear there is no need to choose between 'state' and 'society'-centric theories of national identity (indeed, Greenfeld's foundational approach has always recognised this).

Second, as noted at the outset of the chapter, the approach I promote here has the added advantage that it renders moot another false dichotomy, the one that juxtaposes strategic or 'rational choice' theories (e.g. Hechter 2000; Laitin 2007) to those that posit national identity and nationalism as fundamentally 'irrational' (e.g. Connor 1993). The culturalist and social–psychological arguments developed by Greenfeld – which I have tried to build on here – transcend that false dichotomy. In other words, they are simultaneously consistent with the principles of methodological individualism (modelling society as the aggregate product of individual action) and mechanism-based explanation that have subsequently been identified as key to 'analytical sociology' (e.g. Hedström and Bearman 2009; Hedström and Udehn 2009), *and* they acknowledge that people seek more than material payoffs when choosing whether or not to select and live out their identities. It is not that nationalists are irrational, of course, but that they are motivated by a variety of concerns beyond the material payoffs they can receive based on their identities.

Conclusion

Given how widely this chapter has ranged, a general summary might be in order. In keeping with the goals of this volume, I began by asking whether and to what extent contemporary left-leaning regimes in Latin America have come to transcend nationalism as a source of legitimation. I focused on the Chavista regime in Venezuela and the Morales regime in Bolivia, and argued that in neither case do we see nationalism transcended. The Chavista regime (including the rhetoric of both Chávez himself and Maduro since Chávez's death) draws frequently on nationalism and blends this with fairly traditional Marxist language. The Morales regime – despite the emphasis on Bolivia's status as a 'plurinational state' – also makes great use of (Bolivian) nationalism and national identity in its official rhetoric. In neither case did I find any fundamentally novel alternative rhetorical strategy for regime legitimation.

I turned from these basic descriptive findings to sketch a speculative theory about the persistence of regimes' use of national identity that is inspired by reflections on Latin American cases but potentially applicable elsewhere. This theory draws on previous work in emphasising that identity can be thought of as a kind of ongoing coordination of beliefs, and that successful cases of this are valuable for many actors, including regimes. As such, all else equal, regimes have an interest in maintaining national identity once it is established. Efforts to transcend nationalism are risky because (a) they involve foregoing the use of national identity for strategic purposes and (b) they may provoke resistance from populations that bear those identities. In successful 'identity equilibria', populations too have an interest in maintaining the status quo. However, if exogenous shocks lead to identities becoming problematised – whether through stigma or inconsistency – identity transformation is possible.

The author gratefully acknowledges the support of a summer Lenfest Grant from Washington and Lee University.

Notes

1. Here I follow in the footsteps of Laitin (2007: 41) who sees national identity as 'a product of cultural coordination' and, like Laitin, I draw on Schelling (2006[1978]) in thinking about how identities might be conceptualised as conventions that solve coordination problems. However, my focus is different from Laitin's. He tries to explain identify shifts in which the overarching identity categories are stable (shifts among languages, or between competing national identities) whereas I am also interested in alternative identity systems as conventions, much like Meyer *et al.* (1997) or Wimmer and Feinstein (2010), in their focus on the spread of the nation-state. It is not just particular instances within classes of identities that solve coordination problems, but the selection of classes of identities themselves.

2. For accounts of the Morales regime as deeply transformational, see Artaraz 2012 and Harten 2011. For a more sceptical view, see Webber 2011.

3. There are a number of works dealing with this theme. A good place to start is Smilde and Hellinger 2011.

4. http://www.comunicacion.gob.bo/?q=discursos. Due to space limitations I do not cite each of those speeches individually in the references to this chapter, but at the time of writing (July 2015) they are still available on the government's website. In the few instances of the textual discussion here in which I cite particular speeches I refer to them by date.

5. In rare instances (e.g. 4 November 2013) he seems to reference Bolivia itself as a *nación*.

6. I certainly do not mean to suggest that the Morales regime never adopts a polarising strategy. See Klein 2011: 295–6.

7. In other words, that there is a relevant community that would accept this identity.

8. For example, via dissonance reduction, as discussed in the classic work of Festinger (1985[1957]).

References

Akerloff, G. A. and Kranton, R. E. (2010) *Identity Economics: How our identities shape our work, wages, and well-being*, Princeton, NJ: Princeton University Press.

Ari, W. (2014) *Earth Politics: Religion, decolonization, and Bolivia's indigenous intellectuals*, Durham, NC: Duke University Press.

Artaraz, K. (2012) *Bolivia: Refounding the nation*, London: Pluto Press.

Bates, R. (2008) *When Things Fell Apart: State failure in late-century Africa*, New York: Cambridge University Press.

Bell, D. A. (2001) *The Cult of the Nation in France*, Cambridge, MA: Harvard University Press.

Benoit, O. (2007) 'Ressentiment and the Gairy social revolution', *Small Axe* 22: 95–111.

Breuilly, J. (1993) *Nationalism and the State*, Manchester: Manchester University Press.

Carrera Damas, G. (2006) *Venezuela: Proyecto nacional y poder social*. Mérida: Publicaciones del Vicerrectorado Académico.

Centeno, M. A. (2002) *Blood and Debt: War and the nation state in Latin America*, University Park: The Pennsylvania State University Press.

Chwe, M. (2001) *Rational Ritual: Culture, coordination, and common knowledge*, Princeton, NJ: Princeton University Press.

Connor, W. (1993) 'Beyond reason: The nature of the ethnonational bond', *Ethnic and Racial Studies*, 16(3): 373–89.

Coronil, F. (1997) *The Magical State: Nature, money, and modernity in Venezuela*, Chicago: University of Chicago Press.

— (2011) 'State reflections: the 2002 coup against Hugo Chávez', in T. Ponniah and J. Eastwood (eds) *The Revolution in Venezuela: Social and political change under Chávez*, Cambridge, MA: DRCLAS/Harvard University Press, pp. 37–65.

Corrales, J. (2011) 'Why polarize? Advantages and disadvantages of a rational-choice analysis of government–opposition relations in Venezuela', in T. Ponniah and J. Eastwood (eds) *The Revolution in Venezuela: Social and political change under Chávez*, Cambridge, MA: DRCLAS/Harvard University Press.

Dávila, L. R. (1993) 'Rómulo Betancourt and the development of Venezuelan nationalism (1930–1945)', *Bulletin of Latin American Research*, 12(1): 49–63.

Eastwood, J. (2006) *The Rise of Nationalism in Venezuela*, Gainesville, FL: University Press of Florida.

— (2007) 'Contextualizando a Chávez: el nacionalismo venezolano contemporáneo desde una perspectiva histórica', *Revista Mexicana de Sociología*, 69(4): 605–39.

Elster, J. (2007) *Explaining Social Behavior: More nuts and bolts for the social sciences*, New York: Cambridge University Press.

Festinger, L. (1985[1957]) *A Theory of Cognitive Dissonance*, Stanford, CA: Stanford University Press.

Gintis, H. (2011) *The Bounds of Reason: Game theory and the unification of the behavioral sciences*, Princeton, NJ: Princeton University Press.

Goffman, E. (1963) *Stigma: Notes on the management of spoiled identity*, New York: Simon and Schuster.

Greenfeld, L. (1992) *Nationalism: Five roads to modernity*, Cambridge: Harvard University Press.

— (1993) 'Transcending the nation's worth', *Daedalus*, 122(3): 47–62.

— (2001) *The Spirit of Capitalism: Nationalism and economic growth*, Cambridge, MA: Harvard University Press.

— (2013) *Mind, Modernity, Madness: the Impact of culture on human experience*, Cambridge, MA: Harvard University Press.

Greenfeld, L. and Eastwood, J. (2007) 'National Identity', in C. Boix and S. Stokes (eds) *Oxford Handbook of Comparative Politics*, New York: Oxford University Press.

Harten, S. (2011) *The Rise of Evo Morales and the MAS*, New York: Zed Books.

Hawkins, K. (2010) *Venezuela's Chavismo and Populism in Comparative Perspective*, Cambridge: Cambridge University Press.

Hechter, M. (2000) *Containing Nationalism*, New York: Oxford University Press.

Hedström, P. and Bearman, P. (2009) 'What is analytical sociology all about? An introductory essay', in P. Hedström and P. Bearman (eds) *Oxford Handbook of Analytical Sociology*, New York: Oxford University Press, pp. 3–24.

Hedström, P. and Udehn, L. (2009) 'Analytical sociology and theories of the middle range', in P. Hedström and P. Bearman (eds) *Oxford Handbook of Analytical Sociology*, New York: Oxford University Press, pp. 25–50.

Herbst, J. (2000) *States and Power in Africa: Lessons in authority and control*, Princeton, NJ: Princeton University Press.

Klein, H. (2011) *A Concise History of Bolivia*, second edition, New York: Cambridge University Press.

Laitin, D. (2007) *Nations, States, and Violence*, New York: Oxford University Press.

Meyer, J., Boli, J., Thomas, G. M., and Ramírez, F. (1997) 'World society and the nation-state', *American Journal of Sociology*, 103(1): 144–81.

Schelling, T. (2006[1978]) *Micromotives and Macrobehavior*, New York: W.W. Norton and Company.

Shayo, M. (2009) 'A model of social identity with an application to political economy: nation, class, and redistribution', *American Political Science Review*, 103(2): 147–74.

Smilde, D. (2012) 'From national to international to national liberation: Lenin, Chávez and twenty-first century socialism', *Regular Session on Nations and Nationalism*, American Sociological Association, August 18.

Smilde, D. and Hellinger, D. (eds) (2011) *Venezuela's Bolivarian Democracy: Participation, politics, and culture in Venezuela's Bolivarian democracy*, Durham, NC: Duke University Press.

Tilly, C. (1994) 'States and nationalism in Europe 1492–1992', *Theory and Society*, 23(1): 131–46.

Solt, F. (2011) 'Diversionary nationalism: economic inequality and the formation of national pride', *Journal of Politics*, 73(1): 821–30.

Vom Hau, M. (2009) 'Unpacking the school: textbooks, teachers, and the construction of nationhood in Mexico, Argentina, and Peru', *Latin American Research Review*, 44(3): 127–54.

Webber, J. (2011) *From Rebellion to Reform in Bolivia: Class struggle, indigenous liberation, and the politics of Evo Morales*, Chicago: Haymarket Books.

Weber, E. (1976) *Peasants into Frenchmen: the Modernization of rural France, 1870–1914*, Stanford, CA: Stanford University Press.

Weber, M. (1978) *Economy and Society: An outline of interpretive sociology*, Vol.1, G. Roth and C. Wittich, (eds). Berkeley: University of California Press.

Wimmer, A. (2013) *Waves of War: Nationalism, state formation, and ethnic exclusion in the modern world*, New York: Cambridge University Press.

Wimmer, A. and Feinstein, Y. (2010) 'The rise of the nation-state across the world, 1816–2001', *American Sociological Review*, 75(5): 764–90.

Chapter Eleven

Political Islam: From Transnational Movement to Nationalism ... and Back

Jocelyne Cesari

Browsing through the ever-growing literature on political Islam at least since the 1970s, we see that the dominant apprehension is that political Islam and its synonymous Islamism are religiously based opposition movements to secular states.

The present chapter challenges this approach by arguing that political Islam is better understood as religious nationalism that can be traced back to the building of the nation-states after the collapse of the Ottoman Empire. It will also demonstrate how the global forms of radical Islam embodied today in groups such as Al Qaeda, Boko Haram or ISIS are the most recent iterations of political Islam that have shifted religious nationalism to religious transnationalism.

The chapter agrees with scholars who do not consider nationalism an ideology, but rather an habitus, i.e. the sum of memories, emotions, and values that align the cultural and political identity of people with a certain territory and institutions that control this territory (Rokkan 1988). Its goal is to shed light on the specifics of Muslim political cultures by exploring the historicity of political Islam and showing its enmeshment with nation building. Nation-states emerged in Muslim lands following the collapse of the Ottoman Empire and are the outcome of the importation of western concepts that can be dated back to the insertion of the Ottoman Empire into the Westphalian system of states (Eisenstadt 2006; Sachsenmaier *et al.* 2001; Otmagin and Ben-Ari 2012). Thus, as shown by Vali Nasr or Bobby Said (Said 2003), the adoption of the Western concept of nation-state in Muslim-majority countries is the consequence not only of war or colonial power but also of the inclusion of Muslim polities into the international system. The effects of this adoption on the politicisation of Islam have been much less examined. To do so, our study analyses the diffusion of the nation-state concept and, following this, its embodiments in institutions and political practices.

At the core of Islam's politicisation lie the structural changes unleashed by the transition from pre-modern political entity to modern nation-state. This transition led to the rise of authoritarian 'promethean' regimes in which state actors imposed upon their societies very invasive social and cultural transformations. The outcome has been the construction of strong monist national ideologies with Islam at their centre.

The use of Western terms or Western techniques or cultural styles should not bounce us into thinking that some of these countries went through a differentiation between religion and politics, as was experienced in Western democracies.

Actually, quite the opposite occurred. The use of Western secular techniques in law and the constitutions created a strong connection between Islam and politics, and contributed to redefining Islam *as a political norm* in ways unknown under the Muslim empires (see Yavuz 2003: 52). My position, then, is that the making of Islam as a modern religion, whereby norms, organisations and actors have been defined as Islamic, has been closely related to the making of the modern state.

One of my major conclusions drawn from the data analysis that will be presented below is that modern religion in Muslim countries is positioned on the platform of the state. The institutionalisation of religion occurs through the reconfiguration of relationships between people, property, and organisations that were 'religious' but formerly outside the political control of the state apparatus (Ashiwa and Wank 2009: 45). The state actions described in the following highlight the efforts by the modern nation-state to make Islam into both an organisational framework and an ideology of practice (Ashiwa and Wank 2009: 70). Modernity is thus not constituted by a one-sided state-driven project to discipline people's thoughts, but 'multiple projects or, rather a series of interlinked projects' (Ashiwa and Wank 2009: 45) whereby states and religions reshape each other and, in the process, redefine themselves. While this recalibration of religion by the modern state happened everywhere, in the West its outcome was autonomy of religious institutions from the state, whereas, in most Muslim countries, the trajectory has been in the opposite direction. This counter-trajectory is a challenge for the dominant Western theories of secularisation and democratisation.

The difference between the Western experience and the Muslim countries lies in the institutional arrangement of state–religion relations. In the West, secularism has translated into a legal order that preserves the right both to believe and not to believe, in essence defending their practical equality, even as the balance between competitive sets of beliefs is challenging to maintain, as illustrated by the claims of Christian fundamentalists or the European tensions around Islamic dress codes in public spaces. In Muslim countries on the other hand, the building of the nation-state led to the fusion of Islam and political institutions, in ways that were unknown in the pre-modern era. As a consequence, the 'secular age' came to be embodied in a ubiquitous hegemonic version of Islam, even in countries considered secular, such as Egypt, Turkey, and Iraq, which will serve as case studies in the analysis that unfolds.

Making the state, making the religion[1]

Prior to the states, it is possible to detect the diffusion of western concepts of politics during the Ottoman Empire's reign and amid the rise of Western imperialism. The symbolic moment of this process was the inclusion of the Ottoman Empire within the Westphalian order under the Treaty of Paris in 1856. The treaty itself ended the Crimean War and was the first time the Ottoman Empire participated as a 'state' in the Westphalian order. Hence, it opened the possibility for non-European polities to be part of the international legal community and form alliances with the west (Burgis 2009: 40). In the aftermath of this symbolic inclusion, three disparate factors contributed to the adoption of the Westphalian state system in the Middle East in the first half of the twentieth century: the fall of imperial governments in the region; the rise of local nationalist movements in urban centres, such as Cairo, Tunis, Baghdad, and Damascus; and the emergence of states with demarcated territorial boundaries that pursued self-interests and experienced hostile territorial disputes with neighbouring states. Pro-western, liberal 'civilisationalism' also became the dominant paradigm of the Ottoman modernists and reformists, despite strong internal resistance and protests against the imperialism of Western powers. This opposition was present because of the population's objection to the western critique that the Caliphate was not 'civilised' enough to gain the loyalty of its Christian subjects, which subsequently led to two different movements: Pan-Islamism and Pan-Arabism (Aydin 2007: 32).

Pan-Islamism and Pan-Arabism were reactions to the rise of western liberalisation rhetoric and imperialist threats in the Ottoman Empire. Pan-Islamism was an intellectual and political movement that viewed the universal Islamic community (*Ummah*) as the ideal basis and source for modern political unity, in which the life and works of the Prophet Mohammed and his first four successors served as the model for the political project. Towards the end of the Ottoman Empire, a western threat became more acute with the European incursions into Egypt and Tunisia in 1798 and 1881, respectively. These imperialist exploits greatly impacted nineteenth-century reformers, such as Jamal al-Din al-Afghani (1838–97) and his disciple Muhammad Abduh (1849–1905), who urged all Muslims to unite under *al-Wahda al-Islamiyya* (Muslim unity) in the face of western imperialism in their journal *al-Urwa al-Wuthqa* (The Firmest Bond) (Aydin 2007: 61). The popularity of the Ottoman Caliphate also increased, as the Caliph was recognised as the head of the Muslim State, on a diplomatic par with the western powers (Aydin 2007: 33). Accordingly, the Pan-Islamic ideology refashioned the concept of the Caliph, emphasising his status as the Prophet Muhammad's vice-regent, in order to buttress the Empire's legitimacy in the international state system.

Thus, in direct resistance to the international norm of the nation-state, Pan-Islamism became an ideological approach to the political community in the Ottoman lands, and the transnational vision of Pan-Islamic solidarity served as a geopolitical tool (Aydin 2007: 60). For example, at the onset of World War I, the Ottoman Empire initiated propaganda that utilised pan-Islamic ideas and fomented Muslim disobedience against the Western colonisers (Aydin 2007: 109–10). As a result of the establishment of Muslim states after World War II, 'a rethinking of the feasibility of political pan-Islam gradually led to a search for alternative propositions, more acceptable to Muslim entities. The political goal of a unitary Islamic State was replaced by a goal of unity in Islamic policies' (Landau 1990: 249). However, Pan-Islamism in the form of calls to recreate the *Ummah* by political leaders, activists, and Islamist ideologues was maintained, recreated, and gradually became associated with the increasingly fundamentalist Salafiyya movement. Additionally, it is important to note that, even after World War I, Pan-Islamism was not an ideology of indiscriminate hatred or rejection of the West. The reformulation of Pan-Islamism as a categorically anti-western ideology happened after World War II and formed the basis for the anti-modernist and reactionary positions of future Islamist groups, such as al-Qaeda. In this perspective, Pan-Islamism shared with its secular counterparts of Pan-Arabism or nationalist movements, the idea that the West had to be emulated. Western politics or culture was not 'wrong' or bad; its domination was.

Emerging at the same time as Pan-Islamism, Pan-Arabism was a political movement which reached its height in the 1960s, and was centred on the idea that all Arab peoples, as a linguistic and cultural community, should unite under one banner. Its origins were in the *al-Nahda* cultural renaissance that took place during the late nineteenth and early twentieth centuries with the revival of Arabic poetry and literature and the rise of the print media (Khalidi 1991). This cultural 'awakening', as a rejection of Western cultural norms, was partially a response to the Western influence. But, politically, Pan-Arabism was first endorsed by Sharif Hussein bin Ali (1908–17), the Sharif of Mecca, who wanted to gain independence from the Ottoman Empire. In espousing an Arabist political vision, he inspired the Arab Revolts of 1916. As the ideology of Arab nationalism gained popularity across the Middle Eastern province, and the British began to ally with the Arabs, the Ottoman Empire began to slowly crumble (Wilson 1991: 204–31). Pan-Arabism inevitably competed with Pan-Islamism, and, from then on, political projects diverged between those based on the *Ummah* and those based on cultural and territorial nationalism (Willis 2010: 711).

As Acharya's localisation framework suggests, local actors in Muslim-majority countries resisted Western norms because of fears that these new norms could undermine existing beliefs and practices. As a result, both the Pan-Islamic and Pan-Arab movements came to shape resistance to foreign domination in all Muslim-majority countries after the collapse of the Ottoman Empire. Hence, campaigns of resistance against the West framed and depicted European modernisation, along with its nation-building and secularisation components, through the lens of Islamic terminology, as in opposition to an essential Arab identity in the Middle East.

A brief review of the resistance movements in Egypt, Syria, Iraq, Turkey, and Tunisia illustrates this point. Egypt became the core location of the Salafiyya intellectual and political movement, which employs a revivified Islamic ethos as a major tool against a Western imperialism that would influence the whole Muslim world. Mohammad Abduh (1849–1905), a disciple of the 'father' of Pan-Islamism al-Afghani, reinterpreted the basic principles of Islam in the light of modern reason (Harris 1964: 116). While arguing that Islamic principles were consistent with modern Western rules of logic, Abduh simultaneously promoted an intellectual and cultural programme to fight Western imperialism, rather than a physical war. In 1905, one of Abduh's followers Shaykh Rashid Rida (1865–1935), founder of the journal *al-Manar*, continued Abduh's legacy, but added a more activist element (Harris 1964: 130). Reflecting on the 'Golden Age' of Islam when the Caliphate was the sole spiritual and political authority for the entire Islamic community (Eickelman and Piscatori 1996: 31). and acknowledging that resurrecting such a Caliphate would be impossible given contemporary realities, Rida called instead for the unity of all Muslims under the leadership of a renewed Caliph.

These ideas strongly influenced the activism of Hassan al-Banna (1906–49), the founder of the Muslim Brotherhood. From its inception in 1928, the Brotherhood's objective was to provide an Islamic alternative to the influence of Western culture and politics. Al-Banna borrowed from Abduh and Rida the idea that Islam could be a tool of intellectual resistance to Western culture and imperialism. At the time of its creation, the Brotherhood's objectives competed with more secular nationalist agendas. This was especially true when, as a sign of King Faruq's (1936–52) Pan-Islamist ideals, an alliance between the monarchy and the Muslim Brotherhood took place in the 1940s to counter the nationalist and secular Wafd party (Mitchell 1993: 16).

However, the Muslim Brotherhood also went through several phases of conflict with various nationalist groups and leaders of the nation-state over the course of the following decades. During and after World War II, the Muslim Brotherhood society created a private military apparatus to support the Arab revolts against the British colonial presence, and allied with Germany, which led to accusations of disloyalty against the Brotherhood by King Faruq. The conflicts with the State increasingly intensified under Gamal Abdel Nasser (1956–70) and his successors.

In Syria, the creation of the Ba'ath Party in 1956 was the direct outcome of the political influence of Pan-Arabism. At this time, this was the 'creed of all political activists' in the region, and the founders of the Ba'ath Party Michel Aflaq (1910–89) and Salah Bitar (1912–80) came to embody this broad-based territorial–nationalist movement and reiterated the threat of cultural and political Westernisation to the Pan-Arab ideal. This political project led to tentative unifications such as the United Arab Republic (1958–61) between Egypt and Syria. The relations of the early Ba'athist leaders with Islam were ambiguous. On the one hand, Aflaq was a secular Christian, but on the other hand, he considered Islam as an integral component of the Arab nation (Anderson and Stansfield 2004: 66). As Aflaq envisioned it, Arabism was an ideology 'whose Spirit is Islam' (Anderson and Stansfield 2004: 66). Despite this inclusion of Islam in the Pan-Arabist ideals, the party's political and governing structures were secular.

Similarly, in Iraq, the Ba'ath Party gained power due to the widespread belief in Pan-Arab nationalism, in addition to popular resistance to foreign influences on the government and the strong desire to break the power of the oppressive, ruling elite (Devlin 1991: 1404). Such circumstances eventually led to the rise of Saddam Hussein in 1979 as head of state and the construction of Iraq as a unified Arab nation. As biographer Felicia Okeke-Ibezim describes, 'Saddam [saw] himself as a proud Arab nationalist ... the defender of Holy Islam ... [and] a valiant knight leading the Arabs into a battle against the infidel' (Okeke-Ibezim 2006: 9). Thus, Saddam implemented policies that emphasised Arab unity, such as his Arab National Charter in 1980, to increase co-operation towards common goals in the Arab world. Further, with the change of governance in nearby Iran in 1979 and the subsequent Iran–Iraq War (1980–8), the Ba'ath Party agenda faced competition from the Pan-Islamist agenda of the Iranian Islamic Republic. As a result, Saddam's agenda increasingly downplayed Islamic identities in order to foster a nationalism that distinguished Arab Iraq from the neighbouring Islamic republic in Iran.

Turkey offers a different case of norm diffusion because the nation-building project was the direct outcome of tensions and conflicts within the Ottoman Empire around Pan-Islamic and Pan-Arabist trends. The last Ottoman sultans, such as Abdulhamid II (1876–1909), used Pan-Islamic ideas to promote imperial unity and maintain their control over different parts of the empire that had been penetrated by Western political ideas (Karpat 2002: 46, 125). As Kemal Karpat suggests, 'religious' activities were used to 'nationalise' the millets[2] of the Ottoman dynasty (Karpat 2002: 229). Abdulhamid repaired holy sites in Mecca, Medina, and Karbala, renovated mosques and schools throughout the empire, and gave priority to the printing and distribution of the Qur'an to his subjects (Karpat 2002: 231). These activities reinforced his position as the Caliph in the eyes of subjects for whom Islam was a significant marker of identity.

In the final years of the Ottoman Empire, the Young Turk movement (beginning in 1908) emerged as an alternative political project to the reinforcement of the Caliphate. Young Turk Ahmet Riza (1859–1930) was known for his attempts to reconcile Islam with Western ideas. As suggested by Umat Azak, Riza's project was an 'anti-clerical struggle to refashion Islam as a private matter and as a rational belief comparable with modernization' (Azak 2010: 5–6). In other words, the Young Turk movement was not necessarily anti-Islam but fought against the Caliphate's version of the religion–state relationship. Confronted with independence movements (Armenian, Greek, etc.) sprouting throughout the empire, the Young Turks emphasised their own 'Turkishness', spread the idea of a Turkish nation, and promoted a local form of Islam where prayers and sermons would be performed in the Turkish language (Karpat 2002: 305). With the collapse of the Ottoman Empire at the end of World War I, the nationalist movement gained complete ascendancy in the former provinces of the empire and led to the creation of modern Turkey.

In Tunisia, allegiance to the *Ummah* was manifested in a pervasive loyalty to the Caliphate as a way to resist reforms initiated by the modernist elite under French influence, such as Mohammad as-Sadiq Bey (1859–81). From 1864 until 1881, after France became the official protector of the country with the Treaty of Bardo, Pan-Islamist ideals induced continuous unrest against the urban Westernized elites that asserted their supremacy.[3] Subsequently, in the wake of World War I, the sense of transcontinental Islamic belonging, stemming from solidarity with the Ottomans, persisted with the formation of the Destour Party in 1920. The leader of the party Sheikh Abdelaziz Taalbi (1920–34) spoke little French and was a student of the Salafiyya movement (Moore 1956: 27). The party's membership drew from the educated elite who were fluent in Islamic and Arabic cultures (in contrast to the elite that drew its references from the West). Although it ultimately accepted the existence of the French Protectorate, the party elite viewed European influences as obstacles to a Muslim renaissance.

Destour was the predecessor to the Neo-Destour Party that arose in 1934 and spearheaded the nationalist movement under Habib Bourguiba (1957–87). With the formation of the Neo-Destour Party, the Islamic connections to nationalism were minimised and thus began to fade. However, although Bourguiba would later be known for his secular orientation and his dismantling of Islamic institutions and political neutralisation of the *ulama* during the anticolonial movement, he was often referred to as *al-Mujahid ul-Akbar* (the great warrior) (Brett 1998: 126–8).[4] Moreover, Bourguiba relied on Islamic institutions and symbols to mobilise the masses in the anticolonial jihad. For instance, his party held meetings in mosques and *zawiyas* (Sufi meeting places), and urged the public to pray five times a day for the national martyrs (Boulby 1988: 592). This treatment of Islam is in stark contrast with his policy after Tunisian independence in 1956, as the Personal Status Law 1957 abolished *Shari'a* courts, banned the *hijab*, and restricted polygamy. This brought into focus Tunisia's French influences and a secular–nationalist identity over an Arab–Islamic identity (Esposito 1999). In other words, during the fight for Tunisian independence, Islam was part of the rhetoric against colonial powers, but after independence, Islam was typically painted as a symbol of the past; Westernisation was deemed representative of the newly formed country's future.

Nation-building and framing of new norms

Advocates for new norms use language that is familiar to the local community that 'names, interprets, and dramatizes them' to better adapt these new norms to local norms (Acharya 2004: 243). These processes often occur simultaneously and cannot be entirely pulled apart. That is, framing may lead to adoption of a new norm, and adoption of a new norm may in turn lead to more framing.

The nation-building process in Muslim countries resulted in a decisive re-organisation of the society–state–religion nexus that was unknown in the pre-modern era. Under the Caliphate, Islamic institutions and clerics had not been subordinated to political power. Most scholars of political history (Enayat 2005; Lapidus 2002) argue that divisions of labour and hierarchies of power between temporal and spiritual authorities were fairly well established by the tenth century. In the medieval period, there were certainly 'official' *Ulama* working on behalf of political rulers and providing religious justification for their policies, which is similar to the modern period. However, the major difference with the modern time is that religious authorities and institutions were financially and organisationally independent from the political power.

The Caliphs also acknowledged the cultural and religious diversity of society, although it did not translate into an egalitarian legal and political status for all religions and ethnicities. The *Ummah* was defined as the sum of the territories and populations under the Caliphate rule, hence encompassing an extensive distribution of ethnic, cultural, and linguistic groups, including Muslims, Christians, Jews, Zoroastrians, Bahais, and Druzes. Even though the Caliphate represented the example of the original community that followed the message of the Prophet Mohammad, in reality its power was limited by geography and comparable to that of any secular dynasty ruling multiple ethnic and religious groups (Hourani 1988: 12). This tension between the ideal (of a community following the model of the Prophet) and the political reality was apparent in the distinction between *Shari'a* and *Syar* forged by the juris-consultes. *Shari'a* referred to the laws that apply to

Muslims, while *Syar* designed the laws that apply to non-Muslims living under Caliphate rule, or to the relations between the Caliphate and the non-Muslims at the international level (Burgis 2009: 40). In contrast, the modern vision of the *Ummah* is removed from this imperial definition; the consensus among Muslim scholars is that the *Ummah* refers to a spiritual, non-territorial community distinguished by the shared beliefs of its members. The *Ummah* is therefore often seen as a type of citizenship that all Muslims have, independent of territory (Hassan 2002: 94). Contemporary theologian Yusuf al Qaradawi, in the context of the Palestinian national movement, illustrates this more contemporary and predominant vision of the *Ummah* as a transnational alliance of Muslims that excludes non-Muslims: 'Supporting the Palestinian people in Gaza is a religious duty on every Muslim individual [from Morocco to Indonesia] according to his capabilities, and no one is exempted from that duty' (Hassan 2002).

As the Ottoman Empire collapsed, the emergence of the state as the central political institution went hand in hand with the homogenisation of the different national communities. That is, nation building systematically omitted and sometimes eradicated particular ethnic, religious, and linguistic groups in order to create one nation defined by one religion and one language. This homogenisation process also led to a politicised narrative of religion, i.e. political Islam. In this regard, Muslim countries are not exceptional; with the advent of the modern nation-state, the rules of engagement between religion and politics have been redefined everywhere. However, this does mean that, contrary to the dominant liberal narrative, religion has not become politically irrelevant (Eliade 1961: 205–6).[6]

At the same time, the architects of the new nation-states outside of the Western world had to determine to what degree the 'core' collective identity of the country should be sacrificed in exchange for the Western institutions and technologies necessary to strengthen the state both militarily and economically (Duara 1995). Each state that faced this dilemma has responded differently. In the case of nations built after the collapse of the Ottoman Empire, the diffusion of international norms of statehood was decisive in the fabrication of Islam as a political religion. The emergence of new political norms tied to nationalism generally resulted in state narratives that either referenced Islamic terminology or were diversely articulated within an Islamic framework. Localisation of these norms occurred as state actors employed strategies of entrepreneurship and reframed them using local vocabulary (Acharya 2004: 239–75). As noted above, both Pan-Islamism and Pan-Arabism contributed to the broad appeal of nationalist discourse (Mufti 1996). In other words, Islamic references and norms were used to 'localise' the nation-building process and legitimise state actors and policies. The outcome of such localisation was the redefinition of Islam within the new state institutions.

The adoption of outside norms into local contexts involved both grafting and pruning, two tactics often employed by local actors to institutionalise external norms by associating them with pre-existing ones. Here, linkages have to be constructed and carefully articulated by proponents of new norms, because the links are not always intuitive or seemingly natural. In Muslim countries, pruning and grafting have primarily taken place through three mechanisms: references to Islam in the Constitution, nationalisation of Islamic institutions, and the incorporation of Islam in the legal system. In sum, the localisation phase has entailed the marshalling of four domains to appropriate Islam as a tool for the elaboration of the nation-state. These domains are:

- the constitutional inscription of Islam
- the nationalization of Islamic institutions and clerics
- Islam in the legal system
- the integration of Islam in public education.

Political Islam as national culture[7]

With the creation of a state education system, the curricula and textbooks of public education have socialised new generations to the idea that national identity and Islamic identity are two sides of the same coin. By inscribing Islam within the public education system, the state posits itself as the protector of the Islamic heritage, and assumes 'the responsibility to provide children and youths with trustworthy religious guidance' (Starrett 1998: 5).

National unity comes from two sources: the first is the cultivation of national brotherhood (internal cohesion) against outsiders, including external and internal threats and enemies, and regardless of sectarian divisions. Because nationalism is about difference, 'the imagined community cannot be all-inclusive' (Durrani and Dunne 2010: 218). As a result, the second source is the exclusivist discourses of nationalism, which have implications for citizenship, access to political power, and the allocation of resources (Durrani and Dunne 2010: 230). This means that the state excludes those who do not belong to the dominant group within its discursive project of establishing ideological hegemony and constructing the national identity through education.

But the underlying and more pervasive source of exclusion is the use of Islam within the education system to homogenise the nation. Despite more recent initiatives to focus on tolerance in the curricula, religious minorities are still neglected and discriminated against within most of the curricula of public education. Also, because the concept of tolerance is only promoted in the religious context, other parts of the curricula (history/social studies) that are also influenced by Islamic terms such as *jihad* remain within a militant context and continue to instil ideas of Islamic supremacy and uniting against 'infidels'.

In this regard, it is important to note that Islamic references are not limited to religious education, but are also incorporated throughout the entire public school curriculum. They permeate history, social studies, civics textbooks, and even appear in mathematics (Daun and Walford 2004: 113). Such a 'functionalisation of religion', as Gregory Starrett terms it (Starrett 1998: 10), illustrates the socialisation process at work, in which the state exerts social control and assumes moral authority by promoting a 'proper Islamic identity', and by extension, cultivation of 'good social behavior' (*âdâb ijtimâ'îya*) of 'good' citizens. For example, in primary school Egyptian textbooks, the school is portrayed as the source of the child's moral learnings, which the child will then share with his/her family (Starrett 1998: 143). Thus, while Egyptian textbooks focus on responsibility and duty as main Muslim values (Pink 2004), these are virtues taught by the schools (and thus, by the state), not by independent groups. Similarly in Turkey, the Directorate of Religious Affairs was created under the office of the prime minister, and its responsibilities include administering Islamic affairs with the objective 'to create "good citizens" with civic responsibility toward the State' (Yavuz 2003: 49). In this way, the Turkish state has tried to control Islam and, through public education, disseminated Islam towards its own nationalising and secularising goals.

We collected and analysed primary and secondary school textbooks from Iraq, Egypt, Turkey, Tunisia, and Pakistan used over the period 2000–03 (Pakistan is not discussed in this chapter). The textbooks we focused on were Islamic education textbooks (reflected in a variety of names: 'Islamic Insight', 'Religious Studies', 'Islamic Culture and Religious Studies', etc.) and history and 'National and Civic Education' textbooks. We performed a content analysis to discover the association between Islamic religious terms (*jihad, ummah*) and political terms (nation, state, citizen); the connotations linked to other religions; and the conception of the West.

Ummah *vs.* nation

References to the *Ummah* in textbooks show that the legitimisation of the national community builds on the concept of the *Ummah*. As a result, however, such a reference complicates issues of citizenship and national identity because, while religious identity bolsters national unity, it also undermines national distinctiveness because of the sense of allegiance to the larger Islamic community. Naureen Durrani and Mairead Dunne sum the topic up capably: 'religious identity transcends national boundaries but national identity requires identification with a particular geographical place'. The idea of Islam as central to one's identity places priority on the *Ummah* over the nation, and, as a result, the state grants symbolic supremacy to the *Ummah* in terms of religious solidarity.

In the case of Egypt, religious educational texts have gone through two phases: the Pan-Arabist focus under Nasser and Sadat, and the nationalist/Egypt-first emphasis under Mubarak. The first phase under Sadat illustrates the political instrumentalisation of the *Ummah* under nation-state regimes while also asserting the primacy of the Egyptian identity. As shown by Olivier Carre, 72 per cent of the content of religious education was devoted to political and social matters (al-Sibai 1969; O'Kane 1972). The texts showed that the *Ummah* is superior to the Arab nation and to the country of Egypt; however, the Arab nation and culture should work for the good of the Muslim *Ummah*, as Arab unity is regarded as an essential article of the Islamic faith. One text quoted in Carre gives this invocation: 'O God! Bring to us unity! O God! Re-unite the Arabs in one nation. When that happens [...] they will form the most powerful, the richest, the most knowledgeable and the most important of nations!' (Carre [date]) The Muslim *Ummah* and the Arab nation inter-mesh and reinforce each other. Carre concludes, 'The texts call young Egyptians to feel and think of themselves as Arabs above all and to apply to their Arabism and their sense of identity with the Muslim *Ummah.*' Moreover, while the textbooks emphasised Arab socialism, Saeed points out that the books and curricula of the Nasser period were marked by a façade of secularism, but are in fact very much influenced by fundamentalist Islamic beliefs (Saeed 1994: 138).

In the second phase, the national identity takes precedence. Even religious textbooks focus on allegiance to Egypt as the *watan* or homeland, and, in the 2002–03 textbooks, there is almost no reference to Arabism or the Islamic *Ummah.* For instance, the first-year primary textbook tells a tale of how Allah saved the *watan* or homeland of the Meccans from the 'Ashab al-Feel' (the People of the Elephant) and concludes with a poem that goes:

And you, Muslim student, have to love your homeland (*watan*)

And defend it if it is attacked by any aggressor

Because you live in it and eat from its food

And drink from the water of its blessed Nile.

The focus on the iconic Nile River clearly promotes national identity, which is in direct contrast to the first phase when education revolved around the central idea of Arab nationalism in order to reinforce Arab over Egyptian identity.

Because the modern state has politicised Islam by conflating national identity with religious identity, the supremacy of the *Ummah* is tempered by the textbooks' promotion of allegiance to the state and the state's version of Islam. At the same time, there is still a tension between the *Ummah* and the nation in national identity formation in the varying levels of reference to the *Ummah* among the different countries' curricula. Even when the textbooks depict the *Ummah* as the point of reference, it is important to note that they also propagate each particular state's version of Islam as the true Islam of the *Ummah.* Moreover, the tension between the *Ummah* and the nation is simultaneously manipulated and manifested by many Islamists' rival political agendas to the state and the competing nationalist (modernist) and Islamist (traditionalist) approaches to education.[8] Islamists believe and criticize that 'Islamic education' has been confined to a separate subject instead of rightfully defining the outlook of the entire educational system.

Thus, each state propagates a unique representation of the Muslim identity tailored to forge national identity, promote national unity and cement state authority. Furthermore, each country's curriculum reflects local histories, the degree of Islamist clout in educational policy as well as the specific policy interests of the state. However, the textbook representations of Muslim identity do share four common characterisations of Islam, which further promote unity and reinforce state authority: blurring of sectarian divisions to promote a singular and unified Islam; fostering national 'uniqueness' through a master narrative of victimisation to inculcate a sense of unity against oppressors and representations of conflict, which often includes discussion of *jihad*; building this uniqueness on the implicitly or explicitly proclaimed superiority of Islam; and, relatedly, misrepresenting or omitting Christians and Jews.

Islam as singular and monolithic

No country is religiously homogeneous, but textbooks in Muslim-majority countries essentialise Islam as a monolithic religion and deny through omission the existence of Islamic sects. Since Christian minorities are often acknowledged by state laws, Christian students are exempted from Islamic education or are sometimes offered alternative Christian education. However, Islamic sectarian minorities are not exempted from Islamic education classes, which teach a tradition that is not their own. Although each country's curriculum espouses a different version of Islam, they all avoid sectarian distinctions by simultaneously promoting a singular representation of Islam and scrupulously not mentioning any Islamic sect by name. As a result, Islamic references are used to forge a fictitious and homogeneous community within the state and in the *Ummah*.

In all countries studied, religious education is compulsory, and, for adherents of all Islamic sects, the Sunni tradition of the dominant group is taught as the sole version of Islam. Perhaps most interesting is the case of Turkey, which, as a 'secular' state, promotes Islam as primarily Turkish, 'existing in a vacuum apart from its Middle Eastern context, oblivious to existing sectarian or minority differences, and serving as a locus of identity for feelings of Turkish nationalism' (Altan 2007: 212). Hakan Yavuz terms this Turkification of Islam as 'internal secularization' because the state imagines and promotes this vision of Islam in terms of modern concepts such as nationalism (Yavuz 2003: 5). On the flipside, Islamic intellectuals and movements engage in the 'vernacularization of modernity', which means redefining the discourses of modernity (such as nationalism and secularism) in their own Islamic terms (Yavuz 2003: 5). Thus, the contradiction of a secular state with compulsory religious education is reconciled by the fact that 'Islamic knowledge is reformulated and presented in a way that functionalizes Islam, equating religious study with any other subject' (Yavuz 2003: 202). Religious instruction is advertised as necessary and obligatory because Islamic values are practical and useful to society. Moreover, religion acts as divine legitimisation 'for the pillars of the official ideology of the "secular" State' (Yavuz 2003: 212).

According to Article 24 of the Turkish Constitution:

Education and instruction in religion and ethics shall be conducted under State supervision and control. Instruction in religious culture and moral education shall be compulsory in the curricula of primary and secondary schools. Other religious education and instruction shall be subject to the individual's own desire, and in the case of minors, to the request of their legal representatives.

(Kocak 2010: 245).

While the last part of Article 24 is an important caveat, it is clear that it is not upheld, especially towards Alevi students who are required to attend lessons in religious culture and ethics promoting Sunni Islam (National Secular Society 2007). Thus, the teaching of religion allows the state to further its vision of a Turkish–Sunni society by using compulsory religious education classes to teach Islam as a Turkish religion reflecting the Sunni Islamic interpretation. As a result, the textbooks emphasise the conflation of Turkishness and Islam by including pictures of mosques and holy shrines in Turkey and presenting all Muslim scholars as Turkish, while cutting off Islamic history after the Turks accepted Islam (Altan 2007: 203). In addition to inculcating the idea of Turkish Islam, textbooks do not mention sectarian divisions within Islam or the religious minorities of Turkey, implying that there is no alternative to the Turkish–Sunni identity.

Egypt, Tunisia, and Iraq constitutionally declare Islam as the state religion, but the teaching of Islam in each country varies according to the social and religious features of the society as well as of the political orientation of the regime. In Tunisia and Egypt, under authoritarian rulers, compulsory religious education was aimed at discrediting Islamists within their own societies. During Saddam's regime in Iraq, textbooks emphasised homogeneity and denied the Sunni–Shi'a sectarian divide in order to impose unity on Iraqi society.

While both Islam and Christianity are taught in Egyptian public schools, parents cannot choose the religion their children are taught at school. According to Article 19 of Egypt's constitution: 'Religious education shall be a principal subject in the courses of general education'. If one of the parents is Muslim, the child is considered Muslim and will be placed accordingly. The tradition of Islam taught in schools is Sunni Islam, without distinction between the different schools or any mention of Shi'ism (Aldeeb 2000). According to Toronto and Eissa's study on Islamic education in Egypt, 'the curriculum, from beginning to end, leaves Muslim students with the impression that Sunni Islam is the only and correct version of Islam in existence' (Toronto and Eissa 2007: 44). Such teaching contradicts the reality that Egyptian students live in. Although there are not many Shi'ites in Egypt, there are several mosque-shrines dedicated to Shi'ite figures that are visited and celebrated by Sunni and Shi'ite alike. Additionally, the lack of information on Sufism in public religious education is in stark contrast to the Sufi influence and presence at all levels of Egyptian society (Toronto and Eissa 2007: 45). Nowhere are sectarian identities discussed, lest they induce fragmentation and subsequent instability of the national identity, and instead, the majority Sunni Islamic tradition is offered as 'the' Egyptian norm.

The educational system was one of the main arenas of tension and competition between the state and the Islamists (Toronto and Eissa 2007: 30). Thus, while the Egyptian state's education focuses on national identity over the idea of belonging to the greater *Ummah*, the Islamists argue, the focus in Islamic education should not be to reinforce national identity but rather to uphold the nation-transcending Muslim community (*Ummah*) (Saeed 1994: 224). However, school textbooks in Egypt maintain the state's religious legitimacy, because they reflect adherence to traditional methods of education: memorisation and oral recitation, and source materials such as the Qu'ran, Hadith, biographies of prominent Muslims, and *Shari'a*. Additionally, the objectives of the curricula include teaching the proper recitation of the Qu'ran, rituals, and correct Islamic dress and behaviour.

Despite this traditionalist approach, the main purpose of the curriculum is not to teach the Islamic tradition but to provide religious legitimacy to state policies. For example, at some specific political periods, textbooks were directed towards fighting and discrediting extremist Islamist groups, in an attempt to win the hearts and minds of the people. Hence, public education in Egypt aims to construct an identity based on the pre-eminence of Sunni Islam as a source of values for a national identity (Toronto and Eissa 2007). For example, textbooks stress the importance of 'loving the homeland which God bestowed on us. ... Our noble religion commands us to develop it, to work for its glory and to defend its land and people' (Seventh year, second semester Islamic education textbook 2002–03: 30). In a lesson to first graders about the topic of love, the textbook offers a row of illustrations about recommended objects of love, the first being 'the flag of my country', followed by the teacher, family, and friends (Pink 2004).

Under Saddam Hussein, a Sunni version of Islam was promoted in Iraqi textbooks, despite the fact that the majority of the population is Shi'a. It included Sunni prayer stances and a certain bias towards the Sunni version of Islamic history. Further, most books contained Saddam's image, and all social studies, civics, history books – as well as Islamic history – included substantial content on the history and ideology of the Baath party. Students were instructed in the importance of 'loyalty to the (Arab) people and to the leadership of "the Party" and the revolution' (Iraqi Ministry of Education 2001a: 29). Islam was used consistently to support such indoctrination: the party's history was presented in the context of early Islamic history (lessons on the first Muslims were taught alongside that of modern-day Iraq) (Iraqi Ministry of Education 1988: 33), while the party's ideology was presented within that of Islamic teachings. Modern Iraqi and Baath party history were taught alongside early Islamic history, with Saddam depicted as their champion. The Iran–Iraq war of 1980–8 was presented in Arab and Islamic history textbooks as a modern version of the seventh-century Arab–Islamic victory over the Persians in the battle of Qaddisiyya:

The battle of Qaddissiya of our ancestors was repeated by the champion of Arabism and Islam, our leader Saddam Hussein (may Allah protect and guide him) against the Persian enemy.

(Iraqi Ministry of Education 1999: 58)

The Saddam curriculum also aimed to indoctrinate students with the belief in a homogeneous Iraqi society. Ethnic and cultural diversity was downplayed and little mention was made of any distinct groups. On the other hand, proclamations of coexistence and cooperation were frequent. Students were told that 'Iraqis feel unified; they cooperate and are proud of their deep connection to one another.' This so-called camaraderie, a common theme especially at the primary level, was taught by way of discounting distinct characteristics and maintaining an appearance of an homogeneous Iraq. The theme in the excerpt below, taken from a seventh grade social studies book, is echoed throughout the curriculum:

> The people of Iraq are a single firm unit – from the north to the south ... Living together for thousands of years generated unity between (the Iraqi) people. Iraqi blood was fused in its defense.
>
> (Iraqi Ministry of Education 2001b: 12)

Despite the proclaimed secularism of Baathist ideology, Islamic references were often used to facilitate its legitimation. Quotes from the Qu'ran were interspersed throughout lessons highlighting Baath principles. A lesson instructing students to limit their materialistic consumption for the sake of their country and nation (*umma*) is accompanied by the Qu'ranic saying, 'Those who squander are the brothers of Satan'. By conserving and avoiding materialism, students were taught, they will 'triumph against the greed of the American, British, and Zionist enemies' (Iraqi Ministry of Education 2001b: 37).

After the United States invaded Iraq and ended the Saddam regime in 2003, the new Ministry of Education's General Curriculum Directorate, in partnership with UNESCO and USAID, established a committee for curriculum development in order to drastically change the nature and content of religious teaching. The committee comprised Iraqi educators and education experts chosen by the US, who consulted with other local leaders in education, particularly Islamic education (Hadithi 2010: 58; 'A new history of Iraq', *The Guardian* 2003). The massive endeavour to provide Iraq's 16,000 schools with revised study materials began with the removal of all images of Saddam Hussein and Baath content from textbooks. A subsequent step involved the introduction of new materials that would promote tolerance, respect, and appreciation for a pluralistic Iraqi society by recognising its religious and ethnic components rather than discounting them.

In a broad sense, the prevalence of abstract concepts of tolerance in the Saddam-era curriculum was likely a factor in the decision to continue the use of some old textbooks, with revisions, in the new curriculum (this is especially the case with regard to Islamic studies). A significant shift however, is evident in the new curriculum with regard to specific Iraqi social groups, which were conspicuously ignored in the Saddam-era textbooks. This shift includes revisions in civics, social studies, and history texts teaching students about Iraq's 'ethnic and religious diversity' (Sixth grade social studies, *iraqicurricula.org*: 14), mentioning different Iraqi ethnic and religious groups by name, such as Kurds, Turkmen, Yazidis, Sabians, and Christians (Seventh grade civics, *iraqicurricula.org*: 8). While Saddam-era textbooks also mention Christians, they do so only in the context of ancient Islamic history and Jesus as a Muslim prophet. Jews, despite having been a significant component of Iraqi society for centuries, are mentioned in a limited sense in both the old and new curricula, in the context of relations with Mohammad in ancient Islamic history and with regard to the Zionist movement and Palestine.

One of the major revisions in Iraqi textbooks has been the recognition of Shi'a groups, as opposed to the original textbooks, which contained a Sunni bias. This recognition of religious and sectarian diversity, while being a goal in itself, is also the basis for a unified, stable Iraq and has been out of reach since the end of the Saddam Hussein era. Since 2003, the curriculum has undergone continuous change and several revised versions have been printed, only to be retracted due to public opposition. Many claim that the changes have been politically motivated, and a significant number of politicians, along with religious authorities, have been at the centre of what has become a high profile debate (*Niqash* (2010) 'Throwing old textbooks out'). And while most opponents claim that the new texts promote Shi'a interpretations of Islam at the expense of Sunni Islam, complaints run the gamut of the political and religious spectrum: some feel that Sunnis are being discriminated against, while others assert that not enough has been done to rectify Sunni bias against Shias (*Google* Answers. 'What are Iraqi students learning in regards to Islamic classes and history?' *Arabic Translation*). Still others claim that, despite years of revisions, the curriculum still closely resembles that of the Saddam era (Personal conversation with Dr. Jalal). Many also felt that the US was overstepping its boundaries with regard to Iraq's internal affairs, especially in 2003 following reports that USAID had demanded that religious reference be limited or banned from certain texts (Wang 2005). Some Islamic religious authorities, already wary of US interference, saw the curriculum project as an American plan to westernise Iraqi schools. Sheikh Abdul Settar Jabber, who headed a leading Sunni religious group at the time, called the curriculum project a US attempt to 'break Iraqi identity' (*The Guardian* (2003) 'A new history of Iraq'). At the time of writing, the debate continues and no consensus has been reached on the content of the curriculum (Mohammad 2010).

One of the most contentious points of the debate has been over the way in which prayer is taught at the primary level. Though prayers under Saddam followed Sunni doctrine, the instructional images that accompanied them were ambiguous and could not be identified with either the Sunni or Shi'a sects (Iraqi Ministry of Education 2001c, 2000–02). Elements that would distinguish the prayer as belonging to either of the two were conspicuously missing – a decision that was perhaps made with the regime's authoritarian aims in mind (Tavernise 2008).

The new curriculum has addressed the imbalance in a number of ways. A revised Islamic studies textbook that was in circulation in 2008 depicted both ways of praying. Yet another textbook depicted two brothers, Mohammad and Ahmad, praying according to Sunni and Shi'a guidelines alongside one another (*Al-Raeed* (2010) 'Sectarian change programs influence Iraqi curricula'). While a more inclusive approach to Islamic studies was the stated reason for the change, the move backfired and triggered a wave of accusations that the changes were politically motivated and that the Shiite-led government was deliberately 'fostering injustice and sectarianism' by differentiating between the Sunnis and Shiites (Google Answers, 'The changing of the Islamic studies curriculum in Iraq to teach prayer based on Shia practice ... with pictures', *Hanin Network*, Arabic Translation). Parents and teachers accustomed to instruction under the Saddam regime, especially Sunnis, expressed concern that 'teaching more than one way of praying might confuse children' and 'lead to discrimination and sectarianism'. They said they hoped children would be taught about Islam in a more general way that 'did not differentiate between sects' since Muslims were 'one people with one religion and one God' (*Al-Sharq Al-Awsat* (2009) 'Widespread criticism from parents and teachers over Iraqi curriculum').

Politicians and religious authorities immediately joined the dispute, fuelling even more the suspicions that changes to the curriculum were politically motivated (*Niqash* (2010) 'Throwing old textbooks out'). Sunni politicians criticised the Shiite-led Ministry of Education of fomenting sectarianism, and Shiite leaders responded in kind. Ayatollah Ali al-Sistani stated publicly that he supported changes, and that a single curriculum should reflect 'all the beautiful colors of Iraqi society' rather than being separate for Shias or Sunnis (*Al-Sharq Al-Awsat* (2008) 'Shiite authorities demand changes to Iraqi curricula'). Statements by Internet commentators followed that Sistani was 'colluding [with] the (US) occupiers', since they 'sought sectarian strife' in Iraq (*Al 3 Nabi* 'Sistani and what I learned from him'). And though most complaints were lodged by Sunnis who felt they were discriminated against by Shias, the new books were also denounced by one of Iraq's leading Shi'a clerics the Grand Ayatollah Bashir al-Najafi who said that they fostered sectarianism by imposing one sect's control over another.

A Sunni member of parliament and chairman of the Committee on Education Alaa Makki also said that the new curriculum could worsen sectarian relations, and that it should focus instead on 'the shared aspects (of Islam)' (Mohammad 2010). Makki accused the Education Ministry of distributing the books without his knowledge. The charge was vehemently denied by Iraq's Minister of Education at the time, Islamic Dawa Party member Khudayr al-Khuzai. Al-Khuzai (who held the controversial position of the country's third vice-president under Prime Minister al-Maliki) was later accused by internet commentators of facilitating undue Iranian influence in the revision process by having the new textbooks published in Iran rather than Iraq. Some secular leaders have since criticised the involvement of religious figures. For example, Mithal al-Alusi, a former independent Sunni legislator, argued against what he claimed was undue Shi'a influence, saying that the curriculum should not be decided by clerics and politicians, but by education experts (Mohammad 2010).

The lessons were eventually retracted. Those that replaced them were redistributed for the first time in 2010–11 and, ironically, relied on images nearly identical to those used during the Saddam regime that could not be identified with either sect. In addition, parents were instructed to teach their children how to pray. In some revised lessons, however, both Shia and Sunni prayers accompanied the ambiguous images. Still other books included Shia, rather than Sunni versions, with notes to students that only 'some Muslims' follow the specific tradition depicted ('Accelerated learning track: Islamic Studies', *iraqicurricula.org*, Level 3: 81). The impasse clearly remains unresolved and in some ways was a prefiguration of the violence between Sunni and Shi'a brought upon Iraq by ISIS.

More generally, this nationalisation of Islam at the core of social identities has also refashioned the Islamist project from Pan-Islamist to national, at least until the rise of global movements such as Al Qaeda (Pratt 2007: 167). As a result, Islamist opposition groups constructed political Islam as a national project, a tool to achieve what they see as social justice, by fighting corrupted rulers.

Islamism as a national or counter-national project

As mentioned above, Islamism was, at the time of its inception, opposed to nationalism, perceived as a Western imported concept. However, after the de-colonisation process, the nation framework became the 'natural' political space, instead of a 'foreign' or Western invention. Islamist opposition movements would use Islam more as an alternative to the secular nationalism promoted by state elites, and less as a way to promote a pan-Islamic Caliphate. In this sense, they have increasingly operated within the context of the newly defined national political community.

In Egypt, the Muslim Brothers believed they held the key to the 'true' Islam, and therefore to the rightful authority, whereas the state policies were impure. Hassan al-Banna argued that the purest period of Islam was during the 'Golden Age' when Muhammad and his successors, the Four Rightly-Guided Caliphs, ruled the *Ummah*. Thus, the Muslim Brotherhood's ultimate political goal was to create an 'Islamic Order' or *al-nizam al-islami*, which emphasised a foundation in *Shari'a*. While al-Banna advocated the implementation of *Shari'a*, the Brotherhood's programme also recognised the non-legal aspects of their vision, and worked to improve the social, economic, and political aspirations of the Egyptian people.

That is why the Muslim Brothers declared, 'Egypt was the logical and historically right place for Islam to base itself ... Egypt had a unique role to play in Islam's resurgence' (Mitchell 1993: 217). Al-Banna illustrates this point in the following argument:

> The Muslim Brothers, true to the faith, plead that the nation be restored to Islam. Egypt's role is unique, for just as Egyptian reform begins with Islam, so the regeneration of Islam must begin in Egypt, for the rebirth of 'international Islam', in both its ideal and historical sense, requires first a strong 'Muslim State' (*dawla muslima*).

> (Mitchell 1993: 232)

It appears that, although Hasan al-Banna's project was to build an Islamic political system, his vision was not entirely a pan-Islamic one, and it explains why the Muslim Brotherhood would operate more and more within the national Egyptian framework.

As a result, domestic politics had strong effects in shaping the Muslim Brotherhood ideology over time. After the death of al-Banna in 1949 and the Free Officers' coup in 1952 to remove the monarchy from power, the relationship between the Brotherhood and the state changed from one of cooperation to one of mistrust. At first, the Muslim Brotherhood was allowed to continue as an organisation under Nasser, despite the abolition of existing political parties in 1953. However, the Muslim Brotherhood's refusal to grant legitimacy to a regime that did not implement *Shari'a* soon led to organised demonstrations against the regime. In October 1954, a young member of the Muslim Brotherhood allegedly attempted to assassinate Nasser and the Brotherhood was subsequently outlawed. Members were arrested, jailed, and some even received death sentences. This political change modified the Muslim Brotherhood's strategy to directly oppose the state. This event also accounted for the divisions in the movement on how to approach the nation's government.

In the same vein, the turn towards radicalisation, largely caused by the increased repression of the state, reinforced the nationalisation of the Islamist strategy by focusing on the fight against the ruler. Sayyid Qutb's (1906–66) redefinition of *jihad* as the fight against the unjust ruler was instrumental in this evolution. In *Milestones* (1964), Qutb argued that Egyptian society was steeped in *jahiliyyah*, or ignorance (Qutb 1964: 23). Therefore, Egypt was living under a *takfir* regime, or a regime that had renounced Islam (Zollner 2009: 86). Qutb called for *jihad* to battle the *jahiliyyah* of the Nasser regime, because, to Qutb, the Egyptian state was standing in direct opposition to the ideal Islamic political community. However, Qutb's vision led to several schisms within the Muslim Brotherhood, as several groups such as the Islamic Jihad, and al-Takfir al-Hijra (Zeidan 1999). adopted the *jihad* against the unjust ruler strategy as their priority (Rubin 2002: 56).

Muhammad abd al-Salaam Faraj (1954–82), the founder of the Islamic Jihad, which assassinated Anwar Sadat in 1981, went even further in his national *jihad* approach. In his text, *The Absent Obligation*, Faraj argues that the present Egyptian rulers had been 'brought up over colonial tables be they Christian, Communist or Zionist. What they carry of Islam is nothing but names, even if they pray, fast and claim to be Muslims' (Faraj 2000: 25). Furthermore, Faraj argued that the time to restore the Caliphate of Islam was immediate, and it was 'obligatory upon every Muslim to do his utmost to implement [it]'(Faraj 2000: 17). Faraj promoted *jihad* as a sixth pillar of Islam, meaning that every Muslim was obligated to immediately undermine the state and replace it with a Caliphate. This conception of *jihad* became global when some of these radical opponents, including Ayman al-Zawahiri, left Egypt to join the *jihad* in Afghanistan, which led to the formation of Al-Qaeda in 1998 (Gerges 2005).

In contrast, the mainstream Muslim Brotherhood operated under the guidance of Hasan al-Hudaybi (1891–1973),[9] who, in his book *du'a la quda* (Preachers, Not Judges), published after his death, explicitly criticised the *takfiri* ideology of Qutb (Zollner 2009: 62). Al-Hudaybi *directly* questions Qutb's idea of *jihad*, and instead preaches faith, patience, and perseverance. He argued that the duty of all Muslims is 'to enact all of God's orders and statutes and to pave the way for the establishment of His religion' (Johnston 2007: 43). More specifically, under Hudaybi, the Muslim Brothers began to discuss their involvement in Egyptian political life, their compromise with the Egyptian state, and the acceptance of democratic rules regarding women and minorities.

The creation of Al Qaeda, the most recent evolution of the Islamist project, comes from the combination of the jihadi guerrilla of Qutb and Faraj and the salafi doctrine of Islam from Saudi Arabia. Today, the conditions for communication and the circulation of people and ideas make the *Ummah* all the more effective as a concept, especially considering the fact that nationalist ideologies have been on the wane. The Imagined *Ummah* takes a variety of forms. The most influential of these forms are fundamentalist in the sense that they place an emphasis on the revealed text. The most successful globalisations are the wahabism/salafism and global *Jihad* movements.

What all of these movements indicate is the emergence of fundamentalism as a global phenomenon. Global fundamentalism is defined, above all, by an exclusive and hierarchical vision of the world, as well as by a taxonomy of religions that places Islam at the top. The expanded use of the term 'kafir' (infidel, heretic), for example, is very common among Wahhabis. In the classical Islamic tradition, this term is used only for polytheists, not for members of competing monotheistic faiths. In globalised fundamentalist groups, however, it has been extended to include Jews, Christians, and sometimes even non-practising Muslims (see Cesari, 2004). Thus the world is divided into Muslims and infidels, and the image of the West, automatically associated with moral depravity, is always a negative one. Also common to these movements is a worldview that separates the various aspects of life – family, work, leisure – and classifies everything according to the opposition between *haram* (forbidden) and *halal* (permitted). Everything that did not already exist or happen during the time of the Prophet is an innovation, thus *haram*. All share the vision of homogeneous, superior Islam now denationalised and globalised to the *Ummah*.

Conclusion: modern Islam is political Islam

The outcome of the homogenisation process described above is a politicised narrative of religion, or political Islam. Under these conditions, the dominant Western narrative of modernisation cannot help explain this process because it contains an inherent assumption that secularisation leads to the decline of religion in the political sphere. The invention of Islam as a modern religion is closely associated with the building of the nation-state. The efforts by these 'secular' states to limit the social influence of religion actually led to a nationalisation of religious identities and, therefore, to their politicisation, defying the expectations of earlier modernisation theories (Lawson 2006: 1–2, 7, 12; Burgis 2009: 76–7).

From the time of nation building, Islam has been acknowledged in most constitutions and has often been inscribed into the constitutional foundations as the religion of the country. Thus, it is recognised as the religion of the state, and such recognition occurred even when the state founders maintained a very secular orientation. What followed were the nationalisation of Islamic institutions, state-ordained religious education in public schools, and the enduring legacies of

Shari'a law in the legal system. As a result, the political development of Muslim nation-states leads to a more complex approach to secularity than the separation of church and state principle.

In this regard, political and social modernisation in Muslim countries stands in stark opposition to the dominant Western narrative, according to which, the religious identity of the individual departed from national identity and became increasingly privatised with the expansion of political and civic rights (even though this story does not reflect the diversity and nuances of historical processes in European and American nations). In other words, there is often a correlation of national and religious identities in present day Muslim countries. As a result of this fusion, a moral hierarchy is established, in which the national government intervenes in the personal lives of its citizens on topics that range from dress and social relations, to culture.

Charles Taylor has superbly demonstrated (Taylor 2007) that Western secularity is the culmination of a historical progression of ideas about religion, such that 'authentic' religiosity became increasingly associated with personal commitment and a conception of the world as immanent. The separation of the 'worldly' from the 'transcendent' led to the private vs public disjunction. This separation was accelerated through the Reformation and laid the groundwork for the ascendance of a neutral, self-sufficient secular order, leading to the contemporary situation where belief in God is considered to be one among many viable spiritual options. An environment in which private and public are separated in this way does not necessarily prevent believers from enjoying the right to full expression of their religious identity, although they can occasionally face challenges in this regard that non-believers do not. For instance, *The Satanic Verses* or Danish cartoons crisis are signs that some Muslims who live in Western secular democracies are struggling with this framework of the immanent at the personal level (Klausen 2009).

In contrast, modern religion in Muslim countries is positioned on the platform of the state with the consequence that the latter has defined modern Islam as a code of public morality. In all of the countries surveyed, a combination of culturally constructed values (*adab*) and Islamic Law creates social customs, which emphasise the social over the individual being. In other words, daily interactions reinforce the idea that the self is subdued to social obligations. This standard extends to the very definition of equality. Whereas in the West equality is defined by uniform sets of individual rights, in the countries studied, equality is the equal obligation of individuals to promote communal welfare. Hence, the moral obligation of the family allows no room for the 'promotion of self' above the interests of the community. Any conceptions of female emancipation, therefore, are regarded as dissonant with the cultural values of the nation, often defined in religious terms. A case in point is the controversy created by Prime Minister Erdogan in May 2012, when Mr Erdogan told a gathering of the women's branches of his Justice and Development party that 'each abortion is one Uludere' – a reference to air strikes on a village on the Iraqi border that killed 34 civilians in December. Abortions, said the PM, were, 'a sneaky plan to wipe the country off the world stage'.[10] The same rhetoric is also present in western democracies, as shown by the political agenda of Christian fundamentalist groups in the United States. But these claims do not operate (until now) within the same legal and political environment.

Generally speaking, gendered roles in the family reflect a hierarchy of social positions and purposes that directly impact on women's lives in both the private and public spheres. For example, at the core of the nationalist ideology of the countries surveyed, there is an element of self-preservation, in order to secure moral capital in a rapidly Westernising world. Globalisation and consumerism both pose threats to the social composition of these respective regions of the Muslim world, which, in their instability, regard this trend as one of moral depravity. In this globalising cultural setting, in which the terms and values of social relations are mutating, the reflex in most Muslim countries is to subordinate the rights of individuals, frequently women, to the general social cohesion and political welfare. Government officials, therefore, have relied upon the pre-established moral capital of religion and familial structure to control the social upheaval stirred by Western influences. Consequentially, women's behaviour and sexuality often become restricted.

Presently, the control of women's bodies and sexuality has guaranteed both continuity and stability in the public sphere. Securing a gendered moral hierarchy in the private sphere likewise safeguards social harmony and political stability. Religious and political leaders alike reinforce this presumption of the women's role in family and society. The result is continuous tensions over the legitimate definition of women rights, opposing the advocates of the empowerment of self to the protectors of the political community defined in Islamic terms.

It is important to note that the body is a topic through which many Islamic religious authorities and institutions have critiqued postmodern society (Meijers 2009). In this light, Islam serves as a countercultural voice that simultaneously rebukes Western cultural hegemony and serves the respective political interests of Islamic religious authorities. In other words, Islam is conveniently used by both politicians and religious authorities in Middle Eastern countries to critique Western and secular values with the woman's body being the major site of this cultural and political tension between the West and Islam, past and present, and individual versus collective rights.

At the same time, religious norms and references cannot be completely controlled by the states, especially at a time of facilitated global communication and expedited circulation of ideas that increase the debate on Islamic orthodoxy. In other words, state policies are increasingly challenged by transnational ideas and agents which are currently deeply influencing the national contexts of Islamic religiosity, with consequences still unknown.

Notes

1. This section is an excerpt from chapter 1 of my book, *The Awakening of Muslim Democracy*, Cambridge University Press, 2014.

2. Millets were religious communities regulated by their own civil rules. They were the cornerstone of the Ottoman political system.

3. Signed on May 12, 1881 between France and Mohammad as-Sadiq Bey, by which Tunisia became a French protectorate.

4. He was also known as *Combattant Suprême*, which reveals the French connotations of Bourguiba's anticolonial character.

5. The concept of *Syar* was developed in the early centuries of Islam by Al-Shaybānī (748–805) and later codified by Al-Sarakhsī (d. 1101) and refers to relations of believers to unbelievers and rebels.

6. This dominant political narrative does not reflect the cultural and political evolution even in the West.

7. The data from this section come from chapter 5 of my book, *The Awakening of Muslim Democracy*, 2014.

8. The leader of the Islamicisation agenda in education has often been the Muslim Brotherhood.

9. Al-Hudaybi was the second 'General guide' for the Society of Muslim Brothers, best known for *Preachers, Not Judges* (*Du'at la Qudat*), a refutation of Sayyid Qutb's *Milestones*.

10. Justin Vela (2012) '"Abortions are like air strikes on civilians": Turkish PM Recep Tayyip Erdogan's rant sparks women's rage', *The Independent*. It should be noted that abortions are currently legal in Turkey.

References

Acharya, A. (2004) 'How ideas spread: whose norms matter? Norm localization and institutional change in Asian regionalism', *International Organization*, 58.

Aldeeb, S. (2000) 'Religious teaching in Egypt and Switzerland', symposium organized by the Movement for Human Rights, Beyrouth.

al-Sibai, M. (1969) 'Islamic socialism', in S. A. Hanna and G. H. Gardner (eds) *Arab Socialism*, Leiden: Brill pp. 66–79.

Altan, O. (2007) 'Turkey: sanctifying a secular state', in E. A. Doumato, and G. Starrett (eds) *Textbooks and Religion in the Middle East*, Boulder, CO: Lynne Riener Publishers pp. 197–214.

Anderson, L. and Stansfield, G. (2004) *The Future of Iraq? Dictatorship, democracy, or division*, New York: Palgrave Macmillan.

Ashiwa, Y. and Wank, D. L. (2009) *Making Religion, Making the State: the Politics of religion in modern China*, Stanford, CA: Stanford University Press.

Aydin, C. (2007) *The Politics of Anti-Westernism in Asia: Visions of world order in Pan-Islamic and Pan-Asian thought*, New York: Columbia University Press.

Azak, U. (2010) *Islam and Secularism in Turkey: Kemalism, religion and the nation state*, London: I.B. Tauris.

Boulby, M. (1988) 'The Islamic challenge', *Third World Quarterly*.

Brett, M. (1998) 'Review of Norman Salem's work *Habib Bourguiba, Islam and the Creation of Tunisia*', *African Affairs*, 87: 346.

Burgis, M. (2009) 'Faith in the state? Traditions of territoriality and the emergence of modern Arab statehood', *Journal of the History of International Law*, 11: 37–49.

Carre, O., (1972) 'L'Ideologie Politico-religieuse Nasserienne a La Lumière Des Manuels Scolaires.' *Politique Etrangere* 37: n. pag.

Daun, H. and Walford, G. (eds) (2004) 'Education strategies among Muslims in the context of globalization: some national case studies', *Muslim Minorities*, 3.

Devlin, J. F. (1991) 'The Baath Party: rise and metamorphosis', *The American Historical Review*, 96: 1396–407.

Duara, P. (1995) *Rescuing History from the Nation: Questioning narratives of modern China*, Chicago: University of Chicago Press.

Durrani, N. and Dunne, M. (2010) 'Curriculum and national identity: exploring the links between religion and nation in Pakistan', *Journal of Curriculum Studies*, 42(2): 215–40.

Eickelman, D. and Piscatori, J. (1996) *Muslim Politics*, Princeton, NJ: Princeton University Press.

Eisenstadt, S. (2006) *The Great Revolutions and the Civilizations of Modernity*, Boston: Brill.

Eliade, M. (1961) *Myths, Dreams and Mysteries: the Encounter between contemporary faiths and archaic realities*, New York: Harper & Row.

Enayat, H. (2005) *Modern Islamic Political Thought*, New York: I.B. Tauris & Co.

Esposito, J. (1999) *Islamic Threat: Myth or reality?*, New York: Oxford University Press.

Faraj, M. (2000) *Jihad: the Absent obligation*, Birmingham: Maktabah al Ansaar.

Gerges, F. (2005) *The Far Enemy: Why the Jihad became global*, New York: Cambridge University Press.

Hadithi, A. (2010) 'Shaikh Dr. Hamid Abd El Aziz, the director of the department of Islamic education, in an interview with Al-Raed, *Al-Raed Magazine*.

Harris, C. P. (1964) *Nationalism and Revolution in Egypt*, Stanford, CA: Houton & Co.

Hassan, R. (2002) *Faithlines: Muslim conceptions of Islam and society*, Oxford: Oxford University Press.

Hourani, A. H. (1988) *Arabic Thought in the Liberal Age, 1798–1939*, Cambridge: Cambridge University Press.

Iraqi Ministry of Education (1988) *tarikh al-arabi al-islami lil saff al-khamis al-ibtidait*.

—   (1999) *tarikh al-arabi al-islami lil saff al-thani al-mutawasat*.

—   (2001a) *tarbiyya wataniyya saf chamis ibtidaiya*.

—   (2001b) *al-tarbiyya al-wataniyya lil saff al-khamis al-ibtidai*.

—   (2001c) *al-Tarbiya al-islamiya lil-saff al-awal al-ibtida'I*, First grade Islamic Studies.

—   (2000–02) *al-Tarbiya al-islamiya*, Islamic Studies Grade 2–6.

Johnston, D. L. (2007) 'Hassan al-Hudaybi and the Muslim Brotherhood: can Islamic fundamentalism eschew the Islamic State?' *Comparative Islamic Studies* 3(1)

Karpat, K. (2002) *The Politicization of Islam: Reconstructing identity, state, faith, and community in the late Ottoman state*, Oxford: Oxford University Press.

Khalidi, R. (1991) *The Origins of Arab Nationalism*, New York: Columbia University Press.

Klausen, J. (2009) *The Cartoons That Shook the World*, New Haven, CT: Yale University Press.

Kocak, M. (2010) 'Islam and national law in Turkey', in J. Otto (ed.) *Sharia Incorporated*, Amsterdam: Leiden University Press.

Landau, J. M. (1990) *The Politics of Pan-Islam: Ideology and organization*, Oxford: Clarendon Press.

Lapidus, I. M. (2002) *A History of Islamic Societies*, second edition, Cambridge: Cambridge University Press.

Lawson, F. (2006) *Constructing International Relations in the Arab World*, Palo Alto, CA: Stanford University Press.

Meijers, R. (2009) *Global Salafism: Islam's new religious movement*, New York: Columbia University Press.

Mitchell, R. (1993) *The Society of the Muslim Brothers*, New York: Oxford University Press.

Mohammad, A. (2010) 'Iraqi schoolbooks criticized for sectarian bias', *Institute for War and Peace Reporting*.

Moore, C. H. (1956) *Tunisia Since Independence: the Dynamics of one-party government*, Berkeley, CA: University of California Press.

Mufti, M. (1996) *Sovereign Creations: Pan-Arabism and political order in Syria and Iraq*, Ithaca, NY: Cornell University Press.

National Secular Society (2007) 'Compulsory religious education and abuse of human rights, says European Court' http://www.secularism.org.uk/compulsoryreligiouseducationanab.html.

O'Kane, J. P. (1972) 'Islam and the new Egyptian constitution: Some Discussions in al-Ahram', *Middle East Journal*, 26: 137–48.

Okeke-Ibezim, F. (2006) *Saddam Hussein: the Legendary dictator*, New York: Ekwike.

Otmazgin, N. and Ben-Ari, E. (2012) *Popular Culture and the State in East and Southeast Asia*, New York: Routledge.

Pink, J. (2004) 'Nationalism, religion and the Muslim–Christian relationship: teaching ethics and values in Egyptian schools', *Center for Studies on New Religions*.

Pratt, N. (2007) *Democracy and Authoritarianism in the Arab World*, Boulder, CO: Lynne Rienner Publishers.

Qutb, S. (1964 [2005]) *Milestones*, Gaziabad: Islamic Book Services.

Rokkan, S. (1988) 'Dimensions of state formation and nation-building: a possible paradigm', in C. Tilly (ed.) *The Formation of National States in Western Europe*, Princeton, NJ: Princeton University Press.

Rubin, B. (2002) *Islamic Fundamentalism in Egyptian Politics*, New York: Palgrave MacMillan.

Sachsenmaier, D., Riedel, J., and Eisenstadt, S. (eds) (2001) *Reflections on Multiple Modernities: European, Chinese, and other interpretations*, Leiden: Koninklijke Brill.

Saeed, J. (1994) *Islam and Modernization: a Comparative analysis of Pakistan, Egypt, and Turkey*, Wesport, CT: Praeger Publishers.

Said, B. S. (2003) *A Fundamental Fear: Eurocentrism and the emergence of Islamism*, second edition, New York: Palgrave, 2003).

Starrett, G. (1998) *Putting Islam to Work: Education, politics, and religious transformation in Egypt*, Berkeley, CA: University of California Press.

Tavernise, S. (2008) 'Young Iraqis are losing their faith in religion', *New York Times, 3rd March*.

Taylor, C. (2007) *A Secular Age*, Cambridge, MA: Harvard University Press.

Toronto, J. A. and Eissa, M. S. (2007) 'Egypt: promoting tolerance, defending against Islamism', in E. A. Doumato and G. Starrett (eds) *Teaching Islam: Textbooks and religion in the Middle East*, London: Lynne Rienner Publishers.

Wang, T. (2005) 'Rewriting the textbooks: education policy in post-Hussein Iraq', *Harvard International Review*, 26(4).

Willis, J. (2010) 'Debating the Caliphate: Islam and nation in the work of Rashid Rida and Abul Kalam Azad', *The International History Review*, 32: 711–32.

Wilson, M. C. (1991) 'The Hashemites, the Arab Revolt, and Arab nationalism', in Rashid Khalidi (ed.) *The Origins of the Arab Nationalism*, New York: Columbia University Press.

Yavuz, M. H. (2003) *Islamic Political Identity in Turkey*, Oxford: Oxford University Press.

Zeidan, D. (1999) 'Radical Islam in Egypt: a comparison of two groups', *Middle East Review of International Affairs*, 3(3): 1–10.

Zollner, B. H. E. (2009) *The Muslim Brotherhood: Hasan al-Hudaybi and ideology*, New York: Routledge.

Chapter Twelve

Pakistani Nationalism: Land, People, and History

Aayesha Noor Mian

The unprecedented, historic rise of the power of Islam and its adherents up to the seventeenth century, followed by a gradual and virtually consistent decline afterwards, can be considered as the most important factor in the formation of Muslim consciousness in the subcontinent. Islam reached South Asia in the tenth century, and it remained under Muslim rule up to the arrival of the British colonialists in the eighteenth century. Throughout this period, Muslims never considered themselves to be a minority surrounded by an overwhelming Hindu majority; they thought of themselves as culturally, intellectually, and politically superior to the majority and thus with the right to rule over it. The arrival of the British rulers and the gradual transition of political institutions towards a Westminster-style system made the Muslims acutely aware of their numerical minority status. Heirs to great traditions of art, architecture, music, poetry, literature, and philosophy, they were not ready to accept a subordinate status in the polity. The historic milestone of the fall of Islam's politico-cultural power was of course the fall of the Ottomans.

The great linguistic diversity of the new country stretching from Afghanistan to Burma at its peak, made the British East India Company promote English as the lingua franca, for use by the locally trained persons acting as workers, soldiers, clerics, civil servants, and in countless other capacities. While the Hindu majority welcomed English, the new language, with open arms, bracing for new opportunities, the Muslims did not accept it. Their court and religious languages had been Persian and Arabic respectively, and departure from them in favour of a new medium meant parting with the Islamic tradition and heritage. The opposition came from Muslim community and religious leadership, symbolised by the stance of the great Deoband school of Islamic studies in central India.

Almost a century after the arrival of the British East India Company in Bengal, a small event in Meerut cantonment flared into a nation-wide mutiny, called the war of independence by the locals. There was a strong protest by Muslim soldiers who were made to orally unplug pork-laden cartridges for muzzle-loaded guns, followed by an equally strong reaction by the colonialists. The British now decided to declare India a Crown Colony, adopting measures to control the locals, especially the Muslim population. Muslim political elites and aristocracy were divided and evidently confused, with glory of the past an historical memory and the possibility of a post-colonial India dominated by the Hindu majority. Considering mutiny to be primarily a Muslim adventure, the rulers made of the Muslim population an example, with thousands hanged in public places or blown up with cannons. The city of Delhi was destroyed and converted into ruins. The last Mughal Emperor Bahadur Shah Zafar, though unwilling and too frail to accept the leadership of Muslims, was still treated as the figurehead and sentenced to exile in Burma where he lies buried in Yangon.

In post-1857 India, the Muslims were a dejected and demoralised lot, looking inwards and far removed from the realities of the day. For them, the acceptance of English as a medium of instruction and communication was tantamount to accepting British superiority as a conquering nation, as well as vindicating them of the crimes they had committed against Muslims. The Hindu majority had no such complex. Having been presented with an unprecedented opportunity of countless jobs as labourers, skilled workers, soldiers, civil servants, etc., they whole-heartedly accepted the educational part of the package and learned English with vigour and enthusiasm. There was, however, a voice of dissent against the traditionalists – a reformist Muslim group, spearheaded by Sir Syed Ahmad Khan. A progressive educationist who had founded the 'Mohammedan Anglo Oriental College' in 1877, which still exists as the 'Aligarh Muslim University, Agra', he looked upon this situation with grave concern, concerned that Muslims had derived minimal benefit from European science and literature. Sir Syed Ahmad Khan appeared before the Education Commission of the Central Legislative Council in 1882 and presented a memo with data based upon the representation of Muslim students in the largest educational institution of India, Calcutta University. The memo showed that there was no Muslim among 6 Doctors of Law and 4 Honours in Law, and among the Bachelors and Licentiates of Law, there were only 8 and 5 Muslims out of 705 and 235 respectively. There was not a single Muslim graduate in engineering or medicine. In Masters and Bachelors of Arts, there were only 5 and 30 out of 326 and 1343 respectively. Based upon the population coverage of Calcutta University, the number of Muslims was only 57 as against the expected 1262 (British Council Pakistan).

In this historic memo, presented by Sir Syed Ahmad Khan only twenty-four years after the end of eight centuries of Muslim rule in South Asia, he pleaded not for more jobs for the Muslim population but for assistance from the government for their educational improvement and growth. Sir Syed appreciated that the group of Hindu notables who had met under the leadership of Raja Ram Mohan Roy had rejected the government proposal for starting a Sanskrit college and had instead requested more English colleges.

As a result, when the Muslims learned that the rulers intended to introduce English teaching in all schools, in 1835, an application signed by 8000 Mullahs of Calcutta was submitted to the rulers. Their opposition was based upon the argument that the logic and philosophy propounded by modern education were contrary to the teachings of Islam: Muslim students learning English, in the applicants' opinion, was just slightly less than embracing Christianity.

This was also an era of retrospection for the Muslim religious elite, led by great Islamic seminaries such as the Deoband in north-central India, who started their analysis from the days of Emperor Akbar who had created a new faith, the *Deen e Ilahi* which attempted to bring the two great religions of India, Hinduism and Islam, together. They declared the inclusion of Hindu influence into Islam to be the root cause of the plight of Muslims in South Asia; to them, salvation lay in a return to the puritanical faith of the early Islamic period. This fundamentalist message continues to date.

Though a considerable minority of Muslims adopted Western education and ways with the passage of time in the days of the Raj, the two communities continued to practise different systems, the Muslims sending large numbers of their sons to madrassas and preferring to keep their daughters at home, while the Hindus benefitted from the opportunities provided by the growing public education system. The entrenchment of the Raj and the accompanying strengthening of the Hindu majority created two different perceptions in the Muslim population of the subcontinent. There were those who treated the concept of nationalism in the territorial sense. They agreed that the Hindus and the Muslims of India professed different religions but still thought India to be their combined homeland and Indian their national identity. Most of those who thought so joined the Indian National Congress, the secular, largest political party of India. Since its formation in 1885, it had a small minority of Muslims in its leadership ranks. The other Muslim leaders and elite, however, thought that, although the Hindus and Muslims inhabited the same country, they were culturally and traditionally so different from one another, that they were different nations altogether. This was the core argument, which formed the basis of the 'two nation theory' used effectively by the leadership of Muslim League to get a separate homeland for the Muslims out of Hindu India, on the eastern and western flanks of India.

Most of the Muslim political elite of India came from the modern, Western-educated aristocracy, quite different as such from the traditional ultra-conservative Muslim religious elites of the Mughal era. Sir Syed Ahmed Khan was, of course, a shrewd Muslim political strategist, who strongly believed that the Muslims, being a political minority, could only safeguard their interests and survive honourably if they aligned themselves with the ruling British regime. Sir Syed was a moderate in many ways; he promoted Western education amongst the Muslims, being despised for that by the Muslim clergy, and had many close friends from the Hindu community. The later generations of Muslim leaders harboured antagonistic and paradoxical views on Muslim identity and the nature of nationalism in the South Asian context. The Westernised and progressive Bombay barrister, who became the real force behind the Muslim League, Mohammad Ali Jinnah was a well-known socialite and had several Hindus and Parsis (Zoroastrians) in his close circle. The same held true for most other members of the Muslim political and intellectual elite of India at that time. Still they went ahead with the 'two nation theory', sharply dividing the subcontinent on religious grounds for all time to come. Strangely enough, most of the secular and liberal leaders of Pakistan almost painlessly accepted a deeply religious identity for their new homeland as against their previously held secular ideals (Muhammad 1969).

The Westminster-style parliamentary democracy introduced by the colonial rulers had divided the great country into constituencies based on territorial units in which legislators were elected on the basis of majority votes. The Muslim voters were unevenly spread and in the minority in most constituencies, so the elected legislators were mostly Hindus, quite in excess of their overall percentage in the population. A long-standing deep distrust of Hindus, combined with some kind of paranoia, led the Muslim leadership to demand guarantees of a separate electorate for their community, to ensure that they had a certain minimal representation in the legislative assemblies to safeguard their interests against a larger, richer, better educated, and more powerful majority. The concerns of the Muslim political elite could only be addressed either through ensuring a minimum number of minority members in each political party or through the creation of a separate electorate for them.

Under the leadership of Sir Agha Khan, a delegation of Muslim leaders from all around India called on the Viceroy Lord Minto and presented their demand for a separate electorate. The acceptance of this demand led to the provision of a separate electorate in the 1909 Minto–Morley reforms. This was seen as a success and a progressive step by the Muslims; however, the Indian National Congress saw it as a negative strategy of the British, aimed at distorting the evolving national identity of the Indians. Due to the lack of universal suffrage, the existence of a separate electorate did not affect the ordinary citizens in the beginning; however, it did lead to a cleavage and a sense of political separation from their respective religious counterparts. This initial crack was soon to develop into a wide gulf between the two major communities of India.

With no idea as such of a separate homeland for Indian Muslims yet in sight, the Muslim political elite founded the All India Muslim League in Dacca, the capital of today's Bangladesh, which was the practical first step towards a formal political entity to safeguard the interests of the Muslim minority community against a much larger Hindu majority The first demands of the All India Muslim League pertained to the creation of separate electorates for the Muslims and also for the reservation of seats in legislatures of provinces with a Muslim minority as well as their essential inclusion in any discussion on the future of India. The Muslim League participated in the first provincial parliamentary level elections in India in 1936, believing that they would win enough parliamentary seats to validate their claim as the 'sole spokesman' for the entire Muslim population of British India, according to the renowned historian Ayesha Jalal (Jalal 1994).

The dream of getting an electoral victory for the Muslim League in the 1936 elections was not realised, but, instead of sapping their spirit, the defeat, paradoxically, revitalised it. Shifting from their earlier stance of getting guarantees for separate electorates and reservation of seats in Muslim minority provinces, they now started asking for an equal right to be involved in discussions pertaining to the political future of India, on a par with the numerically superior Hindus. There was a new vigour and determination in the Muslim League to pursue the ideals of the 'two nation theory' and be treated as a separate nation entity of India in the process of the determination of its future.

The 1946 elections were key to the determination of the political future of the subcontinent, as to who would rule it after the imminent departure of the British rulers. Representing the minority and anxious to show its might, the

Muslim League took the 1946 elections very seriously to prove to everyone, including the Muslims, that they were the sole voice of Indian Islam in political affairs. Their political campaign across the territories and regions of the vast Indian land mass, in which the Muslims lived virtually everywhere, in small or large numbers, was intended to highlight the existence of two separate nations in the subcontinent. The Muslim population itself was a very diverse group, based upon their ethnic, linguistic, cultural, historic, and geographic differences; the All India Muslim League used the strategy of emphasising the differences between Muslims as a whole and Hindus, thus comprehensively downplaying the intra-Muslim diversity. Unprecedented explicit expression of uniform Islamic identity in symbols and slogans became the hallmark of the campaign for the 1946 elections. In one of his campaign speeches, Muhammad Ali Jinnah, the President of the All India Muslim League, warned Muslims, 'If you want Pakistan, vote for the Muslim League candidates, and if you don't, you are doomed to live like the Shudra (low caste Hindus) and Islam will be vanquished from the Sub-continent' (Gilani Research Foundation). Islam thus became the drive, the ambition and, finally, the foundation stone for the understanding of nationalism among Indian Muslims. Nationalism as defined by Rourke and Boyer has certain characteristics, one of which is to establish values about what is good and bad (Rourke and Boyer 2008: 72, 72, 81). The adherents of Islam in India were effectively reaching a consensus as to what role their religion would play in the state of Pakistan. To reconcile the ideas of a modern nation-state and a religious state, the Muslim League initially attempted to galvanise support for a sovereign state as envisioned by Jinnah based on the outcome of elections in India conducted by the British (Haqqani 2005). To gain the support of mostly illiterate backward followers of Islam in India, Jinnah openly reached out to the powerful clergy in various parts of the country and reassured them that the new state he wished to create would be run in accordance with Sharia laws. Thus, in a way, in an attempt to expand his support base, Jinnah himself undermined his own secular and liberal vision of a Pakistan through alliances with the clergy, because the clergy and religious lobbies consider God, and not the people, as sovereign over any political entity.

The All India Muslim League reached out to the Muslim elite from diverse backgrounds, such as the feudal lords (Nawabs, Sardars and Khans), chiefs of the traditional castes of India (the beradaries), which still existed amongst Muslims, and traditional hereditary religious elites (the Pirs and Sajjadanashins) in its campaign. The way Jinnah countered the popular, secular, liberal political influence of Khan Abdul Ghaffar Khsan (Bacha Khan) of Congress in the North Western Frontier Province is a good example of the League strategy. On the advice and recommendation of Pir Syed Jama'at Ali Shah of Saydan Pur, Srinagar, Kashmir, Jinnah contacted Amin ul Hasnat (the Pir of Manki Sharif) and assured him that no laws or policies repugnant to Islamic Sharia will be adopted in Pakistan. Convinced, the Pir now called his trusted and influential religious allies such as Syed Abdullah Shah of Hazara, Maulana Musleh ud Din, Maulana Shaista Gul among others to his Manki Sharif abode and convinced them to toe the Muslim

League line; the latter two leaders went around the subcontinent, spreading the League message.

The three-day political moot of the Muslim religious elite at Manki Sharif was a mega event in which almost five hundred leading ulemas and Pirs participated, including such luminaries as Syed Jama'at Ali Shah, Maulana Shabbir Ahmad Usmani, Maulana Badshah Gul of Akora, Hazrat Gul of Dosehra, Faqir Abdul Waseh of Bannu, Maulana Musleh ud Din, Maulana Abdul Sattar Khan Niazi of Mianwali, Pir Abdul Latif of Zakori Sharif, Maulana Shaisa Gul, Naeem ud Din Muradabadi and Maulana Abdul Hameed Badayuni. The conference proposed to form a religious party, Jamiat ul Asifa, with Pir of Manki Sharif as its convener, Pir Jama'at Ali Shah as its president and the Pir of Golra sharif as its vice president.

Jamiat ul Asifia aimed at relating the demand for the creation of Pakistan with adherence to the principles of Quran and Sunnah. Thus the support of Pir of Manki and his associates for the Muslim League was conditional upon the enforcement of Sharia as the supreme law in Pakistan.

Pir Sahib of Manki Sharif, through his emissary Qazi Abdul Hakeem Khattak, apprised Jinnah of the proceedings of the moot and the conditionality of support, and Jinnah quickly responded in the following words:

> I am greatly thankful to you for the powerful support which you have been pleased to give to All India Muslim League. ... as regards your preliminary question of Pakistan being established is settled, it will not be the Muslim League that will frame the constitution of Pakistan but inhabitants of Pakistan in which 75 per cent will be Musulmans and therefore you will understand that it will be a Muslim government and it will be for the people of Pakistan to frame the constitution under which the Pakistan government will come into being and function.

> Therefore, there need be no apprehension that the Constitution making body which will comprise of overwhelming majority of Muslims can ever establish any constitution for Pakistan other than one based on Islamic ideals, nor can the government of Pakistan when it comes into being act contrary to Islamic ideals and principles.

(Ahmed 1997)

Jinnah signed an accord with the Islamic scholars and clergy on 25 November 1945 which declared that every law in the state of Pakistan would be consistent with Islamic Sharia and would not be repugnant to the teachings of the Holy Quran or Sunnah. Any bill concerned with an issue relating to Sharia would have to be presented to President of Jamiat ul Asifa for endorsement before it could be presented before the Constituent Assembly for further consideration and necessary process. Concerning the question as to what type of constitution Pakistan would have, Jinnah responded with a speech:

Let me be clear that Muslims believe in one God, one Prophet, and Holy Quran. Islamic principles are the Constitution, which we inherited from our Holy Prophet thirteen centuries before, so there will be nothing but only Quranic principles as our Constitution. In order to achieve our goal you should vote in favor of Muslim League candidates. Regarding legislation I will say that when you elect your representatives to the Parliament they make laws in conformity with the Quran and Sunnah ... If concerted efforts are made by all, the achievement of Pakistan is not difficult.

(Ahmad 1960: 241–3)

The founding father Mohammad Ali Jinnah had actually created a beast, which was to turn into a Frankenstein's monster. The use of religion by the Muslim League as a political tool to get a separate homeland for the Muslims of India gave rise to the basic question, if Islam was to be the foundation of the nascent state, whose Islam and which Islam? Once Islam was incorporated as the key element in the ideology of Pakistan, nobody could get rid of this question for all times to come. The religious character given to Pakistan's nationalism has created a problem that is virtually impossible to resolve and that has haunted the politicians and statesmen of this country ever since.

The next landmark in Pakistan's history was the Objectives Resolution approved by the Constituent Assembly in 1949, which explicitly stated the guiding principles of the future constitution and defined boundaries within which the new state would function. It was interesting that articulation of the core objectives of Pakistan had taken two years to be decided upon and finalised. This document once and for all decided the character of the polity to be Islamic, by declaring that sovereignty belonged to Allah and not to humans, and directed the state to ensure that it would enable its citizens to pursue their collective and individual lives according to the principles laid down by Islam. The controversial document was opposed by the East Pakistanis, one-fifth of whom were non-Muslims, and the progressive liberal lobbies; however, it did become the preamble of the next three constitutions of Pakistan and was eventually made into an integral part of the constitution, thirty-six years later in 1985.

The first Prime Minister of Pakistan Nawabzada Liaqat Ali Khan, Shaheed e Millat (Martyr of the nation, as he was assassinated in 1951) prepared a speech to the Constituent Assembly at the time of passage of the Objectives Resolution, which he had himself presented, on 9 March 1949, of which some important portions are quoted below:

In the name of Allah, the Beneficent, the Merciful;

WHEREAS sovereignty over the entire universe belongs to God Almighty alone and the authority which He has delegated to the State of Pakistan through its people for being exercised within the limit prescribed by Him is a sacred trust;

WHEREIN the principles of democracy, freedom, equality, tolerance and social justice, as enunciated by Islam, shall be fully observed;

WHEREIN the Muslim shall be enabled to order their lives in the individual and collective spheres in accord with the teachings and requirements of Islam as set out in the Holy Quran and the Sunnah;

Pakistan was founded because the Muslims of this sub-continent wanted to build up their lives in accordance with the teachings and traditions of Islam, because they wanted to demonstrate to the world that Islam provides a panacea to the many diseases which have crept into the life of humanity today.

We, as Pakistanis, are not ashamed of the fact that we are overwhelmingly Muslims and we believe that it is by adhering to our faith and ideals that we can make a genuine contribution to the welfare of the world. Therefore, Sir, you would notice that the Preamble of the Resolution deals with a frank and unequivocal recognition of the fact that all authority must be subservient to God.

But we, the people of Pakistan, have the courage to believe firmly that all authority should be exercised in accordance with the standards laid down by Islam so that it may not be misused.

You would notice, Sir, that the Objectives Resolution lays emphasis on the principles of democracy, freedom, equality, tolerance and social justice, and further defines them by saying that these principles should be observed in the constitution as they have been enunciated by Islam.

When we use the word democracy in the Islamic sense, it pervades all aspects of our life; it relates to our system of Government and to our society with equal validity, because one of the greatest contributions of Islam has been the idea of the equality of all men.

The next clause of the Resolution lays down that Muslims shall be enabled to order their lives in the individual and collective spheres in accord with the teachings and requirements of Islam as set out in the Holy Quran and the Sunna.

It is quite obvious that no non-Muslim should have any objection if the Muslims are enabled to order their lives in accordance with the dictates of their religion. You would also notice, Sir, that the State is not to play the part of a neutral observer, wherein the Muslims may be merely free to profess and practice their religion, because such an attitude on the part of the State would be the very negation of the ideals which prompted the demand of Pakistan, and it is these ideals which should be the corner-stone of the State which we want to build.

1. The State will create such conditions as are conducive to the building up of a truly Islamic society, which means that the State will have to play a positive part in this effort. You would remember, Sir, that the Quaid-e-Azam and other leaders of the Muslim League always made unequivocal declarations that the Muslim demand for Pakistan was based upon the fact that the Muslims had a way of life and a code of conduct. They also reiterated the fact that Islam is not merely a relationship between the individual and his God, which should not, in any way, affect the working of the State.

    Indeed, Islam lays down specific directions for social behavior, and seeks to guide society in its attitude towards the problems, which confront it from day to day. Islam is not just a matter of private beliefs and conduct.

    (Khan 2005)

One of the most important Islamic religious intellectuals of pre-partition India and the founder of the religious political outfit, Jamat e Islami,[1] Maulana asyed Abul Ala Maududi had been one of the main opponents of the creation of Pakistan, largely because of the secular outlook of the All India Muslim League, the party responsible for the movement which led to the creation of Pakistan. But once Pakistan became a reality, Maududi and his party saw it as a fertile empty field for the possible implementation of their fundamentalist ideals and for turning a polity into a theo-democracy. The Jamat e Islami could never muster enough political support to be able to rule but kept on pursuing its ideals by influencing the educational institutions as well as the civilian and military bureaucracy, whose members did not feel uncomfortable as they could accommodate Jamat's ideals without having to concede political space.

The very idea that Pakistan was created on the basis of Islamic ideology and that the purpose of the state was to effectively implement and safeguard this ideology has been a favourite slogan for all of Pakistan's military and civilian rulers and leaders. Nawabzadah Liaqat Ali Khan, the first Prime Minister of Pakistan, would often refer to the importance of Islam in the special ideology of Pakistan. The Sandhurst-trained Field Marshall Ayub Khan, who, as the army commander-in-chief, had been a key figure in the political and military affairs during the earlier years of Pakistan and assumed power through martial law to rule over it for eleven years (1958–69), was also firmly of the view that Pakistan had to be ruled according to the Muslim ideology. Ayub had said:

Pakistan was created on an Islamic ideology and since the state had failed to meet primary responsibility to safeguard Islamic ideals, the nation had suffered as a result. A man's greatest yearning is to have an ideology for which he should be able to lay down his life; for Pakistanis, that ideology was Islam, on the basis of which we had fought and got Pakistan, but having got it, we had failed to order our lives according to it.

(Khan 1967: 196–7)

General Ayub Khan and General Yahya Khan's martial law regimes were followed by Pakistan's first general elections and the democratically elected government of Zulfiqar Ali Bhutto (1928–79), a Westernised ideologue and popular charismatic leader. Political analysts and scholars had high expectations that he would arrest the tide of state-sponsored journey towards fundamentalism. But Bhutto disappointed the secular and progressive liberal lobbies of Pakistan; he propounded his own political theory of 'Islamic Socialism', which he could neither appropriately define nor put into actual practice. Bhutto, however, convinced the oil-rich Gulf monarchies and Sheikhdoms to provide economic support for Pakistan; his theme of Islamic Socialism was aimed at toning down the anti-religious impression made by the politics of the left on religious lobbies, domestically and internationally, and raising the new slogan of Islamic Brotherhood.

In 1972, more than 90,000 Pakistanis performed Hajj and Bhutto was quick to demand of his people, 'make this country an Islamic state, the biggest Islamic state, the bravest Islamic state and the most solid Islamic state' (Burki 1988).

The Berkley-and-Oxford-qualified Bhutto was instrumental in promulgating the most Islamic constitution of 1973 in the history of Pakistan, wherein Islam was to be the religion of the state and serving Islam was the state's core duty, as he was in ensuring that all existing laws were brought into conformity with the injunctions of Islam; an Islamic Advisory Council was set up for the purpose. For the first time in the history of Pakistan, a ministry for religious affairs was established and Islamic studies was made compulsory reading for all children attending school, including those from the minority communities. The national assembly passed an act in July 1973 to ensure 'error free publication' of the Holy Quran. Explicit guidelines were given to the general public regarding disposal of torn or damaged pages of the holy book. Lahore, the second largest city of Pakistan, was host to the Islamic Summit Conference in 1974; informally, this was also the time when the nuclear strategy of Pakistan was referred to as the 'Islamic bomb'. After a lengthy parliamentary debate, the Ahmadiya community beliefs were declared non-Muslim, primarily under pressure from Saudi Arabia.

Bhutto's policy of reaching out to Islamic states yielded economic dividends through aid as well as permission to skilled and un-skilled labour from Pakistan to work in Islamic countries, especially Saudi Arabia, Kuwait, Qatar, Bahrain, the United Arab Emirates and Libya. An international 'Seerat Conference' was also held in 1976 by the Bhutto regime. Threatened by the rise and success of the Pakistan National Alliance, Bhutto went ahead with quite an extensive Islamisation agenda, banning alcohol, horse racing and gambling and declaring Friday as the day for the weekly holiday. His Pakistan Peoples Party founded 'Musawat' in an attempt to reach out to the hardliner religious lobbies. He translated his political slogan of 'Islamic Socialism' into 'Musawat e Muhammadi'.

Facing the dual challenge of stabilising the post-1971 Pakistan and the ever-growing strength of religious hardliners, Zulfiqar Ali Bhutto attempted to appease the Islamic hardliners. His support for the second amendment, which declared the Ahmadis[2] as non-Muslims, and pursuit of a more active role for Pakistan in the Islamic world were strategically aimed at softening the extreme religious right pitched against him. Bhutto even threw extreme leftist elements out from his own political party during this phase, which had very negative effects in the sense that it not only weakened the secular, liberal, and progressive elements in Pakistan but also gave the religious lobbies the taste of success. These lobbies' unabashed pursuit of fundamentalist objectives has remained successful in Pakistani politics ever since. His policy of appeasement yielded nothing positive for him, and the hardliners continued to prosper, ultimately pushing him to the wall in 1977.

Bhutto's failure to deliver on political and governance frontiers led to the 1977 martial law of Gen Zia ul Haq, who was to execute Bhutto following an unfair trial in 1979. From his rise to power till his death in a plane accident in 1988, Zia followed an unprecedented one-track Islamisation agenda and tolerated no opposition or criticism of his policies. 'The ideology of Pakistan is Islam and only Islam, there should be no misunderstanding on this account, we should all in sincerity accept Islam as Pakistan's ideology, otherwise Pakistan will be exposed to secular ideologies', he said (Rakisits 1988: 79). The sweeping, unabashed, bayonet-led agenda of Islamisation that continued for more than a decade reshaped, de-shaped, and transformed Pakistan's institutions, culture, and politics for all times to come, ripe for fundamentalist, extremist, and terrorist adventurers to invade from all across the globe.

Though the Objectives Resolution laid down the foundation stone of Islamic identity as the basis for nationalism in Pakistan, it was nine years after independence, in 1956, that Pakistan was constitutionally declared the 'Islamic Republic of Pakistan' and finally put on the track on which the role of Islam as the determining factor in political affairs has been constantly reinforced as the state policy. Ever since, the Pakistani leadership has steadfastly tried to use Islam as the cementing agent for the nation. In fact the strong desire to create a unified basis for national identity was natural, due to the fact that almost all the major ethnic identities forming Pakistan, such as the Kashmiris, Punjabis, Sindhis, Baluchis, and Pashtuns, have large counterpart populations in India, Afghanistan, and Iran, the neighbouring countries, virtually negating the very rationale for the foundation of the new state. Providing the religious basis for national identity, Islam became the policy of the state in its desire to create 'one nation, one language and one religion' (to quote a popular slogan). The imposition of religion on the polity as its key identity has, however, come at the cost of other attributes of the nationalities comprising the union, especially the minorities whose languages and cultures were severely marginalised to make space for the new venture.

In retrospect, Pakistan's attempt at unification based upon a religious affiliation turned out to be a colossal failure, as it has provided the ground for regular episodes of serious political unrest, violence, and even civil war during the 68 years of its existence. Though a multitude of causes and historic events were responsible for the separation of East Pakistan and creation of Bangladesh in 1971, the Bengali resentment over suppression of their ethno-linguistic identity and cultural heritage was definitely the key factor. The Pakistani army was and is largely Punjabi and Pashtun at the soldier level and Punjabi, Pashtun and Mohajir[3] at the officer level. The Punjabis and Mohajirs similarly dominate the civil services. For most people even today, Pakistani identity is actually a Punjabi–Mohajir nexus. The Muslim political elite who had founded Pakistan invited all Muslims of India to join, but the vast expanse of the country, where Muslims were spread out in every nook and corner, made immigration difficult for many of them. The challenges for potential immigrants were not merely geographic in nature; the Hindus and Muslims of the subcontinent had a millennium of combined history and traditions, whereas the new state of Pakistan had little if any history or heritage that was all its own and which could form the basis for its national identity. After the 1947 partition, Muslims in the eastern and western wings of Pakistan were far removed from Central India, now predominantly under the Hindu majority, which had been the seat of the Muslim rulers and South Asian Islamic traditions as well as of their cultural heritage. The fact that one third of South Asian Muslims were left behind in Hindu-dominated India contradicted the Muslim League's declaration of Pakistan as the homeland for South Asian Muslims. The first major jolt to the two-nation theory was received from the struggle for autonomy by the Bengali Muslims of East Pakistan, resulting in the creation of Bangladesh in 1971.

No geographic features such as mountain ranges or water bodies demarked the frontiers of the eastern and western wings of Pakistan from an India of which they had been integral parts for thousands of years and with which they shared their history and a great heritage of language, culture, and ethnicity. Now the architects of Pakistan's national identity were confronted with a dilemma, either to accept the combined history and heritage or to create a new historical narrative. Choosing the former would have challenged the very existence of Pakistan: considering the commonalities, the slogans of the Muslim League for the creation of the new state would have seemed superfluous, and the very basis of Pakistan could have come into question. Hence a new historical narrative was created to cater to the needs of constructing a new state with new ambitions and a new vision. An almost completely new history was created, based upon magnification of the Islamic component in the history of India, tracing and citing out episodic evidence to provide the *raison d'être* for the new entity. The new historic narrative, being virtually artificial, needs constant beefing up and rationalisation, making it a target for criticism and mockery by historians not only locally but also internationally.

The 'two nation theory', which had effectively provided the basis for the partition of India and the resultant creation of Pakistan by mobilising the largest minority against the majority population, also determined the brand of nationalism that each new state was to follow in times to come. Led by secular socialists, such as Mahatma Gandhi and Jawaharlal Nehru, and religious conservatives, such as the Hindu Sardar Vallahbhai Patel and the Muslim Maulana Abul Kalam Azad, the Indian leadership had a territorial or geographically defined view of nationalism. This secular and essentially non-religious outlook on nationalism helped the Indian government effectively run the great land mass of the new state with numerous ethnic, linguistic, and religious identities spread over three dozen provinces and territories, and their leadership quickly managed to get down to the practical aspects of statecraft such as writing its constitution and implementing its economic and foreign policy agendas. "In Pakistan, Muslim identity became an important feature of citizenship. Jamaat-e-Islami (JI), started to operate within the newly defined national political community. JI which had initially opposed the idea of the creation of Pakistan made the Islamization of the political institutions and the society as its major agenda. A state for Muslims, as envisioned by the founding fathers of Pakistan saw the emergence of an Islamic state, the activism of JI coupled with the Islamising policies of Zia-ul-Haq brought a major shift in the ideology of Pakistan" (Cesari 2014). General Zia-ul-Haq (1977-88) wanted Pakistan to be an ideological state and a "global centre for Political Islam", he had declared, "Pakistan, which was created in the name of Islam, will continue to survive only if it sticks to Islam......I consider the introduction of the Islamic system as an essential prerequisite for the country" (*Pakistan Times*, July 6, 1977).

Notes

1. The Jamaat e Islami was founded in 1941 by Maulana Abul Ala Maududi. Maududi believed that Islam was not just a religion and faith but a way of life. Maududi's ideal political system was a 'theo-democracy', which meant 'limited people's sovereignty under the suzerainty of God'.

2. Ahmadis or Ahmadiyyas follow the teachings of a nineteenth-century messiah Mirza Ghulam Ahmad – whom they consider a prophet – and their two main points of disagreement are that they do not acknowledge the finality of the Prophet Muhammad and do not accept the obligation of *jihad*.

3. Mohajir is a term which in the Indian subcontinent refers to those Urdu-speaking Indian Muslims – from Muslim minority provinces – who migrated from India to Pakistan at the time of Partition. Though many Bengali and Punjabi Muslims also migrated across the border, most of them settled down in Pakistani Punjab and Bengal and are not normally referred to as Mohajirs.

Bibliography

Ahmad, J. (ed.) (1960) *Speeches and Writings of Mr Jinnah,* Vol I, Lahore: Ashraf.

Ahmed, A. S. (1997) *Jinnah, Pakistan and Islamic Identity: The Search for Saladin,* London: Routledge.

British Council Pakistan. *The Next Generation.* Full report available at http://www.britishcouncil.pk/pakistan-Next-Generation-Report.pdf.

Burki, S. J. (1988) *Pakistan under Bhutto, 1971–1977,* London: Macmillan.

Cesari, J. *The Awakening of Muslim Democracy*, Cambridge University, 2014.

Gilani Research Foundation. Religion and Governance: Islamization of Society. Jamil u-Din. Full report available at http://www.gallup.com.pk/Polls/31-05-11.pdf.

Haqqani, H. (2005) *Pakistan: Between mosque and military*, Washington, DC: Carnegie Endowment for International Peace, The Brookings Institution Press.

Jalal, A. (1994) *The Sole Spokesman: Jinnah, the Muslim League and the demand for Pakistan*, Cambridge: Cambridge University Press.

Khan, H. (2005) *Constitutional and Political History of Pakistan*, Karachi: Oxford University Press.

Khan, M. A. (1967) *Friends Not Masters: A political autobiography*, Karachi: Oxford University Press.

Muhammad, S. (1969) *Sir Syed Ahmad Khan: a Political biography*, India: Meenaksi Parkashan.

Rakisits, C. G. P. (1988) 'Center province relations in Pakistan under President Zia: the government's and opposition's approaches', *Pacific Affairs*, 61(1).

Rourke, J. T. and Boyer, M. A. (2008) *International Politics on the World Stage*, Seventh Edition, New York: McGraw Hill.

Chapter Thirteen

With God on Their Side: The Nationalism of Contemporary Islamic Extremism

Chandler Rosenberger

Political movements that interpret Islam as a call to arms against the West are frequently dismissed as 'medieval', while their emphasis on religious belief is understood to be a rejection of modernity. Such movements are, however, far more modern and secular than is commonly assumed. A range of movements considered to be primarily theocratic – from Ayatollah Khomeini's Islamic Republic of Iran to Osama bin Laden's 'Islamic Nation' – were consciously framed as a reaction to secular nationalism. Whether by accident or design, they ended up adopting and adapting many, if not all, of the fundamental principles of nationalism.

This chapter, an exercise in historical and comparative sociology, will examine the writings of intellectuals behind several of the most prominent examples of political Islam: Ayatollah Khomeini, the leader of the Islamic Revolution in Iran; Hasan al-Banna, the founder of the Muslim Brotherhood; Sayyid Qutb, a former member of the Brotherhood in Egypt; Ayam Zawahiri, cofounder and now leader of al-Qaeda; and Osama bin Laden, the now-deceased al-Qaeda leader. Although they vary in the degree to which they have incorporated nationalist ideas into their worldview, these Islamists treat nationalism as the organising principle of the societies they hope Islamic government will transform. Every one of them ends up framing his own vision of the social order around nationalism's principles, even when appearing to reject it.

This is surprising for several reasons. First, nationalism requires at least nominal respect for the notions that the people are, to quote Liah Greenfeld, 'the bearer of sovereignty, the central object of loyalty, and the basis of collective solidarity' (Greenfeld 1992: 3). Any thinker who advocates for God's sovereignty over a community is thus challenging nationalism's focus on the affairs and wishes of men and the secularism that ensues from this focus on the mundane world. In societies that put a premium on avoiding logical contradictions, such as Western monotheisms (including Islam), one must, at some point, choose between the rule of God and the rule of man. The thinkers discussed here reveal themselves to be well aware of this dilemma. Most, surprisingly, resolve it by turning to their co-nationals rather than to their God.

This secular orientation of some of the world's most influential political Islamists is easy to miss. Their political language, after all, is infused with piety; many of their followers, moreover, are sincerely religious and faithfully turn towards a God who transcends this world. The thinkers themselves, however, are concerned with worldly issues such as a nation's status in a world pecking order and their own position as potential leaders of these nations (Greenfeld 2006). They are prickly, sensitive to slights that no one secure in the primacy of God's favour would deign to notice. In their determination to right worldly wrongs, these thinkers do, of course, invoke the will of Allah. Such is their confidence in the justice of their cause, however, that they rarely change direction because God has told them to. God, in other words, is on their side, backing their every move. They are only on God's side to the extent that obedience to a transcendent God helps advance their worldly agendas.

These five thinkers adopt, adapt, or adapt to, nationalism in differing ways. Some, such as Khomeini, al-Banna, and Zawahiri, show a deep familiarity with nationalism; they are also comfortable discussing how their own campaigns will advance their nations' interests. The others, Qutb and bin Laden, are less obviously influenced by nationalism. Bin Laden speaks vaguely of an 'Islamic Nation', while Qutb is openly hostile to a concept he knows well. This variety among the five cases might be taken as proof that nationalism is merely incidental to them all. When we consider the social worlds in which each thinker began shaping his ideology, however, the variety proves nationalism's salience. The thinkers we consider are nationalist to the same degree that their societies are nationalist. Three of the five – Khomeini, al-Banna, and Zawahiri – grew up in societies (Iran and Egypt) steeped in nationalism; even as Islamists later in life they continued to find a role for their nations in their thought. A fourth, Qutb, also grew up immersed in nationalism, that of his native Egypt; he only rejected nationalism once his political competitors, secular Arab nationalists, had secured the people's mandate for themselves. Only bin Laden, the Saudi, shows a weak grasp of nationalism's principles, but he is the exception that proves the rule. Saudi Arabia imprinted its image of social order on the young bin Laden; even as he struggled to remove the House of Saud from power, he imagined leading a state that would imitate its theocratic and dynastic structures. This imitation, explicit or implicit, of the social principles one has internalised can, of course, also be seen in the other four of our thinkers – men who supposedly rejected the secular nationalism. Nationalism marked them as much as its absence marked bin Laden.

Nationalism is a secular form of consciousness. It inspires us to seek status and meaning primarily in the mundane social order. It assumes that political and social legitimacy arises in this world, from the 'people', the primary object of loyalty and source of solidarity. If we find ideologues and revolutionaries mostly justifying their cause with reference to the fate and interests of the people, we can assume that their orientation is secular, even if those same leaders also invoke God's will. The difference between the secular-minded 'Islamist' and a genuinely religious thinker is a matter of logical priority. In the case of most political Islamists, we will find that religious ideas and images are invoked primarily to demonstrate the distinctiveness of what really matters to them – that is, one nation or another. To the modern political Islamist, Islam is precious primarily because it defines the character of society in a way that appeals to the religiously minded. Islam is useful as a test of citizen's loyalty and character, or as a source of solidarity against the imperialist West, or as bulwark of morality within the modern state bureaucracy (itself an inherently secular institution). Whether or not the creator of the universe has actually mandated a particular social order is almost beside the point. Islam, we will see, is good because it is good for the Iranians, or the Egyptians, or the Arabs, or whichever secular nation it is called on to support. Political Islamists almost never allow their faith to make a case for its own inherent value.

Ayatollah Khomeini's Iran is usually cited as one of world's most robust Islamist states; in seeking to explain the Islamic Republic's strength, most analysts note that the regime has counted on the support of pious former villagers who moved en masse to Iran's cities in the twentieth century. But Iran's version of political Islam also has deep roots in the country's vision of nationalism. Iranian political Islam emerged at the turn of the twentieth century from the Muslim clerics, the *ulema*. It was a new form of social consciousness – one that inherited ideas of personal and family morality from the traditional faith but one that also took its ideas about the overarching social order from nationalism, the secular vision then being imported from the West.

At the end of the nineteenth century, the Persian *ulema* had good reason to seek a new political vision; the Qajars, the latest royal family to pair with the *ulema* in upholding a peculiarly Shia empire, were in a state of collapse. The Qajars were unable to protect possessions in Central Asia and the Caucasus from Russian intrusion, nor could they resist the entreaties of British mercantilists determined to win new monopolies for British industry. In 1890, when the Qajars gave the British control of all tobacco sales in the Persian empire, the *ulema* broke with the imperial family, siding instead with the merchants of the bazaar and secular intellectuals eager to explore ideas of popular sovereignty. The Qajar dynasty could no longer uphold the traditional Persian imperial vow to protect the realm of Shia Islam; instead, the *ulema* would join constitutionalists and nationalists in using 'the people' as a restraint on imperial whim (Nasr 2006).

In breaking with the imperial house, the *ulema* were stepping into unknown territory. For four centuries, the Shia clergy had governed hand in hand with Persian royalty. Turning to the people instead required them to invent – or rather, to help invent – a new social order. This turn to the people, moreover, had inherent contradictions. In helping constitutionalists to establish a parliament, for example, were the *ulema* not establishing an institution that could create laws of men, laws that could well contradict the laws of God? What if this parliament legalised the sale of alcohol? 'The people' might well be a brake on a capricious and weak monarchy, but who could serve as a brake on them? The *ulema* initial solution was to embed piety into the definition of the people and its institutions. So long as the parliament was known as the House of Justice the *ulema* could believe that their mandate to supervise laws for compatibility with Islam was more than just lip service. The *ulema* also worked to define the electorate as a 'society of believers' and thus to prevent non-Muslims from voting. Bolder secular nationalists, however, such as the authors of the 1907 Tabriz constitution, pushed past such compromises. To them, parliament was 'The House of the Nation,' and owed sharia law nothing (Nasr 2006).

Lost without the royal allies they had betrayed and unable to trust the nationalists with whom they had allied, the politically active among the *ulema* arguably spent the rest of the twentieth century searching for a way to reconcile themselves to the inherently secularising force of nationalism. Their every move seemed to undermine their cause. In 1925 the clergy supported the restoration of the imperial throne – this time as the Pahlavi dynasty – in hopes of also restoring an alliance that had secured their own authority as, for example, judges of local courts. Much to their surprise, however, the Pahlavis proved as nationalist as the constitutionalists, and competed with parliamentarians for the claim to defend the interests of the Iranian people. The clergy may have persuaded Reza Khan to establish an imperial throne, with its vestiges of religious sensibility, rather than the Kemalist presidency he had imagined, but they could not prevent him from opening Iran's first secular universities or removing the *ulema* from judging cases of family law. When British and Russians forced Reza Kahn abdication in favour of his son, the *ulema* remained supportive of the dynasty, especially as an alternative to the truly frightening prospect of a secular nationalist such as Mossadegh unseating all competitors to a sovereign parliament. But *ulema* loyalty to the Pahlavis was repaid only in further marginalisation and secularisation, as the dynasty pursued its own nationalist vision. Populist campaigns such as the White Revolution (1960–3), which extended the franchise and abolished serfdom, were designed to win the loyalty of secular Iranian nationalists, expected to thank the royal household for removing traditional barriers to their advancement (Ansari 2003).

Caught between the shah and the people, the politically ambitious among the *ulema* needed an ideology that would allow them to compete with the royal household for the loyalty of the people. After seven decades of nationalist fervour, that new ideology would have to accommodate ideas of popular sovereignty. Much as some clerics might have (and still do) regret the fact, the consciousness of ordinary Iranians could no longer accommodate deference to mosque and throne. Each might still rule without regard for the welfare of individual Iranians, but each could only do so if it seemed to fulfil the destiny of the collective Iranian nation. The case would have to be made that the Shah's populism was insincere and that the Pahlavis, like the Qajars before them, were in fact selling out the national interest for their own gain.

Awkwardly, the intellectuals making this argument most forcefully were the secular socialists of the Tudeh Party and affiliated groups. Such avowedly atheistic movements were anathema to the clergy. They had also lost much popular support after the end of World War II, when they supported Soviet claims to territory in the northwest populated by ethnic Azeris (whom the Soviets hoped to include in a greater Azerbaijani soviet socialist republic). To attentive and creative minds among the clergy, however, the anti-Western, Third World populism of Iran's revolutionary left suggested a way to recast the Pahlavis as traitors to the Iranian people. Islamic ideologues would just need to recast Islam not as a buttress of a stratified society, but instead as a revolutionary doctrine in its own right, one that could better secure the dignity of the people than any monarch could.

Some intellectuals from the secular left also formulated a new, explicitly nationalist vision of Islam. In his 1962 essay *Occidentosis*, former Tudeh ideologue and novelist Jalal ali-Ahmad luridly described an Iranian nation that was being consumed by 'the Machine', a rationalism that devoured the economic and cultural resources of the Third World. Ahmad had broken with Tudeh over its support for the Soviet Union; in *Occidentosis*, he portrayed communist and capitalist states as allies against the Third World. Steeped in the *ressentiment* of an apostate, Ahmad searched for inherent qualities of the Iranian people that would allow them ultimately to resist this global conspiracy. His search led him back to the Islam he had mocked as a younger writer. Islam, Ahmad decided, was the finest characteristic of Iran – not, as one might argue, because it accurately portrayed God's relationship to man, but rather because it was a culture the West could not digest. Islam, that is, was not valuable for its own sake; it was valuable as a bulwark of Iranian sovereignty (ali-Ahmad 1984).

The dilemma of the *ulema* – that they had thrown in their lot with Iranian nationalism only to be marginalised by nationalism's inherently secular orientation – was finally resolved by the 1979 Islamic revolution led by Ayatollah Khomeini. Given Khomeini's own background as a cleric, his powerfully religious rhetoric, and the enormous authority that his revolution invested in religious men, his overthrow of the Shah has understandably been interpreted as the most compelling example of desecularisation – that is, the return of the sacred as the primary source of orientation in public affairs. While there is little reason to doubt that millions of Iranians understood the revolution through the lens of a national culture infused with Shia imagery, we will lose the thread of continuity of Iranian national consciousness unless we understand that Khomeini succeeded not by abandoning Iran's nationalism, but rather by resolving its contradictions. Khomeini himself was certainly religious, in that he felt the hand of Allah working through him. But that hand struck to redress wrongs that were profoundly secular – wrongs of aggrieved personal and communal pride, of insufficient stature and influence in worldly affairs – wrongs, in short, that traditional Shia clerics had considered beneath the interest of an omnipotent God.

Khomeini's early personal experience embittered him to Iran's secular nationalism, but these experiences also made nationalism, however irritating, his frame of reference. Born to a prominent Shia family that had lost influence as the Shah purged the *ulema* from public institutions, Khomeini was orphaned by the age of 16. As an aspiring cleric, Khomeini studied Islam in Qom, enshrined as the centre of Iranian Shi'ism after 1920, when the newly independent nation of Iraq had claimed Najaf, the heart of traditional Shi'ism. In Qom, Khomeini showed a deep interest in classical and contemporary Western philosophy, especially Aristotle. He also studied Shia mysticism, particularly the writings of Mulla Sadra. While apparently otherworldly, Sadra's thought actually prepared Khomeini well for his future as mundane politician. The mystic, Sadra wrote, is led upward toward God and opens himself to divine wisdom. He then returns to act in the world, united with God and reflecting divine attributes. One need not accuse Khomeini of cynically using religion for worldly authority; we can instead just note that this particular mystic found his deepest satisfaction applying the sacred to mundane national affairs (Nasr 2007).

Despite being motivated by the wisdom of tradition, Khomeini cast his social commentary entirely in the modern idiom of nationalism. In one of his first speeches on national affairs – 'A warning to the nation' (1941) – Khomeini lamented that having a royal household at all placed one man 'no different in outward appearance' above all other Iranians. The shah's rule should be replaced with sharia law, Khomeini wrote, because then 'everyone … would cooperate with the government and strive earnestly to attain the independence and greatness of the nation'. If all laws contrary to sharia were abandoned, Khomeini wrote, 'the country would move forward with the speed of lightening' (Khomeini 1981: 171).

Indeed, the speech that finally forced the Shah to send Khomeini into exile was a nationalist denunciation of a 1963 'Status of Forces' agreement between Iran and the United States. Like other agreements between the US and governments accepting help from US advisors and soldiers, this 'Status of Forces' agreement stipulated that American personnel in Iran would be tried in US courts for any crimes they committed. To Khomeini, this legal arrangement was an inexcusable violation of Iranian sovereignty. The US and Pahlavi regime 'have reduced the Iranian people to a level lower than that of an American dog', Khomeini wrote. 'If someone runs over a dog belonging to an American, he will be prosecuted. Even if the Shah himself were to run over a dog belonging to an American, he would be prosecuted. But if an American cook runs over the Shah, the head of state, no one will have the right to interfere'. Khomeini's new interest in the welfare of the Shah was a familiar expression of his nationalist perspective. Khomeini could no more tolerate the elevation of the Shah above all Iranians than he could the fact that Americans would be set as a class above all Iranians (Khomeini 1981: 182).

In exile in Najaf, Iraq, Khomeini composed his ideas about government – ideas that would help him and fellow clerics replace the Pahlavi dynasty as shepherds of the Iranian nation. The lectures Khomeini gave in Najaf, collected together as the book *Islamic Government* – are usually read as the blueprints for a theocratic state. To some extent, they are just that. Khomeini developed an innovation in Islamic law that would justify a government of clerics. But the work also reflected the degree to which Khomeini had fully reconciled himself to nationalism. In justifying clerical rule, Khomeini's *Islamic Government* makes arguments for the efficacy of clerical rule in nationalist terms.

Clerics should rule Iran not because Allah wanted them to, Khomeini argued, but rather because they could guide Iran to glory and victory over its international enemies. Clerics could uphold the key principle of Mohammed's teachings – the equality of all men (a key element of nationalism). Khomeini agreed with 'red Shia' such as Ali Shariati that Shi'ism had made a critical error in the sixteenth century when it had aligned with a monarchy that promised to defend the faith. Instead, the Shia faith could be used to defend the Iranian nation. The problem with the ideas of popular sovereignty introduced during the Constitutional Period was not that they allowed for elections – Khomeini too would have provisions in his Islamic constitution for popular sovereignty. The problem, rather, was that foreign agents had helped to write the first constitution specifically to 'keep us in our present miserable state so they can exploit our riches'. Drafters of a new constitution should not pay attention to 'xenomaniacs' who admired Western law. Westerners 'do not want us to be true human beings', Khomeini lamented, 'for they are afraid of true human beings'. Restoring the stature of the *ulema* within an Iranian national constitution would help Iran to hold its own among other nations. Sharia judges, for example, were far more efficient and honest. With the *ulema* serving again as the judiciary, Iran would again enjoy the kind of penal provisions that 'keep great nations from being destroyed by corruption' (Khomeini 1981:34, 38, 39, 33).

With such faith in the abilities of the *ulema* to govern, Khomeini might have been expected to abandon all pretence of popular sovereignty. But he did not. Instead he created a new governing principle – the Veleyat-e Faqih, or 'Rule of the guardians' – that would give the *ulema* a role that was stronger but similar in kind to that imagined by Iran's early nationalists. The *ulema* would be in a position to correct mistakes of the popular will – annulling laws that contradicted sharia, for example. The people, however, would still provide the government with legitimacy through an elected parliament. To justify both popular sovereignty and its clerical corrective, Khomeini took a principle of family law and transplanted it to constitutional theory. Under sharia, an orphaned child could be taken care of by a cleric until he reached maturity. The people of Iran, Khomeini argued, had been orphaned. Shia had enjoyed just Islamic government until their leader, a twelve-generation descendent of Mohammed's, had disappeared in the ninth century. Since that time, the Shia had awaited the return of their missing imam. In his absence, they had been abused and misled. In taking control of Iran's government, the *ulema* would merely be protecting the interests of the people as any one cleric might have cared for an individual orphaned child – correcting its mistakes but allowing some autonomy. Together the people and the *ulema* would await the twelfth imam's return (Nasr, 2007).

The constitution that Khomeini approved also left elements of popular sovereignty in place. Iran continued to have an elected parliament, for example. An unelected twelve-member council of guardians could annul laws if they were found contrary to sharia, but parliament could appeal such annulments to another appointed council. Iran's chief executive – the Supreme Leader – would be a cleric, but in theory he could be removed by an eighty-six-member assembly of experts that was directly elected. Khomeini, in other words, reasserted the right of the *ulema* to guide the nation, a role they had sought since the Constitutional Period in the early twentieth century. But he did not abandon the principle of nationalism. If anything, he sacralised it.

Given that the principle of 'veleyat-e faqih' places clerics ultimately in charge of the Iranian state, it might seem strange to ask whether the idea justifies a theocracy or, instead, a nationalist government that is ultimately, in some sense, secular. Strictly speaking, 'veleyat-e faqih' justifies a theocracy. Clerics have ultimate control of the Iranian state; they, presumably, answer to God. Considered in the light of Khomeini's other ideas, however, the case is not so clear cut. Throughout

Khomeini's political writings, Islam is celebrated as a culture and way of life that will help the Iranians – and Middle Easterners more broadly – preserve their sovereignty. The Constitutional Period and the Pahlavi reign had allowed so many foreign ideas to enter Iranian culture that the country lost its identity and strength. Iran should restore Islam's place in government – and welcome the *ulema* back to power – because only Islam could preserve the people's true character, and thus guarantee their wellbeing. Such arguments hardly dislodge the people from the centre of Iranian society; if anything, concern for their ability to resist foreign intrigue suggests that Khomeini thinks the people, taken as a collective whole, are genuinely an agent of destiny. Khomeini and the *ulema* might need to guide those people since they, like Khomeini himself, had been orphaned, but Khomeini makes his case for religious leadership in a profoundly worldly way. Khomeini fears for the character of his nation as if Iran were a teenager loitering in a bad neighbourhood. If one prescribes religion as a means to protect a child's virtue, one is arguably still more interested in the child than in God's will (Nasr, 2007).

In the Iranian case, nationalism and political Islam seem to be forces that were easily aligned. Shia Islam was a natural choice for nationalists hoping to distinguish Iranians from Sunni Arabs and Turks and, as we have seen, Islamists were happy to have a neatly defined polity from which to begin their international revolution. In the case of the Arabs, however, Islam and nationalism seem to be implacable foes. Arab Islamists denounce the secular Arab nations that emerged from the Ottoman Empire and European colonialism – states such as Algeria, Libya, Syria, Egypt – as incorrigibly corrupt. Secular nationalists did not rescue Arabs from European rule, the Islamists argue; instead, the very separation of mosque and state imposed by secular nationalism embedded a distinction between the worldly and the transcendent that itself was profoundly European. Arabs would only have just governance again, Islamists have argued, once the state apparatus of secular nationalism was dismantled and Muslims lived again in a pan-national *umma*.

Whatever vision of Arab unity the Arab Islamists promote, however, their lives and writings reveal that the national idea left a profound mark on their own visions. Although their ideologies argue for the erasure of national boundaries, each writer's pan-national vision congealed within the mould of a particular nationalism. As a result, they too are usually far more secular than they might appear to be. Worldly slights and frustrations, especially slights to their nation, figure as much in their ideologies as any transcendent God. More importantly, each of the major Arab Islamists describes communities united in common destiny, equality of membership and mutual solidarity – all the hallmarks of nations.

It is also telling, if ironic, that the call to abolish national boundaries comes loudest from thinkers influenced by nationalism. Three of the most effective Arab Islamist groups of the past century – the Muslim Brotherhood, Egyptian Islamic Jihad, et al – have their intellectual roots in Egypt, arguably the most robustly nationalist of the Arab societies. No doubt Egyptian secular nationalists have given Islamists much to oppose, but they have also provided much to mimic, whether consciously or not.

The Egyptians have a good claim on being the first Arabs to appreciate the force of nationalism. Napoleon's invasion in 1798 revealed that even a vastly outnumbered European military expedition could prevail over a much larger Ottoman army. The French certainly enjoyed technical advantages, but they were also far more fluid and coordinated on the battlefield. What kind of society, Arabs were left to wonder, could generate so much spontaneous and flexible order? The British who helped expel Napoleon in 1802 made a similar impression. Upon the expulsion of the French, Muhammad Ali, the Ottoman general tasked with assisting the British, declared himself viceroy of Egypt and Sudan and began to modernise his province of the empire along proto-nationalist lines. Ali sent civil servants to France for training, opened secular schools for transmission of European ideas, encouraged industrialisation of the economy, brought the first printing press in the Arab world and oversaw the *Nadha*, or 'Awakening', in Egyptian culture. Ali's campaigns, all conducted with great popular support, arguably made Egypt the first of the Arab nations and cultivated expectations for national dignity and sovereignty (Cole 2007).

Whenever these expectations were disappointed, would-be reformers explicitly sought to change the Egyptian national culture with the aim of strengthening the Egyptian nation – even if the cure was to make the state more 'Islamic'. As Ali's successors took on openly royal trappings and steeped their inherited throne in corruption, rebels – even Islamists – staked their claim to power on bids to better represent the interests of the people.

Nationalism is plainly apparent, for example, in the writings of Hasan al-Banna (1906–49), the founder of the Muslim Brotherhood. Egypt had been a British protectorate since the end of World War I, but, in the face of a nationalist uprising, the British granted Egypt its political independence in 1922. The country's nominal sovereignty could not, however, disguise the many Western characteristics that had been consciously imported or that had streamed in over the century since Napoleon. Egypt had a written constitution, a parliament, political parties, and a free press. It might have won formal independence but, to Islamists such as al-Banna, it could only truly be sovereign once its culture was purged of corrupting Western influence and infused instead with Islam.

Al-Banna was especially aware of British influence. He taught in a primary school in Isma'iliyya, the capital of the one stretch of Egypt – the zone around the Suez Canal – that remained under British control. As a leader of discussions in coffeehouses, private homes and mosques, al-Banna built the Muslim Brotherhood as a potent army for self-assertion. As al-Banna's writings make clear, that recovery of authentic culture would take a distinctly nationalist tone.

This tone is apparent in everything al-Banna wrote but it is perhaps most striking in the essay 'Toward the light', an open letter that al-Banna addressed to King Farouk and his prime minister in 1947. Egypt, al-Banna writes, must choose between continuing to imitate the West or – the better option – to follow the way of Islam, 'its fundamental assumptions, its principles, its culture and its civilization'. For a nominally religious figure, al-Banna commended Islam for benefits that were remarkably secular. Islam would allow a 'pride in nationalism and the extolment of sincere patriotism', al-Banna wrote, 'for then we will construct our lives on our own principles and fundamental assumptions, taking nothing from others. Herein lie the highest ideals of social and existential independence, after political independence' (al-Banna 1978: 105).

Islam, it turns out, offers everything needed to help a 'renascent nation' – whether that nation be Egypt particularly, the Arabs as a whole, the Islamic community ('umma'), or humanity writ large. The 1,300-year-old doctrine shows how to improve public health, turn science into powerful technology, strengthen the military, improve the economy, and, perhaps most importantly, redress the millennia-old wrong that the West should have come to dominate the East at all. 'Truly the weakest of nations', al-Banna wrote, 'if it heard these good tidings and read the real stories pertinent to them, would absolutely emerge thereafter as the strongest of nations in faith and spirit' (al-Banna 1978:108-9).

We might suspect al-Banna of emphasising the secular consequences of his programme when writing to secular men, but there is no mistaking the nationalist frame of reference – especially the collectivist and ethnic elements of both the Egyptian and Islamic nationalisms that he switches between. Al-Banna's ultimate object of loyalty is something he calls the 'Islamic Fatherland', but this, he concedes, is a multifaceted thing, in which one owes loyalty to 'the particular country first of all', then to the broader community of Islamic nations, the former empires, and finally the entire world. Islam, in other words, need not preclude nationalist sentiments; it has 'reconcile[d] the sentiments of local nationalism with that of common nationalism'. Al-Banna's Egyptian nationalism was imagined as part of a larger identity, but it was nonetheless sincere (al-Banna 1978: 110).

As al-Banna himself acknowledges, it also bears a resemblance to other, secular nationalisms. Like Mussolini's fascism and Hitler's Nazism, al-Banna's 'Islamic nationalism' preaches the revival of a collective, homogeneous in membership, which has been denied its freedom and sovereignty. After its reawakening, the nation will be newly united, unhampered by the egotism of individuals, and thus able to compete with other nations and get back to pursuing the destiny that had provided its greatest moments in the past. While tolerant of quiescent minorities, the Islamic nation will repress any 'internal enemy' who sows discord and disrupts the nation's 'internal organization'. As a collective that adds up to more than merely a sum of its individual members, the Islamic nation cannot depend on popular opinion or elections to determine its will. Instead, like Germany, Italy, and the Soviet Union, the Egyptian and then Islamic nations will need to be led by a rightly guided vanguard – specifically, the Muslim Brotherhood al-Banna had founded. Such leadership will end 'party rivalry' and will instead channel its political forces 'into a common front and a single phalanx'. State employees will be surveilled to ensure moral conduct; plays, films, and literature will be censored for moral content. Journalism will be given its 'proper orientation'; public broadcasts will feature only songs and lectures that educate the nation in a 'virtuous and moral way'. Al-Banna claimed that his Islamic nation would be distinguished from the totalitarian states of World War II since his would be guided by God; in every other respect, however, al-Banna imagined a collectivist nation guided by an unchallenged political elite who, while inspired by Islam, would not even be clerics. Even the founder of the Muslim Brotherhood, in other words, saw Islam primarily as a means to an end, a culture that could guide his people – Egyptian and/or Islamic – out from under the oppression of the West and back to the stature and glory that Muhammad Ali had first pursued (al-Banna 1978: 119-131).

Under al-Banna, the Brotherhood had sought a way to reconcile Islam with nationalism; they had ended up with a doctrine that, like Khomeini's, treated Islam primarily as a defence of national sovereignty. Islam was good, al-Banna wrote, because it was good for Egypt and the 'Islamic Nation' of which Egypt was a part. After al-Banna's death in 1949 and the Brotherhood's suppression, al-Banna's successors as Brotherhood ideologues were increasingly inclined to drop the Egyptian nationalist element of the founder's thought. But in transferring their loyalties completely to the Islamic umma, even at the expense of Egypt, such thinkers did not abandon nationalist principles. Instead they rewrote their pan-national Islamism as a cause to unite peoples into an Islamic nation, an umma, which could yet defeat the West.

Sayyid Qutb is perhaps the most influential of these revisionists. Qutb, a poet, literary critic, and later chief ideologue of the Brotherhood, had often expressed Egyptian nationalist sentiments while working for the Ministry of Education in the 1940s. Although fond of Hollywood films and Western classical music, literature, and science, Qutb worried that Egyptian identity was being engulfed. He despised Egypt's former colonisers, the British and French, as well as European powers that had subdued peoples elsewhere. At first the United States seemed less objectionable, but Harry Truman's support for the founding of Israel soon changed that. 'I hate those Westerners and despise them!' Qutb wrote. 'All of them, without any exception: the English, the French, the Dutch, and, finally, the Americans, who have been trusted by so many' (Wright 2006: 9).

Qutb nonetheless took an offer to study at the University of Northern Colorado for three years. There he found still more reasons to dislike the Americans: their promiscuity, insincerity, and perhaps above all, their lack of appreciation of his home country. Writing for a student literary magazine, Qutb told a parable of an undutiful child who had attacked the very mother that had nursed him. 'She is Egypt', Qutb wrote, 'and the little boy the world'. Egyptians had been 'very advanced' and had 'possessed a great civilization before any other country'. Egypt taught Greece, Greece taught Europe. Still, the ungrateful world – the boy of the parable – threw out his nurse and tried to kill her. The world sided with Britain in its occupation; it helped the Jews in their 1948 war against the Arabs. 'Oh! What an undutiful world!' Qutb concluded. 'What an undutiful boy!' (Wright 2006: 21).

Returning home in 1951, Qutb witnessed Nasser's overthrowing of the Egyptian monarchy just a year later. At first Qutb was delighted with Nasser. In time, however, Qutb and the Muslim Brotherhood came to oppose Nasser's secular and socialist nationalism. When the Brotherhood attempted to assassinate Nasser in 1954, the organisation was banned and Qutb was arrested. He would be executed in 1966.

While in prison, Qutb wrote *Milestones*, the work that became the central document of the Egyptian Islamic Jihad, the most effective of the Brotherhood's splinter groups. *Milestones* is not the work of a nationalist, at least not an intellectually coherent one. Qutb rejects, for example, several of the compromises that allowed al-Banna to mix Islamic theocracy and popular sovereignty. By treating Islam as a key element of Egyptian and Arabic culture, rather than as an ahistorical faith, al-Banna could call for the faith's revival as chief trait of a reborn people. Qutb, on the other hand, condemns those who reduce Islam to mere 'cultural information'. Muslims should not read the Koran for academic enjoyment but rather as a soldier reads reports from a battlefield. Qutb also condemns any notion of popular sovereignty, whether as nationalism or democracy. Democracy is merely 'worship of some people by others'. Al-Banna was happy to put Egypt at the centre of concentric circles of loyalty, but, to Qutb, Egyptian nationalism is now the enemy. 'A Muslim has no nationality', Qutb writes, 'except his belief'. "[I]n the sight of Allah', he also wrote, 'all other relationships based on blood or other considerations disappear' (Qutb 2006: 103, 101).

Yet traces of Qutb's once-virulent Egyptian and Arab nationalism remain, even in *Milestones*. Chief among them is his enormous wounded pride, and confidence that Allah will avenge the wrongs. Qutb once condemned the world for not appreciating Egypt properly; in *Milestones* he wrote that Islam lifts people up who might otherwise feel inferior to the West. To be a Muslim, Qutb writes, 'means to feel superior to others even when weak, few and poor, as well as when strong, many and rich'. 'Allah does not leave the believer alone in the face of oppression to whimper under its weight', Qutb wrote. And what held for the individual held for the 'Islamic nation' as a whole. The West might appear to be much stronger than the Arab and/or Muslim peoples, but to Allah, these great powers are 'like playthings'. 'The Muslim loses his physical power and is conquered', Qutb writes, but 'if he remains a believer, he looks on his conqueror from a superior position'. Qutb promises new recruits a new, higher, and secure status as soldiers in a critical war; they now feel empowered by their new 'nobility' even if those lost in pagan ignorance cannot see any actual change in their worldly lot. For all of his suspicion of secular nationalism, Qutb ends up relying on one of nationalism's most appealing psychological rewards– the sense of dignity that comes from attaching oneself to a confident, powerful, and sovereign society (Qutb 2006: 121-138).

Books such as *Milestones* made Qutb arguably the most compelling ideologue of Islamic extremism worldwide. By proclaiming that 'a Muslim has no nationality but belief', Qutb opened the recruiting doors of jihadist movements to all comers. Qutb's 'Islamic nation' would bear some resemblance to the secular powers it was destined to fight, but it was at least meant to overcome loyalties that divided believers.

It is one final irony, then, that the men who have been most determined to fulfil al-Banna's vision have been no more able to escape the frameworks of their own particular nationalisms than Khomeini was able to loosen the bonds of Iranian national identity. For men who claim to follow only the will of Allah, many Islamist leaders find that God is remarkably determined to redress the very particular slights to their own pronounced dignity. Men like Ayman al-Zawahiri and Osama bin Laden cite Qutb as they try to tear down the national boundaries dividing Arab states. And yet each of these leaders envisions such a unified Islamic state differently. These jihadists may long to destroy the physical checkpoints dividing states, but the borders among their mental worlds survive.

Ayman al-Zawahiri, a founder, along with bin Laden, of al-Qaeda, came to his new venture out of Egypt, where he had been the leader of a group that had broken with the Muslim Brotherhood over its moderation. Although Zawahiri left Egypt in the 1980s, Egypt has remained with him. His autobiography, *Knights Under the Banner of the Prophet* – composed while on the run from US forces in Afghanistan shortly after 9/11 – reveals a continuing obsession with Egypt as the potential centre of a unified Islamic umma. Even as he was hiding out in Afghanistan, al-Zawahiri was mentally living in Egypt.

Perhaps the most compelling evidence of Zawahiri's continuing nationalism is his obsession with that great hero of Egyptian life, Muhammad Ali. Every Islamist movement has its own conspiracy theories about the founding of Israel: in Zawahiri's version, Napoleon himself so feared the power of Ali and the Egyptians that he planted the seeds of Zionism so as to place a Jewish barrier to unity between Egypt and France's occupation of Syria. The British too saw the wisdom of supporting Israel to 'separate the Ottoman Empire and the ambitions of Muhammad Ali and his allies'. Pasha Ali had grown so strong that, by 1838, Zawahiri reports, the British were determined to prevent him from taking over and strengthening the Ottoman Empire. Egypt returned as a threat to the West after Qutb's martyrdom, Zawahiri writes, which was the spark that launched the modern jihadist movement – not just in Egypt, but worldwide. Egypt would be the natural home of a new Caliphate: 'If God wills it, such a state as Egypt, with all its weight in the heart of the Islamic world, could lead the Islamic world in a jihad against the West' (Zawahiri 2001).

Unlike Qutb, in other words, Zawahiri had neither despaired of nationalism nor of Egypt. As befits a man who had experienced the egalitarian character of the Arab world's most robust nation, Zawahiri warns throughout the book against spiritual elitism – nearly a direct criticism of Qutb's own writings but true to Zawahiri's ultimate goal of winning over his co-nationals:

In waging the battle the jihad movement must be in the middle, or ahead, of the nation. It must be extremely careful not to get isolated from its nation or engage the government in the battle of the elite against authority.

Zawahiri also harkens back to al-Banna's tradition of seeing particular nationalism as one expression of a greater Islamic umma. Jihadists should unite with movements of national liberation, Zawahiri writes, since it worked in Afghanistan, Chechnya, and Palestine, where 'the jihad movement has moved to the center of the leadership of the nation when it adopted the slogan of liberating the nation from its external enemies and when it portrayed it as a battle of Islam against infidelity and infidels' (Zawahiri 2001).

It is ironic that, in his very fealty to the Egyptian nation, Zawahiri has criticized Qutb, his co-national but a man who gave up on Egypt as Zawahiri never quite did. It is equally ironic that the man who was more loyal to Qutb's vision was, in fact, a Saudi by birth. This irony, however, is perhaps more understandable. Everything about Osama bin Laden's own experience in Saudi Arabia confirmed Qutb's vision of a militant elite that disdains popular opinion.

Born and raised in Saudi Arabia, one of the few modern human societies that is not organised as a nation, bin Laden's experiences arguably had more in common with that of a Habsburg prince than with that of his colleague Zawahiri. Like the nobility of nineteenth-century Vienna, the elite of Saudi Arabia found social stature in their affiliations to the royal family – in bin Laden's case, the House of Saud. Growing up, bin Laden was tantalisingly close to the royal family but firmly separated from it. On the one hand, he was a son of Mohammed bin Laden, the construction magnate who had won the royals' loyalty and patronage by reconstructing such landmarks as Mecca. On the other hand, bin Laden was a son by his father's fourth wife, a Syrian who had never been welcome at court. When bin Laden's parents divorced, Osama was sent to live with his mother and her new husband, a low-ranking employee in his biological father's firm (Wright 2006).

It is well known that, after university, bin Laden found a way to seek glory far from home – as an 'Afghan Arab' fighting the Soviet Union in Afghanistan. Few, however, appreciate how much Saudi Arabia remained on bin Laden's mind while away, and how much he still hoped to be welcomed at court. In 1990, after the Soviets had withdrawn from Afghanistan but just as Saddam Hussein was threatening to invade Saudi Arabia, bin Laden offered to bring 4,000 of his Afghan veterans to the kingdom to defend it. All bin Laden asked in return was to be appointed as Saudi Arabia's Minister of Defence. Bin Laden's offer to bring his own personal army to Saudi Arabia was – perhaps not surprisingly – denied. Noting his increasingly erratic behaviour, the Saudis sent him into exile in 1992. From that point on, bin Laden's loyalty to his homeland transformed into an obsession with replacing its royal household. Bin Laden began to refer the country as 'The Land of Two Holy Places', a name that conveniently left the name of the Saud family out. Instead of loyalty to the Saudis, bin Laden offered his loyalty to the ummah, which he sometimes referred to as the 'Islamic Nation' (bin Laden 2005).

From the time of his exile, bin Laden committed himself to unifying Muslims under one government; like Zawahiri, he appears to have imagined his own homeland – Saudi Arabia rather than Egypt – as the natural centre of such a state. Unlike Zawahiri, however, bin Laden did not have a natural feel for the language and imagery of nationalism. His embrace of the Islamic ummah was tentative and vague, especially compared to his fascination with the *ulema* as a source of legitimacy. When the Saudi government cracked down on dissident clerics – the so-called *sahwa* – bin Laden complained to the chief Saudi mufti, bin Baz. 'You are well aware', bin Laden wrote, 'what a great status the scholars, the men of knowledge, have been given by God'. The scholars bin Laden supported had been justified in challenging Saudi law, he wrote, since they were merely complaining about man-made laws that amounted to the 'setting-up of a rival authority to God'.

Bin Laden's vague formulation of an 'Islamic Nation' was somewhat reminiscent of Qutb's own ambiguity: like Qutb, he showed little interest in paying even lip service to the people, preferring the authority of clerics to legitimacy derived from popular sovereignty. But, having never known a first love for a secular nation, as Qutb had once loved Egypt, bin Laden was even more incoherent on what the 'Islamic Nation' might be (bin Laden 2005: 4, 6).

In one critical respect, however, bin Laden's vision, like the visions of Khomeini, al-Banna, Qutb, and Zawahiri, was shaped by the triumph of nationalism as the predominant organising principle of modern societies worldwide. The major ideologues of political Islam had varying depths of exposure to nationalism and varying commitments to creating an Islamic form of it. For Khomeini, al-Banna, and Zawahiri, it was natural to seek political legitimacy in the nation, be they nations of Iranians, Muslims, Egyptians, or Arabs. Qutb wrote as a disaffected nationalist and redirected his earlier ardour for Egypt to a future global ummah, one that would be ruled by an unelected elite. With little experience or apparent affection for nationalism, bin Laden nonetheless hoped to lead something he called the Islamic nation into a war with the West. While these ideologists may have differed in the degree to which they accepted the principles of nationalism, all organised their political visions within the secular frame that nationalism had built. All wrote and acted as if victories in the secular sphere mattered most.

The Iranian *ulema* followed Khomeini because he found a way to restore their authority within a nationalist frame that for seventy years had pushed clerics to the periphery of political life. Al-Banna and Zawahiri could both imagine personal, worldly triumph as leaders of an Egyptian nation that finally used Islam to redress the humiliations of Western dominance. Qutb and bin Laden were more reluctant to turn to the people for their legitimacy as leaders, but they were nonetheless driven to rebel against their home governments that seemed to have sacrificed their sovereignty to Western nations. Since both Qutb and bin Laden had experienced personal humiliation as a result of their homelands' weakness, they were all the more inclined to imagine worldly revenge in terms of both personal and communal war. Neither asked whether Allah was just in punishing them or their societies. Allah was not imagined as an independent authority whose will could not be questioned; He was imagined instead, to put it plainly, as the servant of their own ambitions and the redresser of their own very worldly grievances.

Over the past four decades the success of Islamist movements inspired by the men discussed here has upended both the academic discipline of sociology and the more practical world of foreign policy planning. In a welcome development, more thinkers in both fields now acknowledge that culture provides institutions such as states with their legitimacy and that it is therefore worth understanding. Acknowledging culture's salience, however, requires that we analyse it with the same empirical rigour that has so often been used in dissecting institutions. The very significance of culture requires that we resist the temptation to treat it as an unknowable black box, or that we accept the movements that emerge from culture uncritically and on their own terms. To use our current case as an example: just because a movement claims to be oriented towards the heavens does not exclude the possibility that its attention is in fact turned almost exclusively toward earth. Taking a thinker's ideas seriously does not require that we believe those ideas fit together the way he claims they do.

In sociology, such sceptical empiricism should encourage us to hesitate before we abandon pillars of the field such as the secularisation theory. If evidence from the empirical world contradicts social theory we should, of course, modify or abandon such theory; if anything, sociology has been far too reluctant to abandon theories that fail to explain reality. But a close look at the realities of political Islam suggests that the modern monotheistic world at least is just as secular as we think it is. In the struggle between the rule of God and the rule of man, even political Islamists orient themselves primarily according to mundane human interests. God may cheer them on, but He does not call the plays. The rise of political Islam should not encourage us to discount the explanatory power of the secularisation thesis. We might instead reconsider what we mean by secularisation. Casanova's account of secularisation (Casanova 1994), for example, can help explain political Islam; it is surely more fruitful to consider the affect of religious men entering a world of secular institutions than it is to imagine that the secularisation is merely a Western illusion.

On the policy side, understanding the secular orientation of political Islamists will allow us to distinguish them from traditional Muslims. Understanding the secular orientations of the ostensible theocrats of the recent past will also help us understand the obsessions of their imitators, such as Iraq's Islamic State. Like the Islamists discussed here, the 'Islamic State' tears down borders in the name of a new supranational 'caliphate' but much of its program – particularly its fierce repressions of Shi'ism – has roots in the very Ba'athist nationalism that brought Saddam Hussein to power in the first place. Ba'ath Party founders such as Michel Aflaq had celebrated Islam as the 'flame of the Arabs' (Makiya 1998) but such a formulation, like others we have seen, demonstrates an overriding interest in the strength of the nation and mere ancillary respect for Islam as something that keeps the nation strong.

It is perhaps no wonder that the Islamic State is led by many former Ba'athists who are also from Iraq's Sunni minority and who plainly seek revenge for their displacement from power after Saddam's fall. For such men, God is on *their* side. They are only on *God's* side to the degree that He helps them win this world.

References

Al-Banna, H. (1978) 'Toward the light', in *Five Tracts of Hasan Al-Banna (1906–1949)* (trans. by Charles Wendell), Berkeley, CA: University of California Press.

ali-Ahmad, J. (1984) *Occidentosis: a Plague from the West*, Berkeley, CA: Mizan Press.

Ansari, A. (2003) *Modern Iran Since 1921: the Pahlavis and after*, London: Pearson.

bin Laden, O. (2005) *Messages to the World: the Statements of Osama Bin Laden* (trans. and edited by Bruce Lawrence), London: Verso.

Casanova, J. (1994) *Public Religions of the Modern World*, Chicago: Universtiy of Chicago Press.

Cole, J. (2007) *Napoleon's Egypt: Invading the Middle East*, New York: Palgrave MacMillan.

Greenfeld, L. (1992) *Nationalism: Five roads to modernity*, Cambridge, MA: Harvard UP.

—   (2006) 'The modern religion?' in *Nationalism and the Mind: Essays on modern culture*, Oxford: Oneworld.

Khomeini, R. (1981) *Islam and Revolution: Writing and declarations of Imam Khomeini*, Berkeley, CA: Mizan Press.

Makiya, K. (1998) *Republic of Fear: the politics of modern Iraq*, Berkeley, CA: University of California Press.

Nasr, V. (2006) *Democracy in Iran: History and the quest for liberty*, Oxford: Oxford University Press.

—   (2007) *The Shia Revival*, New York: Norton.

Qutb, S. (2006) *Milestones*, New York: Islamic Book Service.

Wright, L. (2006) *The Looming Tower: Al-Qaeda and the Road to 9/11*, New York: Knopf.

Zawahiri, A. *Knights under the Banner of the Prophet*. Serialised in *Al-Sharq al-Awsat*, London, 2 December 2001. Translated and reprinted by Foreign Broadcast Information Service, 2 December 2001 (Document number FBIS-NES-2002-0108).

Chapter Fourteen

Birth and Development of Chinese Nationalism

Zu Guo-xia and Wei Wan-lei

Introduction

Many western and Chinese scholars have analysed Chinese nationalism since the middle of the twentieth century. A consensus has emerged among the Western scholars that nationalist ideas were introduced into China in the second half of the nineteenth century from the West and Chinese nationalism developed as a passive reaction to foreign countries' aggression against it. The Xinhai Revolution that occurred in 1911 and overthrew the Manchu Regime of Ch'ing Dynasty was the key event in this development.[1] While most Chinese scholars agree with Western scholars on the time of the rise of Chinese nationalism, they tend to make a distinction between 'modern nationalism', which refers to the nationalism that came into being after that event, and 'pre-modern nationalism' which they believe had existed for thousands of years and had exhibited explicitly Chinese national consciousness, reflected in the famous '*Hua-Yi* Distinction', an ancient Chinese conception that tried to differentiate the Chinese from the barbarians (Jiao 1996: 97–105). In this chapter, which accepts the agreed-upon timing of the rise of Chinese nationalism (or, for Chinese scholars, 'modern nationalism'), we propose a new explanation of this development. We argue that Chinese nationalism arose in the second half of the nineteenth century due to the change in the mood among Chinese intellectuals, who experienced an intense sense of identity crisis and status inconsistency after Ch'ing regime introduced a series of reforms in the face of foreign conquest. The analysis is based on Liah Greenfeld's theoretical framework and understanding of nationalism. This chapter also briefly discusses the development of Chinese nationalism after the epoch-making Xinhai Revolution and points out that the proper ways for China's self-realisation and modernisation are still being negotiated.

The betrayal of the intellectuals: the birth of Chinese nationalism

Human beings, as Greenfeld reminds us, in distinction to other animals, live in a cultural reality, a multidimensional fabric of symbolic systems formed in history in the process of the transmission of human ways of life. The human mind is also part of culture. It is the culture of the brain or individualised culture. The 'mind' is a collective name for the complex interaction of separate symbolic processes, including identity, will, and symbolic imagination, among which identity is a central process. It is the symbolic self-definition, the image of one's position in the socio-cultural space in relation to others, providing information regarding one's social status, expectations, moral standards, etc. People's identity is usually stable, but when one is in an anomic situation, it can be seriously shaken. Widespread social anomie, i.e. the gross inconsistency within the system of social stratification which defines individuals' positions in the world, may lead to social turmoil, as people try to readjust the stratification to eliminate these inconsistencies and ensure for themselves the healthy development of identity. Nationalism, which is the framework of modern culture, has resulted from such an effort to resolve an anomic situation (Greenfeld 2006: 212–9).

In this analysis, nationalism was first created in England in the sixteenth century and then imported to other countries. Nationalism has three basic principles: secularity, popular sovereignty, and egalitarianism. The word nation, in its modern sense, means a sovereign people consisting of fundamentally equal individuals. There are several types of nationalism, depending on how the nation is defined (individualistic versus collectivistic) and criteria for membership in it (civic versus ethnic). Individualistic nationalism emphasises individual rights, giving rise to political institutions whose purpose is to safeguard them, while collectivistic nationalism conceives of the nation as a collective individual, an independent moral agent with its own rights, will, and interests that the individual persons who compose it should submit to. Civic nationalism equates nationality with citizenship, the commitment to which is a matter of individual choice. But, in ethnic nationalism, nationality is independent of individual will, being fundamentally a matter of race (Greenfeld 1992: 10–13).

As elsewhere, Chinese nationalism was a result of anomie among social elites.[2] It falls into the type of collectivistic–civic nationalism as defined by Greenfeld. The discussion in this chapter will focus on the elite status of intellectuals in pre-modern China, their identity crisis in the second half of the nineteenth century, and the shaping of China's nationalism under the influence of the leading intellectuals.

Status of intellectuals in traditional Chinese society

As is known, China experienced a very long absolutist (in Marxist terms, feudal) period, from the Qin Dynasty to the early twentieth century. Imperial China was far more unified and centralised, as compared to the feudal systems in Europe. Though occasionally subject to revolts and changes of dynasties, on the whole, unity and centralisation was the dominant feature of its history, due to its unique social structure and the predominant role of the intellectuals in it. As a result, pre-modern China was unfamiliar with anomie.

Pre-modern Chinese society was strictly hierarchical. The classification of its social classes was based on Confucian doctrine, which, excluding the emperor and the nobility, divided the general population into four broad social classes according to their occupations: the merchants (*shang*), the artisans (*gong*), the peasants (*nong*) and the intellectuals (*shi*).

The merchants were the lowest class in the Confucian classification, who made their living by trading in other people's products. They were even regarded as parasites, believed to live off other people instead of labouring on their own. In the western Han dynasty (202 BCE–9CE), the merchants were explicitly forbidden to ride horses, take carriages, and wear silk clothes. Their offspring were deprived of the right to take the civil service examinations.

The artisans, or the craftsmen, composed the second-lowest class. They enjoyed a higher social position than the merchants, but their production range was very restricted because a high proportion of them worked in state-run factories only catering to the needs of the ruling class since western Han Dynasty. The production capacity of the self-employed was also very limited. They could never become an important force.

The third class was the peasants, who comprised 80 to 90 per cent of the population. Having no land of their own, most of them rented it from the local gentry, but there were no personal dependence relations between the two classes. The peasants had to pay land tax in commodities, which was the major source of state revenue. They kept the remaining food for their own use, and focused on their own needs. Therefore, although the huge empire depended on them, they could not become the organising force in it either.

The intellectuals or scholars, comprising about 1 per cent of the Chinese population, were the top and the only literate common class of Chinese society. The purpose of learning for them was to pass examinations. The so-called imperial, or civil service, examinations were based on Confucius's texts and selected candidates for government positions. These examinations were for men only and were organised on three levels: county, provincial, and national. Those who succeeded could be awarded titles and appointed to government positions, which would in turn bring them and their family wealth, power, and prestige. A person would get the title of *xiucai* after he passed county-level examinations, and would get more social privileges than the commoners. Success at provincial level would make him a *juren*, qualifying him for appointment as an official of low rank. Those who succeeded in passing the national level were called *jinshi* and were usually given higher rank positions directly. After that, further promotions were based on merit. Though numerous honest and upright intellectual officials have been recorded in the history of pre-modern China, the pursuit of status and fortune was the goal of most. The well-known Chinese proverb 'When one attains officialdom, even his pets ascend to heaven' attests to the high status of intellectuals with appointments. The intellectuals' commitment to the system ensured the exceptional stability of pre-modern China.

What explained this commitment was, first, that, though in some dynasties there were emperors who held autocratic power, more often than not the small civil bureaucracy staffed by intellectual officials (about 0.5 per cent of the total population) constituted the national elite and really ruled China (Jin and Liu 1984: 25). Civil officials chosen from intellectuals who had passed the examinations were directly appointed and paid by the emperors. As the ruling class of China, they were the most devout supporters of its imperial regime for thousands of years.

Second, this class was highly mobile and built on the idea of meritocracy. Except for a few top scholar officials, most would retire and, upon retirement, usually returned to their home districts and joined local elites (or gentry – *Shen*). However, their titles and positions were not hereditary. Their descendants, in order to obtain the same title and status, would have to take the examinations and secure chances of appointment by themselves. The accumulation of wealth within one family could not last for many generations either, because, under the traditional Chinese inheritance system, a father had to distribute his wealth and land equally among his sons upon his death and his sons among their sons. To acquire status and wealth, everyone had to take the examinations given by the central government, which therefore had a monopoly on the prestigious titles and held the loyalty of the social elites.

Most importantly, this system provided a channel for upward mobility of the learned men from almost any social stratum and prevented structural anomie among them. The examinations were designed as a most open system. In principle, any male adult in China, regardless of his family background, was entitled to take them and embark on the path to officialdom, fame, and positions. It frequently happened that individuals rose from a low social status to political prominence through success in the examinations. So this system was a double-win device for the empire and the educated, recruiting talent for the administration and meanwhile providing an outlet for talented individuals' aspirations. Even those who failed in the examinations could find peace within the system: there was no limit to the age of the candidates and one could take them as many times as he wished; as one of the handful of literate people, they enjoyed higher social status than their illiterate countrymen. The civil service system was a nearly perfect crisis-prevention mechanism in imperial China, ensuring the fluidity of the society and avoiding widespread anomie among its elites.

One feature of the Confucian classification of Chinese social classes was that it did not assign noblemen to any stratum; these were either relatives of the emperor or had made an unusually significant contribution to the empire, and held peerage titles of different ranks, only some of which were hereditary. The nobility enjoyed little social and political influence under China's unique bureaucratic recruitment system. They could only acquire influence after passing the examinations and becoming professional bureaucrats, just like the candidates from common families. In most cases, the bearer of the title of nobility was given a fixed income paid by the state or a piece of land, enjoying a care-free and honoured life, but was not expected to involve himself in the empire's politics. Even so, noble status and titles could hardly be kept for long because of the change of dynasties. In China, though customarily the emperorship would be transmitted from a father to his oldest son, it was not at all unusual for emperors to be replaced by rebel leaders, leading to changes of dynasty. When an old dynasty collapsed, the majority of the nobility were either killed in civil wars or executed after the new rulers were enthroned, and the minority who survived were invariably reduced to the status of commoners and lost their privileges. Therefore, the ancient aristocracy of Europe had no counterpart in China.

In a word, in traditional Chinese society, the scholar stratum, or the intellectuals, were the social elite. This included the scholars who were waiting to be appointed to offices, those who held offices, and those who became local gentry after retirement. They commanded the lion's share of the country's political and cultural resources and part of its economic resources, and were known as the first of all occupations. The change of their mentality would inevitably lead to the change of the country's consciousness.

Identity crisis of Chinese intellectuals in the final years of the Ch'ing regime

In the second half of the nineteenth century, Chinese society experienced dramatic changes. As a reaction to Western invasions, the Ch'ing dynasty implemented a series of reforms, especially in education and examinations. These reforms disrupted the equilibrium of the Chinese social structure and placed the intellectuals in the situation of anomie, a mismatch between their personal expectations and wider social requirements. To assuage their sense of alienation, foreign-educated intellectuals imported nationalism from the West and spread it to the huge number of domestically educated ones. Together they brought about the revolution in China in the first two decades of the twentieth century.

Since the 1830s, China had become a target of the aggression of Western powers. It suffered a series of defeats in the resistance wars and had to sign humiliating treaties. The First Opium War (1839–42) concluded with the Treaty of Nanking, forcing China to pay an indemnity, open four ports and cede Hong Kong to Britain. The Second Opium War with Britain and France (1856–60) was even more humiliating: the capital was occupied by foreign troops and more treaties undermining China's sovereignty were signed. The Ch'ing regime was determined to carry out self-improvement reforms to prevent similar humiliation in the future. Among the innovations, two were aimed at the intellectuals, which eventually led to the rise of Chinese nationalism.

One was sending students abroad. China's defeats in the wars made some enlightened officials, such as Li Hung-chang, realise that only adopting Western military technology could strengthen China against the West. The simplest way to achieve this was to learn it at the source. From 1872, students, supported by the government, began to travel overseas. Before 1895, small groups of students were sent to America and Europe, but after 1896, the movement gained momentum, with the majority going to Japan.

In the first three years, 120 Chinese boys nine to fifteen years of age were sent in four groups of thirty to America to study for fifteen years. Hosted in fifty-four Connecticut families, they attended American public schools, but also learned Chinese classics at the headquarters of the educational mission in Hartford (Wang 1966: 44). They worked diligently and excelled both academically and socially. By 1880, more than half of them had entered American colleges and universities, 22 going to Yale, 8 to MIT, 3 to Columbia, and one to Harvard. Their academic achievement was matched by excellence in sports. They were good at baseball, swimming, skating, soccer, and rowing (Luo 2007: 16–17).

Their academic progress was accompanied by rapid Americanisation. Some even refused to review Chinese lessons, or cut their long pigtail braids. A number converted to Christianity, a few dated American girls. Deciding that this violated the mission's regulations, the imperial court recalled the students in 1881. In 1882, ninety-four of them returned to China. By then, only two students had finished their university education, but many were expecting to finish in one or two years (Luo 2007: 25). They were appalled by the government's action.

What upset them even more was the chilly reception upon their return. Arriving in Shanghai, they were shut in a school building like prisoners, not even allowed to attend the mid-autumn festival. The sharp contrast between the free life in America and the punishing treatment in China proved traumatic. Huang Kai-jia, one of the boys, wrote to an American friend: 'only in sleep could we get a moment free from the severe pain and misery' (Qian and Hu 2010: 118). Then, regardless of their majors in American schools, they were allocated to random schools and offices: twenty-one were sent to a telecommunication bureau to learn the technique of the telegraph, twenty-three were employed by the Shanghai Dockyard and Machinery Bureau, and fiftly were sent to work in the navy (Luo 2007: 25). Though a number of them became leading figures decades later in politics, technology, and engineering in the Republic of China, they all experienced much hardship and frustration. For example, Jeme Tien-yow, who had majored in engineering and was later honoured as the father of the Chinese railroads, was first assigned to teach English in the navy. He was able to return to his profession only eight years later.

This inconsiderate treatment and positions incommensurate with their education undermined the boys' identity and disaffected them from the regime. Huang complained in the letter of being assigned to work in Shanghai for a meagre salary of ten taels of silver a month, with which he had to support his whole family, while even the children studying in the arsenal could get five taels a month: clearly, the government did not value return students (Qian and Hu 2010: 118). The feeling of status-inconsistency in the group was pervasive.

Those sent to study in Europe were in no better situation. From 1875 to 1897, eighty-five students, trained for a couple of years at Foochow Arsenal, were sent to Europe for three or six years to become military, navigation and manufacturing experts. Though they had better employment opportunities than the Chinese-trained upon return, they did not feel adequately appreciated. Before 1890, many were retained at the arsenal as teachers and technicians, but then, as a result of financial problems, were discharged and told to seek employment elsewhere. Some were even reported to be unemployed in 1896 (Wang 1966: 85–6). They had hoped to join the national elite soon after their return. The contrast between their expectations and reality placed them in a problematic situation, the more problematic the more talented they were. They felt they had to find a solution and put an end to their alienation. Some focused on the political system as the root of their dissatisfaction, feeling something must have gone wrong with it. They turned to Europe and saw it as the model for China. Yen Fu, one of the most talented among this group, introduced nationalism to China.

From 1896 to 1911, a larger number of Chinese students, either government-supported or self-funded, went to study in Japan. China's defeat in the First Sino-Japanese War (1894–5) stunned many Chinese officials, who realised that, while China had modernised somewhat under the self-improvement movement, it could not match the rapid progress made in Japan under the Meiji Restoration. Some top literati were provoked to take action, and helped the enlightened emperor Guangxu to carry out a more radical reform. In 1898, Guangxu issued a series of edicts for the purpose of modernising China through military, educational and constitutional innovations. Of them, the educational reform, aiming at the creation of modern education and a modern examination system, was given the priority. The reform movement only went on for a hundred days before being overturned by the conservative forces, headed by the Empress Dowager. However, even the conservatives realised that reforms had to be implemented to some extent to ensure the survival of the regime. In August 1900, the Empress Dowager began to issue decrees calling for basic educational reforms.

As a part of the reforms, the imperial government sent more students to Japan than to America and Europe, because its proximity allowed more to be sent abroad for a given cost and made possible more convenient supervision. In 1896, the first group of thirteen students was sent by the Ch'ing government to Japan. After that, many provincial governments sent students from their own provinces. A growing number of self-supported students also chose to study in Japan. The large-scale self-funded overseas study was warmly encouraged by the government, which, in an edict in 1901, stipulated that all students, whether government-supported or self-funded, should be awarded traditional scholar titles upon return in accordance with the diplomas they got in their overseas studies and could therefore become candidates for government positions. So now studying overseas seemed to be a shortcut to officialdom. By September 1906, the number of Chinese studying in Japan had reached 15,000, among whom most were short-term trainees, only interested in acquiring scholar titles and not in actual study (Li 2010: 390; Wang 1966: 64).

To place them after they returned to China, a type of examinations, called 'metropolitan examinations', were held annually between 1905 and 1910. Those who passed were given positions of different ranks according to their results. The top students were given top positions in the bureaucracy, while the majority had to settle for less important posts, such as teachers. In the first year, only fourteen Japan-trained students took them. All passed and were granted scholar titles and government positions. In the second year, fifty-three took examinations, thirty-two passing and appointed to positions. These successful students immediately became the centre of other students' attention and admiration. The number of examinees increased dramatically in the following years and the number of passing students also increased accordingly. From 1905 to 1910, in total 1,380 succeeded in the examinations and joined the bureaucracy (Li 2010: 403). However, in view of the large number of returning students at this time, the proportion of the successful ones was rather low. So the majority were not satisfied. They had been openly instrumental and utilitarian in studying abroad, believing that the overseas study was a quick way to high government positions. But the number of leadership positions was limited – they could not be attained by all. In a culture that highly valued people's 'face' – status– the less successful intellectuals experienced enormous pressure: the failure to get a decent job meant the loss of face and a disgrace to one's family. So they soon developed a strong sense of resentment and jealousy of those who were successful in the bureaucracy, and despaired of ever securing an acceptable position themselves, which finally turned them against the regime.

The second most important educational reform of the Ch'ing Regime was the opening of new schools. These have produced a huge number of new intellectuals in the past fifty years, who also became an important anti-regime force and firm supporters of nationalist ideas. Between 1862 and 1894, twenty-five new schools were set up by the government under the pressure of the self-improvement movement, focusing on Western languages, such as English, French and Russian, or Western technical skills, especially ship building, machinery, telegraph, military arts, and medicine (Sang 1997: 2). Because the civil service examinations were still the only way of selecting officials, these schools were not very popular at first. To recruit more students, the government tried to make their placement more attractive. For instance, through the 'Proposed regulations regarding the newly created schools of combined learning' in 1862, outstanding graduates from the three-year Beijing School of Combined Learning (set up in 1862) could be recommended to be officials of seventh, eighth or ninth ranks (Bai 1998: 923).

The government was determined: 150 new schools were created between1895 and 1899 (Sang 1997: 2). After 1899, more new schools of higher education that taught more subjects were set up, notably, the Imperial University of Peking and Nanyeng College. A comprehensive education system composed of elementary, middle and higher education was established in 1903, under which children went to elementary schools at the age of six and graduated from universities at twenty-six. In 1905, the civil service examination system was abolished as one of the major educational reforms. To select candidates for official positions, it was decreed that university graduates be conferred the title of *jinshi*, high school graduates *juren*, and middle school and higher-elementary school graduates *xiucai*, making them qualified for positions of different ranks (Bai 1998: 947). These reforms made the number of the educated increase at a drastic rate. The total number of graduates from higher elementary schools and beyond, entitled to official recognition, rose to about 300,000 in the country by 1911, causing the widespread comment that soon there would be no commoners in the country. Experiencing great difficulty in placing all these, the government decided to stop awarding official positions to graduates of the Chinese schools after 1911 and cease the examinations for returning students in 1912 (Wang 1966: 70–1). Thus the only channel of upward mobility for this huge number of people was obstructed.

For over one thousand years, officialdom has been the pursuit of Chinese intellectuals. Since this official-rank-oriented social mentality was still in place, the government's decision to stop awarding official positions was a heavy blow for them. The graduates from new schools looked forward to being appointed to official positions but the majority were doomed to be frustrated because the social structure of the Ch'ing dynasty was not mature enough to absorb all of them. Therefore, similarly to the overseas-trained students, the domestically trained intellectuals were also stuck in an anomic situation and this anomie was pervasive throughout the country, because, in the last ten years of the Ch'ing regime, the new comprehensive education covered the entire territory, even the most remote provinces (Sang 1997: 3). The students and graduates were disappointed and angry with the regime. The failure of China in international competition gave direction to their malaise. It seemed that only a revolution could change the fate of the individuals and the country as a whole, and they were eager for one. Equipped with the newly arrived ideas of nationalism, this previously elite class and devout supporters of the old regime changed their loyalties. As an important and most articulate force in China, they soon made their voice heard by other, voiceless, classes in Chinese society and drew them in. So the 1911 revolution was basically a revolt of the intelligentsia suffering from identity crisis and longing to safeguard their status against the old, but changing, regime.

Birth of Chinese nationalist thinking

Among the great number of Chinese intellectuals attempting to change their lot via nationalism at the turn of the twentieth century, three, Yen Fu, Liang Qi-chao, and Sun Yat-sen, who had all suffered from identity crises of different degrees and all of whom studied or lived abroad, were especially influential.

Yen Fu was the first person who introduced Western nationalistic ideas to China. In comparing Chinese and Western cultures in articles and translating works of Darwinism and social Darwinism into Chinese, he convinced the Chinese literati that only by becoming a nation and replacing traditional government by an impersonal (representative) state could China meet the menacing challenge flung at it by other nations.

Born in 1853 into a poor family near Fuzhou, Yen had received some Chinese classical education in his childhood from his grandfather and uncle. His father had no scholar title and tried to support the family by practising traditional Chinese medicine; his death in 1866 left the family poverty stricken. So at the age of thirteen, Yen decided to take the entrance examination to Foochow Arsenal School, which offered stipends of four taels per month for students (Wang 1975: 1). Excelling in all subjects and demonstrating great ability, Yen was selected to be among the first group of students to go to Europe in 1876 and was admitted to the Royal Navy College at Greenwich. Having broad interests, he read Darwin, Spencer, and others, and tried to become acquainted with British society. On his return to China in 1879, he was first assigned to teach at the Foochow Arsenal, but soon was transferred to Beiyeng Naval Officers' School at Tianjin. Though already an expert on the West of some renown, Yen did not have a civil service degree and his road to promotion was rocky. Under the system that still valued civil service examination and belittled new school graduates, the highest position he could secure in the school was that of the provost. Hoping to rise through the civil service and get more prestige, he sat for the provincial exam four times between 1885 and 1893 but failed every time. He had no choice but to buy a civil service degree with money borrowed from his friends and finally became the president of the school in 1890. However this bought position could not ease his feeling of depression and frustration: he took to smoking opium and became addicted. After the 1894 war, he came to see his personal frustration as an expression of common suffering, and attributed both to the failings of the Chinese system and culture.

Yen's nationalist thinking was clearly expressed in his four articles first published in the newspaper *Zhibao* in 1895 and his translation of Huxley's *Evolution and Ethics*, published in 1896. In the articles, he criticised Chinese traditional culture and its political system, arguing that China should learn from the West. In the first one, entitled 'On the speed of world changes', he argued that what made China lag behind was not technology and science, but values and ideas: the Chinese attached no importance to progress, worshipping antiquity and belittling everything contemporary, while westerners tried every means to make the contemporary better than the past; Chinese rulers, committed to reducing strife and creating social harmony, made all possible efforts to tame the masses and prevent them from realising their rights, while westerners extolled individual liberty and equality (Yen 1986a: 2–3). Yen insisted that to survive the 'perilous change' that it had never experienced during the past 3,000 years, China had to follow the example of Western countries and develop individual liberty.

His second essay, 'On strength', discussed Darwin's *On the Origin of Species* and spoke highly of Spencer's sociology. He emphasised that, as the aggregate of individuals, a country's strength and fate were decided by the quality of these individuals, namely, their intelligence, bodily vigour, and moral virtues, the lack of which resulted in China's repeated defeats in the wars. Citing the war with Japan as an example, he wrote that one could clearly see Chinese people's defects in this war, and the top priority for China was to promote these qualities among the whole population. To achieve the first two goals, China would have to abandon opium smoking and foot binding, encourage empirical learning and abolish the civil service examinations. To develop virtue, people should be made free and equal through political and social reforms, and in turn cultivate the sense of self-respect and patriotism (Yen 1986b: 17–19, 28–31). Here he implied that free and equal people would regard themselves as the holders of the country's sovereignty and popular sovereignty would give rise to popular patriotism. In his third and fourth articles, 'On our salvation' and 'In refutation of Han Yü', Yen further criticised the 'eight-legged essays', which were the basis of Chinese learning, and the institution of monarchy, comparing the monarch to a thief stealing sovereignty from people. Thus modern Western ideas of nation, state, and social contract made their way into China.

Though Yen did not use the word nationalism, his writings reflected national consciousness. Deriving most of his ideas from Western thinkers, such as Spencer and Rousseau, he believed that China had to change its traditional values and reform its culture and the existing system, granting people liberty and equality, and uniting the individuals of the whole country as one if it wished to survive. But Yen did not advocate revolution; monarchy, he believed, should remain temporarily, because the people were not yet able to govern themselves.

Yen's influence among Chinese intellectuals was immense, especially after his translation of Huxley's *Evolution and Ethics* was published. His work was extremely popular in China at the beginning of the century; the theory of social evolution was epoch making. There were more than thirty editions of Yen's translation of *Evolution and Ethics* in the final years of Ch'ing. His ideas were accepted and developed by another talented intellectual, Liang Qi-chao, the first to use the term 'nationalism' and 'Chinese nationality' explicitly.

Liang was born in 1873 into a lower gentry family. A person of remarkable intelligence, he passed the provincial civil service examination at the age of sixteen, but failed in the national examinations in 1890, thus being barred from further traditional honours. He began to read books on Western culture from then, enthusiastically following Yen Fu's writings. Yen's ideas of evolution and political gradualism impressed Liang so much as to lead him beyond criticism of the Manchu Regime and advocacy of political reform in journals, to political activism. In 1898, he, with several others, helped the emperor carry out the reforms mentioned earlier in this paper. After the reform movement failed, six intellectuals were arrested and executed, but Liang escaped to Japan. He stayed there for thirteen years, plotting against the Empress Dowager and arguing for constitutional monarchy.

After 1901, Liang turned into an explicit advocate of nationalism, believing that it was nationalism that had empowered the West. He argued that in the past 400 years, nationalism had risen and gradually developed in western countries – to such a degree as to become the most important idea in modern world. The countries which had accepted it all thrived while those who had not were failing. He distinguished between nationalism and nationalist imperialism, insisting that the former was just and righteous, and that only nationalism could prevent China's demise and resolve its crisis. Liang also distinguished between broader nationalism and narrower nationalism. The former meant unity among all ethnicities in China, while the latter contrasted the Han population with others. He proposed that China should adopt broader nationalism and build a multi-ethnic nation so that it could have enough power to resist the aggression of foreign nations. For him, national survival was China's top priority; its achievement required that all ethnicities, including the Manchu, be united as a whole. Liang believed that, to prepare for nationalism, the Chinese had to be enlightened, becoming a new people. There were deficiencies in Chinese traditional morality, which could be divided into two kinds, the private and the public. Private morality pertained to the relationships between individuals, while public morality governed relationships between an individual and the whole group. He argued that, for a nation, public morality was more important because ultimately the purpose of morality was to benefit the group. Deficient in this regard, the Chinese had to develop a new mentality that would place the wellbeing of the group above all other considerations (Liang 1992a: 105–6,113–4). This led him to the formulation of a collectivistic and civic national idea: China set up as a nation that accepts people of all ethnicities on the basis of equality, with all Chinese enlightened as new people for whom the interest of the whole was the highest interest.

The popularity of Liang's writings among Chinese intellectuals was based on his harsh criticism of the Manchu Regime. His influence reached its peak around 1902, when the great majority of Chinese students in Japan belonged to the Emperor Protection Society which he had founded along with Kang You-wei in 1899 (Wang 1966: 226). Though he was a fugitive wanted by the Ch'ing government, many officials in China kept in touch with him secretly and solicited his advice on many matters. Many radical journals reacted to the term 'Chinese nationality' ardently and had heated discussions on what this meant. Students became nationalist zealots and there was much radical activity. But after 1903, Liang's political influence and popularity gradually declined, because he was opposed to revolution and advocated reformism like Yen Fu. Frustrated intellectuals wanted a more radical movement, which would break all established institutions and bring drastic changes to China immediately. Sun Yat-sen and his *Tungmenghui* (Alliance Society) began to attract the young intellectuals' attention.

Sun was born into a poor farmer's family in Canton in 1866. In 1879, his elder brother who had immigrated to Hawaii brought him to Honolulu, where he first went to a British missionary school and then an American school. He returned to Hong Kong in 1883 and had five years of medical training in Canton and Hong Kong from 1887. Graduating from British Medical College at Hong Kong in 1892, he began his professional life as a surgeon in Macao. However, his medical career was brought to an end in a few months, because a Portuguese diploma was required for the legitimate practice of medicine there. Returning to Canton, he was determined to find a position at a medical college in north China by seeking the patronage of Li Hung-chang but failed. His ambition for professional life so soon checked, and his road to advancement closed, the disappointed Sun decided to leave medicine and embark on the road of revolution.

In November 1894, Sun founded a secret organisation, the Revive China Society, aiming to overthrow the Ch'ing regime through revolution. But it had very few members. In 1897 Sun went to Japan, establishing close relations with the Chinese students there, and, along with Huang Hsing, set up the Alliance Society, which had four aims: overthrowing the Manchu, restoring China, establishing democracy, and equalising the land rights. Later Sun summarised his ideas as three basic revolutionary principles: nationalism, democracy, and people's livelihood.

The key content of Sun's nationalism was anti-Manchuism. He believed that the Manchu were not Chinese. They were foreign invaders and their rule was therefore illegitimate. China could become a nation only after they was overthrown. Democracy, or government by the people, to Sun, represented a Western constitutional government. The principle of livelihood meant that the government should take care of the people and ensure their welfare. This principle had a strong tint of socialism to it, for it proposed to equalise land rights and limit the wealth of 'capitalists' (Sun 1966: 69).

The nationalist ideas of Liang Qi-chao and Sun Yat-sen were different, in that Liang supported civic nationalism and nationalism through reform, while Sun was in favour of ethnic nationalism and nationalism through revolution. But both thinkers embraced collectivistic nationalism.

Sun believed that in China the problem was not that people did not have liberty, but that they had too much liberty, which made the people 'a heap of loose sand'. Liberty was not to be given to individuals, but to the nation as a whole. In a speech in 1924, he argued that the country should get complete freedom. He said, 'Only when our country can act freely, would it be rich and powerful. To achieve this, individuals will have to sacrifice their freedom' (Sun 1966: 690). Liang also held that, although individual rights were a universal value and the basis of the rights of the nation, people should sacrifice their own interests for the sake of the nation. To protect individuals' freedom, people had to protect the nation's freedom as a whole (Liang 1992a: 131). Freedom belonged to the group rather than individuals. In our opinion, three factors accounted for their collectivistic nationalism.

The ideas of these architects of Chinese nationalism were formed when China faced a critical situation, suffering from humiliating aggression from outside and a series of troubles inside. The emphasis on the interests of the nation as a whole would draw people to the cause of China's independence, the prerequisite of a nation state.

Connected to this historical context were the models of nationalism they had followed. Liang got his nationalist inspiration mainly from Germany and Italy, because the nationalism of these two countries also took shape in the course of fighting for national unity and the establishment of an independent country. Similar social contexts made German and Italian models more acceptable to the Chinese than those of British or French nationalism. In his essays, Liang frequently used Germany and Italy as examples, and thought highly of German Prime Minister Bismarck, praising his authoritarian methods and writing that 'to seek the independence of Germany, he resorted to despotism, even dismissing the parliament several times. Although he was again and again stuck in the swirl of public opinion, he didn't retreat from his cause' (Liang 1992b: 210). As for Sun, though he spent many years in America and Japan, he was mostly influenced by French and Russian nationalisms. He endorsed Rousseau's ideas on liberty. Unlike Rousseau, Sun believed that human rights were a result of historical development rather than naturally endowed. But, like Rousseau, he insisted on the supremacy of the general will, because individuals were collectively the authors of the general will which could ensure their freedom. He wrote that Rousseau's advocacy of the original idea of democracy was one of the greatest contributions to government in all history (Sun 1966: 673).

Russian nationalism was preferable to those of Britain and America. In his eyes, Russian revolution was a complete success, while in Britain and America, the revolution did not bring happiness to the majority of workers, but only to the minority of capitalists. He claimed that the workers' suffering in these two modern nations was even harsher than that of people in despotic societies (Sun

1966: 84–5). In short, all early nationalist thinkers followed collectivistic models of nationalism.

The third factor was the influence of Confucianism. Though both Liang and Sun tried to break the dominance of Confucianism in the Chinese people's mind and replace it with brand-new Western consciousness, they were inevitably influenced by it since it had actually been dominant in their own minds. Both of them had received traditional education in their youth. Collectivism, as one of the core ideas of Confucianism, was only reinforced by Liang and Sun, who no longer stressed the idea of hierarchy in the collective.

Since 1905, Sun's revolutionary ideas proved increasingly popular among Chinese intellectuals. Military uprisings occurred one after another, and those who had studied in Japan took an important part in them. In the Wuchang uprising, organised by Sun and Huang Xing, the turning point of the Xinhai Revolution, most New Army officers who commanded the troops in occupying Wuchang city had been trained in Japan and were affiliated with the Revive China Society, and in every provincial campaign several key individuals belonged to it (Wang 1966: 303). When, after the abdication of the 'Last Emperor' *Puyi* on 12 February 1912 and the beginning of China's Republican era, twenty-two provinces declared independence, the governors or general commanders of seventeen had been overseas students in Japan (Li 2010: 450). They became the national elite, performing important functions in government departments after the revolution.

It is noteworthy that, although the revolution was called an anti-Manchu revolution, its target was only the Manchu regime, and not common Manchu people. No genocide or racial massacre happened in China. This was, we believe, directly linked with Sun's definition of the revolution, in which he explicitly distinguished the Manchu people from the Manchu government. He told his supporters that the purpose of the revolution was not to expel Manchu, but to drive away those, whether from Han or Manchu, who tried to impose their rule upon all Chinese (Sun 1966: 79).

Liang and Sun exerted crucial influence on the development of nationalism in China. Liang's influence was so immense that Chinese scholars commented that 'In the past fifty years, every intellectual in China has been influenced by Liang Qi-chao. There was no exception at all' (Cao 1997: 97). As the father of the Chinese nation, Sun's pivotal position in Chinese thinking is also beyond doubt. Their collectivistic and civic nationalism became the mainstream of China's national consciousness in the following century despite frequent internal and external disturbances.

Epilogue

Though the Xinhai revolution theoretically set up a republic and ushered in a new era in China in which political power rested with the people, it was crippled over the next two decades by a decentralised government and warlordism. Yet, in 1919, nationalism surged again, culminating in the students' May Fourth Movement. As a prelude to China's New Democratic Revolution, this Movement can be divided into two stages, the 'new culture' movement and the 'anti-imperialism patriotic' movement, with the central task of the former always being defined by Chinese scholars as enlightenment of people's thoughts while that of the latter as national salvation. The rival Communist Party and National Party sprang up in China in this period and started their nation-building efforts. The Communist Party of China (CPC) was the eventual winner.

Li Da-zhao from the north and Chen Du-xiu from the south were the creators of the CPC. For Chen, the essential problem was that 'the belief of equality in human rights', which was the basis of Western society, was incompatible with Confucianism which underlay Chinese society. To foster new ideas, old ones had to be destroyed, which meant the social basis for the existence of Confucianism had to be eradicated, for there was no possibility of reconciling the contradiction between the old and the new (Chen 2009: 252). This criticism of traditional Chinese culture and social structure became the basis for the acceptance of Marxist ideology.

It is interesting that Marxism, which became the guiding doctrine of nationalists within the Chinese Communist Party, is in essence a theory advocating a kind of cosmopolitanism, spreading universal values. Karl Marx famously predicted that the change of modes of production, communication and division of labour, brought about by big industries, would destroy 'the former natural exclusiveness of separate nations'. He also insisted that 'the working men have no country' (Marx and Engels, 1976a: 73, 1976b: 502). Such rhetoric was obviously very different from the aspirations of the workers' movement led by CPC. Chen interpreted Marx's latter statement as containing three layers of meaning. First, up to the present, no country protected workers, the governing power everywhere being held in the hands of either the feudal landlord class or the bourgeoisie. Second, the workers of the whole world should be united in class struggle. Third, no worker should support imperialism. This interpretation diminished the contradiction between cosmopolitanism and nationalism. In his old age, Chen broke away from the Communist Party and oscillated between cosmopolitan Marxist and national considerations. This reflected the inner conflicts of his role: as a political figure on the margins speaking for the ordinary public on the further margins, he stressed distribution and justice, advocating democracy and welfare of the general public; as an elite intellectual he had to shoulder the responsibility of the ruling class, give more consideration to production and order, and strive for the nation's advantageous position in international society against the background of world conflicts.

Li Da-zhao's cosmopolitanism was less contradictory. Chen in 'Patriotism and self-awakening' and Li in 'World-weariness and self-awakening' discussed patriotism almost simultaneously. Chen believed that love of one's nation implied knowing its 'situation' and 'objective'. Li held that people should first build a nation worth loving. He advised the young to have a long-term view, avoid narrow patriotism, regard the world as their family, but reform by renovating the spiritual and material life of their own nation. The movement that stimulated love for humanity was more important than the one that stimulated love for one's nation, but the former would lead to the creation of the 'young China' (Li 1959: 238).

The significant result of the CPC movement was the founding of the People's Republic of China. For about thirty years, ideology allowed nationalism to be discussed only under the name of patriotism. As a sentiment, it was cultivated as the brotherly love for socialist countries and hatred for capitalism. Until 1959 it also implied a sense of belonging to the united socialist camp. Later, with the Sino-Soviet split, China began to adopt the policy of 'fight with two fists', regarding the two super-powers, the United States and the USSR, as enemies, and only developing countries in Africa and Latin America as friends. Chinese nationalism gradually became more narrow till the melting of Sino-Soviet and Sino-America relations in the 1970s.

Nationalism was not a separate current of thought among others in China, but a consciousness suffusing all kinds of 'isms'. Under the guise of radical communism, it inspired CPC's revolutionary mottos of 'destroying the old and establishing the new' and 'it is right to rebel'. Since the 1980s, based on reflection on the 'Cultural Revolution', most elite intellectuals held high the flag of enlightenment, trying to continue the unfinished task of the May Fourth Movement. Nationalism in this period, focused on modernisation, was expressed as criticism of traditional Chinese culture and admiration for Western culture. The influence of the Tiananmen Incident of 1989 split the enlightenment intellectuals into the liberal and 'new left' camps with different judgments and opinions regarding China's needs and interests, highlighting the inner tensions in Chinese nationalism. The present Chinese government, for its part, explicitly adopts the nationalist agenda, declaring the 'Great Rejuvenation of the Chinese nation' as its fundamental aspiration and national sentiment as the necessary means for the achievement of this goal and the people's unity.

Notes

1. The first to propose this view were John King Fairbank and Joseph Levenson (Levenson 1968).
2. It should be noted that China has been secular politically and culturally since the Western Zhou period (1046–771 BCE).

References

Bai, S. Y. (1998) *The General History of China* (Volume 11, book 1 on modern China), Shanghai: Shanghai People's Press.

Cao, J. R. (1997) *Fifty Years of Chinese Literary Arena*, Shanghai: Dongfang Publishing Center.

Chen, D. X. (2009) 'Constitution and Confucianism', in J. S. Ren (ed.), *Selected Works of Chen Du-xiu* (Book one), Shanghai: Shanghai People's Press pp. 248–52.

Greenfeld, L. (1992) *Five Roads to Modernity*, Cambridge, MA: Harvard University Press.

— (2006) *Nationalism and the Mind: Essays on modern culture*, Oxford: Oneworld.

Jiao, R. (1996) 'On modern Chinese nationalism', *Social Science Journal*, 18(4): 97–105.

Jin, G. and Liu, Q. F. (1984) *Prosperity and Crisis: the Super static structure of China's feudal society*, Changsha: Hunan People's Press.

Levenson, J. J. (1968) *Confucian China and Its Modern Fate* [Volume one], Berkeley, CA: California University Press.

Li, D. Z. (1959) '"Youth movement" in Young China', in *Selected Works of Li Da-zhao*, Beijing: The People's Press pp. 235–8.

Li, X. S. (2010) *History of Chinese Overseas Study* (Volume on late Ch'ing Dynasty), Guangzhou: GDPG, Guangdong Education Press.

Liang, Q. C. (1992a) 'On new people', in X. H. Xia (ed.) *Collection of Liang Qi-chao's Essays*, Beijing: Chinese Broadcasting Press pp. 102–64.

— (1992b) 'Bismarck and Gladstone', in X. H. Xia (ed.) *Collection of Liang Qi-chao's Essays*, Beijing: Chinese Broadcasting Press pp. 210–11.

Luo, Y. Z. (2007) 'Young children studying in America: review of the first group of Chinese students in America during the latter period of the Qing dynasty', *Tamkang Journal of Humanities and Social Science*, 9(31): 1–46.

Marx, K. and Engels, F. (1976a) 'The German ideology', in *Collected Works*, Moscow: Progress Publishers pp.15–539.

— (1976b) 'Manifesto of the Communist Party', in *Collected Works*, Moscow: Progress Publishers pp. 477–519.

Qian, G. and Hu, J. C. (2010) *Chinese Education Mission Students*, Beijing: Dangdai China Press.

Sang, B. (1997) *Students in the New Schools of Late Ch'ing and Social Evolution*, Shanghai: Xuelin Press.

Sun, Y. S. (1966) *Selected Collections of Sun Yat-sen*, Beijing: The People's Press.

Wang, S. (1975) *A Biography of Yen Fu*, Shanghai: Shanghai People's Press.

Wang, Y. G. (1966) *Chinese Intellectuals and the West*, Chapel Hill, NC: The University of North Carolina Press.

Yen, F. (1986a) 'On the speed of world changes', in S. Wang (ed.) *Collections of Yen Fu's Works* (Book one), Beijing: Publishing House of China pp. 1–5.

— (1986b) 'Revised version of "On strength"', in S. Wang (ed.) *Collections of Yen Fu's Works* (Book one), Beijing: Publishing House of China pp. 15–32.

Chapter Fifteen

Reunification with Taiwan: An Unexamined Aspect of Chinese Nationalism

Yu Peiji

Introduction

In the past twenty-five years, we have witnessed the decline of the struggle for ideological supremacy and the rise of globalisation. One aspect of this in China has been the spread of passionate competitive nationalism. In the course of these twenty-five years, China rose impressively to be a global power, while gradually abandoning the key line of ideological command and concentrating on economic development. Today, as in many other countries, nationalism lies behind the major political developments in China, and its spread as a sentiment and motivation can clearly be seen. It shows as both the memory of the worst bitterness of a century-long national humiliation and the great ambition of building China into a strong and prosperous country. Specifically, attitudes to geo-political issues, such as reunification with Taiwan, are now both perceived and experienced as expressions of forms of Chinese nationalism, with the current view projected into the past.

The demand for reunification with Taiwan has been regarded as a mainstay of Chinese nationalism since Taiwan and Mainland China became two de facto independent political entities in 1949.

In the past few years, the cross-Strait relations have been greatly improved through unprecedented economic integration and multiple personal ties. Meanwhile, the rise of China as a political, economic, and military world power was accompanied by a surge of nationalism among both the leadership and the general population. This could not fail to affect attitudes to reunification. This chapter provides an in-depth investigation of, first, the continuity of Beijing's policy toward Taiwan; second, whether the traditional assumption that 'all mainland people wish for reunification' still holds; and, finally, whether this aspect of Chinese nationalism is susceptible to uniform characterisation.

Conceptualisation of Chinese nationalism and its political orientations

Chinese nationalism can be analysed along two dimensions, the vertical state–popular dimension and the horizontal left–right one. In China, nationalism, on the one hand, has been imposed top-down on the population by the state. This state nationalism, 'demanding that citizens identify themselves with that nation and subordinate their individual interests to those of the state' (Zhao 2004: 26), has been both idealistic and pragmatic. The former because of the sincere belief in the legitimacy and greatness of the CCP as primarily responsible for making China strong, washing away previous national humiliations, and thus being the embodiment and object of patriotic sentiment (Seckington 2005: 25). The latter because of the actual practice, 'behavior disciplined by neither a set of values nor established principles' (Zhao 2013: 537). This latter, pragmatic, nationalism 'does not have fixed, objectified and eternally defined content, nor is it driven by any ideology, religious beliefs or other abstract ideas' (Zhao 2008a: 3). It tries to maintain political stability and economic prosperity in domestic governance and to advance national interests in foreign policies. Except for issues of historical sensitivity, involving China's dignity and considered vital, Chinese state nationalism has been flexible and even accommodative in policy making.

On the other hand, China has experienced a surge in popular nationalism, reflecting sentiments of the citizens and ideas developed and upheld by them independently from the state and sometimes in opposition to it. Such critical opposition, according to Zhao Suisheng, 'has a tendency to include liberal ideas and be led by liberal nationalists' (Zhao 2013: 539). Liberal nationalists understand the nation as a 'composition of citizens who not only have a duty to support their state in defending national rights in the world of nation-states, but also to pursue greater individual rights of participation in the government' (Zhao 2005: 133). As to spontaneous public sentiment, it reflects perceived national triumphs and humiliations and is deeply rooted in the suspicion of Western conspiracy to prevent China from becoming powerful (Zhao 2013: 539).

The relationship between the Chinese state and popular nationalisms in the past two decades developed as follows: on one hand, a 'positive interaction' was reached between state nationalism and popular nationalism. Both are determined to make China a prosperous, strong country with a prominent position in international competition. Popular nationalism recognises the contribution of the party state to the nation's standing and supports the authorities in the defence of national interests. Meanwhile, the state uses popular nationalism as a tool for social management and party control in addition to deflecting pressures from Western powers. At the same time, the divergence between state nationalism and popular nationalism is also obvious. While the state adopts a pragmatic position and refuses to make China's domestic and foreign policies hostage to emotional rhetoric or decayed ideologies when there are crises at home and abroad, emotional popular nationalism conflicts with that. In recent years, despite Beijing's effort to maintain control over popular nationalism, it has been growing, generating a widespread feeling of frustration and disappointment. Popular nationalist protests have focused increasingly not only on foreign policy but also on domestic social and political problems, fanning opposition to both the West and the party. 'The increasing assertiveness of popular nationalism has thus posed a daunting challenge to a communist government clinging to its monopoly on power', says Zhao (2008b: 53).

The state–popular dimension of nationalism is also criss-crossed by the dimension of left–right political orientations.

Table 15.1: Political orientations of Chinese nationalism

Type	Xenophobia towards foreign powers	Attitude towards contemporary government policy	Attitude towards Chinese traditional culture	Attitudes towards Western values
Radical Left	Very Strong	Against	Strongly Against	Strongly Against
Moderate Left	Strong	Support	Support	Against
Moderate	Neutral	Neutral	Neutral	Neutral
Moderate Right	Moderate	Moderate	Moderate	Moderate
Radical Right	Weak	Against	Strongly Against	Strongly Support

Source: Le, Y. and Yang, B. X. (2009) 'Zhongguo wangmin de yishixintai yu zhengzhipaibie' *Er shi yi shi ji ping lun, 112: 22–34.*

While in the West 'left' seems to connote change and 'right' stands for order, in China the definition is quite different. 'Left' in China refers to the advocates of orthodox socialism, a Maoist orientation, stressing social equality, protection of the poor and democratic centralism under the leadership of the CCP. In contrast, 'right' is commonly equated with (classical) liberalism. Rightists in general support ideological emancipation, socialist market economy, private property, global participation, and access to the WTO (Chen 2004). Additionally, they embrace universal values and ask for more political freedoms. Active rightists in China strive for human rights and individualism, the rule of law and balance of government powers.

Based on this definition scholars distinguish five types of Chinese nationalism, namely 'radical left', 'moderate left', 'moderate', 'moderate right', and 'radical right', which also considers the intensity of xenophobia regarding foreign powers, and attitudes towards contemporary government policies, Chinese traditional culture, and Western values. Details are illustrated in the table.

Clearly, attitudes towards reunification with Taiwan reflect these different types of nationalism at the state as well as the popular levels. Conversely, the issue of reunification provides a useful lens through which one can analyse today's Chinese nationalism.

Analytical framework and methodology

Taiwan-related policy papers, issued by the organs of the state, and speeches of Chinese political leaders provide the empirical basis for the analysis of state nationalism. The two sources differ, in that policy papers offer a clear statement of the official position, while speeches provide some latitude for accommodating it to specifics of the situation.

Figure 15.1: Analytical framework for analysing Chinese nationalism on political reunification with Taiwan

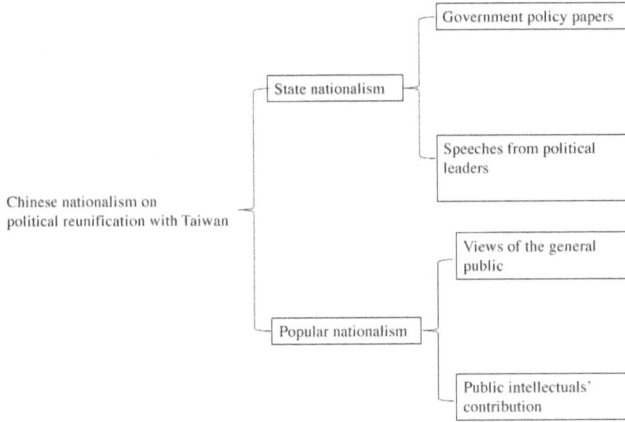

The empirical basis for the analysis of popular nationalism are, on the one hand, internet forums which reflect 'views of the general public' and, on the other, views of independent intellectuals without official affiliations[1] – popular writers, lawyers, and scholars from universities – published in newspapers, journals, and formal social commentary websites.

For the purpose of this research, all the effective white papers and political documents at central level referring to Taiwan issues were collected, as well as all the relevant formal speeches of leaders in the Standing Committee of the CCP Political Bureau[2] from 20 May 2008 to 31 December 2014.[3, 4] The access was based on the investigation of the database of the official website of the Taiwan Affairs Office of the State Council.

For the study of the views of general public, I sought netizens' expressions from online forums with different political orientations.[5] Selected forums ranged from left to right in political orientation, so that they could represent as many views as possible.[6] Note that the population under investigation here is not all Chinese online forums but all netizens' views expressed on the different forums. They cover a wider and comprehensive political orientation on the issue of reunification with Taiwan. Each selected forum had at least some advanced search functions to filter the unwanted information among the tens of thousands of posts. In the end, four forums were selected. They are Utopia (烏有之鄉)[7] for the radical left, Tiexue (鐵血論壇)[8] for the moderate left, Tianya (天涯社區[9] for the moderate right, and Kaidi (凱迪社區)[10] for the radical right. The next step was to locate, identify, and delineate relevant expressions by reviewing the posts related to the reunification issue. Three topics were investigated through searching key words, namely political reunification, the arguments of the Cross-Strait Service Trade Agreement (also known as the Sunflower Movement), and the Taiwan mayoral elections of 2014.[11] The first topic is directly relevant, while the last two are used as proxy for public sentiment towards reunification.[12]

Figure 15.2: Range of attitudes to reunification with Taiwan in the framework of Chinese nationalism

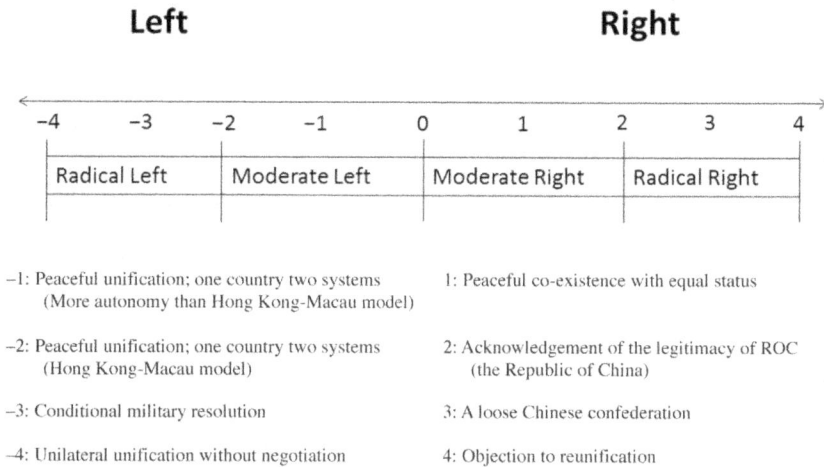

Left   Right

-4	-3	-2	-1	0	1	2	3	4
Radical Left		Moderate Left			Moderate Right		Radical Right	

−1: Peaceful unification; one country two systems (More autonomy than Hong Kong-Macau model)

1: Peaceful co-existence with equal status

−2: Peaceful unification; one country two systems (Hong Kong-Macau model)

2: Acknowledgement of the legitimacy of ROC (the Republic of China)

−3: Conditional military resolution

3: A loose Chinese confederation

−4: Unilateral unification without negotiation

4: Objection to reunification

The procedure of screening the posts on the four selected forums was, first, checking whether there is a specific Taiwan column. If yes, I searched with the key words of 'Taiwan unification' (Taiwan tongyi, 台灣 統一), 'Cross-Strait Service Trade Agreement' (fu mao服貿) and 'mayor elections' (jiu he yi, 九合一) respectively in that column through the function of the advanced search engine. If there was no such column, then I directly searched the three key words through the advanced search engine. There were three criteria for choosing the posts for investigation on the four forums: (1) time frame: posts written from 20 May 2008 to 31 December 2014; (2) relevance: posts had to express personal opinions on reunification (posts on the history of cross-Strait relations, news reports, comments on democracy, and analysis of governance models without reference to the attitude to reunification were excluded); (3) content: selected posts had to be written from a clear standpoint, with logic and supporting evidence (they had to be of a certain length: no fewer than five sentences. Posts merely containing slogans without arguments were excluded).[13] A quantitative summary was made for the distribution of political orientations and a qualitative one for the analysis of major points.

The study of intellectual contribution was based on articles from the social commentary website, the Consensus Website (共識網). This website is a daily updated opinion aggregator that operates through collecting influential articles written in magazines, websites, newspapers, and blogs, regardless of their political orientations. It is the platform for exchanging insights on art and social science in the Greater China area. There is a special column for Taiwan, which collects the articles from officials, establishment intellectuals, and independent scholars in the Greater China areas and overseas.[14] I used three criteria to select from it articles to study which gave the opinions of public intellectuals: (1) time frame: from

20 May 2008 to 31 December 2014; (2) authors: independent intellectuals without official affiliations in mainland China; (3) topic: articles had to express personal opinions on reunification with Taiwan. Political orientations were summarised quantitatively and major points qualitatively.

To aid in conceptualisation, I designed a model of the range of attitudes to reunification with Taiwan in the framework of Chinese nationalism.

In this model, 0 represents neutrality. The negative number range represents Chinese nationalism informed by left-driven or orthodox party-dominated ideation. The smaller the number the more radical the stance is or, in other words, the less space for negotiation and compromise on unification. Basically, the range from 0 to −2 means the moderate left stance that prefers peaceful unification, while the range from −2 to −4 suggests acceptance of military force. For numbers 0 to −4, there is no requirement for reforming the current social–political system or fundamental political compromises regarding reunification.

In contrast, the positive number range represents Chinese nationalism informed by liberal thinking. The larger the number, the more liberal the stance is, or, in other words, the more space and tolerance there is for compromise on reunification. The range from 0 to 2 represents a moderate right stance reflected in the acknowledgement of political facts across the Strait. The range from 2 to 4 represents radical right nationalism, comparatively indifferent to reunification. For numbers 0 to 4, the current socio-political system requires major reform and mainland authorities must be ready to a compromise on reunification.

Interpreting Chinese nationalism on reunification with Taiwan

State nationalism

There were five effective Taiwan-related policy papers in the database of the Taiwan Affairs Office of the State Council, and they are listed chronologically as follows: *A Message to Compatriots in Taiwan* (1979), *Constitution of the PRC* (1982), *The Taiwan Question and Reunification of China* (1993), *The One China Principle and the Taiwan Issue* (2000), and *Anti-Secession Law* (2005). *A Message to Compatriots in Taiwan*, *Constitution of the PRC* and *Anti-Secession Law* are constitutional documents ratified by the National People's Congress. *The Taiwan Question and Reunification of China* and *The One China Principle and the Taiwan Issue* are White Papers issued by the State Council. Despite the different category and issuing agencies, they are legally binding and represent the fundamental standpoint of the state on the reunification issue. The table gives the highlights of these policy papers.

I now give greater detail. First, the government's stance of 'trying the best to realise political reunification under the One China Principle' and 'no tolerance for Taiwan's independence in any form' remains unchanged. Second, the rhetoric of policy papers shows a clear change from soft to tough and from active to passive. While the first three policy papers actively create conditions for political unification, the last two are passively 'establishing the bottom line for preventing separation'. Third, the people and the state of Taiwan are treated differently.

Table 15.2: Highlights of the policy papers

Time	Document	Core idea (if first introduced or any distinction from the others)	Commonality
1979	*A Message to Compatriots in Taiwan*	Hope to establish a dialogue with the Taiwan authority.	To achieve political reunification under the One China Principle of using peaceful means.
1982	*Constitution of the PRC*	Taiwan is part of the territory of the PRC;The State may establish Special Administrative Regions when necessary.	No recognition of the legitimacy of the Republic of China (ROC) under the One China Principle.
1993	*The Taiwan Question and Reunification of China*	Emphasise peaceful reunification, One Country Two Systems; on the premise of one China, both sides can discuss any subject.	No tolerance of 'Taiwan Independence' in any form or name.
2000	*The One China principle and the Taiwan Issue*	Continue the stance on peaceful reunification and set the red line for using military force under three conditions.	
2005	*Anti-Secession Law*	Legalise the use of military force to defend sovereignty.	

The tone of the policy papers in regard to the people of Taiwan is friendly. Beijing regards them as compatriots who share Chinese blood. It trusts the people of Taiwan to welcome reunification. In contrast, friendliness towards the Taiwanese state is noticeable only in the 1979 *Message to Compatriots in Taiwan*, when Taiwan was under the authoritarian regime of the KMT (the then ruling political party in Taiwan originated from Mainland China). With the further development of cross-Strait relations, democratisation, and the change of ruling parties in Taiwan, all expressions of friendliness disappeared. Importantly, the name 'China' refers to the PRC only. It does not implicitly or explicitly stand for any other part of China, suggesting no possibility of the recognition of the Republic of China in the post-1949 era.

As to the speeches of political leaders, from 20 May 2008 to 31 December 2014, there were six transcriptions which appeared on the official site. Made by party/state leaders at the level of the Standing Committee of the CCP Politburo, they include *Let us join hands to promote the peaceful development of Cross*

Table 15.3:Highlights of the political leaders' speeches

Time	Speech	Core ideas (if go beyond the policy papers)	Commonality
2008	Hu Jintao's six points	Attempt to negotiate with pro-independence Democratic Progressive Party (DPP); to end the state of hostility and reach a peace agreement; to make pragmatic explorations in political relations under the special circumstances in which the country has not yet been reunified.	Adherence to 'One China Principle' under '1992 Consensus'.[16]
2009	Jia Qinglin's address on the first Straits Forum.	–	
2012	Jia Qinglin's address on fourth Straits Forum.	–	
2012	Jia Qinglin's address on the eighth Cross-Strait Economic, Trade, and Culture Forum.	–	
2013	Yu Zhengshen's address on the fifth Straits Forum	–	
2014	Xi Jinping's speech *To Realise the China Dream of the Great Rejuvenation of the Chinese Nation*	Injection of Xi's governing philosophy of realisation of the Chinese dream	

Strait relations and strive with a united resolve for the great rejuvenation of the Chinese nation by Hu Jintao (2008),[15] the addresses to the First (2009) and Fourth (2012a) Straits Forum, the address to the Eighth *Cross-Strait Economic, Trade and Culture Forum* (2012b) by Jia Qinglin, the address to the Fifth *Straits Forum* by Yu Zhensheng (2013) and the speech *To Realize China's Dream of the Great Rejuvenation of the Chinese Nation* by Xi Jinping (2014). Of these speeches, two were made by the supreme party/state leaders, while the other three were made by chairmen of the Chinese People's Political Consultative Conference (CPPCC). The core ideas of these speeches are summarized in Table 15.3.

Additionally, it may be noted that, first, that party leaders' speeches, which are not legally binding, adjust the official discourse on reunification to the latest domestic situation and current evaluation of the political–economic conditions in Taiwan. Second, in distinction to policy papers, which use rigid and explicitly defined terminology, the language of the speeches is vague, rhetorically providing much space for negotiation. For instance, while the policy papers explicitly identify 'China' as the People's Republic of China, in speeches this is only implicitly assumed. Third, the speeches of supreme party/state leaders (Hu Jintao and Xi Jinping) attempt to influence the general thinking on reunification, justifying

Figure 15.3: State nationalism's attitude to reunification with Taiwan in the framework of Chinese nationalism

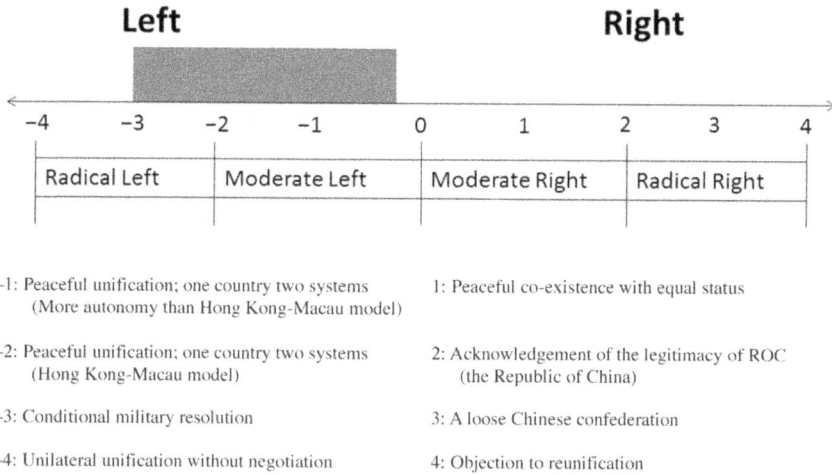

Radical Left	Moderate Left
Moderate Right	Radical Right

−1: Peaceful unification; one country two systems (More autonomy than Hong Kong-Macau model)

−2: Peaceful unification; one country two systems (Hong Kong-Macau model)

−3: Conditional military resolution

−4: Unilateral unification without negotiation

1: Peaceful co-existence with equal status

2: Acknowledgement of the legitimacy of ROC (the Republic of China)

3: A loose Chinese confederation

4: Objection to reunification

Table 15.4: The overall distribution of political orientations of total selected main posts

Political Orientations	Radical Left	Moderate Left	Moderate Right	Radical Right
Percentage and posts number	41% (81)	37% (71)	17% (34)	5% (10)

their positions theoretically and introducing new concepts. By comparison, the speeches of the CPPCC chairmen are auxiliary in nature, aiming at the promotion of the latest CCP policy.

On the whole, state nationalism as reflected in the reunification discourse may be characterised as moderately left with some radical left leanings and mapped on the proposed model thus:

Popular nationalism (views of the general public)

The three criteria for post selection were satisfied by 196 posts. Thirty of these were selected from Utopia, 85 from Tiexue, 55 from Tianya, and 26 from Kaidi. Overall, the political orientations of these 196 posts from the four forums were distributed as follows:

On the radical left side, the majority preference is for military annexation of Taiwan. Usually, netizens argue that if diplomatic efforts are exhausted, or the Taiwanese authorities are dragging their feet, the mainland government should use military force. This is almost identical with the official rhetoric. Netizens believe that military action would accomplish reunification most effectively. They argue that the People's Liberation Army (PLA) is powerful enough to conquer Taiwan without much trouble. They also think that Beijing's current Taiwan policy produces nothing but deadlock. For instance:

> So far I have been totally disappointed by all political parties in Taiwan. It is impossible for them to voluntarily return to the motherland ... and it is the same situation for people in Taiwan, ... I think our government should take measures to force Taiwan (into submission), perhaps military unification is the only way.

Some netizens are led to this conclusion by the perceived anti-mainland sentiment in Taiwan, demonstrated in the Sunflower Movement and the crushing defeat of the pro-mainland Kuomintang (KMT) in the mayoral elections. These netizens generally think that the Taiwanese are brainwashed and should be punished. For example:

> I know some Taiwan people, their impression of the mainland is 'no democracy' and 'poverty' ... and they use 'China pig' as a mantra. I don't even hate the Japanese like that. ... we may as well use the military to demonstrate our power.

> The essence of the students' campaign (against the Service Trade Agreement) is against exchange and integration with Mainland, and to resist the reunification with the motherland ... if the internal opposition worsens, (Mainland) should send troops to suppress it, according to the *Anti-Secession Law*.

> KMT's crash in the major elections signifies the policy of 'No Unification, No Independence and No Military' is severely challenged by people in Taiwan. But it is a good opportunity for Mainland. ... As long as Taiwan marches towards independence, it is time for China to achieve a quick and clear reunification.

Some ardent patriots argue unconditionally for military action, regarding war as glorious and inspiring, and deprecating peaceful unification as a sign of weakness and compromise. For example:

> Decision-makers should have the determination and courage to have a great war, nuclear war and even world war (for the Taiwan issue).

> Mao's Taiwan policy (liberating Taiwan) is correct. The reunification was almost accomplished. ... The slogan 'we must liberate Taiwan' best reflects the strong determination of the Chinese people.

> The reunification war will be a war that determinates the destiny of the Chinese nation. Under the firm support of patriotic Chinese people all over the world, the Chinese government and the PLA will win this great war. China and the Chinese nation must put an end to secession and march toward a brilliant future.

Some turn to China's historical experience, declaring that political reunification was always achieved by means of war and that no case can escape from this logic. For example:

Looking back for the past 3000 years, peaceful reunification is nonsense. It never happened.

Only fools will imagine so called 'peaceful reunification'. ... peaceful reunification can be tried, but all reunifications in Chinese history were achieved by force.

Finally, military action is justified as good for China's international prestige. Some believe that no state in world history became a superpower only by peaceful means. The great rejuvenation of the Chinese nation cannot be realised without national reunification. Military reunification with Taiwan will be the starting pointing for the rise of China. It will help China obtain necessary geopolitical strategic advantages. For example:

Taiwan allows the West to stand in the way of China's rise. Military unification will eliminate this problem. After reunification, China can control the West Pacific more easily.

Military reunification enables (Mainland) to obtain Taiwan's military facilitates and its outstanding navy bases. After that, Mainland may have its will in Diaoyu Island and South China Sea. (Military reunification) is also good for developing China's oceangoing navy.

Radical left netizens also support the economic war by means of economic sanctions and trade isolation to bully the island into submission. (Note that this is fundamentally different from the economic integration advocated by moderate left, which will be illustrated later. While economic integration presupposes mutual benefit, the purpose of economic war is annihilation.) For example:

The current economic power of Mainland can make Taiwan totally marginalised and isolated. After that, reunification will be rather easy.

While Mainland netizens generally acknowledge the Democratic Progressive Party (DPP) as the pro-independence force which should be suppressed, some of them also show hostility towards the KMT, which is assumed to be pro-Mainland, demanding that Beijing abandon its close cooperation with it. For example:

It is very horrible that many mainlanders still hold unrealistic expectations of KMT, thinking they can be relied on. If (we) continue so, there will be a lot of compromise and appeasement and mediation with the sacrifice of principle.

In sum, war, economic pressure and hostility towards KMT constitute the radical left netizens' position. War is the preferred method of reunification with Taiwan. Though most of the radical left opinions are expressed in an emotional language and plenty of them are apparently unrealistic under current circumstances, some attempt to support their views rationally.

Netizens in the moderate left group believe the best strategy for reunification would be bringing the Taiwanese to the realisation of their Chinese national identity. Those Taiwanese who contribute to Chinese national reunification will be remembered as heroes, they argue. Those who oppose it will be forever considered traitors. Taiwan's reunification with the mainland is a milestone in the great rejuvenation of the Chinese nation. As members of the Chinese nation, the Taiwanese will share in its glory and rise in international status. The Taiwanese, they hold, are Chinese, and national reunification is a general historical trend, thus internecine friction is meaningless and counterproductive; the best way is to understand their unity. The commonly used phrases in this category of posts are sentimental: 'treasure island', 'blood is thicker than water' and 'unity based on flesh and blood'. Here are some examples:

(During the Beijing Olympic Games), when people across the Strait stood up and sang the March of Volunteers together, it was as if we had returned to the 1930s, the era of national catastrophe when all Chinese people united and fought against the Japanese invaders. People across the Strait, only by uniting will we realise the great rejuvenation of the Chinese nation.

The realisation of the reunification across the Strait is the last common aspiration of both the KMT and CCP leaders. It is also the common aspiration of the Chinese people. To truly achieve the rise of Greater China, we sincerely call you, please come back, Taiwan, my compatriot and brother!

The moderate left favour 'Peaceful reunification and one country, two systems'. Within this position one can distinguish three types. First, the compromise 'One country, two systems' offers an economical alternative to costly military action:

Even if Mainland owns overwhelming military supremacy, there is no need to have internal frictions within the Chinese nation again. Hence we may as well sign a contract with the KMT, Taiwan must return (to China) in name and essence, and to become a special administrative region under PRC.

Second, many netizens genuinely believe that the arrangement of 'One country, two systems' is in Taiwan's interest. With it, the people of Taiwan can not only enjoy a high degree of autonomy, but also better develop their economy under Mainland's generous support:

The 'One country, two systems' has achieved great success so far (in Hong Kong and Macau). This system is designed for peaceful reunification with Taiwan. Given this past success, should we also adopt it in Taiwan? Of course! Taiwan can even enjoy greater autonomy (than Hong-Kong and Macau).

Is reunification that horrible? 'One country, two systems' is genuinely no harm at all. I don't understand (why people in Taiwan refuse to accept it)!

Third, the moderate-left netizens appeal to the rationality of the Taiwanese. 'One country, two systems' shows the benevolence of Beijing and, more importantly, it is the best option for Taiwan given the nature of international politics. In distinction to the friendly tone of the second type, this view is expressed in a condescending and threating manner:

Do Taiwan people think clearly? 'One country, two systems' is asking Taiwan to make concessions. However, these concessions still allow Taiwan to negotiate for its political name, flag, or even military. There is no sense requesting similar concessions from mainland China ... the maker of the rules of the game cannot be forced. After a few years, you (Taiwan) will have no bargaining power and face unconditional surrender.

Moderate-left netizens pragmatically believe in economic integration as the least expensive reunification method; directed by the objective economic determinism, political reunification is an irresistible natural process:

when all the food, clothing, electronic devices and loans of the Taiwanese come from the motherland, when Taiwanese economists are proud to own certificates from mainland business schools, there will be no obstacles to reunification. Globalization and EFCA are more convincing than millions of troops.

In sum, moderate-left netizens stress the Chinese national consciousness, the 'One country, two systems' model, and economic integration. Their views, however expressed, generally align with those of the mainland government.

On the moderate-right side, netizens are more liberal, tolerant, and flexible in regard to the reunification issue. The typical position here combines a firm belief in reunification with the conviction that it requires political compromise on the part of the mainland authorities. This compromise is twofold: political reform of mainland China itself and greater accommodation of Taiwan's interests after reunification. As regards political reform, these netizens consider the differences between the Taiwanese and Chinese regimes and Taiwan's distrust of authoritarianism a great obstacle to reunification. Beijing, they believe, should initiate some reforms to make mainland China a freer and more democratic society politically, more liberal economically, and more impartial legally. As for accommodating Taiwan, they believe Taiwan should be given more autonomy than the 'One country, two systems' model allows. Compared with the views of the left, this view requires the mainland authorities to give up some of their demands and make some liberal reforms. For example:

(After reunification), with the prerequisite of supporting the constitution and maintaining national unification, all political parties and people in China should be equal. They should develop their organisations and participate in national elections freely ... the military should not belong to any political party.

The condition of realising the Mainland's aspiration of reunification with Taiwan is actually very simple: it is no more than implementing democratic principles (in the Mainland), commonly embraced in most countries. This means a great deal for mainland people as well ... Peaceful reunification is not only in the interest of the Chinese nation, but also a common aspiration of the general public across the Strait.

Another characteristic of moderate-right views on the net is that, while the general attitude is still pro-reunification, netizens prefer reunification to be delayed. This is explained by the perception of a great disproportion regarding Taiwan between Beijing's huge effort in reunification work and the very limited progress in achieving political agreement. Additionally, it reflects the consideration that mainlanders would benefit, both economically and politically, from Beijing focusing on China's internal development. Taiwan's anti-Mainland sentiment, especially demonstrated during the anti-Service Trade Agreement campaign, strengthens this attitude. For instance:

China is now at a crucial stage of national development. It will not hurt China if reunification is delayed. When to resume (the process)? It will not be too late when the Chinese people can afford (the cost to do the united front work).

Some netizens on the moderate-right side regard reunification as conditional on what promotes the wellbeing of all concerned. For instance:

Ultimately, regardless of whether we are united or split, ... the state must be responsible for the security, freedom, and dignity of each individual and the whole community.

In brief, moderate-right netizens still favour reunification with Taiwan. However, in distinction to orthodox thinking, they see it as conditional on political reform in mainland China, granting Taiwan greater autonomy, as well as on not compromising China's own development or the interests of both communities. They are less emotional than netizens on the left and care more about human rights and individual interests. Their position on reunification diverges from the mainland government's current Taiwan policy.

Finally, though fewer in number than netizens in any other group, those on the radical right also represent the views of a section of the general public. These netizens are no longer in favour of political reunification with Taiwan. They either accept Taiwan independence or actually prefer it. Remarkably, though, none of them object to reunification due to an appreciation of Taiwan's democratic system or civil society. Their pro-independence position is based on the rational calculation that the status of the split may be favourable for the future development of mainland China and for the masses of ordinary mainlanders. For example:

My mother comes from the countryside. She asked whether we could collect tax from Taiwan after reunification when we watched the Taiwan election on television. I said no, and she replied 'then why we do we need reunification?

There are so many earthquakes and we may need to give them money. That's a bother.'… I think my mother's point represents many mainlanders' reunification view.

I want to say, if a son (Taiwan) has grown up, wants to be independent and leave his mother, let him go … if he is an unfilial son, he will be a scourge if he stays at home. Just let Taiwan go.

Taiwan and mainland China have been separated for more than six decades. Peaceful reunification is merely wishful thinking. This is as if you kicked your brother out of the house and he had his new home outside. It is impossible to reunify as the same family.

These posts demonstrate that, though the views expressed are politically radical, abandoning reunification altogether, the reasoning is non-emotional and practical. This small group contradicts the assumption that today 'all mainland people are looking forward to a reunification with Taiwan'.

To reiterate, the investigation of opinions on different online forums allows us to characterise popular nationalism as expressed on the issue of reunification thus:

First, the most popular position among the general public remains the preference for military action. This position is presented emotionally, rather than rationally, fuelled by strong nationalistic sentiment, and is especially prominent among those who consider war a good in its own right and as contributing to China's prestige.

Second, contrary to the assumption that all mainlanders uniformly support reunification with Taiwan, the Chinese general public no longer manifests such uniformity. On the radical right, some object to reunification and even openly prefer an independent Taiwan. Their main arguments are practical, rather than ideological: democratisation, civil society, and national self-determination receive no mention. Though the 'pro-independence' group in our investigation is small, it reflects a new trend in popular nationalism. It also reflects the negative perception of Beijing's current Taiwan policy.

Third, the general public's views on reunification show a polarisation and limited overlap with the current policy. Though the mainland authorities still preserve the possibility of using military force if all other options fail, most supporters of military intervention among the general public prefer it. Judging by the conditions for using force they mention and the methods of fighting, the public's views are far more radical than those of the government. As for the views of the public on the moderate and radical right, they are obviously unacceptable to the government. This means that the state and the public agree only on aspects of 'One country, two systems' and economic integration.

Fourth, popular nationalism revealed in the public views on reunification is highly emotional across the spectrum. Arguments for military reunification and appeals to national consciousness are emotionally driven, but so are seemingly rational calls for political reform or Taiwan's independence, the salient emotion in this case being dissatisfaction with state nationalism.

Figure 15.4: Political orientation span of popular nationalism (general public)

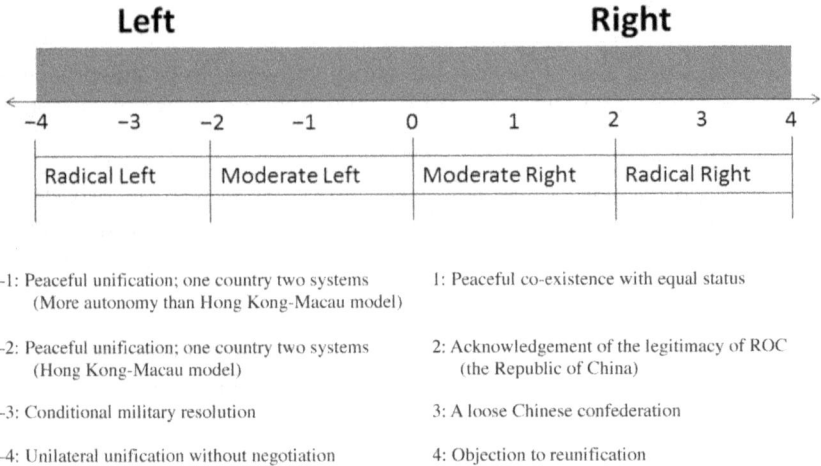

−1: Peaceful unification; one country two systems
    (More autonomy than Hong Kong-Macau model)

−2: Peaceful unification; one country two systems
    (Hong Kong-Macau model)

−3: Conditional military resolution

−4: Unilateral unification without negotiation

1: Peaceful co-existence with equal status

2: Acknowledgement of the legitimacy of ROC
    (the Republic of China)

3: A loose Chinese confederation

4: Objection to reunification

Table 15.5: The distribution of political orientations in public intellectuals'
contributions

	Radical Left	Moderate Left	Moderate Right	Radical Right
No. of articles	4	17	29	1
Percentage	8%	33%	57%	2%

Finally, while, as is agreed, post-2008 cross-Strait relations have been unusually friendly, this is not reflected in the friendliness of the general public's views on reunification. On the contrary, precisely because of the new situation across the Strait, mainlanders have become more aggressive towards Taiwan and its people, and more radical on the reunification issue. The majority of supporters of military reunification, almost all the nationalistic enthusiasts and supporters of 'One country, two systems', however, seem to be unaffected by the improvement of cross-Strait relations in the past few years.

Mapped on our model, contemporary popular nationalism revealed through the prism of reunification spans the full range of political orientations.

Popular nationalism (public intellectuals' contributions)

To investigate the contribution of public intellectuals, I selected fifty-one articles in total from 20 May 2008 to 31 December 2014 from the Taiwan Study column, the Consensus Website. The following two tables offer the distribution of political orientations and major views in these articles.

Table 15.6: Highlights of public intellectuals' contributions

Orientations / Typologies	Radical Left	Moderate Left	Moderate Right	Radical Right
Legal Principles	–	–	Support One China by the international law; face the de facto existence of the ROC; acknowledge the legitimacy of the ROC	–
Views of Taiwan Independence	Condemn both KMT and DPP as pro-independence forces;'Economy first' or 'One China, different interpretations' is acquiescence to Taiwan independence	DPP is pro-independence force and it should amend its mainland policy	Should not equate Taiwan local sentiment with the independence of Taiwan; respect the de facto existence of the ROC and their proposals	–
Proposals	Establish Unification Department and impose further deterrence measures	'One country, two systems'; looser version of 'One country, two systems'; transitional proposals to promote reunification	Cooperation with DPP; initiate political reform in Mainland; enhance soft power; call for the principle of political equality	An integration based on the EU model

In detail, the articles exhibit the following characteristics. All public intellectuals support reunification with Taiwan and are moderate in their views on the issue, but liberal (right) views predominate. Though the majority is moderate, a few public intellectuals embrace the radical-left position. Though serving 'outside the bureaucratic system' and independent, their way of thinking and rhetoric are virtually identical with those of the government. Some of these intellectuals' views are more radical than those of the government. For example, they suggest the replacement of the Taiwan Affairs Office of the State Council with a new Unification Department, which shows an uncompromising determination to reincorporate Taiwan. They also advise Beijing to strengthen its military, bully Taiwan into submission, and ruthlessly suppress Taiwanese pro-independence forces politically and economically.

On the moderate left, the public intellectuals' core ideas overlap with the state agenda. However, they are more flexible and pragmatic as to the means of its realisation. This is especially evident in proposals for transitional changes promoting cross-Strait reconciliation. Typically they include establishing *Cross-Strait Relations Laws of the PRC* to legalise cross-Strait interactions and facilitate reunification, reaching an agreement on military confidence across the Strait for defending the common economic and strategic interests threatened by foreign states, and signing a diplomatic treaty between Beijing and Washington to require the US to openly support Mainland's peaceful reunification with Taiwan in exchange for China's promise of greater contribution to international society and allowing the US to continue playing a major role in Asia Pacific and the globe.

On the liberal side, public intellectuals, on the one hand, also show pragmatism, which is mainly illustrated in their honest recognition of the unpleasant facts of ROC's existence as an independent political entity and effective administration of Taiwan, and the Taiwanese general lack of a sense of identity with the PRC and reluctance to reunify with it. On the other hand, they openly support universal values and democracy in Taiwan. Thus, their reunification suggestions often include calls for political reform in China. In many cases, while declaring themselves in favour of reunification, they in effect acknowledge the existence of two Chinas and imagine the reunified Chinese state as being from both PRC and ROC. Some views – for instance, the proposal of integration based on the EU model – even by neutral standards, can hardly be interpreted as supporting national reunification, because the sovereignty of Taiwan is assumed.

Figure 15.5: Political orientations in popular nationalism (public intellectuals)

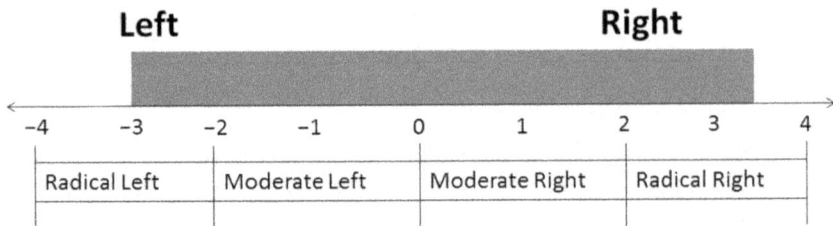

−1: Peaceful unification; one country two systems (More autonomy than Hong Kong-Macau model)

1: Peaceful co-existence with equal status

−2: Peaceful unification; one country two systems (Hong Kong-Macau model)

2: Acknowledgement of the legitimacy of ROC (the Republic of China)

−3: Conditional military resolution

3: A loose Chinese confederation

−4: Unilateral unification without negotiation

4: Objection to reunification

In sum, the nationalism of public intellectuals as expressed in their views on reunification mostly reflects a moderately right orientation, with some addition of moderate-left views and a limited number of radical positions.

Conclusion

In the framework of Chinese state nationalism today, the settlement of the Taiwan issue and the realisation of the complete reunification of China represent fundamental national interests. Reunification along the 'One country, two systems' model under PRC sovereignty through peaceful negotiation is the ideal option, and the mainland government pursues it with the greatest sincerity and utmost effort. It reserves the option of achieving these goals by military means, but only as the last resort. Considering the political reality across the Strait, as long as Taiwan acknowledges the 'One China principle,' the mainland authorities are willing to make accommodations.

By comparison, popular nationalism is ambiguous on reunification. On the one hand, the desirability of reunification is largely accepted. However, there is no consensus regarding how to achieve it: a clear division exists between the conservative (left) and liberal (right) positions. The left insists on the dominance of the PRC and believes that Taiwan should become a local administrative unit after reunification. It further believes that the mainland government is justified in using military force, though reunification may also be achieved peacefully along the 'One country, two systems' model, mainly through economic integration. On the other hand, liberals think that it cannot be realised without political compromise on the part of the mainland authorities, meaning that Beijing should either reform itself or allow Taiwan to have more autonomy than in the 'One country, two systems' model. Some liberal opinions, though ostensibly pro-unification, acknowledge the reality of 'Two Chinas,' or a de facto independence for Taiwan. Some openly object to reunification. This proves wrong the assumption that 'all mainlanders desire reunification with Taiwan'.

Popular nationalism and state nationalism differ in two additional ways. First, popular nationalism is polarised in the political orientation of views on reunification. While state nationalism can be characterised as falling on the moderately left side, popular nationalism tends to the radical left and moderate right. The overlap between state nationalism and popular nationalism is limited. The state heavily favours 'One country, two systems' through peaceful reunification. It considers the radical-left option of military force only if other options fail. But the general public favours use of force (the majority clamouring for war without even attempting peaceful negotiations), while public intellectuals, for their part, prefer political compromise.

The other difference is that popular nationalism reflects rapid changes in cross-Strait relations post-2008, while state nationalism does not. Among the public, the perception of the disproportion between the Mainland's effort and the limited political outcome leads many away from the established position. They either become convinced that nothing but military force will do, or give up on reunification altogether. Meanwhile, the unprecedented openness across the Strait enables mainlanders to better observe the political and social differences between the two sides and makes quite a few of them conclude that only political reform in China will make reunification possible. In contrast, the position of the state remains unchanged. No Taiwan-related legal document has been released since 2008. Even though the supreme political leaders gave speeches to keep pace with the time, these speeches reflected the established Taiwan policy based on pre-2008 legal documents.

Today, under the authoritarian rule in mainland China, a split exists between state nationalism and popular nationalism. The latter is beyond the total control of the state authorities and develops on its own. This reveals that the Chinese people no longer take the proclamations of the party and the state on issues such as reunification with Taiwan for granted, but rather question them and reach their own conclusions.

Notes

1. Because of the contemporary Chinese political system, intellectuals in China can also be establishment (non-independent); they serve the official affiliations and institutions that directly work for the CCP and the government, playing the function of mouthpiece for the party states. Typical institutions are the *People's Daily*, the China Academy of Social Sciences, *Hongqi* (紅旗) magazine, *Qiushi* (求是) magazine, etc. In this light, we can regard the voice from official intellectuals as unlikely to be independent but to provide theoretic justification and to makes propaganda for state nationalism.

2. This part does not count the speeches from officials at provincial and ministerial levels because the quantity is too large and, due to the centralised political system in China, lower ranking officials' talk on the Taiwan issue is merely to convey the spirit of the central government.

3. The first date is the start of Ma Ying Jeou's first presidency in Taiwan, 20 May 2008, and the end date is practically chosen to be most up to date according to the writing of this chapter.

4. Since speeches from political leaders always keep pace with the times, a fixed time period is needed as a restriction to make sure the points summarised are the latest. However, policy papers with legal effect are part of a programme and intended to be long lasting; they should not be restricted by a fixed time period.

5. Under the current social–political system in China, it is very difficult to implement surveys or interviews, a commonly acknowledged scientific method to study public opinion on political issues such as national unification. Therefore, the internet becomes the sole effective platform in China for people to present their opinions and exchange ideas on this issue.

6. Apparently, almost all websites in China do not openly declare their political stances but justify their standpoints as 'objective' and 'representative of the voice of people'. The political orientations of the four selected forums are largely publicly assumed in China, based on their major expressions. In addition, it needs to be noted that the political orientations of posts on a website do not necessarily accord with the assumed political orientation of that website.

7. See http://www.wyzxwk.com/.

8. See http://www.tiexue.net/.

9. See http://www.tianya.cn/.

10. See http://club.kdnet.net/index.asp.

11. It is also termed as 'jiu he yi' 九合一 in Chinese.

12. The fundamental purpose of choosing these three key words is to include multidimensional discussions on reunification as much as possible. After all, the general discussion on reunification may have its roots in historical rhetoric or military analysis, while reunification-related discussions inspired by the specific cases of the Sunflower Movement and mayoral elections are more likely to be based on reflections on aspects such as the difference of political systems across the Strait or the gap between generations.

13. This is mainly based on the consideration that political expressions on the Chinese internet can be intervened in by government-hired internet commentators, the so called 50 cent party (五毛党). In most circumstances, expressions from the 50 cent party are pro-establishment slogans and refutations (of the pro-liberal expressions) with limited paragraphs.

14. See the Consensus Website: http://www.21ccom.net/articles/about.html.

15. Also known as Hu Jintao's six points.

16. The '1992 Consensus', on the 'one-China' principle and its respective verbal wording on both sides, was reached in a meeting in November 1992 held in Hong Kong by the Association for Relations Across Taiwan Straits of the mainland, headed by Wang Daohan, and the Straits Exchange Foundation of Taiwan, led by Koo Chen-fu. The consensus was that 'both sides of the (Taiwan) Straits adhere to the "one-China principle" and orally explain the principle respectively'. See: Taiwan Affairs Office of the State Council. (2004) *Backgrounder: '1992 Consensus' on 'one-China' principle*. http://www.gwytb.gov.cn/en/Special/OneChinaPrinciple/201103/t20110317_1790114.htm (accessed 23 April 2015).

References

Chen, L. (2004) 'The debate between liberalism and neo-leftism at the turn of the century', *China Perspectives*, (55).

Hu, J. T. (2008) *Let us join hands to promote the peaceful development of Cross Strait relations and strive with a united resolve for the great rejuvenation of the Chinese nation.* http://www.gwytb.gov.cn/zt/hu/201101/t20110125_1732427.htm (accessed 1 April 2015).

Jia, Q. L. (2009) *The address for the first Strait Forum.* http://www.gwytb.gov.cn/speech/speech/201101/t20110123_1723986.htm (accessed 1 April 2015).

—— (2012a) *The address for the fourth Strait Forum.* http://www.gwytb.gov.cn/wyly/201206/t20120617_2746943.htm (accessed 3 April 2015).

—— (2012b) *The address on the eighth Cross-Strait Economic, Trade and Culture Forum.* http://www.gwytb.gov.cn/speech/speech/201207/t20120729_2862602.htm (accessed 3 April 2015).

Le, Y. and Yang, B. X. (2009) 'Zhongguo wangmin de yishixintai yu zhengzhipaibie', *Er shi yi shi ji ping lun*, 112: 22–34.

NPC (1982) *Constitution of the PRC.* http://www.npc.gov.cn/englishnpc/Constitution/node_2825.htm (accessed October 2014).

—— (2005) *Anti Session Law.* http://www.npc.gov.cn/englishnpc/Law/2007-12/13/content_1384099.htm (accessed 28 March 2015).

NPC Standing Committee (1979) *A Message to Compatriots in Taiwan in Taiwan.* http://www.gwytb.gov.cn/gjstfg/xfl/201101/t20110123_1723995.htm (accessed 1 October 2014).

Seckington, I. (2005) 'Nationalism ideology and China's fourth generation's leadership', *Journal of Contemporary China*, 14(42): 22–33.

Taiwan Affairs Office of the State Council (1993) *The Taiwan Question and Reunification of China.* http://www.gwytb.gov.cn/en/Special/WhitePapers/201103/t20110316_1789216.htm (accessed 23 March 2015).

—— (2000) *The One China Principle and the Taiwan Issue.* http://www.gwytb.gov.cn/en/Special/WhitePapers/201103/t20110316_1789217.htm (accessed 25 March 2015).

Xi, J. P. (2014) *To Realise the China Dream of the Great Rejuvenation of the Chinese Nation.* http://www.gwytb.gov.cn/wyly/201402/t20140219_5697134.htm (accessed 5 April 2015).

Yu, Z. S. (2013) *The address for the Fifth Straits Forum.* http://www.gwytb.gov.cn/wyly/201306/t20130617_4327750.htm (accessed 20 March 2015).

Zhao, S. (2004) *A Nation-State by Construction: Dynamics of modern Chinese nationalism*, Stanford, CA: Stanford University Press.

—— (2008a) 'Chinese pragmatic nationalism and its foreign policy implications', *Annual Meeting of the American Political Science Association.* University of Denver. http://www.lsu.edu/arsci/groups/voeelin/society/2008%20Papers/Suisheng%20Zhao.pdf (accessed 12 March 2014).

—— (2008b) 'The Olympics and Chinese nationalism', *China Security*, 4(3): 48–57.

— (2013) 'Foreign policy implications of Chinese nationalism revisited: the strident turn', *Journal of Contemporary China*, 22(82): 535–53.

Appendix. Online sources used for quotation

Chenwulor (2010) *Taiwan shenme shihou cai keyi huigui.* http://bbs.tiexue.net/post2_4258001_1.html (accessed 25 April 2015).

Fankongtejing (2008) *yiwei lao jiangjun: duiyu Taiwan wutong bi hetong hao.* http://bbs.tiexue.net/post2_3160793_1.html (accessed 25 April 2015).

feichang2020 (2014) *Taiwan jian xing jian yuan.* http://club.kdnet.net/dispbbs. asp?boardid=124&id=10600772 (accessed 28 April 2015).

Fengxuexingzhe (2014) *Jiuheyi Taiwan guomingdang baixuan shi dalu de fuyin.* http://club.kdnet.net/dispbbs.asp?boardid=1&id=10542587 (accessed 25 April 2015).

Guanrichanghong (2009) *A Jiakuai tuijin liangan tongyi jiasu tuidong zhongguo jueqi.* http://bbs.tiexue.net/post2_3970475_1.html (accessed 26 April 2015).

Hanshuangdeyanlei314159 (2013) *Lai yingguo liangnian, Chuguoqian dui Taiwan baoyou yisi haogan, xianzai juedui zhichi wuli tongyi.* http://bbs.tianya. cn/post-333-292518-1.shtml. (accessed 22 April 2015).

Herou (2013) *Xian jieduan bu zancheng Taiwan tongyi.* http://bbs.tianya.cn/post-333-314740-1.shtml (accessed 27 April 2015).

Huazi (2014) *xinnian heci guojia de zhengyi—jiantan Taiwan wenti.* http://bbs. tianya.cn/post-333-401407-1.shtml (accessed 27 April 2015).

Laobing778 (2008) *Zhongguo dalu de xiongjin shi Taiwan wuhuakeshuo: Huge qidu ling xiaoma zicanxinhui.* http://bbs.tiexue.net/post2_2974424_1. html (accessed 26 April 2015).

Leidawang (2009) *Xinsiwei: Taiwan huigui, dalu chengnuo guomindang zhitai.* http://bbs.tiexue.net/post_3595733_1.html (accessed 27 April 2015).

Liu, Y. W.(2010)*Jianliliangansanjunshihuyin, gaishanxitaipingyanganquanhuanjing.* http://www.21ccom.net/articles/zgyj/thyj/article_201004298702.html (accessed 2 June 2015).

Markli (2010) *Taiwan mashang jiuyao tong yi la.* http://www.wyzxwk.com/Article/zatan/2010/04/141120.html (accessed 27 April 2015).

Neijukongziwaishukongzi (2014) *Cong jiuheyi daxuan jieguo kan Taiwan zhengzhi shengtai yu zouxiang.* http://bbs.tianya.cn/post-333-588037-1. shtml (accessed 25 April 2015).

Peng, N. (2010) *Zai xinqidian shang de Taihai zhanlue taolun.* http://www. wyzxwk.com/Article/guoji/2010/01/122185.html (accessed 20 April 2015).

Rujinwuzhangsang (2014) *Taiwan xueyun benzhi shi kangju tongyi, dalu bixu jingjue.* http://club.kdnet.net/dispbbs.asp?boardid=1&id=9944168 (accessed 24 April 2015).

Shibaziage (2009) *Kuai huijia ba Taiwan, Women de tongbao xiongdi.* http://bbs. tiexue.net/post2_4013953_1.html (accessed 26 April 2015).

Shuai33 (2014) *zuowei dalu ren, hen bu lijie weishenme Taiwan bu xiang yao tong yi.* http://bbs.tianya.cn/post-333-540979-1.shtml (accessed 27 April 2015).

Tang, S. P. and Shi, Z. Y. (2011) *Zhuazhu zhanlue jiyu, Kaipi liang'an guanxi xin jumian.* http://www.21ccom.net/articles/zgyj/thyj/article_2011092245760.html (accessed 2 June 2015).

Tian, F. L. (2013) *Liangan renmin guanxi tiaoli de lishi kaocha yu xiugaizhanwang.* http://www.21ccom.net/articles/zgyj/thyj/article_2013031879280.html (accessed 30 May 2015).

Wang, Q. (2012) *Ruhe caineng jiakuai zuguo tongyi Jincheng.* http://www.wyzxwk.com/Article/shiping/2012/01/279371.htm (accessed 21 April 2015).

windonson45 (2009) *Kanle jintian dalu jiaoshou he Taiwan jiaoshou jiaoliu de xinwen, shiwangtouding: jiang tongyi jinxingdaodi.* http://bbs.tiexue.net/post2_3941664_1.html (accessed 25 April 2015).

Woqixiaoyangyang (2012) *Lao ma dui he tongyi Taiwan de kanfa.* http://bbs.tianya.cn/post-333-163798-1.shtml (accessed 28 April 2015).

Yangguangrenshi (2014) *Taiwan tongyi hen jiandan.* http://club.kdnet.net/dispbbs.asp?boardid=1&id=9911693 (accessed 27 April 2015).

Youyongmalasong (2010) Wo xiwang dalu yu Taiwan yi yizhong xin xinshi jinkuai tongyi. http://bbs.tianya.cn/post-333-31596-1.shtml (accessed 27 April 2015).

YuYeGuiHua (2011) *ping Taiwansheng bowen 'qianxi zhonggong 'shixian guojia wanquan tongyi"* http://www.wyzxwk.com/Article/shiping/2011/01/200753.html (accessed 20 April 2015).

Zhao, Y. S. (2014) *Taiwanwenti de lishi ji fansi.* http://www.21ccom.net/articles/zgyj/thyj/article_201001202030.html (accessed 28 May 2015).

Zhongguoxinqingnian (2014) *Guomindang jiuheyi xuanju canbai, taidu weihe chengwei zhuliu minyi?* http://club.kdnet.net/dispbbs.asp?boardid=1&id=10539224 (accessed 28 April 2015).

Zhucebuzhidao (2013) *Gao Taiwan tongabo shu: Bawo ji hui, heping tongyi.* http://bbs.tianya.cn/post-333-285000-1.shtml (accessed 27 April 2015).

Chapter Sixteen

'One Country, Two Systems': Politics of Democratisation and Identities in Hong Kong Since the Handover

Yiu Chung Wong

Introduction

Geographically situated at the southern tip of the mouth of Pearl River Delta, Guangdong Province, China, Hong Kong has been traditionally a part of the province and the bulk of population are Chinese. Though hardly 'a barren rock', when the British came, Hong Kong's population was at most a few thousands, mostly fishermen (Endacott 1964). For the imperial Qing Government, HK was too far away to warrant serious attention, and its distance from Canton (now Guangzhou), the provincial capital, is a little more than 150km. For the British, the small island served as trading outpost with no restrictions, unlike in Canton, to handle its mercantile trade (Endacott 1964: 3–19). However, the fate of HK was completely transformed because of the British seizure. In the course of development, the British were to acquire two more pieces of land: namely the Kowloon Peninsula and the New Territories, where the lease of 99 years from 1898 marked the issue of disputed sovereignty in 1997 between the British and Chinese governments (Wesley-Smith 1980).

Historical relations with successive governments in China

Although the ceding of Hong Kong was viewed as a humiliation for China by the Qing government and patriots, it made a tremendous contribution to China's modernisation, right up to the present date. Without doubt, China had existed for more than 3,000 years before the Western invasions in the nineteenth century and early twentieth century. It was unified two centuries BC. With a system of agricultural farming, Confucianism as the ruling ideology, and a large bureaucracy with the Emperor at the apex, the polity was maintained for thousands of years through the circulation of elites by a system of public examination. The dynastic cycles repeated almost every 300 years and followed the pattern of expansionism, reform, decay, and peasant revolutions (Hsu 1995: 45–79).

By the mid-nineteenth century, the high point of Qing power had passed and history seemed to be falling into the familiar dynastic cycle of reform and decay. China was thrown into a century of defeat and humiliation. To be truthful, the country that was to take away most Chinese territories was Russia, not the Western powers. In fact, the USA was the most benign foreign power in China, neither taking away Chinese lands nor setting up concessions in big cities. British economic imperialism came to play a progressive role in the Kingdom of Heaven despite the humiliating treaties China signed with victorious powers. The British injected elements of new civilisation into ancient feudal Chinese soil. The British defeat of the Qing government and capture of Hong Kong for trading purposes heralded a new era, bringing to China both humiliation and enlightenment (Warren 1980).

Here is a civilisational conflict: an industrial Britain, with superior military weaponry, sophisticated navigation techniques and advanced economic production, conquering a feudal peasantry, corrupt and outmoded equipment, and servile officialdom. For Hong Kong, British colonisation charted a different developmental path, with consequent repercussions for mainland China. Hong Kong became a fertile ground for the transmuting of modern/industrial ideas to autarkic China. By comparison, the island was a much better governed place than the mainland under the decayed government of the Qing. Many prominent modern Chinese thinkers, such as Hu Shih, Lu Xun, Kang Yu-wei, and Liang Chi-chao,[1] had unreserved praise for the British governance of Hong Kong at the end of nineteenth century and early twentieth century. It was in Hong Kong where the revolutionary ideas of Sun Yat-sen,[2] the founder of modern Republican China, were born and developed. As a small enclave ruled by Britain, Hong Kong served as a refuge for dissidents or revolutionaries who were opposed to the incumbent governments from the Qing era (Fok 1990: 36–53).

The Republic of China was founded in 1911. However, parliamentary democracy repeatedly failed to take root, being followed by movements to restore the monarchy and ending in the personal dictatorship of Chiang Kai-shek, leader of the Kuomingtan (KMT, or GDM, the Nationalist Party), who overwhelmed different warlords and unified the country in 1927. The Chinese Communist Party (CCP) was founded in 1921 and struggled for twenty-eight years to gain political power in the Mainland. Ideologically equipped with Marxism and Leninism and its sinicization – Maoism – the CCP was able to capture the support of intellectuals through nationalism and drove the KMT to Taiwan in 1949 (Li 1987: 7–49). Both the Republic of China (Taiwan) and the People's Republic of China (PRC) have co-existed since then.

In the course of fierce power struggles, the KMT was relentless in persecuting CCP members, and again Hong Kong under the British rule served a safe haven for CCP dissidents and revolutionaries. Particularly in the period of the civil war between 1945 and 1949, thousands of famous intellectuals within the CCP and sympathisers took refuge in Hong Kong and waited for the end of hostilities. It was only after Mao took over Beijing and tried to set up a coalition government that those staying in Hong Kong were called back to Beijing to be crowned (Kong 2011, 2012: 168–78, 203–20, 259–302).

The free flow of immigrants was stopped in 1949, the borders closed and the PRC adopted a policy of 'inclining towards' the Soviet Union. Despite it autarkic politics, Mao was adamant in stopping the People's Liberation Army (PLA) from entering HK in 1949. He publicly said that 'he had decided to defer the seizure of the colonial bastions of Hong Kong and Macau because of their economic value' (quoted from Steve Tsang, 70–1). Taking a long-term strategic view, Mao's policy towards Hong Kong was 'keep the status quo and for a long-term purpose'. In retrospect, Mao's astute foresight proved right and Hong Kong has indeed been extremely 'useful' in the different developmental stages of the PRC contained by alliances led by the USA after the Korean War (1951–3) (Yahuda 1995).

Before the reform era, Hong Kong provided the country with nearly one-third of foreign exchange reserves when China practised command economy, and contributed tremendously to China, being its 'window' to the West. Since the reform period, Hong Kong has served as a centre of financial capital investment, syndication, and management skills transfer, and more recently, as an international financial centre, helping China's drive for the internationalisation of the Reminbi currency (Lee 2005: 1–6).

The emergence of the 1997 sovereignty issue

The 1997 issue was rooted in the Treaty of Extension of the New Territories, by which they had been leased to Britain for ninety-nine years in 1898. Hong Kong had been called a 'borrowed place on borrowed time' (Hughes 1976). The days of the treaty were numbered. The negotiation was started by the British side. As administrator of Hong Kong, the British were aware that commercial property leases required a long-term payment period with fifteen years as the minimum demand by the real estate developers. The PRC responded to the initiation as a 'provocation' and hastily summoned experts to study the options available (Wong 2014a).

Hong Kong's fate from very beginning was sealed. Britain's options were limited and its trump card seemed to be the threat that, once taken over by the PRC, Hong Kong's value to China's modernisation was to be totally destroyed. However, the Chinese negotiators stood firm and even counter-threatened that, if Britain rejected the terms set unilaterally by China, China might take over HK earlier than 1997 (Wong 1997b).

Implementation of the 1C2S since the handover

When the PRC announced the formulae of 1C2S to resolve the issue of 1997 sovereignty in the midst of the Sino-British negotiation, Britain was quick to embrace this concept. Mrs Thatcher considered it 'imaginative'. The agreement resulted in the Sino-British Joint Declaration concluded in 1984, which was registered in the United Nations. It took five years for the National People's Congress (NPC) to draft the Basic Law – the mini-constitution for post-1997 Hong Kong – and it was promulgated in April 1990.

The articles of the Basic Law reflected all the features of the system existing in HK at that time, but its essence could be summarised as 'One country, two systems, Hong Kongers ruling HK, high autonomy', which China pledged to keep for 'fifty years unchanged', (The Basic Law, first chapter, General principles).[3] The concept seemed satisfying to all sides. However, the key issue that remained unresolved was the issue of the political system, namely the elections of the chief executive (CE) and the legislature after the handover.

The Sino-British Declaration was vague regarding the election of the top leader. The leader could be selected either by election or consultation (Sino-British Joint Declaration, para. 3.4), which opened the room to deception and manipulation by CCP officials in future.[4] On the democratisation of the legislature, the Basic Law was more specific. The Legislative Council (LegCo) members and the CE would be ultimately elected by universal suffrage (Basic Law, article 45). The first CE was elected by a small election committee of 400 in 1997, with the electorate to be progressively enlarged to 'universal suffrage'. The democratisation process would be incremental.

The Basic Law further outlined the gradual democratisation process, both for the CE and the legislature within the ten years after the handover (The Basic Law, Annex 1 and 2). In the past eighteen years, four indirect elections of the CE were held: 1997 (Tung Chee Hwa, 1997–2002, 2002–5); Donald Tsang (2005–7, 2007–12), Leung Chun Ying, 2012–present) and the legislature expanded from sixty members to seventy members in 2012, with thirty-five members elected by geographical constituencies (direct elections) and thirty-five members by functional constituencies (indirect elections).

Three periods can be delineated since 1997 in terms of the PRC's policy orientation towards 1C2S: non-interventionist (1997–2003); increasing interventionism (2004–11); comprehensive intervention (2012–present). The first and second periods were characterised by politics of democratisation, and the third period by identity politics.

In the first period, the PRC kept its promise. Besides changing the flag and replacing the Governor with the CE, almost the entire team of senior officials (at the Secretary level) remained intact, except that the post of Attorney-General was replaced by the new Secretary of Justice. However, there were two big changes: the introduction of the Accountability System of the Principal Officials in 2002 (Fong 2014) and the first interpretation of the Basic Law by the NPC in 1999, in which the Court of Final Appeal was deemed no longer final. The impact was huge because this heralded the beginning of political intervention through legal channels (Ghai 2000: 189–230). The 1 July 2003 rallies/marches in opposition to the enactment of the Article 23 marked the end of the first period and the beginning of the second.

Politics of democratisation

The most dramatic intervention by Beijing at this stage was the second interpretation of the Basic Law on the constitutional development of HK in 2004, which was exclusively concerned with the electoral methods of the CE and legislature in 2007 and 2008.[5] In the original Basic Law, constitutional change of the electoral methods required only three steps, namely, the submission of the relevant bills to the LegCo, two-thirds majority consent of the LegCo members, and the approval of the NPC (Basic Law, Annex 1). The second interpretation of the Basic Law, however, brought the central government into the centre, three steps becoming five steps: namely, first, the CE submits a report which outlines the necessity of the constitutional development to the NPC (or Standing Committee) for approval; second, the HK Special Administrative Region (SAR) government submits the relevant bills to the LegCo; third, a two-thirds majority is required; fourth, the consent of the CE; fifth, the ordinance is submitted to the NPCSC for approval (Wong 2014b).

The interpretation was different from the previous one in that it required an active intervention from the NPC. Aside from interpreting the original provisions, the NPCSC also made new laws for HK in 2007. In one of the decisions, for example, in any future LegCo elections, an increase in the geographical constituency (direct elections) had to have a proportional increase in the functional constituency (indirect elections), a move that would perpetuate indirect seats in the LegCo in future (*Apply Daily*, 30 December 2007). In hindsight, the second interpretation was the most important, for it shaped how HK would be moving in constitutional development.

In 2005, the NPCSC again intervened to interpret the Basic Law for the third time regarding the term of the CE. This time, it was also widely speculated, even though it has never been proven beyond doubt, that the Liaison Office was heavily involved, lobbying in the District Council elections. On the one hand, increasingly more pro-establishment councillors were appointed by the government to the District Councils, and, on the other hand, fraudulent methods proliferated, such as mainlanders coming and registering in HK addresses not intended as homes in an attempt to increase the numbers of eligible voters (*Apple Daily*, 21 November 2011; *Ming Pao*, 24 November 2011). The outcome of the elections in 2011 was a drastic reduction in the seats for pro-democracy councillors and the Democratic Alliance for the Betterment and Progress of HK (the disguised underground party of the CCP and the largest political party in HK) grabbed the largest number of seats. Pro-government parties have dominated grass-root/district politics since then. Most significant of all was the high visibility in the mass media of the Liaison Office officials, in particular its Director Zhang Xiaoming, a symbol of the Beijing authorities.

The third phase of the development began with the election of C. Y. Leung as the CE in 2012. The compromise reached in 2010 between Beijing and HK pro-democracy legislators enabled the elections of the CE and the LegCo to advance one step forward in 2012, expanding the Election Committee from 800 to 1200 members, though it was still a small-circle election. The number of LegCo seats increased from sixty to seventy, with five additional seats allotted to the geographical constituency and five new seats to the functional constituency.

According to a motion passed by the NPCSC, HK 'may' have a 'universal suffrage' election of the CE in 2017 and LegCo elected by 'universal suffrage' by 2020. Nevertheless, it has been widely expected by the HK community that in 2017 HK would directly elect the CE, followed by the direct election of all LegCo members.

As 2017 would be the year to elect the CE by 'universal suffrage', the HKSAR government in 2013 formed a three-member special task force, headed by Carrie Lam, Chief Secretary, with Chi-keung Yuen, Secretary of Justice, and Chi-yuen Tam, Secretary for Constitutional Development and Mainland Affairs, in charge of forging a consensual constitutional package. The task force launched a consultation period of three months for the new electoral method of 'universal suffrage' for the CE starting early in 2014. On 15 July 2014, the HKSAR government published the summaries of the results of the first consultation on electoral reform, and the CE officially submitted the report to the NPC, thereby formally starting the first step of the five-step process for constitutional development.

However, this time Beijing seemed to have no patience for negotiating with the HK Community in general, and the pro-democratic camp in particular. Beijing wanted to dominate the process. At the outset, in June 2014, the State Council in Beijing published a White Paper, 'The Implementation of "One Country, Two Systems" in the HKSAR', which practically abolished the Basic Law as the supreme constitutional document for Hong Kong but inserted it as the fundamental policy paper that becomes the corner stone of the 1C2S (Information Office of State Council (IOSC) 2014). This was a blatant violation of the pledge made before. The White Paper claimed that the PRC is a unitary state, the central government in Beijing has 'comprehensive governing power' over HK (IOSC 2014: 7), that 'all powers in HK are derived from the Central government', and that 'no residual power' exists in HK (IOSC 2014: 31). It also demanded that the concept of 1C2S be understood and implemented in a 'comprehensive and correct way'(IOSC 2014: 32). As expected, the White Paper was heavily criticised by the Hong Kong public, particularly the legal professionals. The White Paper had violated the spirit of HK legal system and 1C2S and arbitrarily inserted the Chinese Constitution into HK's legal system. In retrospect, the publication of the White Paper was a prelude to further intervention in the constitutional development of HK.

Since the early 1980s, there has been consensus in HK that HK should have full democracy as quickly as possible after the handover. However, Beijing was an obstacle. In relation to the public consultation on the new electoral method of the CE in 2017, the HK public had agreed that the election must comply with the 'international standard' prescribed by the United Nations Charter of Human Rights, giving all eligible citizens the right to participate and compete for the top leadership post. The public had long considered the small circle of a 800 or 1200 member election committee and functional constituency in the LegCo archaic, undemocratic and in need of being overhauled or abolished. People demanded a genuine implementation of the Basic Law.

During the consultation period, more than a dozen electoral reforms were proposed by non-partisan scholars, political parties, social groups, and professional bodies. These proposals were all ignored by the NPC which, on 31 August 2014, set up three restrictions on the universal suffrage for the election of the CE in HK in 2017, namely that the candidate must be supported by half of the members of the Nomination Committee; that the structure of the nomination committee should be modelled upon that of the Election Committee which elects the CE and the ratio of the four categories of memberships and size (1200) of the Nomination Committee had to remain unchanged; and that there would be two or three final candidates. The public were furious at the restrictions and vehemently protested to the Mainland authorities. Even the moderate factions were disappointed. Aside from the procedural matters, most significantly, the NPC imposed an ideological bottom line: the elected CE must be 'patriotic' and 'love motherland and HK' (*Apple Daily* 1 September 2014).

The Umbrella (Occupy Central) movement

The Umbrella movement (UM), initially called the Occupy Central with Love and Peace movement (OCM), became the largest civil disobedience movement in the history of Hong Kong in terms of participant numbers and length of time. The OCM was initially organised by Benny Tai, a law professor at the University of Hong Kong, Kin Man Chan, a sociology professor at the Chinese University of HK, and Yiu-ming Chu, a pastor. The idea of organising it was raised first in January 2013 in a newspaper article by Tai as a strategy for bargaining with Beijing for full democracy, particularly for the election by 'universal suffrage' of the CE to be held in 2017 and of the legislature in 2020. After months of deliberation and planning, the three organisers initially staged a sit-in of about 10,000 people on the streets of the Central, Hong Kong's financial district, in order to paralyse the area on 1 October 2014, the national day of the PRC. By adopting a strategy of civil disobedience and non-violence, the participants would offer no resistance if the police arrested them. Because of this, the three organisers received death threats from the anonymous public (*Apple Daily* 31 July 2014).

On 22 September 2014, in protest at the three restrictions on the universal suffrage election of the CE, the Federation of Students, the conglomerate body of HK's university students, decided to launch a class strike at all the local universities. Students framed their demands with the slogan 'I want true universal suffrage' (Au 2014: 69–91).

On 25 September 2015 (Au 2014; Lam 2015), the last day of the class strike, a few hundreds of students who were staging a sit-in nearby wished to end it by marching towards the Central Government Office (CGO) building. Some students, headed by Joshua Wong, convener of Scholarism, stepped inside the fence surrounding the area they called 'civic square' in front of the CGO. On 26 September 2015, these students refused to leave the civic square. Next morning, after the forced clearance of the area by police, thousands of citizens rushed to support the students. Some students, including Joshua Wong, were arrested. About 50,000 protesters encircled the CGO and Benny Tai and Kin-man Chan came to support the students. On the morning of 28 September at about 1.30 a.m., Benny Tai, urged by the protestors, and three days before his scheduled date, declared the OCM as started. The news spread and thousands of citizens came to show support. The area was so crowded that people began to spill over to the street (Harcourt Road, the main road connecting the east and west parts of HK Island). The police strengthened their forces and attacked the protesters with pepper spray and tear gas. The tear gas did not deter the protestors, who had practically taken over the Admiralty building but had only umbrellas to protect themselves from the police.

Thus, the OCM was transformed into the Umbrella Movement. The UM swiftly spread to other parts of HK Island and Mong Kok (the most crowed area in Kowloon). The movement lasted for seventy-nine days; luckily, despite frequent scuffles between police and protestors, it ended without serious bloodshed.

For years, the Hong Kong police had been relatively mild in dealing with protestors and were respected as effective and professional throughout the Asian countries, but this time it exhibited unprecedented violence. Policemen were fully equipped with baton and helmet, sometimes even with handguns. The brutality was evident not only in the use of tear gas; in addition, Ken Tsang, a young member of the Civic Party, was severely beaten by seven policemen in a dark corner, which was filmed and broadcast by TV journalists *(Ming Pao*, 15 October 2014).[6]

The movement was conspicuous in its defiance of the Beijing authorities, the will to have Hong Kong control its destiny, and the strong sense of HK identity. Despite the size of the movement, Beijing did not back down, but neither did the protesters. Though they seemed to have achieved none of the UM goals, they certainly galvanised the younger generation, determined to master their future. In fact, 'mastering our own destiny' was one of the most popular slogans during the OCM.

The rise of localism and identity politics

Demographic changes in Hong Kong generally followed the shifting political situation in mainland China. Most Hong Kong residents came from Mainland, as refugees, in particular after 1949 when the CCP established a Marxist–Leninist one party-state dictatorship. During the three decades of Maoism, the PRC was plagued by internal factional struggles and political purges. Millions died of starvation. What the refugees wanted was just a place where they could live and work peacefully, hoping, through hard work, to raise their living standard. Many of them, in fact, saw Hong Kong as a temporary shelter, while their ultimate destinations were the developed industrialised countries, e.g. USA, Canada, and Australia.

Two riots occurred in HK in the 1950s and 1960s, both quashed by the colonial government. The first was engineered by pro-KMT elements retreating to Hong Kong, while the second was a spillover of the radical politics of the Cultural Revolution in China (Kong 2012: 92–6, 197–230). The appointment of new governor MacLehose in 1971 (1971–82) heralded a new era in Hong Kong. In the aftermath of the riots, the new governor implemented a series of progressive social and economic policies that enabled Hong Kong to become one of the four 'Asian Tigers' by the end of the 1970s – one of the most advanced economies in Asia. The outstanding social–economic achievements paved the way for the emergence of what is now called 'localism'– a strong sense of HK identity and consciousness (Kong 2015: 185–90). In 2011, during the 1 July rallies and marches, for the first time, young protestors hoisted the British colonial flag as a sign of nostalgia for the past when the British ruled over HK.[7]

The Chinese Party–state socialist regime has followed another developmental path. The regime was a total disaster in the Mao decades. More than 30 million people died of starvation in the late 1950s. More than 200 million people were persecuted and victimised and millions died in factional fighting and persecution during the Cultural Revolution.

Even after Mao and opening up, China's authoritarian political system remained unchanged. It imprisoned thousands of people, including the Nobel Peace Laureate Liu Xiaobo. The rampant corruption and cronyism have been appalling, the land has been degraded, and more than 70 per cent of the rivers poisoned. Hong Kong has been the exact opposite: a vibrant international city where east meets west, ruled by law, a strong civil society, a free city although with only partial democracy. That is why the concept of 1C2S was created by Deng Xiaoping to make these two contradictory systems co-exist.

HK's developmental model is based on the model of liberal democracy: societal pluralism, rule of law, separation of powers, emphasis on human rights, growth of civil society, etc. In contrast, China adopted a totalitarian model in the Maoist era and an authoritarian model in the reform period: monopoly of political power by an oligarchy of the party elite, a state-dominated market economy, a large coercive machinery, hegemonic state ideology, judiciary as a tool for oppression of dissidents, etc.

In hindsight, however, the crucial event that divides the two societies is the 4 June 1989 massacre in Beijing. It may be seen as the defining moment in HK for the rise of localism. Bordering mainland China, HK people watched the brutal slaughter of the students and common folks by tanks and military armoured vehicles. Two marches of one million people each were launched in HK (on 21 May and 28 May 1989) in protest against the PRC government. The massacre was on full display before the eyes of HK people through TV broadcasts. Hong Kongers have never been able to forget and forgive what transpired in Tiananmen Square that night. The following table shows the number of people participating in the 4 June candlelit vigil night held every year in commemoration of the victims of Tiananmen in Victoria Park, Hong Kong.

Table 16.1: Number of participants in the candlelit vigil on 4 June for the past 26 years in Victoria Park

Year	Themes	Figures by HK Alliance in support of the Patriotic Democratic Movement in China (10 thousands)
1990	Release pro-democracy participants, rehabilitate 89 pro-democracy movement, hold the butchers accountable for the killings, end one-party dictatorship, build a democratic China	15
1991	Release pro-democracy participants	10
1992	Release pro-democracy participants	8
1993	Release pro-democracy participants	4
1994	We'll come back	4
1995	Rehabilitating 4 June	3.5
1996	Go beyond 1997	4.5
1997	Fight to the end	5.5
1998	Rehabilitating 4 June	4
1999	Don't forget the tenth anniversary of 4 June, move towards a new century	7
2000	Pass to another generation	4.5
2001	Educate the younger generation, nurture them into becoming democracy fighters	4.8
2002	Let the youth know history and don't forget 4 June	4.5
2003	Don't forget 4 June, oppose article 23	5
2004	Rehabilitate 4 June, let people have direct elections	8.2
2005	Know history and rehabilitate 4 June	4.5
2006	Rehabilitate 4 June, defend our rights	4.4
2007	Rehabilitate 4 June, defend our rights	5.5
2008	Same world, same rights, same dream, rehabilitate 4 June	4.8
2009	Don't forget 4 June, inherit the wills of pro-democracy fighters	15
2010	Release Liu Xiaobo, oppose political prosecution, support 2008 Charter	15
2011	Revolution has not succeeded yet, building democracy is still needed	More than 15
2012	Preserve the truth, democratic currents cannot be resisted	More than 18

Table 16.1: *(continued)*

Year	Themes	Figures by HK Alliance in support of the Patriotic Democratic Movement in China (10 thousands)
2013	Never give up, rehabilitate 4 June	15
2014	Fight to the end	18
2015	People united to fight for democracy	13.5

Source: 1990-2013 figures retrieved 27 August 2015, from http://www.sopawards.com/wp-content/uploads/2014/05/%E5%AE%88%E4%BD%8F%E7%87%AD%E5%85%89.pdf.

2014 figure retrieved 27 August 2015, from http://www.bbc.com/zhongwen/trad/china/2014/06/140604_64_alliance_hk_vigil.

2015 figure retrieved 27 August 2015, from http://hk.apple.nextmedia.com/realtime/news/20150604/53816138.

In general, the number of participants varies each year but in the first three years, due to fresh memories, the number was higher than the following years. Commemoration of the fifth and tenth anniversaries attracted more people than in the other years. In recent years, the anniversaries have attracted increasingly large numbers of young people, which shows the success of publicity campaigns among the younger generation by the pro-democratic political parties. However, in the past few years, young people began to question the annual formalistic ritual, asking how effectively they could transform the authoritarian regime in the north. Organisers in the pro-democracy camp were criticised as representing 'pan-ethnic Chinese chauvinism', ignoring the roots and sentiments of localism which many young people claim to embrace.

The 4 June massacre was the defining moment for Hong Kong localism: Hong Kongers began to be aware of the significant value differences between HK and the Mainland system. They began to see the how brutal the Chinese regime could be and grew alienated from their 'motherland'.

Together with HK's socio-economic development, cultural trends of Cantonese pop songs and martial arts films in the 1970s already provoked some forms of localism.[8] In the 1980s, it was further encouraged by the outcome of Sino-British negotiations when the PRC declared its lenient policies towards HK and promised HK people high autonomy. On the wave of the formation of local political parties, localism grew (Li 2013: 13–16, 208–13). The dominant voice in the HK political scene was 'democratisation against communism (authoritarianism)'. The 4 June massacre exacerbated these sentiments, leading to the first identity crisis among Hong Kongers.

In exploring Hong Kong's identity, four forces may be distinguished: ethnic Chinese identity, national identity (PRC), international identity, and local identities (Cheung 2011: 1–20). I have argued that, traditionally, Hong Kongers have always considered themselves ethnically Chinese, and, even now, as localism grows, consider themselves as ethnic Chinese (Chinese is a complex concept); due to circumstances, Hong Kongers have now begun to negate their Chinese national identity (associated with the PRC) but retain their ethnic Chinese identity (similar to Singaporeans). Regarding the international aspect of identity, accepting ethnic Chinese identity does not mean Hong Kongers are shy of obtaining foreign national passports. It is estimated that more than a million residents have foreign passports (excluding the 300,000 foreign domestic helpers, e.g. Indonesians and Filipinos). The unique character and civility that Hong Kongers possess, however, contrasts with the mainland people. As a colony of the United Kingdom, HK society was deeply influenced by Anglo-American (modern) values and systems. As today the PRC regards the US as the greatest threat to its security, Hong Kongers increasingly see the incompatibilities of the 'two systems' (Chan 2013: 247–50, 254–9).

Amid the struggles for the realisation of 'universal suffrage' in Hong Kong, the politics of democratisation becomes tainted with a touch of identity politics. In political terms, it is relatively easy to define the concept of nation-state, which is composed of four elements: land, people (nation), government, and sovereignty. National identity can be perceived as collective consciousness or the psychological state of affinity with the land where one lives or was born. It could be created, shaped, and reinforced objectively by a variety of factors, such as culture (style of life), religion, language, history, geographical location, social norms and mores, etc. Nowadays, it is difficult to find nation-states with only one homogeneous nation. However, empirically, whether a nation could evolve into an independent nation-state depends on many factors, particularly political situations/conditions, and very often geopolitics. For example, the Jews spread all over Europe until the state of Israel was founded in the Middle East after World War II. Scotland has been part of the United Kingdom for more than two centuries, but the Scottish still wants to become an independent nation-state. Tibet is a distinctive nation and its ethnicity is different from the Han nation in coastal China but Tibet was denied independence by the PRC. On the contrary, a nation-state could become a 'melting pot' of many nations, e.g. USA, Australian, and even British governments have been implementing the 'policies of multiculturalism'.

The chapter argues that the establishment of an independent nation-state depends not so much on the adequate theoretical exposition of the components concerned but rather on the political power involved. It is the power manoeuvring of the various parties that would ultimately pave the way for the emergence an independent nation-state.

Take Taiwan as an example. It is an outlying island outside south eastern China. The Taiwan Strait separates continental China and the Island. In the seventeenth, eighteenth and nineteenth centuries, it was repeatedly occupied by the Portuguese, Spanish, and Japanese. In 1894, the Qing government ceded the island to Japan after its defeat by Japan, which colonised the island for fifty years until the end of World War II in 1945, when the island was surrendered to the Republic of China.

Table 16.2: The survey on the question: would you identify yourself as a Hong Konger/English/Chinese in HK/Hong Konger in China (per poll)

Date of survey	Total Sample	Sub-sample	Hong Konger	Hong Konger in China	Chinese in Hong Kong	Chinese	Mixed Identity	Other	DK/HS
15–18/6/2015	1003	678	36.3%	27.4%	13.1%	22.1%	40.5%	0.3%	0.8%
10–16/12/2014	1016	660	42.3%	24.3%	15.0%	17.8%	39.3%	0.6%	0.0%
6–12/6/2014	1026	660	40.2%	27.1%	11.6%	19.5%	38.7%	0.2%	1.3%
9–12/12/2013	1015	628	34.8%	27.6%	15.0%	21.8%	42.6%	0.8%	0.1%
10–13/6/2013	1055	677	38.2%	24.3%	12.0%	23.0%	36.3%	1.1%	1.6%
14–17/12/2012	1019	687	27.2%	33.1%	16.1%	21.3%	49.2%	0.6%	1.7%
13–20/6/2012	1001	560	45.6%	22.8%	11.5%	18.3%	34.3%	1.1%	0.7%
12–20/12/2011	1016	541	37.7%	25.3%	17.8%	16.6%	43.1%	0.6%	2.1%
21–22/6/2011	520	520	43.8%	21.3%	10.3%	23.5%	31.7%	0.4%	0.6%
13–16/12/2010	1013	1013	35.5%	27.6%	13.8%	21.1%	41.4%	0.4%	1.5%
9–13/6/2010	1004	1004	25.3%	31.3%	14.8%	27.8%	46.0%	0.4%	0.5%
8–11/12/2009	1007	1007	37.6%	23.9%	13.1%	24.2%	37.0%	0.2%	1.0%
8–13/6/2009	1002	1002	24.7%	32.0%	13.3%	29.3%	45.3%	0.2%	0.4%
9–12/12/2008	1016	1016	21.8%	29.6%	13.0%	34.4%	42.6%	0.5%	0.7%
11–13/6/2008	1012	1012	18.1%	29.2%	13.3%	38.6%	42.5%	0.1%	0.7%
11–14/12/2007	1011	1011	23.5%	31.5%	16.0%	27.2%	47.5%	0.7%	1.1%
8–12/6/2007	1016	1016	23.4%	31.8%	16.7%	26.4%	48.5%	0.3%	1.4%
6–12/12/2006*	1011	1011	22.4%	24.3%	20.1%	31.8%	44.4%	0.6%	0.7%
13–15/6/2006*	1018	1018	24.8%	25.1%	14.9%	34.6%	40.0%	0.3%	0.3%

Table 16.2: (continued)

Date of survey	Total Sample	Sub-sample	Hong Konger	Hong Konger in China	Chinese in Hong Kong	Chinese	Mixed Identity	Other	DK/HS
9–14/12/2005	1017	1017	24.8%	26.5%	16.9%	30.7%	43.4%	0.0%	1.1%
6–8/6/2005	1029	1029	24.0%	21.2%	14.7%	36.4%	35.9%	0.5%	3.3%
6–9/12/2004	1007	1007	25.9%	23.1%	16.2%	31.6%	39.3%	0.4%	2.8%
7–11/6/2004	1027	1027	28.0%	21.2%	14.3%	33.0%	35.5%	0.4%	3.1%
10–14/12/2003	1059	1059	24.9%	23.4%	15.6%	32.5%	39.0%	0.3%	3.3%
13–18/6/2003	1043	1043	36.7%	19.2%	11.9%	29.0%	31.1%	0.7%	2.5%
1–4/3/2003	1035	1035	28.5%	22.3%	15.0%	32.3%	37.3%	0.3%	1.6%
13–18/12/2002	1026	1026	31.1%	21.3%	14.3%	29.7%	35.6%	0.6%	3.0%
2–5/9/2002	1017	1017	28.9%	22.0%	15.0%	32.5%	37.0%	0.4%	1.2%
4–5/6/2002	1067	1067	32.2%	18.1%	13.0%	32.5%	31.1%	0.4%	3.9%
12–13/3/2002	1024	1024	27.5%	23.3%	17.9%	28.3%	41.2%	0.0%	3.0%
7–9/12/2001	1052	1052	31.9%	20.5%	10.4%	31.5%	30.9%	0.3%	5.4%
13–21/9/2001	1025	1025	26.1%	27.9%	17.6%	25.8%	45.5%	0.4%	2.1%
1–5/6/2001	1053	1053	36.1%	18.3%	13.3%	28.4%	31.6%	0.0%	3.8%
22/3–2/4/2001	1014	1014	31.4%	21.7%	16.0%	28.2%	37.7%	0.4%	2.3%
4–12/12/2000	1040	1040	35.6%	19.1%	13.8%	25.2%	32.9%	0.9%	5.5%
21–25/9/2000	1087	1087	37.0%	26.8%	14.5%	17.4%	41.3%	0.4%	3.9%
7–8/6/2000	1074	1074	35.5%	22.9%	14.0%	22.8%	36.9%	0.7%	4.1%
6–7/4/2000	570	570	38.7%	21.4%	14.2%	20.4%	35.6%	0.2%	5.1%
1–2/2/2000	566	566	38.3%	23.2%	19.5%	13.8%	42.7%	0.5%	4.6%

Table 16.2: (continued)

Date of survey	Total Sample	Sub-sample	Hong Konger	Hong Konger in China	Chinese in Hong Kong	Chinese	Mixed Identity	Other	DK/HS
13–15/12/1999	529	529	39.0%	20.9%	17.2%	19.9%	38.1%	0.2%	2.8%
26–27/10/1999	535	535	31.2%	23.7%	16.2%	25.5%	39.9%	0.7%	2.6%
6/8/1999	596	596	30.3%	23.3%	17.5%	25.3%	40.8%	0.3%	3.2%
8/6/1999	538	538	39.9%	25.0%	11.2%	17.0%	36.2%	0.6%	6.3%
15/4/1999	527	527	43.4%	20.0%	13.1%	18.0%	33.1%	0.4%	5.1%
8–9/2/1999	513	513	41.0%	20.9%	15.3%	17.6%	36.2%	1.2%	3.9%
21/12/1998	544	544	40.7%	22.3%	15.1%	17.2%	37.4%	0.6%	4.2%
29/9/1998	517	517	39.4%	22.9%	15.5%	20.6%	38.4%	0.4%	1.2%
14/8/1998	526	526	29.7%	25.2%	19.6%	22.0%	44.8%	0.2%	3.2%
22–24/6/1998	1042	1042	30.2%	18.0%	16.1%	31.6%	34.1%	0.4%	3.8%
3–4/6/1998	544	544	34.2%	18.6%	18.7%	24.8%	37.3%	0.2%	3.4%
8–9/12/1997	500	500	35.8%	22.9%	18.9%	18.2%	41.8%	0.2%	3.9%
28–29/10/1997	536	536	36.6%	22.6%	20.1%	17.5%	42.7%	0.2%	3.0%
23–24/9/1997	512	512	36.2%	24.2%	20.3%	17.5%	44.5%	0.2%	1.6%
26–27/8/1997	532	532	34.9%	24.8%	20.1%	18.6%	44.9%	0.4%	1.3%

Source: The University of Hong Kong, public polling http://hkupop.hku.hk/english/popexpress/ethnic/eidentity/poll/datatables.html (accessed on 16 June 2015).

The Taiwanese people were happy to be back in China. However, the independence movement began to emerge in 1947, when the 28 February massacre took place by the KMT army in Taiwan of Taiwanese elites and the general public.[9] Since then the movement has never subsided and, in the past three decades, because of the democratisation of the political system, the views of 'independence' were articulated openly and even gained popularity. During the tenure of President Chen Sui-bien (2000–8), in fact, an 'independence' line of policies was pursued but was fiercely opposed by the PRC. It is still part of the political platform of the DPP, the main opposition party in Taiwan. Is it possible to establish a 'Republic of Taiwan'? The four textbook components of a nation-state are all available, but there is the PRC opposition. If not for the strong objections of the PRC, given Taiwan's large population (24 million), its area (more than 34,000 sq. km), democratic politics, legitimate government and standing armed forces, it could have evolved into an independent nation-state. Similar arguments can be made for Tibet as well.

In spite of its status as a British colony for 155 years, a very small percentage of HK residents define themselves as British, though many of them may have British passports. The bulk of the population prefers 'Hong Kong local identity' or 'Chinese Hong Konger identity'. The rise of localism could be seen from the preference for Hong Konger identity in the previous survey.

According to these surveys, those defining their identity as 'Chinese' never exceed 40 per cent, and the three years exceeding 30 per cent could be explained by the economic and medical assistance sent by Beijing during the SARS years. Since C. Y. Leung became the CE, the ratio declined to 10 plus per cent, a record low percentage. In most of the years since the handover, the combined number identifying themselves as Hong Kongers and Hong Kongers in China exceeds 60 per cent, with the percentage reaching a new high in recent years.

From the second half of 1997 to the first half of 2008, the percentage identifying as Hong Konger and Chinese Hong Konger decreased gradually, while the Chinese and Hong Kong Chinese categories rose to a new high, at times almost to half. However, it is apparent that 2008 – the year of the Olympics in Beijing – was the landmark year and thereafter the percentage declined. The relatively high acceptance of Chinese identities in these periods was explained by the absence of Beijing intervention, e.g. the successful withdrawal of Article 23, and the increasing activities of civil society.

More surprisingly, in a survey on political nationalism conducted by the undergraduate publication of the University of Hong Kong Student Union regarding the political system HK should adopt, 68 per cent accepted 'One country, two systems' but 15 per cent chose 'HK should become independent'. On the referendum question regarding HK independence, 37 per cent said HK should become independent, even if Beijing rejects the result, and 42 per cent, if Beijing accepts it (Undergrad, HKUSU 2015: 78). Of those polled, 48 per cent characterised their nationalism as 'localism' and 15 per cent as 'pan Chinese nationalism' (Undergrad, HKUSU 2015: 20–1).

After 2003, civil society became more vibrant, with numerous organised social movements that actively promoted localism. These movements were often nostalgic about the colonial past, hoisting the British flag. The so-called post-1980s generation has played an increasingly prominent role in them. An observer remarked:

> Post-1980s are young people who doubt the rationality of the existing institutional design. ... They are not satisfied with the existing political order and demand the government tackle issues such as rising property prices, the gap between rich and poor, cultural heritage and the road map of democracy development.

(Lau Calvin: 386)

However, after the successful hosting of the Olympics in 2008, China began to tighten its grip on internal dissenting voices. In May 2008, a strong earthquake shook Sichuan Province and thousands of children died because of collapsed school buildings, attracting large donations from the Hong Kong public. Bribery and embezzlements by officials in building construction materials were revealed, but the investigators probing into these cases were prosecuted, found guilty of subversion of the State, and imprisoned by the PRC (Li 2013: 214–15). In 2010 it was found that a poisoned milk product had endangered thousands of children's lives and that again corruption and the collusion of businessmen and officials were involved. Zhao Lianhai, a Beijing resident whose child suffered, tried to organise groups to investigate the case but was arrested and imprisoned. He was eventually released due to the intervention of Hong Kong NPC Deputies. Another case was that of Lee Wanyang, imprisoned for his pro-democracy activities during the 4 June crackdown. In May 2012, he was released after twenty-two years in jail. The next day, he was interviewed by a journalist on Cable TV and the day after that found dead in suspicious circumstances. The official source declared cause of death 'suicide'. This followed on the heels of imprisonment of the Nobel Peace laureate Liu Xiaobo in 2010. These cases angered the Hong Kong public who felt frustrated and powerless. The PRC was perceived to be completely corrupt, arrogant, and without any justice. This negative image contributed to the alienation of the great bulk of young Hong Kongers and their unwillingness to identify as 'Chinese'. Several groups advocating HK independence emerged (Li 2013: 52–77) e.g. Passion Citizens, Young Aspiration, etc. (Undergrad, HKUSU 2015).

Theoretical discourses: minimalists vs maximalists

The official Chinese view is that Hong Kong is an inalienable part of China, 1C2S has been implemented successfully, and the Basic Law should be correctly understood and implemented. In HK, there are two prevalent discourses on the political status of Hong Kong, one minimalist and the other maximalist, both criticised by the PRC officials as 'independence' views. The minimalists champion the view that the concept of 1C2S should be defined as clearly as possible and that its genuine implementation should be able to guarantee the actual high autonomy of HK. The official view is a distortion of the Basic Law. The CCP /state should not meddle in the internal affairs of Hong Kong. Hong Kong has an edge in global competition, as evidenced by its recognition as one of the 'Little Asian Tigers' from the early 1970s to the mid-1990s. Even now, it is still one of the world's financial hubs, with an important role to play. The logic of One country/ 2 systems implies that the two systems are really equal and one-sided integration of HK by the Mainland destroys the 'golden egg' and harms both sides. HK and Mainland must benefit reciprocally. The CCP has destroyed Chinese traditional culture, becoming a nation of deception. With a high degree of autonomy, HK would have independent financial, fiscal, social, and education policies, which should enable it to develop a new kind of Chinese culture, protecting values and norms which have been poisoned by the Party/state cronyism. Left alone, HK should be able to become a self-sufficient political/economic/social entity (Chin 2015: 166–74, 196–200, 228–54). In effect, this view advocates a 'federal Republic of China' (Chin 2015: 224).

The maximalists, in contrast, want to totally break relations with Mainland. They want complete independence, abolition of the Basic Law, and HK's own constitution. Ethnically, Hong Kongers are Chinese, but this does not mean that HK cannot become an independent country. Singapore is a good example. As a sovereign nation state, Singapore is 85 per cent ethnically Chinese. The importance of the 155-year-long rule by the British cannot be overestimated; it shaped a new 'Hong Kong nation' which may be historically linked with China ethnically and culturally, but developed a new culture of its own under British rule. To safeguard and preserve HK values and norms, political independence is required. Modern Chinese authoritarianism, in fact, is a mixed product of Marxism–Leninism and traditional despotic feudalism.

The maximalists insist that Hong Kongers should have the right of self-determination and that Hong Kong has already developed a unique legal system, social institutions and cultural values, different from Mainland (Lee 2015: 63–76). However, neither of these theoretical positions contains a strategy for Hong Kong's disentanglement from Chinese Mainland. The integration between the two entities has resulted in their almost becoming inseparable. Hong Kong has come to depend on mainland China to the extent that its survival may be at stake if the two are now separated. Above all, will the PRC tolerate such separation? With the Chinese media repeatedly expressing criticism of 'independence' views, could the CCP party/state simply stand and watch the drama unfold? Certainly not. On 30 July 2015, the PLA for the first time conducted military exercises, fighting against separatist/terrorists in the urban area. More than 500 guests were invited to watch the drill, including the vice-chancellor of the Chinese University of Hong Kong (*Ming Pao* 31–30 July 2015). I believe that China would not hesitate in cracking down on a Hong Kong separatist movement.

Whither Hong Kong localism?

The CCP counts Hong Kong's 'independence' movement among the four independence movements in contemporary China, the others being Tibetan,

Taiwanese and Xinjiangese. Evidently, Hong Kong's movement is in essence different from these three (*Ming Pao*, 30 September 2015). In geographical size, HK is the smallest among the four areas; in population, however, it is, with 7.5 million, second to Taiwan with its 23 million. Tibet and Xinjiang are comparatively underpopulated. More significantly, their populations are ethnically different, while Hong Kong and Taiwan are predominantly Han. The four communities have different histories of involvement with foreign powers. The exiled Tibetan government led by the Dalai Lama was supported by most of the Western countries, and Xinjiang's independence movement has links with the radical Islamic movement in Central Asia. Hong Kong and Taiwan were once colonies of the United Kingdom and Japan but now maintain little contact with them. Culturally, however, both have inherited many civic values of their former colonial masters and still feel spiritual affinity with them. As one of the global financial centres, Hong Kong has the most foreign contacts of the four places. The USA, the only superpower in the world, supports the existing systems in Hong Kong and Taiwan, while having relatively little influence in Tibet and Xinjiang.

The weakness of Hong Kong's so-called 'independence' movement is obvious. It lacks organised power and does not have a strong basis. Organisationally, it is hardly a movement, but, rather, a scattered voice in the academe, articulated by a number of social groups with 'independence' leanings, and shared by the younger generation. The minimalists have more influence; sometimes involved in street scuffles with mainlanders, they at most could attract a few hundred young people. After all, 95 per cent of the population in Hong Kong is Han Chinese. Since the handover, more than 900,000 mainlanders have moved into Hong Kong (the formal daily quota for immigrants is 150), excluding informal immigration with different visas and direct entry to Hong Kong by the personnel sent by Beijing. There are also traditional 'leftist' (pro-Maoist/pro-PRC) supporters who account for about 40 per cent of the whole population, which are the 'iron votes' of the pro-government legislators. The forthcoming elections in the LegCo will be a test as to how loyal this pro-Beijing support is.

More significantly, it is questionable how many pro-democracy political parties would support independence. The positions of many were attacked by the young as 'pan-ethnic Chinese chauvinism'. On the other hand, Beijing will do everything possible to counter the trend. The Hong Kong government is required by the Basic Law to enact national security legislation which includes anti-secession and treason provisions. The lack of international institutional support is another factor. Officially, both the USA and UK governments support the policy of 1C2S and can hardly intervene in HK internal affairs. Although there are still a number of NGOs operating in HK and HK's links with international organisations are still strong, considering the close economic connections, such as the imports of foodstuffs from Mainland, water supply from Guangdong Province and electricity, etc., the success of the 'independence movement' is unimaginable. However, I firmly believe that liberal values have been embedded in the structure of society. The CCP/state might wish to reshape Hong Kong, but Hong Kong will remain essentially different from mainland cities in terms of civic sense, openness of mind, degrees of social and political freedom, and vibrancy of society.

Notes

1. Hu Shih (1891–1962); Lu Xun (1881–1936); Kang Yu-wei (1858–1927); Liang Chi-chao (1873–1929).
2. Sun Yat-sen (1866–1925) was the founder of the modern Republic, which was not to last long. Later, he turned to the Soviet Union for fresh ideas on the dissemination of his revolutionary ideas and activities.
3. Deng Xiaoping indeed said that if 'fifty years were not sufficient, it could be an additional fifty years', and 'We want to create several HKs in Mainland', etc.
4. The document said that 'The Chief Executive will be appointed by the central government on the basis of elections or consultations to be held locally'.
5. The late Lu Ping, former director of the HK and Macau Affairs Office, once said that the development of the electoral system in Hong Kong would be purely an internal matter for the HKSAR government in the early 1990s, when Britain and the PRC were negotiating the electoral arrangement in post-handover HK. The Beijing government lied at that time.
6. One year afterwards, the seven policemen were finally charged over the alleged attacks on Tsang. He was at the same time charged over assaults on other policemen and resisting police arrest (*South China Morning Post*, 16 October 2015).
7. I have talked to three young social activists who unanimously reckoned that the first time the 'dragon lion flag' was hoisted in public was in the 1 July 2011 street marches. The 'dragon lion flag' is the British colonial flag with little changes, first designed by a group called the Hong Kong Autonomy Movement.
8. Some argue that localism could be dated back to the end of the nineteenth century (Kin-ming Kwong, 173–4); see also Tsui Shing-yan, 133–4; others believe it was born in 1949 (Anthony Cheung, 2–3).
9. The massacre nearly eliminated an elite of more than 20,000 people. In the mid-1990s the KMT apologised to the Taiwanese people.

References

Au, K.-L. (2014) *Under the Umbrella*, (Chinese), Hong Kong: Enrich Publishing Ltd.

Chan, C.-K. (2013) 'Hong Kong identities and their interaction with the Chinese narratives' (Chinese), in *On the Chessboard: Donald Tsang's legacy for C. Y. Leung (Chinese)*, Hong Kong: City University of Hong Kong Press.

Cheung, A. (2011) 'Hong Kong identities: Fusion of nativism, nationalities and globalisation' (Chinese), in *Hong Kong . Life . Culture* (Chinese), Hong Kong: Oxford University Press.

Chin, W. (2015) *The City State of Hong Kong*, (Chinese), Hong Kong: Enrich Publishing Ltd.

Endacott, G. B. (1964) *A History of Hong Kong*, Hong Kong: Oxford University Press.

Fok, K. C. (1990) *Lectures on History: Hong Kong's role in modern Chinese history*, Hong Kong: the Commercial Press.

Fong, B. (2014) 'Ten years of political development in Hong Kong: the challenges and prospects of developing a political appointment system under a semi-democratic regime, 2002–2012', in *New Trends of Political Participation in Hong Kong*, Hong Kong: City University of Hong Kong Press.

Ghai, Y. (2000) 'The NPC interpretation and its consequences', in J. M. M. Chan, H. Fu, and Y. Ghai (eds) *Hong Kong's Constitutional Debate*, Hong Kong: Hong Kong University Press.

Hsu, C. Y. I. (1995) *The Rise of Modern China*, New York: Oxford University Press.

Hughes, R. (1976) *Borrowed Time, Borrowed Place*, London: Andre Deutsch Ltd.

Information Office of State Council (IOSC) (2014) *The Practise of 'One Country, Two Systems' in the Hong Kong Special Administrative Region'* (Chinese), Beijing: Renminchubanshe.

Kong, K.-S. (2011, 1921–49), (2012, 1949–2012) *Chinese Communists in Hong Kong* (Chinese), Hong Kong: Cosmos Books.

Kwong, K.-M. (2015) *Britain's Governance in Hong Kong*, (Chinese), Hong Kong: Enrich Publishing Ltd.

Lam, M.-W. (2015) *The 79 Days that Disappeared*, Hong Kong: Isiash Publisher.

Lau, C. H. M. (2014) 'Political participation of the post-1980s generation: their protest activities and social movements in recent years in Hong Kong', in Y. S. Cheng, pp. 385–416.

Lee, P. T. (2005) *Colonial Hong Kong and Modern China: Interaction and reintegration*, Hong Kong: the Hong Kong University Press.

Lee, K.-T. (2015) 'Should Hong Kongers have the rights of self-determination?' (Chinese), in H. Undergrad (ed.) *A Narrative on Hong Kongers as a Nation*, (Chinese), Hong Kong: the University of Hong Kong Student Union.

Li, Z. (1987) *Modern Chinese Political Thought*, (Chinese), Beijing: Oriental Chubanshe.

Li, Y. (2013) *Hong Kong Social Thoughts: the Rise and controversies of localism*, Hong Kong: Kwong Yu Publishers.

Tsui, Shing-yan or S.-Y. (2015), *A National History of Hong Kong* (in Chinese), Hong Kong: Roundtable Publisher.

Undergrad, H., HKUSU (2015) *A narrative on Hong Kongers as a Nation* (Chinese), Hong Kong: the University of Hong Kong Student Union.

Warren, B. (1980) *Imperialism: Pioneer of capitalism*, London: Verso.

Wesley-Smith, P. (1980) *Unequal Treaty, 1898: China, Great Britain and Hong Kong's New Territories*, Hong Kong: Oxford University Press.

Wong, M.-F. (1997) 'An interview on Hong Kong's sovereignty change', *Open Monthly*, January: 46–55.

Wong, Y.-C. (2014a) 'Hong Kong 1997 sovereignty issue: who raised it? Could the outcome have been different?', *Journal of Asian Politics and History*, 4: 1–15.

—— (2014b) 'Absorption into a Leninst polity: a study of the interpretations by the NPC in the post-handover Hong Kong', in J. Y. S. Cheng (ed.), *New Trends of Political Participation in Hong Kong*, Hong Kong: City University of Hong Kong Press.

Yahuda, M. (1995) 'Hong Kong: a new beginning for China?', in J. M. Brown and R. Foot (eds) *Hong Kong's Transitions, 1842–1997*, New York: St. Martin Press.

Index